BUYING A HOUSE IN

ITALY

Gordon Neale

Foreword by Joanna Lumley

Distributed in the USA by
The Globe Pequot Press, Guilford, Connecticut

Published by Vacation Work, 9 Park End Street, Oxford
www.vacationwork.co.uk

BUYING A HOUSE IN ITALY
By Gordon Neale

Editor: Victoria Pybus

First Edition 2003
Reprinted 2004
Copyright © 2003

ISBN 1-85458-300-X

Publicity: Roger Musker

Cover design by Miller Craig & Cocking Design Partnership

Illustrations by Mick Siddens

Typeset by Brendan Cole

Printed and bound in Italy by Legoprint SpA, Trento

CONTENTS

PART I
VIVA ITALIA!

LIVING IN ITALY

RESIDENCE AND ENTRY

PART II
LOCATION, LOCATION...

WHERE TO FIND YOUR IDEAL HOME

PART III
THE PURCHASING PROCEDURE

FINANCE

FINDING PROPERTIES FOR SALE

PART IV
WHAT HAPPENS NEXT

FOREWORD

Ever since I heard the song 'The Isle of Capri' when I was eight years old I wanted to live in Italy, or better still be an Italian. This involved riding a scooter without a crash helmet, looking alluring in a full-skirted cotton dress with a silk headscarf knotted under the chin and arguing volubly whilst wearing dark glasses. Years later it also meant speaking the beautiful language fluently and being married to a man with sensational footwear.

To date, I have only achieved one, maybe two, of these criteria: but Gordon Neale, a lifelong Italophile and incidentally my cousin, has morphed into the masculine version of my ideal, but a thousand times better. He taught himself Italian when he was nineteen and speaks it flawlessly like a native. He has bought sold, restored and built properties all over Italy. His passions for history, geography, art, food, wine and society have put him in a unique position, one which he now shares fully with us, to advise how to buy a place in this astonishing country and where to look for it.

For me, the best aspect of this fabulous book is the combination of knowledge and know-how: regional foods and wines, Caesar's Gallic wars, and how to approach a notary; a sort of life study of how to love Italy and know the Italians, how to speak with accuracy and courtesy, where to find help, what to do and (what the *cognoscenti* are always after) where the next Tuscany will be. Read this book even if you live in Iceland; have it in your car, show it to your bank manager. With Gordon I once found a ruined cottage with a terrace and a threshing floor, overlooking a steep wooded ravine with its own olive grove and vineyard. We called it 'Casa Giovanna': in the evening the sun set behind Siena on a distant hill. The time was wrong then to buy and restore my own place in the sun, but that was long ago. Now, reading this book, I find that there are compelling reasons for packing up and setting off for Piedmont, or Umbria, or anywhere as long as it's in Italy. Perhaps a scooter waits for me somewhere, leaning in the black shade of a cypress tree, shrilling with cicadas in the midday sun.

Joanna Lumley.

ACKNOWLEDGMENTS

The author would like to thank everyone who helped with this book especially: Frank Lee, Belinda Scaburri and Charles Butterno for providing their case histories, Guido Cerboni of the Italian Embassy in London for dealing with specific requests for information, Anne Birney for her constant assistance and contribution of chapters, Isabella de Pian for her contributions, Jennifer Hosmer for her superlative word-processing and Mariella Righetti for her information and hospitality in the field.

Special thanks also to Mick Siddens for the illustrations of Italian houses and also to the editor, Victoria Pybus, for her masterly additions and arrangements, and to the publisher Charles James for his encouragement.

The author would also like to acknowledge the following sources:
Calendario Atlante de Agostini 2003; *Ritratto dell'Italia* (Laterza 2001); Editrice de'il Vespro (Palermo) for the regional proverbs taken from the *Regioni in Bocca* series (1976-1981).

Part I

VIVA ITALIA!

LIVING IN ITALY

RESIDENCE & ENTRY

DEDICATION:

To the memory of Rina and Zaverio Nepi,
Italia and Annunziata
and Pietro di Galante

LIVING IN ITALY

CHAPTER SUMMARY

- So familiar a sight were the English in Italy that for generations all foreigners were termed *inglesi* by the Italians.
- **Eating Out.** Sparse or unpretentious decor is common in restaurants and does not reflect the quality of the food.
  - Young children are welcomed and fussed over in Italian restaurants.
- **Getting There.** There are non-stop flights from the UK and USA to over 30 Italian cities.
- **Crime.** The Italian state pays 50 million euros a year for witness protection for trials against the Mafia.
  - Foreign visitors are not normally the target of organised crime and can remain blissfully unaware of its existence.
  - Petty crime (*microcriminalità*) is however, a way of life in the cities and tourist places and on public transport.
- Italian police, especially the *carabinieri*, are much less approachable than UK or US ones.
- **Media.** Italy has no separate Sunday newspapers. Instead the dailies print on Sunday and have Monday off. The quality Italian newspapers are excellent and informative.
  - Italy was a pioneer of the 'violence chip' which filters out television programmes depicting violence when children are watching.
  - Italian television is monopolised by trashy quiz and games shows and soaps and is frequently described as 'crap', though there are some serious news programmes.
- **Post.** The post is much slower than in the USA or UK and you have to pay extra for next day arrival (which doesn't necessarily arrive next day).
- **Social Drinking.** Drunkenness is frowned on in Italy and brawls outside bars are rare.
  - However, drinking wine from a young age is an accepted part of the culture.
- **Health.** Italian state hospitals, except possibly in the north, can be

depressing places with inadequate bathing and feeding facilities.

- ○ In contrast with the public sector, the private sector of the health service is amazingly well organised.
- ○ Most Italian citizens and foreigners in Italy have private health insurance.
- ○ **Schools.** Italian schools do not have a particularly good reputation. The exception is at primary level.
  - ○ 57% of Italian schools do not have a certificate of stability for their buildings.
  - ○ In 2002 Italy revived the apprenticeship system (similar to Germany's) for non-academic children from age 15.
- ○ **Food and Consumer Goods.** Italy tempts the consumer with the best quality products in food and luxury goods the globe can offer.
  - ○ Italy has a dazzling array of small specialist shops.

INTRODUCTION – THE MUTUAL LOVE AFFAIR

The English-speaking peoples have had a love affair with Italy, which goes back over a thousand years. King Alfred the Great, the founder of book-learning in English was inspired by his visits to Rome as a boy (in AD 853 and AD 855). Geoffrey Chaucer befriended the poet Francesco Petrarch near Padua in 1373 and modelled his *Canterbury Tales* on the humorous, bawdy Tuscan fables of Boccaccio's *Decameron*. The people of Verona still think that Shakespeare actually visited their city, so convincing are the images in *Romeo and Juliet*. William Harvey, the discoverer of the circulation of the blood, studied medicine at the University of Padua (1602). John Milton visited the astronomer Galileo Galilei at Arcetri (Florence) in 1639 and composed sonnets in impeccable Tuscan long before he wrote his great English epic *Paradise Lost*.

In the 18th century the Grand Tour – to Italy – became an essential part of the education of English gentlemen, so attractive was Italy's fund of courtly society, classical remains and contemporary art and music. Italian paintings and sculptures were shipped by the cartload to the stately homes of Britain and Ireland, and the Italian language was enriched by words from these English tourists, such as *bistecca* (beefsteak), *rosbif* (roast beef), *ponce* (punch) and *clebbe* (club). Thomas Jefferson, co-author of the American *Declaration of Independence*, could speak *Toscano*, imported olive trees, and built an Italianate villa with an Italian name *Monticello* in Virginia.

In the 19th century, English poets were irresistibly attracted to this *Paradise of Exiles* and made their homes in Italy. Lord Byron went native in Venice, where he wrote his satiric epic masterpiece *Don Juan* (1819-1824), John Keats died of tuberculosis in Rome in 1821, and, after four years in Italy, where he produced

Major Towns and Cities of Italy

GERMANY

AUSTRIA

Bern

Innsbruck

SWITZERLAND

Bolzano

Tarvisio

HUNGARY

Trento

Udine

SLOVENIA

Aosta

Como

Bergamo

Treviso

Ljubljana

Zagreb

Novara

Brescia

Vicenza

Trieste

CROATIA

Milan

Verona

Padova

Turin

Piacenza

Po

Venice

Parma

Ferrara

Genova

Reggio

Reno

Ravenna

BOSNIA-

Savona

Bologna

Rimini

HERZEGOVINA

La Spezia

Pesaro

Sarajevo

Monte Carlo

Pisa

Arno

Florence

San Marino

Split

Mostar

Nice

Livorno

Ancona

Siena

Perugia

Elba

ITALY

Dubrovnik

Corsica

Grosseto

Tiber

Terni

Pescara

Adriatic

Ajaccio

Rome

Sea

Latina

Foggia

Barletta

Ofanto

Bari

Olbia

Andria

Sassari

Naples

Potenza

Brindisi

Alghero

Tirso

Salerno

Taranto

Sardinia

Lecce

Otranto

Tyrrhenian Sea

Cosenza

Crotone

Cagliari

Catanzaro

Messina

Trapani

Palermo

Reggio

Catania

Sicily

Siracusa

| 0 | 50 | 100 | 150 miles |
| 0 | 50 | 100 | 150 | 200 | 250 km |

MALTA

Valletta

Mediterranean Sea

Railway network

Motorway/
Main roads

some of his best poetry, Percy Bysshe Shelley was drowned while sailing in the Bay of Lerici in 1822. The city of Florence (and to a lesser extent Rome) then became the base for a large expatriate Anglo-American community. Long term residents in Florence were the poets Robert and Elizabeth Browning, in Casa Guidi (1846-1861). 'Italy, my Italy' Robert Browning wrote, 'Open my heart and you will see, graved inside of it, 'Italy'.

Alassio, a small fishing port on the Ligurian coast, was transmogrified into an English winter resort, popular with retired folk from India who couldn't face the British climate after a lifetime in the tropics. The church, the library and the tennis club are still there, but the English colony had disappeared by the 1960's. This Riviera, the lakes (Maggiore, Como and Garda), Florence, Asolo, Venice, Capri, Ravello, Amalfi – and Taormina in Sicily – continued to be colonised into the 20th century by English speakers, mainly artists, writers and aesthetes, such as Max Beerbohm, D.H. Lawrence, Bernard Berenson, Osbert Sitwell, Ezra Pound and Aldous Huxley. Ernest Hemingway's *A Farewell to Arms* gravitated to the North West of Italy in World War I, and is still revered in Harry's Bar in Venice. In World War II powerful links were forged between the local partisan populations and fugitive allied servicemen such as Eric Newby, author of *Love and War in the Apennines*. The *liberazione* (liberation) of Italy by the *angloamericani* on April 25 1945 is commemorated by a public holiday and affectionately remembered by the older generation.

So familiar were the English in Italy that the word *inglesi* came to mean foreigners in general. Only recently have Italians learnt to distinguish between *inglesi* (English) and *scozzesi* (Scots), between *irlandesi* (Irish) *islandesi* (Icelandic) and *olandesi* (Dutch), between *australiani* (Australians), *nuova zelandesi* (New Zealanders) and *sud africani* (South Africans). Even the blanket expression *anglosassoni* (Anglo Saxons) in the Italian mind seems to include not only native English speakers but also Dutch, Scandinavian and Germanic people in general. But the important thing is that, thanks to the input of our illustrious antecedents, the *inglesi*, or the *anglosassoni*, and now especially the *americani* are admired – or at least tolerated – by the modern inhabitants of Italy.

It is accepted (but fallacious) wisdom that Italians do not travel much beyond their own shores. While British politicians recharge their batteries in Tuscany in August, their Italian counterparts (such as Sig. Arnaldo Forlani) seek renewal in Edinburgh, Scotland. Italy's greatest living cavalry hero, Amedeo Guillet, has lived in retirement in rural Ireland, near Dublin, since 1975. Italians flock to London, New York, Toronto and Sydney.

When it comes to fashion, many *anglosassoni* yearn for the stylish cut of an Italian designer suit, while Italian men remain faithful to English and American styles.

Italians are deeply attached to American music, and latterly to its British and Irish adaptations: in December 2002, the 1960's English 'progressive' rock group

Procul Harum ('A whiter shade of pale') returned to rapturous acclaim in Italy, *the Cranberries*, a young Celtic-rock group from Limerick Ireland enjoyed a sell-out tour, and Irish folk music, personified by *Craobh Rua*, is pervasively played and sung by young enthusiasts throughout Italy. Italy and the English-speaking world enjoy a strong reciprocal admiration, which can certainly be described as a mutual love affair.

Even the anti-American, anti-capitalist no-global protesters of Italy wear American jeans, listen to American rock music and rap; and they are motivated by the ideology of American gurus such as Noam Chomsky and Ruth Klein.

After the Second World War, during the boom years of the Italian economic miracle, Italy radiated appeal to the Anglo-Saxons. Gregory Peck and Audrey Hepburn idyllically toured Rome on a Vespa in the film *Roman Holiday* (1953). Reacting against the grim world of bad food and rationing in the UK Elizabeth David brought out her inspirational books on Mediterranean Cooking – such as *Italian Food* (1954) – thereby sowing the seeds of the foodie revolution, in which Italy has now replaced France as the favoured hunting ground for gourmets and 'gastronauts'.

In the 1960's a small trickle of English bohemians and hippie escapists, were buying old farm houses in the rustic hinterlands of Tuscany and Liguria, some of them making their own wine and oil. For a while coastal resorts like Rimini enjoyed an influx of mass Anglo-Saxon tourism, but this was soon diverted to Spain, Portugal, Yugoslavia, Greece and Turkey. Italy's own prosperity was the cause of this mass defection. From the 1950's Italians from the towns and cities could afford to buy or rent second homes at the seaside, to send their families away to escape from the *afa* or heat of the cities in July and August, or for the duration of the long school holidays (June to September). It was their birthright and culture. The result was that the coastlines were developed by Italians themselves, for themselves. There were a few Swedish, Dutch, Swiss, German colonies – but hardly any British – who had been lured away to other shores by their entrepreneurial travel agents. Besides, the Italian coastal resorts were too crowded. The Italians had become exuberant with their wealth, and very often their developments were ugly – and you had to *pay* for your deck chair and cabin in the *stabilimento balneare*.

If they didn't go to the seaside the Italians went to the mountains or the lakes for their *villeggiatura* (holiday). This left the hills in the favoured regions to the *inglesi*. The trickle became a flood. Germans, Dutch, Swiss, Americans – and Italians from the North – joined in. Any pretty village was a magnet. Abandoned farmhouses near the villages were the first to go. Then the remoter hovels or barracks.

This process has been going on for thirty years. First in Tuscany, then in Umbria, and now in Le Marche. The colour supplements and the travel sections of the British Sunday papers have articles on these places every week. It is a perk for journalists to write about their holidays. So the demand increases, and prices go up. Then *Under a Tuscan Sun* by Frances Mayes (1996) became a bestseller in the USA. It describes how a writer bought and converted a house near Cortona in Tuscany, and, as a result, more Americans came and bought the best villas and mansions available. This is all very good for the local economy. Country roads are full of builders' vans and trucks. There is work for immigrant Albanians, Poles and North Africans. The conversions are mostly very tasteful. They have to be; local building codes are strict. There are hundreds of estate agents operating – Italian, German, British – but now they are buying and selling finished houses rather than ruins (and if they can find a ruin to sell the price can be over €500,000).

It is estimated that Italy has no more than 100,000 British residents. This compares with an estimated 500,000 British in France and nearly a million in Spain. So Italy has a lot of catching up to do. Central Italy might be saturated, but there are plenty of other regions to consider buying a house in.

The remoter regions of Italy, such as Friuli, Valle d'Aosta, Molise, Abruzzo, Basilicata, Apulia and Sardinia are worth considering because:

○ They have largely escaped the industrialisation, pollution and tourism of the twentieth century.
○ Enlightened local councils now concentrate on the protection of the

environment and on the promotion of intelligent tourism and local produce.

- ◯ They have preserved their architectural, rural, linguistic and gastronomic traditions.
- ◯ They have a rich diversity of vernacular styles and local materials.
- ◯ The Italian reverence for the *centro storico* (old town centre) plus EU money is leading to the appropriate restoration of town and village centres and monuments.
- ◯ Foreigners who buy are welcomed for their contribution to the economy.
- ◯ Houses and land are still cheap.
- ◯ Low-fare airlines have now made these remoter areas more accessible.

IL BEL PAESE – HISTORY

Italy is a young country and was unified only in 1861. Its present constitution dates from 1948. But it has a rich and fascinating history and not without reason or consequences is it known as *il bel paese* (the beautiful country). It was this fatal beauty which has attracted migrants from all directions from time immemorial.

The earliest inhabitants can be traced back 700,000 years to *Homo erectus Aeserniensis*, recently found in Molise. The autochthonous tribes are identified as Ligurians in the North and Sicels in the South. These people lived in round huts of wattle and daub, kept domestic animals and subsisted by hunting and fishing. By 2000 BC other tribes – Indo-Europeans – arrived from the north-east, lake dwellers who lived in huts raised on stilts. They were expert ironworkers, shepherds and weavers. They surrounded their villages with protective earthworks. Called Villanovans after the town they founded near modern Bologna, they spread throughout Central Italy and are believed to be the racial and linguistic forerunners of the Umbrian, Sabine, and Latin tribes. They established several villages *circa* 1000 BC in the area between the mouth of the Tiber and the Bay of Naples, hitherto uninhabitable because of volcanic activity, villages which were perpetually at war with each other. The biggest of these settlements was Alba Longa the capital of the Latins fifteen miles from the sea at the foot of Monte Albano (modern Castel Gandolfo). The Albolongans were the founders of Rome. The first of the famous Seven Hills of Rome that they colonised was the Palatine. The legend of Romulus and Remus (see *The Romans* below) and that of the Rape of the Sabine Women date from this time. The Latins and the Sabines combined forces to fight a common enemy who appeared on the scene at this time – the Etruscans.

The Etruscans

The Etruscans almost certainly originated from Asia Minor, but they remain a mystery because Rome obliterated their culture after centuries of ferocious warfare. The emperor Claudius recorded the speech of some rustics who still spoke Etruscan in about 50AD, but unfortunately his works have been lost and scholars are still struggling to decipher the language from the numerous tombstone inscriptions discovered in the last few centuries. They are inclined to think it is not an Indo-European language. The Etruscan priesthood and the practice of divination persisted as a pagan cult into the Christian era and the priestly *abracadabras* or hieratical language was presumably Etruscan, but the Christian Emperor Honorius ordered the destruction of all Etruscan books in the 5th century from when all practice of the *Etruscan Discipline* was banned.

The Etruscan museum in Tarquinia credits two Englishmen with the rediscovery of the Etruscans: George Dennis, whose *Cities and Cemeteries of Etruria* (1848) described the incredible treasures buried under centuries of undergrowth and neglect, still a superb guide, and D.H. Lawrence, whose *Etruscan Places* (1916) poetically indoctrinates us with an image of the Etruscans as a sensual life-enhancing people, superior to, but defeated by the villainous and boring Romans.

In fact the Etruscans were a formative ingredient of Roman civilisation. The first kings of Rome were from the Etruscan house of Tarquin. Building practices: the arch, sewers, tiles, irrigation, religion, divining from birds and entrails, sacrificing, were Etruscan. Gladiatorial fights to the death originated from Etruscan funeral rituals. The Roman legionaries' early armour, crested helmets, weapons, ball games, wind instruments, chariot racing, jewellery, were all copied from the Etruscans. Banqueting – as on Etruscan sarcophagi, at the feast of life – reclining on couches, served by naked slave children – the Romans continued these practices. They even inherited – and never got rid of – the aristocratic class system itself – whereby men and women of the superior race lorded it over a proto-plebeian class.

As a nation the Etruscans peaked at the end of the 6th century BC expanding northwards into the Po valley where they gave their name to Ravenna (from *Rasna* their own name for themselves). At Bologna their settlement was called *Felsina*. To the south they expanded into Campania (capital Cumae).

But soon pressure from the Gauls in the North and Greeks from the South caused them to retreat to their heartland – roughly modern Tuscany and Umbria – where their aristocrats lived in luxury and their women enjoyed equality with men, to the disdain of the censorious Romans. We have a vivid picture of them through their tombs (at Tarquinia, Chiusi, Cerveteri) whose wall paintings so impressed D.H. Lawrence, the prophet of proletarian hedonism, with their sportive rural scenes.

The contribution of the Etruscans to the psyche of the Italians, though hidden, has been enormous. No other European country has the Etruscans in their genetic make-up. They are unique to Italy. The area they colonised produced through history a disproportionate number of creative geniuses: Giotto, Cimabue, Michelangelo, Leonardo du Vinci, Benvenuto Cellini, Botticelli, Donatello,

Masaccio, Brunelleschi, Piero della Francesca – even Napoleon Bonaparte. It is tempting to think that this pool of talent is Etruscan in origin.

Modern researchers have discovered Etruscan DNA surviving in the populations of the Tuscan hinterland – such as San Quirico d'Orcia – and magazine articles have shown photographically the remarkable physical resemblance between some modern Tuscans and the tombstone busts of their ancestors of 2,500 years ago.

In about 500 BC Rome was invaded by Lars Porsenna the *Lucumon* of Clusium. The legend of Horatius' heroic defence of the bridge is a later invention to cover up Rome's inglorious defeat.

> *Lars Porsena of Clusium*
> *By the nine gods he swore*
> *That the great house of Tarquin*
> *Should suffer wrong no more.*

(from Macaulay's *Lays of Ancient Rome*)

The Roman Republic

The Roman genius for organisation can be traced back to the fusion of Romans, Sabines and Etruscans which was accomplished by Romulus, Rome's legendary founder (753 BC). He created the law making matrix and the embryonic military machine: the Senate and the Legion, which were destined to conquer the whole of the Mediterranean and beyond.

Rome became a republic after the expulsion of the seventh King, the Etruscan Tarquin the proud, in 510 BC. Power now went to two annually-elected, monthly-alternating consuls. The history of the Republic became as much a history of an internal class struggle between the patricians and the plebeians as it was of colonial expansion.

The two orders managed to hold together and their well-disciplined and motivated citizen's army inexorably absorbed and conquered all their neighbours, whether Etruscans, Latins, Æquians, Volscians or Samnites, and by 265 BC the whole of the peninsula south of the Apennines was under Roman control.

Another enemy in Rome's way was Carthage ; the Carthaginians were a Semitic people from Palestine who had colonised North Africa, cruel worshippers of Baal and Moloch, aggressive traders and seafarers, whose sphere of interest now clashed with Rome's. They were defeated by Rome in the first Punic war (264-261 BC). In 261 the Romans built a fleet of a hundred quinquiremes (galleyship with five rows of oarsmen on either side) and twenty triremes in two months, copying a Carthaginian war prize, and discovered sea power. They also acquired Sicily which became their first *Provincia*, and provocatively seized Sardinia and Corsica (238 BC).

The Second Punic War (218-201 BC) – Hannibal's revenge campaign in Italy, and his final defeat at Zama (75 miles from Carthage), in North Africa by Scipio Africanus – is one of the most famous epic struggles in history. Hannibal led an army, with elephants, over the Alps, defeating the Legions twice on the way to his spectacular victories at Lake Trasimene in Umbria (217 BC) and Cannae in Apulia (216 BC). But he failed to march on Rome and frittered away the next few years in the south before returning to Africa and defeat. Carthage was finally annihilated in 146 BC by Scipio Africanus's adopted son and namesake, who razed the city and ploughed up the site. The surrounding coastal strip of land was named the Province of Africa.

The conquest of the Eastern Mediterranean, Greece, and Spain followed, with similar ruthlessness, and then in 133 BC began a century of unrest and civil war ending in the overthrow of the Republic and the establishment of absolute government.

In a second civil war, Julius Caesar became dictator, and was murdered in the Senate in 44 BC. In the power struggle that followed Caesar's nominee Octavius got the better of his rivals, beating Pompey first, then Antony at Actium (31 BC). Antony and his lover Cleopatra, queen of Egypt, committed suicide, and Octavius returned to Rome in 29 BC, the unchallenged master of the Roman world.

The Empire

Octavius was nominated Augustus (the revered) by the Senate, and he presided over the Augustan Age, personified by the poets Horace, Virgil, Ovid, Livy, the historian, and their great Etruscan patron, Maecenas. He beautified Rome, finding it a city of brick and leaving it a city of marble. He kept the senate as his chief support and made a new order of the equites. The Popular party disappeared and even the optimates atrophied. The consuls became honorary. The empire was guarded on its frontiers by a standing army of about twenty-five legions and equivalent auxiliaries and there were two fleets. His long reign was wonderfully tranquil.

ROMAN-THEMED MOVIES

The Roman Empire is familiar to us through the images of Hollywood and Pinewood, which often focus on the monstrosities of later emperors such as Caligula, Commodus or Nero: *Quo Vadis* (1951), *Ben Hur* (1959), *Spartacus* (1960), *Cleopatra* (1963), *Fellini Satyricon* (1969), *Up Pompeii* (1971) and *Gladiator* (2000) give us the picture.

Rome's Decline and Fall

According to Edward Gibbon in his *Decline and Fall of the Roman Empire* (1776) 'The most happy and prosperous period for the human race in the history of the world' was AD 96-180, under the emperors Nerva, Trajan, Hadrian, Antoninus Pius and Marcus Aurelius: 'the Golden Age of Trajan and the Antonius'. The religion was pagan, the emperor was a god, the favourite sports were chariot racing and gladiatorial contests and Christians were outlawed. The supply of slaves was constantly replenished by war-captives. Rich Romans owned regiments of slaves for every conceivable job over whom they had the power of life and death. Runaways were branded, pilloried, beaten or crucified. Slaves were not allowed to own property or marry. But home-born slaves were valued and trusted and superior slaves were often freed. Women and children had to belong to a *paterfamilias*. The profession of teaching was looked down on; it was practised generally by freedmen or Greek slaves. Greeks were despised ('greedy little Greeks' according to the satirist Juvenal), but their language and culture was prestigious, and rich boys were sent to university in Rhodes (for rhetoric) and Athens (for (philosophy). By the time of Constantine there were over 900 bath houses in Rome (*balneae*) and eleven hot baths (*thermae*). The army had built roads to last, and travelling was safe and rapid. Villas were heated by underground flues called hypocausts, fuelled by slave-stoked furnaces. This was a way of life which extended as far north as Britain.

A succession of cruel and corrupt emperors followed the death of Marcus Aurelius, the last of the philosopher kings. Commodus was murdered in a palace

Roman Soldiers. (From Column of Trajan.)

conspiracy and Pertinax was killed by the Praetorian guard, who then put the empire up for auction. A series of 'barracks' emperors ensued, such as the giant Thracian Maximin, chosen for his skill in wrestling by his fellow-soldiers and soon killed off.

Civil war and barbarian invasions caused Valerian to divide the Empire in AD 253. Rome lost its importance. Milan became capital of the West – Nicomedia (Izmit on the Sea of Marmara) of the East. A proliferation of emperors and civil war ended with Constantine, who became a Christian in AD 312 and founded Constantinople as the 'New Rome' in AD 328 at Byzantium on the Bosphorus. In AD 394 Theodosius became emperor of the East and West and finally suppressed paganism. In AD 410 Alaric the Visigoth sacked Rome for three days, reducing the city to rubble, thus ending the history of classical Rome.

What caused the decline of the Roman Empire? The ruling class became effete, stopped having children, were brain-damaged by lead water pipes, possibly, but in fact it was the Roman army that made and unmade the Roman empire. The legions in their long hey-day were an unparalleled military/engineering machine whose veterans also brought order to the land they were granted on their retirement. The focus of their loyalty was their Standard, the Glory of Rome, and later the God Emperor, under the control of the Senate. Chronic anarchy began as soon as the provincial armies started proclaiming their own generals as Emperor, ignoring the deliberations of the Senate. In the 126 years between Marcus Aurelius and Constantine there were thirty-five Emperors – a succession of alpha-males who lived by the sword and died by the sword and left the country derelict.

The Dark Ages

Ravenna replaced Milan as capital of the West in AD 395 when the Emperor Honorius took refuge there. A separate Emperor ruled in the West until AD 476, when Odoacer – an Ostrogoth – became the first barbarian sovereign to rule over Italy.

In AD 535 the great Emperor Justinian, famous for his codification of the laws, invaded Italy with his able generals Belisarius and Narses and fought against the Goths for eighteen years. As a result the Ostrogoths disappear from history, and Italy becomes a province of the eastern Byzantine Empire, its capital Ravenna.

In AD 568, three years after Justinian's death, Italy was invaded by a new and very fierce German tribe, the Langobards or Lombards from the upper Danube (originally from Sweden) under their king Alboin. They conquered the North of Italy, still called Lombardy. In AD 569 there were about 200,000 Lombards in Italy.

At the time of the Lombard invasion, refugees from the Lombards founded Venice. Italian civilisation decayed. Whatever survived of the culture of ancient Rome was preserved by the Church, thanks to the influence of the Papacy and the monastic movement. Monasticism, which had started spontaneously in Egypt and Syria at the beginning of the first century with saints like St Antony of Egypt, was revolutionised in Italy by St Benedict, who was born of a wealthy family in about AD 480 at Norcia, near Spoleto in Umbria. In AD 520 he founded the famous monastery of Monte Cassino and drew up the 'Benedictine Rule' which promoted total obedience to the abbot, forbade excessive zeal and put manual work on a par with prayer and reading, creating an organisation with a life of its own, which proliferated beneficially for the minds and landscape of Italy. Gregory the Great, himself a Benedictine, became Pope in AD 590. (It was Gregory who when told that two blue-eyed boys in the slave-market at Rome were Angles replied 'Not Angles, but Angels'.) Gregory, an aristocratic Roman, inspired respect for the Church amongst the Goths and the Lombards. He was the last of the great Romans. The long and profound influence of the papacy was due to him, just as the influence of monasticism was due to St Benedict, and the influence of Roman Law was due to the Emperor Justinian.

In the centuries that followed Italy was still ruled over by foreigners, and in AD 800 Pepin's son Charlemagne was crowned in Rome as the Holy Roman Emperor. By the oneupmanship gesture of crowning him, Pope Leo III established the precedence of the Papacy.

The Renaissance

From the end of the thirteenth century to the end of the sixteenth century Italy became the most advanced country in Europe economically, commercially and artistically. This was the era of the independent *Comunes* or small city states.

Pisa's maritime empire rose and fell, Genoa was a great sea port, Venice prospered through her oriental trade. Milan boomed – and the great princely families started to dominate, presiding over courts which were the breeding ground of high art and culture: the Viscontis and Sforzas in Lombardy, the Gonzagas in Mantua, the Montefeltros in Urbino, the Estenses in Ferrara and the Medicis in Florence. Artists of fifteenth century Florence sparked off the Renaissance. Brunelleschi built the Dome of Florence cathedral in 1436 – Lorenzo the Magnificent dominated Florence from 1469. This was the age of Leonardo da Vinci (1452-1519) Michelangelo Buonarroti (1475-1564) Niccolò Machiavelli (1469-1527), of ritualised warfare celebrated in the paintings of Paolo Uccello (1396-1475), conducted by mercenaries, or *condottieri* captains such as Sir John Hawkwood (1320-1398) (*Giovanni Acuto*) who never learnt Italian and was sent back to his beloved Essex when he died.

The incredible richness and diversity of the Italian Renaissance would have been unthinkable without this multiplicity of princely courts and petty states. Here we have the origin of Italy's still flourishing regional cultures. It was Francesco Guicciardini, the Florentine historian (1483-1540), who pointed out how beneficial a disunited Italy was at that time.

This advanced culture and lack of military virtues made Italy fatally weak.

Rome was sacked in 1527 by Lutheran German mercenaries , '*Lanzichenecchi*', fighting for the imperial army of Charles V. Florence fell to the Spanish in 1530. The Pope crowned Charles V, the Holy Roman Emperor, with the iron crown of Monza.

In the early eighteenth century the Spanish Wars of succession changed the geopolitical map of Europe and Italy. Italy was a pawn in the game of dynastic rivalry between the Bourbons of France and Spain and the Hapsburgs of Austria. The Treaty of Utrecht in 1713 brought in the Austrians to replace the Spanish in Milan, Naples and Sardinia. But their allies the English put the Duke of Savoy on to the throne of Sicily, which the Austrians forced him to exchange for Sardinia in 1720. The Savoys were thus Kings of Sardinia until 1861 when they became Kings of Italy. In 1734 the Bourbon king, Charles VII became king of the reunited Naples and Sicily. The Hapsburg-Lorraines took over Tuscany from the extinct line of the Medicis, while the Bourbons obtained the Duchy of Parma, Piacenza, and Guastalla.

Foreigners from the North swarmed into Italy on the Grand Tour, attracted as much by the relaxed courtly society, the seductive courtesans of Venice and elsewhere as by the fabulous classical remains – Goethe from Germany in 1786 was struck by 'an Italy timeless in its serene and perfect immobility'. Culture and art and music flourished. This was the heyday of the castrati opera singers; Senesino and Farinelli, contemporaries of Vivaldi (1645-1741), in the early part of the century were the pop stars of their day, fabulously well-paid, followed by virtuoso musicians like the violinist Paganini. Every town had its opera house (*teatro*), from the San Carlo in Naples to La Scala in Milan, many of them still extant 250 years later.

The Risorgimento – Wars of Independence

Feelings against Austrian rule in the North, against Papal rule in the centre, and against the rule of the Bourbons in the South – the status quo – gave rise to the movement that led to the *Risorgimento* or Revival of Italy, orchestrated by the radical republican exile Giuseppe Mazzini (1805-72), the wily Piedmontese politician Camillo Benso Comte de Cavour, the figurehead Savoy King of Sardinia Victor Emmanuel II, (1820-78) and the guerrilla hero from Nice, Giuseppe Garibaldi (1807-82).

In 1859 Garibaldi's volunteer army defeated the Austrians in skirmishes on the hills of Varese and Como with the backing of Cavour, inspired by a battle song whose last line was 'get out of Italy, you foreigner' (*Va fuora d'Italia, va fuora, o straniero*). Garibaldi, who in his youth had been a guerilla leader in Uruguay and a longshoreman in New York, was already the hero of the two worlds, 'adored wherever he went', clad in a red shirt and a poncho, with a mesmerising voice and honest blue eyes that seemed to scan the horizon. His next exploit was the incredible capture of the kingdom of the two Sicilies with the band of a thousand volunteers who had steamed down from Genoa to Marsala in 1860, captured Palermo – having defeated the Neapolitan regular army 24,000 strong at Calatafimi; then proceeded up to Naples with victories at Milazzo and Volturno on the way. Prime Minister Cavour's role in Garibaldi's triumph was ambivalent. He had been reluctant to support him at the start. Having been a 'useful idiot' Garibaldi became a loose cannon, appointing himself Dictator of Sicily. Cavour put pressure on Garibaldi, who sent a famous telegram to King Victor Emmanuel with the word *'Obbedisco'* (I obey), delivered him the Kingdom of the two Sicilies and retired to his smallholding on the island of Caprera on the north coast of Sardinia.

In 1860, Tuscany, Modena, Parma, Bologna and Romagna voted in plebiscites to join the Monarchy. Umbria and the Marches were annexed, and the Kingdom of Italy was proclaimed in 1861.

The end of that era came in August 1914 with the assassination of Franz Josef at Sarajevo. Italy changed alliances at the Treaty of London in 1915 and faced an Austrian army in the North West reinforced by seven elite German divisions, one battalion of which was led by a youthful Erwin Rommel, the future desert fox of World War II, who ran rings round the Italians. Their massive defeat at Caporetto in 1917 was redeemed the next year by heroic Italian victories at the river Piave and Vittorio Veneto where the Austrians were routed. Italy gained Trento and Trieste as promised in the Treaty of London, but the war had cost her six hundred thousand men killed and one million wounded.

Mussolini and Fascism

The rise and fall of fascism with Mussolini is the story of the next quarter century. A school bully from Romagna, Mussolini became a Socialist journalist, then a leader of a political party whose symbol was the *fasces* or rods of office of the lictors of ancient Rome, who wore black shirts and practised terrorism in armed groups called *Squadracce*. Mussolini marched on Rome in 1922 and King Victor Emmanuel III called on him to form a government. In 1924, after the accidental murder of Giacomo Matteotti – an honest parliamentarian – at the hands of a *squadraccia*- Mussolini blustered his way out of his involvement and stepped up the repression by creating a secret police force, the Ceka and a special tribunal to stamp out all opposition. In the 1930s Mussolini aggrandised himself as *IL DUCE* in capitals, imagining himself as Caesar and his officers centurions and consuls.

But he was upstaged by his copycat dictator Adolf Hitler in 1934 with a threat of *Anschluss* or annexation of Austria on Italy's north east border – Mussolini countered by invading Africa and annexing Ethiopia to the delirium of the Italian people and the dismay of the League of Nations. At the same time he sent a large Italian force to help Franco in the Spanish Civil War in 1937. In 1938 anti-semitic racial laws imposed by Mussolini to copy Hitler's disgusted the Italians. The 50,000 Jews in Italy – many of them fascists – were perfectly well integrated into Italian society. In 1939 Italy annexed Albania, in 1940 Mussolini saw Hitler slicing through Czechoslovakia, Poland and France, decided he would back a winner and seized Menton in France as Hitler's ally. But it was only the beginning of the war and not the end.

The alliance with Germany led to the humiliating destruction of the Italian fleet by the British at Taranto, defeat in North Africa by General Wavell at Benghazi, 75,000 Italians lost in Russia on the Don, and a final defeat at El Alamein by General Montgomery. In 1943 the Allies invaded Sicily. Mussolini was relieved of his command by the Grand Council of fascism and bundled into a fortress hideaway in the Gran Sasso in Abruzzo, where he was liberated by a commando unit of German gliders and set up as a puppet by Hitler on Lake Garda as head of the Republic of Salò.

The partisan movement now co-operated with the Anglo-Americans in pushing the Germans northwards out of Italy. There was a fratricidal Civil War between fascists and partisans, trading atrocities. Mussolini tried to escape, in a German uniform, with his lover Claretta Petacci, into Switzerland, but they were recognised, put to death by the partisans and strung up upside down in Piazzale Loreto in Milan on April 28 1945, three days after the official liberation of Italy by the Anglo-Americans.

In 1946 Victor Emmanuel III abdicated in favour of his son Humbert, but it was not enough to save the monarchy. In a referendum on June 2 1946 Italy voted for the abolition of the monarchy and the institution of a Republic. A committee was set up to write a Constitution, which was finalised in 1948.

MODERN ITALY – POLITICS

Since the foundation of the First Republic in 1946 Italy has had more than fifty different 'revolving door' governments characterised by coalitions, horsetrading and a *sottogoverno* or 'undergovernment', of bewildering complexity, of wheeler-dealers and power-brokers in Rome, offering jobs for the boys and girls. *Lottizzazione* – dividing into lots – is the name given to the system whereby a plethora of political parties has carved out shares in the various national spheres of power such as the arts, media and the trade unions. Thus the channels of the state radio and TV RAI 1,2, and 3 each belong to different parties, becoming progressively left wing according to the number. The trade unions UIL, CIGL, and CISL are the same. Even the supermarket chains have political affiliations, the Co-op being left wing and Conad right wing. The system has been called a *partitocrazia*, or rule by political parties. Because of proportional representation each party has a chance of being represented in Parliament; official funding comes from the state according to electoral performance.

The attitude of the man or woman in the street is that politicians are all the same whatever party they belong to – what's the difference between a pear and an apple? (*fra mela e pera ci corre poco*) – they are just in it for the money. The Italian people do not expect their politicians to 'deliver' nor are they curious about the details of their private life or sexual behaviour; the general public simply get on with their lives.

The Economic Miracle

After the war and with the help of Marshall aid from the USA the Italian economy took off in the 1950s and 1960s – the boom years of *il miracolo economico*. Massive internal migrations from country to city and from South to North involving ten million Italians provided the labour vital for the factories of the North, such as the burgeoning FIAT of Turin. Mostly hardy peasants from rural hinterlands, their organisational and working habits translated excellently to the shop floor – and they in turn enjoyed prosperity for the first time. *Rocco and his Brothers* and *La Dolce Vita* (1961) are films which illustrate the spirit of that age.

The Mafia

Aldo Moro saw the beginning of the decline of his party and called it the 'convergence of parallels', ie. the overhauling of the right by the left – which led to Bettino Craxi's socialist-led government in 1983-7. Left wing and right wing coalitions alternated in power. In 1981 there was the scandal of the famous P2 masonic lodge, with its deep implication of the Italian political classes and in 1986 the maxi-trials of the Mafia were sparked off by the confessions of Tommaso Buscetta in 1984. The collapse of communism with the fall of the Berlin Wall in 1989 led to the splitting and renaming of Italian political parties of the left with names like 'Democrats of the Left', (DS) 'Party of Italian Communists' (PdCI) and 'Party of the Communist Refoundation'. In 1991 a crusading magistrate Antonio di Pietro started the so-called 'Clean Hands' campaign (*mani pulite*) bravely exposing corruption in high places, including the systematic and illegal funding of political parties in the *Tangentopoli* or Bribesville scandal. But di Pietro himself was accused of illegal acts and Italian life soon returned to its tacit acceptance of corruption, Bettino Craxi – the ex Socialist party leader and prime minister died a fugitive from justice in Tunisia in 2001. Giulio Andreotti, known as the 'divine Giulio', active in politics since 1946 and seven times prime minister for the Christian Democrats ended his career in 2002 facing a 24-year sentence for complicity with the Mafia in the murder of a journalist. The present (2003) prime minister Silvio Berlusconi (*Forza Italia*) is a defendant in lawsuits, accused of such things as false accounting and bribing judges. Even notaries – who are representatives of the state – habitually recommend the lowest declarable and not the actual price in the conveyancing of real estate. Laws are negotiable. Politicians do not go to prison.

The Present

The two leading forces in Italian politics in 2003 are Silvio Berlusconi and

Umberto Bossi.

Silvio Berlusconi was born in 1936 in Lombardy into a small hard working and religious family. He soon revealed his talents as an innovative property developer, creating a new town called Milano Due; he joined the P2 Masonic lodge and befriended the corrupt Socialist prime minister Bettino Craxi , who gave him a leg up with the acquisition of a TV empire, following the deregulation of state TV monopoly: *Telemilano, Canale Cinque, Italia Uno, Retequattro* TV channels were his power base for the creation of a financial empire *Mediaset* and a political party, *Forza Italia*, with which he became the leader of a coalition government in 1994. He was the richest man in Italy, with the state honorific title of *il Cavaliere*. Berlusconi's most important ally, Umberto Bossi was born in 1941 also in Lombardy, a rough provincial with a raucous voice whose mentor was Bruno Salvadori the Valle d'Aosta separatist and ideologue. Bossi founded the *Lega Nord Padania*: The Lombard League, promoting a separate country to be called Padania i.e. the Po valley, which gained a huge following at the grass roots, taxi-driver level amongst northern Italians who were fed up with *Roma ladrona*, the thieving government of Rome. Bossi was elected to the Senate and is known as *il Senatur*. But he withdrew his support from Berlusconi in his 1994 government, which collapsed.

Four governments followed, of which the Christian Democrat Romano Prodi's was the most distinguished, in 1998 successfully privatising state utilities and monopolies and engineering entry into the Euro monetary union.

At the 2001 elections the centre-right coalition headed by Berlusconi's *Casa delle Libertà* (Home of Freedoms) beat the centre-left coalition *l'Ulivo* (the Olive tree) 365 to 250 seats in parliament and 177 to 128 in the Senate.

With this convincing majority the *Casa delle Libertà* declared a Second Republic. Its manifesto proposed sweeping liberalising reforms, in a 'Pact for Italy' (*un Patto per l'Italia*), but by 2003 it had no money to spend. It had provoked serious hostility from the trade unions (a general strike in April 2002) and from the magistracy (who went on strike in June 2002). It had only succeeded in passing laws directly favourable to Berlusconi's personal interests.

It also tinkered with the Italian constitution in favour of the subsidiarity of the Regions, Provinces and *Comunes* and abolished the ban on the Savoy royal family who were at last allowed to set foot in Italy in 2002.

The Italian people have consistently shown themselves to favour the President above all Italian institutions, ever since the charismatic Sandro Pertini's term in the 1980's. The present incumbent, Carlo Azeglio Ciampi, is equally highly regarded. At the moment (2003) the President is elected by Parliament (for a term of seven years). One of Silvio Berlusconi's parliamentary proposals is that the President should instead be elected directly by the people, which would require a change in the constitution – with his control of the media and marketing skills Berlusconi would stand a good chance of winning, thus gaining for himself the same power that he envies in his buddies George W. Bush and Tony Blair. Berlusconi is surrounded by astute lawyers such as Cesare Previti who help him block and delay prosecutors, and he is an *amicu di li amici* a friend of friends to the Mafia, with mafioso cronies such as Senator dell'Utri. Foreigners are horrified by Berlusconi's dictatorial instincts and breathtaking conflict of interests, but Italians will point out that he is only a grinning presenter with a permatan – he lacks the addiction to violence of the true dictator. *Per fortuna.*

In January 2003 the magistrates throughout Italy demonstrated in silent protest, each one of them brandishing a copy of the Italian constitution. The signal was: don't mess with this, it is a precious document.

In February 2003 a Mediobanca report revealed that only 15 of the world's top 274 multinationals were Italian, the most important of which, Fiat, was in serious difficulties. Even Switzerland and the Scandinavian and Benelux countries were doing better. Only 2.4% of Italy's industrial turnover was ploughed back into research compared with 4.7% in the US and the European average of 3.7%. Further education was starved of funds – there was a brain drain, mainly to the USA sometimes via the UK. The Censis report of January 2003 gave a picture of Italy as a 'dwarf with flat batteries!' Italian capital and Italian industrial plant was emigrating to central and eastern European countries where labour was cheap and welfare poor – not to the *Mezzogiorno* of Italy. Italian entrepreneurs were besotted by countries like Romania (often returning with track-suited child brides).

Economic commentators, including President Ciampi, felt that future prosperity depended on a reform of the labour market, education and research, a massive improvement in the infrastructures and the promotion of big conglomerates. Foreigners were not deterred by this charming pessimism, and continued to flock to the country in droves. Berlusconi is not Mussolini, but Italian trains run on time, as a public service, and they are cheap. Trenitalia, the company that runs them showed a profit in 2001. Italian TV might be *spazzatura* (rubbish), but a whole spectrum of Italian newspapers is engaged daily, not in pursuit of celebrity trivia, but in serious political debate.

The parliamentary opposition, the centre-left coalition *l'Ulivo*, led by the telegenic Clintonesque ex-mayor of Rome, Francesco Rutelli (born in 1954), have not come up with any coherent policies. The *Lega Nord Padania* has as many seats (30) as all the ex-communist parties put together, and, in the extremely unlikely event of Berlusconi's expulsion from office by President Ciampi or at the hands of a triumphant judiciary, the centre left will still have to contend with, the popularity of Gianfranco Fini of the crypto-Fascist *Alleanza Nazionale*, who control more than three times as many seats as the *Lega Nord* itself.

From the outsider's point of view, Italy is going through an interesting period of reappraisal, but it is still buzzing. The collapse of the Fiat motor company, symbolised by the death of its prince, Gianni Agnelli, in January 2003, suggests that Italy was not so good at running large conglomerates, but has a true talent for clusters of small, cutting edge, often family businesses, half in and half out of the black economy, to which the government instinctively turns a blind eye: not so much Fiat cars as Malaguti motorbikes. *L'arte di arrangiarsi* – the national art of getting round the law- is epitomised by Premier Berlusconi, of whom ex-president Francesco Cossiga said: 'It is better to be governed by a clever con-man (*un'imbroglione*) than by an incompetent nice guy. To which the Italian people add a strong dose of civility and altruism, a surviving spirit of mutuality and an idealistic younger generation almost totally opposed to multi-nationals. Italy is still the fifth or sixth largest economy in the world: a *serie 'A'* country.

THE WIT AND WISDOM OF SILVIO BERLUSCONI.

Berlusconi's solution to the Fiat crisis?
Change the name to Ferrari.
Berlusconi's advice to laid off workers?
Get a job in the black economy.
Berlusconi's attitude to magistrates?
They only got their jobs by passing exams: I got mine by being voted in by the People.

Racism and the North South Divide

In Italy there is scant respect for any taboo on social stereotyping. It is recognised by local folklores that different areas produce a different character of person. Historical prejudices persist in static communities. Thus in Tuscany the Sienese regard the Florentines as unprintable epithets, and it is always better to have a dead man in the house than a man from Pisa on the doorstep. This stereotyping by proverb pervades Italy. The Piedmontese have fake manners (*Piemontesi: finti cortesi*) and the people of Vicenza eat cats (*Vicentini magnagatti*). Fierce local loyalties are defined by the word *campanilismo*, the *campanile* being the bell tower in the main square which is the focal point of the community.

Within this context there is an imaginary border 'where Africa begins'. For some this is South of Florence, *'da Firenze ingiù'* or even *'da Bologna ingiù'*, but it is definitely south of Rome. This is the Italian equivalent of the Mason-Dixon line in America, or the north of Watford concept in England.

The qualities admired in the South are feistiness, cunning and swagger; it is despicable to be doltish (*scemo*). In the north on the other hand the quality admired is *Serietà*, seriousness, reliability, honesty with money and so on. Pejorative terms used are *Terroni* (dirt) to describe southerners and *polentoni* to describe northerners. Polenta is maize porridge, a traditional dish of the north. The prejudice is so strong that there have been cases recently where southerners have been bashed up and killed by hooligans in the north who heard their southern accents. It is said that the old car number plates which indicated the car's provincial origin such as PA for Palermo and SS for Sassari were being phased out in 1996 in favour of anonymous Europlates, specifically for the purpose of removing the incitement of tribal identification.

The reaction of an unreconstructed Tuscan to Southern swagger is '*oi oi oi oi oi*' (repeated) or *marocchini!* (Moroccans!). The *Marocchini* are specifically *malvisti* or ill-regarded because of the behaviour of some North African troops under Free French command in the Second World War, added to the atavistic fear of the Saracens and the Barbary pirates, whose slave raids continued into the eighteenth century. This deep antipathy does not augur too well for Italian relations with the growing Islamic community in the post September 11 world. Islam and Rome are both anathema in Padania (the plains of northern Italy).

Immigrants to Italy

Over nine million southerners were absorbed into the north and centre of Italy in the great internal migrations which took place between 1955 and 1971 changing the character of cities like Genoa and Turin. Just as the southerners were indispensable to the success of the Italian economic miracle, so now is the present wave of immigrants, illegal or otherwise, (*extracomunitari, clandestini*) recognised by some as a beneficial movement of labour in the global village of the third millennium, especially in Italy where the birthrate has been declining since 1964. Immigrants are doing the jobs that Italians no longer want to do, from Senegalese fishermen in Trieste to Chinese sweatshop workers in Prato, from Cameroon tannery workers in Croce sull'Arno to Ukrainian carers in Vicenza, from Peruvian houseboys in Radda to Filipino maids in Rome. They are encouraged to pay taxes through come-clean amnesties called *sanatorie*, and according to Antonio Fazio, the governor of the Bank of Italy, they are a 'precious resource' for Italy. But the fact remains that 62.9% of Italians are racist towards Africans, 18.5% towards eastern Europeans, 7.5% towards Asians and 3% towards South Americans (according to a recent survey by the 'National Xenophobia Observatory'). The *Lega Nord Padania* is institutionally xenophobic, and most Italians remain stolidly monocultural; their schools quickly assimilate immigrant children, particularly the offspring of Albanian rural workers. But other groups, Muslims specifically, are not absorbed into the community, their womenfolk literally not showing their faces. Many immigrants with commercial talents prosper – such as the Indians, Bangladeshis, Sri Lankans, Nigerians and Chinese. On Sundays the public parks of Milan are full of men playing cricket – hailing from Sri Lanka and the 'subcontinent'.

GEOGRAPHICAL INFORMATION

Mainland and Offshore Italy

Italy occupies an area of 116,000 square miles (301,278 sq km). As well as the long peninsula, which as most schoolchildren learn, is shaped like a boot, Italy's offshore elements include the island of Sicily situated off the toe of the boot across the Strait

of Messina, the islands of Pantelleria, Linosa and Lampedusa which lie between
Sicily and Tunisia, the island of Elba located off Tuscany, and the rocky, barren
island of Sardinia which lies west of Rome and south of Corsica. The Tyrrhenian
Sea bounds the south west of the peninsula, with the Ionian Sea under the sole
of the boot. The Adriatic Sea lies on the eastern side between Italy and former-
Yugoslavia. Italy shares borders with France, Switzerland, Austria and Croatia.

Main physical features include the Alps, which form much of the the northern
border with Slovenia, Austria, Switzerland and France. Also in the north are Italy's
main lakes: Guarda, Maggiore and Como. An offshoot of the Alps curves round
the Gulf of Genoa and runs spine-like down the peninsula to form the Appenines.
The longest river, the Po, lies in the north and flows from west to east across the
plain of Lombardy and into the Adriatic. On Sicily, the regularly active volcano,
Mount Etna rises to 10,741 feet (3,274 m). Etna has been very active since 2001
and some experts are predicting more eruptions.

Earthquakes & Volcanoes. The European fault line runs right through Italy
from north to south. The main risk areas for quakes are central and southern Italy
(from Umbria to Calabria) where about 70% of the region is susceptible. Tremors
are quite common in Umbria and the Apeninnes. Seismologists claim that the
number, strength and frequency of quakes hitting central Italy is increasing,
which has led to a drop in tourism and house buying by foreigners. Italy's last
big disastrous earthquake flattened Messina in 1908, killing 84,000 people and
causing the shoreline to sink by half a metre overnight. Other serious ones were
Friuli (1976), Irpinia (1980), and Umbria (1997) – the most dramitic recent
quake caused severe damage to the Church of Assisi in front of the television
cameras. Another in Molise in 2002 caused a substandard school to collapse
killing 20 children.

As if this were not excitement enough, Italy has three active volcanoes. The
most infamous of these is Vesuvius near Naples, which buried 2,000 inhabitants
in their hedonistic city of Pompeii in AD79. These days the volcano's rumblings
are under continuous monitoring so there should be plenty of warning before it
pops again. The other volcanoes are comfortingly offshore (unless you live there):
Etna on Sicily and Stromboli on a small island off the western coast of southern
Italy.

Climate

The climate of Italy shows the kind of regional variation one would expect from
a country with its head in the Alps and its toe in the Mediterranean. At the
foot of the Alps in the north is the flat and fertile Plain of Lombardy, which is
also one of the main industrial areas. Cold and wet in winter, those who find
themselves living and working in the north can escape to different climatic
regions to rejuvenate themselves. There are the cold, dry Alps further northwards

for winter sports. The Italian Riviera (Liguria), which is pleasantly mild in winter. Or there is the south, including Sicily, where the winters are even milder and typically Mediterranean. In summer and winter, the middle regions of Tuscany and Umbria, which are home to many expatriates, have the best of both worlds: neither too cold in winter nor too parched in summer. However, the higher areas of even these favoured regions can be cold and snowbound in winter. The far south and Sicily are generally considered too hot for comfort in summer.

Italy, especially its islands, is exposed to winds which can make life very uncomfortable for people and plants depending on the season.

ITALIAN WINDS

Bora. A cold, dry, violent wind which blows from the east-north-east, from the eastern Alps on to the Gulf of Trieste.

Garbino. (see *Libeccio).*

Ghibli. A hot, dry south-western wind from Libya.

Greco. Also called *grecale* is a strong winter wind from the north-east which affects the central and eastern Mediterranean.

Libeccio. An often violent wind from the south-west which affects the centre and north Mediterranean.

Levante. A wind from the east.

Ostro. Also called *austro* is the generic name for a wind from the south. Winds from the Sahara often bring rain full of sand particles which make cars dirty.

Mistral. Also called *maestrale* or *maestro*. Dry, cold, impetuous north-west wind which blows through southern France and Liguria.

Ponente. A fresh wind from the west; the summer breeze from the Tyrrenian Sea.

Scirocco. A hot, wet wind from the south east blowing from Africa across the Mediterranean.

Tramontana. A cold, generally dry and rather strong north wind.

AVERAGE TEMPERATURES

City & Province	Jan	Apr	July	Nov
Ancona (Marche)	42°f/6°c	]56°f/14°c	77°f/25°c	55°f/13°c
Bari(Puglia)	46°f/8°c	57°f/14°f	77°f/25°f°	59°f/15°c
Bologna (Emilia Romagna)	37°f/3°c	56°f/15°c	78°f/26°c	50°f/10°c
Florence (Tuscany)	42°f/6°c	55°f/13°c	77°f/25°c	52°f/11°c
Genova (Liguria)	46°f/8°c	56°f/14°c	77°f/25°c	55f/13°c
Milan (Lombardy)	36°f/2°c	55°f/13°c	77°f/25°c	48°f/9°c
Naples (Campania)	48°f/9°c	56°f/14°c	77°f/25°c	59°f/15°c
Palermo(Sicily)	50°f/10°c	61°f/16°c	77°f/25°c	50°f/16°c
Rome (Latium)	45°f/7°c	57°f/14°c	78°f/26°c	55°f/13°c
Trieste (Friuli-Venezia)	41°f/5°c	55°f/13°c	75°f/25dg]c	52°f/11°c
Venice (Venetia)	39°f/4°c	55°c/13°c	75°f/24°c	52°f/10°c

CULTURE SHOCK

(Some comments listed by an Englishwoman living in Italy)

1. No one dreams of respecting a zebra crossing. If, as a motorist, you stop at one the pedestrian looks at you with amazement and refuses to cross.
2. In the restaurants vegetables come on separate plates. The romantic candle-lit dinner is very rare. Most restaurants have bright fluorescent ceiling lights and a TV blaring.
3. Attractive young girls are complimented all the time, even by complete strangers. But, unlike other Mediterranean men, Northern Italian ones seem to have stopped the practice of touching and pinching foreign women.
4. A lot of people smoke even in no smoking areas.
5. In the country, men in camouflage carrying shotguns, i.e. hunters, seem to trespass everywhere. The hail of shot on roofs makes the foreigners indignant, (but this used to be much worse).
6. The alarming number of feral cats or hedge cats. In Pienza twenty odd cats were being fed by an American woman.
7. The amount of pornography on display at child height.
8. The degrading of women on TV, such as women dancing on a table-top with newscasters behind them wearing suits. Every single programme seems to present women in the same way, as sex-objects. Yet there are no men in the same situations, and why are all male presenters fat and bald? Italian TV is just crap!
9. Black prostitutes on the roadside, black madams in the middle of the country. Hence if you see black women you think they are prostitutes.
10. More small shops than we are used to. We didn't expect to see any MacDonalds.
11. You seldom see drunks or drunken brawls outside bars. Pubs dedicated exclusively to the consumption of alcohol do not exist. Bars are open to all, with all ages welcome.
12. Men sitting in bars not drinking but playing cards.
13. Men urinating in public (the time-honoured *vespasiani* or small urinals have been removed).
14. The beggars in Rome, bands of them especially around the Vatican, hassling people.
15. The way people walk through the town in the evening all dressed up (the *passeggiata*).
16. The *festas* (celebrations) which bridge the generations are delightful. e.g. mothers teaching their young boys how to dance a mazurka. A big community spirit. Perhaps because of their old way of life. Everyone had to club together to harvest the grapes and olives.

17. The long lunch hour; you have to get used to being able to do nothing between 12.30 and 4pm or later. But in compensation all the shops are open until eight o'clock in the evening.

18. The high status of the working men. You see workmen and truck drivers eating at tables with freshly laundered white table cloths. A shock to see their healthy choice of food such as vegetable soups, fresh salads and grilled fish etc.

19. The stand-up coffee habit – surprising that people don't have breakfast. A lot of men drink a glass of water with their espresso.

20. The mutual respect between tradesmen. The plumber would not dream of encroaching on the work of the electrician.

21. Shocked to find there is still a snobby system here. Rich bourgeois people lording it over the *contadini*. But this is fading. The modern generation has lost their deference, and staff has to be immigrant or southern.

22. Hospitals: In the hospitals there may be nowhere to have a shower. They come and give you a bowl of warm water. The bathroom facilities in a modern hospital may not be adequate. They may not put screens round you when the doctor examines you. They expect relations to bring food; they only give you gruel. But they are not sparing of the latest medical technology and treatment and medical attention. What was most shocking of all was the sight of a chain-smoking radiographer.

23. The Carabinieri are not so approachable as our police. If you talk to them they bark back and ask what's wrong? It is not the custom to ask the Carabinieri anything.

24. Having to report to the *Comune* within 48 hours of arrival for members of the EU – and having to carry your passport at all times.

25. Italians' lives are very ordered and organised, they always have their wood stacked up, their apartments are so neat. In England they are knocking down high rise apartment blocks because people couldn't live in them. Here they are flat dwellers. They take a pride in their homes. Their policy of community housing is to put relations near to each other.

26. Young children and babies are welcomed and made a fuss of everywhere, especially in restaurants.

27. Old people are looked after by their children and respected by the young.

28. Italy is the home of Catholicism, but hardly anyone goes to mass.

29. The religious, almost pagan, respect for the dead. On All Souls Day the cemeteries are cleaned up and crowded with people paying respect to their dead.

30. The ambulance service – the *Misericordia* is run by volunteers, a free service which dates back to the Middle Ages, available day and night.

GETTING THERE

By Air

High Street travel agents, the travel pages of most national newspapers and the internet are obvious sources of discounted fares to Italy and there is plenty of choice. Non-stop flights are available from the UK to over 30 Italian cities. If you change to a domestic flight at Milan or Rome, you can reach still more. Due to the constantly changing nature of the airline industry and the spreading network of the budget airlines, it is likely that origin and destination airports will change, and airlines will disappear (like British Airways' budget airline Go, which was absorbed by EasyJet in 2002 and Buzz which was taken over by Ryanair in 2003 and may well not survive as a separate entity). Therefore the information below is for guidance only and should be checked with your travel agent, or direct with the airline well in advance of your departure and before you make concrete travel plans.

Internet tools that regularly scan airlines' websites and download details of fares from different airlines and compare them can be useful. www.skyscanner.net and www.aerfares.net and www.easyvalue.com are such tools, and cover most budget airlines, while Austrian Airlines website has a comprehensive interactive flight planner that allows travellers to find details of most scheduled flights, on any airline, in the world: www.aua.com.

Milan Linate is 10 km east of the city and Milan Malpensa is 46 km north-west of the city. Malpensa to Milan is by Malpensa Express (train) and the Malpensa Shuttle coach.

Most of the airlines listed below allow passengers to book flights online.

Aer Lingus: (☎0845 084 4444; www.aerlingus.com) flies direct from Dublin.
Alitalia: (☎0870 5448259) flies Heathrow and Gatwick to Rome, and Gatwick to Venice and Florence.

BMI: (☎0870 6070555; www.flybmi.com) flies Heathrow to Milan (Linate).
BMI Baby: (☎0870 264 2229; www.bmibaby.com) flies from East Midlands airport to Milan (Bergamo).
British Airways: (☎0845 773 3377; www.ba.com) uses Heathrow and Gatwick.
British European: (☎08705 676 676; www.flybe.com) flies from Southampton to Bergamo (for Milan).
EasyJet: (☎0870 607 6543; www.go-fly.com) uses Stansted, and has the largest number of Italian destinations.
MyTravelLite: (☎0870 1564 564; www.mytravellite.com) new small airline uses Birmingham.
Ryanair: (☎0871 246 0000; www.ryanair.com) uses Stansted.
Virgin Express: 020-7744 0004 (in the UK), 02-482 96 000 (Milan), 800-097 097 (Rome & other areas), www.virgin-express.com.

AIRPORTS/AIRLINES: THE UK & IRELAND & ITALY							
	Aer Lingus	Alitalia	BMI	BMI Baby	British Airways	EasyJet	MyTravelLite	Ryanair
Alghero (Sardinia)								o
Ancona								o
Bergamo Orio Serio (for Milan)				o				o
Bologna (Borgo Panigale airport)	o							
Bologna (Marconi airport)					o			
Brescia (for Verona)								o
Florence (Peretola airport)		o						
Forlì airport (for Bologna)*								o
Genova								o
Milan (Linate airport)	o	o	o		o			
Milan (Malpensa airport)	o	o			o			
Naples					o	o		
Pescara								o
Pisa (for Florence)					o	o	o	
Rimini							o	
Rome (Ciampino airport)						o		o
Rome (Fiumicino airport)**	o	o			o			
Treviso aiport (for Venice)								o
Trieste								o
Venice (Marco Polo airport)		o			o	o		

* Forlì is 45km from Bologna

**Rome Fiumicino airport is also known as Leonardo da Vinci

Airlines offering direct flights from the USA and Canada:
North West: 800-447 4747 (US – international reservations), www.nwa.com
Delta: 800-221 1212 (in USA and Canada) 800-864 114 (in Italy),
   www.delta.com;
Alitalia: 800-223 5730; www.alitaliausa.com.
Air Canada: www.aircanada.ca.

Travel agents specialising in offering discount fares to Italy can be found in the
Travel sections of newspapers such as *The Sunday Times, The Sunday Telegraph*
and *The Mail on Sunday.* The websites of many agents and budget airlines offer
special deals and discounts and special offers change frequently. Ryanair was
offering flights to Ancona in November 2002 for 1p (not a misprint) plus airport
taxes. It is also worth looking at the following websites:
Lupus Travel: www.lupustravel.com
Orbitz: www.orbitz.com
Holiday Choice: www.holidaychoice.co.uk

Approximate Flight Lengths
London to Rome – two and a half hours
New York to Rome – ten hours
Los Angeles to Rome – Fifteen and a half hours
Sydney to Rome – just over twenty-four hours

By Rail
For those who don't care to fly, getting to Italy from Northern European stations
such as Paris and Calais can be a doddle on a direct through train. There are also
sleeper services from Paris and Calais. If you want to take the car but not drive it to
Italy, you can use the Motorail service from Denderleeuw in Belgium. Denderleeuw
is about a 100-mile drive from Calais and the route goes through Belgium, eastern
France and Switzerland. Once in Italy the route goes through Milan and terminates
at Bologna. A useful contact is Railsavers; ☎0870-750 7070; www.railsavers.com.

By Road
You can enter Italy by road from France, Switzerland and Austria. The routes
from Austria and France are open year round. From Switzerland access is via the
Mont Blanc tunnel from Chamonix (France) to Courmayeur in Italy. If you have
a tunnel phobia then from Switzerland access is via the Grand St. Bernard pass,
which can be dodgy in winter when you will almost certainly need snow chains
on your tyres.

Speed Limits. 50 kph (urban roads); 90 kph (other roads); 130 kph (*autostrade*
(toll motorways).

Documents. Note that if driving to Italy it is advisable to carry all your car documents with you, i.e. driving licence, car registration document (known as *patente* and *libretto* respectively), insurance certificate, and certificate of roadworthiness.

Breakdowns. If you break down you can dial the emergency number 116 from a public telephone and the Automobile Club of Italy will come to your aid. You should consider taking out breakdown insurance if you do not belong to an automobile club with a reciprocal assistance agreement with the Automobile Club d'Italia.

The Automobile Club d'Italia: Via C. Columbo 261, 00147 Rome; ☎+39 06 514971; fax +39 06 5123682; www.aci.it).

Getting to the Islands

Ferries. There are regular ferry connections between the mainland of Italy and the islands. Large car ferries run from the ports of Genova, Civitavecchia and Naples to Sardinia and Sicily. There are also ferry connections from the mainland to the smaller Tremiti, Bay of Naples and Pontine islands. The ferries also make international trips from the mainland to Malta, Corsica, Spain, Greece, Turkey, Tunisia, Egypt and Israel. Fares are reasonable although you may have to book well in advance, especially over the holiday season in the summer months. In the winter the number of crossings is greatly reduced. In Italy the tourism office and travel agents can provide information, which can also be found on the website www.traghettionline.net or the websites of the ferry operators, some of whom are listed below.

Minoan Lines: www.minoan.gr

Agoudimos Lines: www.agoudimos-lines.com

Strintzis Line: www.strintzis.gr

COMMUNICATIONS

The Post Office

The Italian postal system, *Poste e telegrafi* (PT) is now being revamped and services are improving, though they still have some way to go to fully escape their old image. Mail deliveries are getting quicker, though overnight delivery can not be relied upon – nor is the system reliable enough to negate the need for courier services for important letters and packages. The overseas service is also slow and mail can take a week or more to arrive at a European or North American destination.

Stamps can be bought from the post office (*ufficio postale*) and also tobacconists (*tabaccherie*). Post office opening times vary depending on location but they are open Monday to Friday (some open at 8am) until 2pm (some until later 6.30/

7pm) and until lunchtime on Saturdays. You can get precise information on post offices' opening times from your municipal website.

There are various postal services for letters and parcels; some internal some both internal and international. Domestic post under 3 kg can be sent *posta celere*, which is supposed to take one day, or priority (*posta prioritaria* – almost guaranteed next day delivery for post less than 2 kg), or ordinary (*ordinaria* – probable delivery within three or four days). With registered post (*posta raccomandata*) the post office supply a confirmation of receipt of your letter at its destination. *Posta assicurata* insures the contents of a letter, within Italy.

Parcel Post. Parcel post can only be insured. For parcels there is *Pacco celere1* – takes a day, less than 30 kg within Italy; *Pacco celere3* – takes 3 days, less than 30 kg within Italy.

International mail. Can be sent by airmail or surface mail – surface mail from any country can take many weeks and Italy is no exception to this rule.

Poste Restante. For those who have no fixed address, the post restante (*fermoposta)* service is useful; just write the addressee's name, then *fermoposta* and the place name on the envelope; the addressee can then pick up his or her mail from the post office after providing a passport as identification. In large cities it is always better to address poste restante mail to the main post office.

Telegraph. The state-run Italcable operates a telegraph service abroad by cable or radio; both internal and overseas messages can be sent over the phone.

Other services offered by the post office. In addition to the regular postal services, larger post offices in major cities are now offering financial services, as do post offices in other parts of Europe. Services offered include bank accounts *(conto bancoposto),* savings schemes, money wire transfers and bill payment services for most bills you are likely to receive (gas, electricity, telephone, rent, etc.).

Telephones

The Italian telephone giant Telecom Italia was privatised in 1997, thus bringing Italy towards liberalisation of her telecommunications market in line with EU directives. Since the early 1990s the Italian phone system has undergone modernisation, and fibre optic cables have been installed throughout the country – except in the usual remote rural districts that always seem to be left somewhere in the past. Public telephones take coins, or more usually, phonecards that are available from tobacconists, news-stands, machines at telephone offices, stations and airports. Coin operated phones are being phased out in favour of the card phones. Note that the sign *guasto,* often posted on public telephones means 'out of order'.

American users will find having to pay as you go for local calls different to the system prevalent in many US locations. Local and long distance calls do not vary much in price, though the time of day affects the cost of a call – out of business hours is cheaper than during them. International calls within Europe cost less after 10pm, though the peak rate for North America finishes earlier in the day. As peak rates and off-peak rates and their applicability vary it is worth checking with Telecom Italia to find the best time to make your calls.

CHEAP TIME

The cheapest time to make calls is from 10pm-8am Monday to Saturday and all day on Sundays. As the cheap rate for evening calls in Italy doesn't come into effect until 10pm, it is quite usual to make long distance calls late into the night. However, there is a price structure known as *Numero Blu* that provides discounts on the numbers you call most often, including your Internet connection number.

DIALING TELEPHONE NUMBERS IN ITALY

Phone users need to dial the complete number of the person they wish to contact, including the area code, even for local calls. This system is common in Europe and possibly heralds the introduction of a seamless European phone system sometime in the future.

Expatriates (*extracommunitari*) who use international phones more than most for keeping in touch with friends around the world have long used call-back services and other alternative phone services. These are advertised in international newspapers and magazines (*International Herald Tribune, Time, Newsweek etc*) and can be a great cost saver.

The latest innovation in reducing telephone costs is the utilisation of the internet for international phone calls. Services such as www.Net2Phone.com allow internet users whose computer is equipped with a microphone and sound card (most computers produced within the last three years allow a microphone/headphone set to be plugged into their soundcard) to log on to their local Internet Service Provider (ISP) and call a standard phone, via the internet, in most countries around the world. The cost of the call is then limited to the cost of being online.

Some phone users even avoid *Telcom Italia* completely by making long distance calls through France Telecom, or Deutsche Telecom or Sprint etc. To do this you need a hardware gadget than allows you to connect direct with the provider. You need to contact a private telecommunications broker to do this (see below) or look in the telephone yellow pages of your city under *telefonia e telecommunicazioni*. The attraction of this is lessening with the increase in quality of internet-to-telephone services.

Mobiles. The mobile phone (*telefonino*) has become the vital accessory without which no self-respecting Italian would dare to be seen. In common with other European countries, Italy has auctioned off mobile phone licences and there are now about ten network providers including Tiscali, Tim, Vodafone, Wind, Clicktel, Infostrada and Eplanet which between them offer a bewildering range of price structures and payment options depending on the type of service required, the amount of time you spend on the phone per month, what time of day you phone and how often you want to phone abroad. The area of coverage also varies between providers.

When choosing a mobile phone it is important to check that the provider covers the areas where you live, work and visit. Tim is the mobile telephone subsidiary of *Telecom Italia* and has the widest coverage for those who travel extensively. Roaming agreements, where you can use the phone outside Italy, are another useful option for frequent travellers. In addition to the coverage, the level of usage needs to be considered. High monthly charges can counteract low call rates for some, while the reverse is the case for other users. If your Italian is not up to it, take someone along to translate for you – or risk facing a large bill.

When dialing Italy from abroad to mobile phones remember to omit the international access and Italian country code (00 39).

International Calls to and from Italy. To telephone the UK from Italy dial 00, wait for the continuous tone and then dial 44 and continue immediately with the UK number, omitting the first number of the UK code. For example, to ring Vacation Work Publications from Italy you would dial: 00-44-1865 241978.

To telephone the US from Italy the country code is 1 followed by the ten digit number, including the area code, e.g. 00-1 123 456 7890.

To telephone Italy from the UK dial 00 39 and then the Italian number. The first zero of the provincial code must be included. For example to ring a Rome number of 06-123456 you would actually dial 00-3906-000000. From the US it is necessary to dial the international access code of your service provider, followed by 39-06-123456.

LOCAL TELEPHONE CODES

Alassio 0182	Naples 081
Aosta 0165	Palermo 091
Bologna 051	Pesaro 0731
Bolzano 0471	Pisa 050
Cagliari 070	Riccione 054
Cattolica 0541	Rimini 0541
Como 031	Rome 06
Cortina d'Ampezzo 0436	San Remo 0184

Diano Marina 0183	Sorrento 081
Florence 055	Taormina 0942
Genoa 010	Trento 0461
Grado 0431	Trieste 040
La Spezia 0187	Turin 011
Lido di Jesolo 0421	Venice 041
Lignano 0431	Verona 05
Milan 02	Viareggio 0584

Emergency & Useful Numbers
Ambulance   118
Breakdown Services   116
Carabinieri   112 or 113
International Directory Enquiries   170
Enquiries for Europe & the Mediterranean 176
Telephone faults/engineers   182

The Internet

Italy was one of the slowest European countries to jump on the internet bandwagon, though it is now catching up – Italian municipalities (e.g. Rome) now have websites where they provide information in English for expatriates.

The internet is a great resource for expatriates and email is an easy, cheap and reliable way to keep in touch with friends and relatives around the world. There are a number of free access (but you pay for the phone call) ISPs in Italy, www.jumpy.it and www.kataweb.it are two, who give away CDs in store to attract new clients. Once you have a CD, insert it in your modem-equipped computer and follow the instructions. Within a few minutes you should have internet access – assuming *Telecom Italia* have installed your telephone line. As in other countries, heavy users may find it more cost-effective to pay for a subscription service as there are special deals available.

Expatriates should be aware that different phone systems around the world are wired differently. Modem sockets have four connectors, different Modems are wired to use either the inside pair or the outside pair. If your modem worked before you arrived in Italy but not after arrival, try changing the connector cable to one that is wired differently. Remember to keep the cable for when you go home again. A useful worldwide internet café search engine can be found at www.cybercafe.com

FOOD AND DRINK

Food. Many myths surround the Italians, and their eating habits are no less liable to exaggeration or misconception than other aspects of their lives. Admittedly, whether the pasta is cooked *al dente* (just right) or *una colla* (sticky and overcooked) is an issue treated with near religious reverence. However, despite the world-famous ice creams, pizzas and pasta dishes, the Italians boast one of the lowest incidences of heart disease in Europe (and consume less ice cream than most of their European neighbours). The basis of Italian eating tends towards quality, and as with all matters of Italian life, is subject to the rigorous demands of *la bella figura* (cutting a fine figure). Just as the majority of Italians look upon drunkenness as a disgusting and unnecessary foreign fetish, obesity is similarly unacceptable, unless accompanied by a corresponding amount of Pavarotti-type charisma. Even so, it is noticeable these days that the increasing problem of obesity in western children includes Italy where a recent article in *Corriera della Sera* claimed that one in three Italian children is now overweight.

Although every Italian region proclaims the excellence of its own cooking, the region of Emilia-Romagna is thought by some to boast the finest and richest of Italian cuisine. However, Tuscany is renowned for its high-quality meat and Genoa for its herb-based dishes while the food of the south is often spicy. The three main meals of the Italian day are treated with varying degrees of importance. Breakfast (*colazione*) is usually a frugal offering of croissant (*cornetto*) or biscuits (*biscotti*), although cereals are gaining popularity in the Italian market. Italians often take breakfast (i.e. a capuccino and a croissant) in a bar. Lunch (*pranzo*) is treated as the main meal of the day in the southern regions although home-cooked food is increasingly being superseded by convenience food. Finally, dinner (*cena*), as in the majority of Mediterranean countries, is eaten late in the evening, usually between 8pm and 10pm, especially during the summer months.

Eating Out. Traditional Italian restaurants are signalled by the *ristorante trattoria* or *pizzeria* signs. Sparse or unpretentious decor is common and does not reflect on the quality of the food or service. When eating out with Italians you should offer to split the bill *alla romana* – dividing it by the number of those present. However, if you have been invited out to dinner, your host or hostess will probably insist on paying the entire bill. As far as giving tips is concerned, service was traditionally added at the customer's discretion, usually at around 10%-15%. These days though, a 10% charge is generally included in the total bill, as is a cover charge per person. The easiest way to tell if service is included is by looking at the bill (*il conto*), it will have *servizio* and *coperto* for service and cover charges respectively.

Italian bars . Bars typically open at 6am and some stay open till 2am. Coffee – espresso – is the favourite drink. Beer is more popular than wine, the ritual of the pre-meal *aperitivo* at midday or early evening, or the post-meal *digestivo*, are still respected. Fine Italian grappas have replaced malt whiskies as the favoured *digestivo*. In the mornings bars are characterised by customers drinking their *cappuccino* and eating their *brioche* or *panino* standing up at the bar. They are unlikely to drink a cappuccino after 11am. In the evening old men will typically be occupying the tables playing cards and not drinking. If you see a group of Italian men sitting around and drinking beer they will most likely be Sardinians (*Sardi*) who have retained a culture of round-buying. Bars often double as tobacconists and paper shops and nearly always serve snacks, toasted sandwiches and even hot pasta dishes (*primi piatti*).

The Slow Food Movement. Italy, more than France which has surrendered to Disney and Macdonalds, is still holding out as a counter culture to the Americanization of Everything. Americans are attracted in Italy by what they miss out on in America, such as fresh produce that has a taste, culinary artisans at work, life in the piazza, and slow food. The Slow Food Movement (whose symbol is a snail) is lobbying against genetically modified organisms, and is pro organic food. Also, through its publishing company (*Slow Food Editore*) it produces a range of books which deal, in encyclopaedic fashion, with all the food traditions of Italy, historical and regional.

Thus, far from fulfilling the image of a nation of pasta-stuffing, wine-guzzling Pavarotti prototypes, the reality of the Italians' eating habits is far more discerning and infinitely more healthy. Italians are still providing a role model for every aspiring *buongustaio* (food and drink connoisseur) the national gastronomic motto seems to be, enjoy, but not to excess. In Italy, Macdonalds is in retreat.
Slow Food Editore: Via della Mendicità Istruita, 45-Bra (Campania); ☎0172 419611; e-mail: editorinfo@slowfood.it; www.slowfood.it

Drinking. As mentioned above, the Italians are not great drinkers and being drunk (*ubriaco*) carries a special disapproval amongst the majority of Italians which would be thought curious by the lager-lout bravados of the British pub and club scene. However, drinking wine from a young age *is* an accepted part of the culture, unlike in the USA. Overall, alcohol sales have flagged in Italy, as mineral water (*acqua minerale*) sales escalate nationwide. Italy is now second only to France in annual consumption of mineral water. According to the Italian Statistics Institute, ISTAT, the majority of men and a significant percentage of women now choose beer above wine. This may be a result (or a cause) of the mushrooming of English-style pubs in the larger cities (there are scores in Rome alone). The new pubs appeal mainly to the twenty-something party crowd of cosmopolitan Europeans that can be found in most major commercial cities of Europe. In contrast to the increase in beer sales, the annual consumption of wine is dropping to such a level that the wine marketing board is now advertising it in order to encourage sales. If you prefer wine-bars then look for the signs *cantina* or *enoteca* above the door.

Wine. Most of Italy is wine country and there is no space to do justice to the many varieties here. Suffice it to say that some areas have gone in for professional production and export while others have kept their traditions and best wines a secret from the outside world. The northwest (Piemonte) is famous for its vermouths and spumantes, and purplish wines and barolo and barbera grapes. The north-east, particularly the part under Austrian influence, has gone in for mass production. Probably the best known wines abroad are those from central Italy, especially the Chianti wines from the Tuscan hills between Florence and Siena. Southern Italy has the Neapolitan wines of Ischia, Capri and red and white wines from the area around Mount Vesuvius. Sicily's best-known wine is probably the sweet and treacly Marsala.

WINE LABEL GLOSSARY

DOCG – *Denominazione di Origine Controllata Garantita:* the highest quality, similar to France's *appellation contrôlée.*

DOC – *Denominazione di Origine Controllata:* the second highest quality.

DS – *Denominazione Semplice* – the equivalent of the French vin de table.

Messo in bottiglia del produttore all'origine: estate-bottled.

Classico: from the central, i.e. best area of the region.

Imbottigliato nello stabilimento della ditta: bottled on the premises of the firm.

Riserva: wine that has been aged for a statutory period.

Wine Colours: *Bianco* (white), *Rosso* (red), *Rosato* (pink), *Chiaretto* (very light red), *Nero* (very dark red).

Secco: dry.

Amaro: bitter or very dry.

Amabile/Abboccato: medium sweet.

dolce: very sweet.

Spumante: bubbly.

Frizzante: slightly fizzy.

Vin/Vino santo: sweet dessert wine made from dried grapes.

Stravecchio: very old, mellow.

Vino liquoroso: fortified wine.

SCHOOLS AND EDUCATION

Education in Italy is a truly democratic system guaranteed by the constitution, compulsory from age 6 to 15, and controlled by the *Ministero dell'Istruzione dell'Università e della Ricerca* (acronym MIUR) the Ministry of Education, Universities and Research).

Recent changes passed through parliament in 2002 are bringing the Italian system more into line with other EU countries:

- State schools now have local autonomy as a constitutional right.
- They are free to organise their own timetables, curricula etc.

○ Each school must produce a plan of the education on offer a sort of identity card.

○ Schools – teachers and children – are to be monitored by a national evaluation institute, with assessment tests on children at 11, 14 and 16. This will be introduced gradually and only covers 25% of schools to start with.

The aim is to keep children longer in education – up to 18 and beyond:

○ by boosting choice and flexibility between disciplines.
○ by giving career guidance (*orientamento*) at all stages.
○ by promoting information technology and language learning.
○ by issuing certificates and diplomas of national and international worth.
○ by offering vocational and apprenticeship options.
○ by offering work experience at home and abroad.
○ by collaboration with local industry.
○ by constant guidance and re-training for teachers.

Strategic objectives are:

○ to realise the spiritual, ethical and cultural potential of all children.
○ to create a valid technical and managerial class for the future.
○ to eliminate the major youth unemployment problem, especially in the south.

The recent earthquake tragedy in Molise (2002), in which a substandard, modern schoolbuilding collapsed and killed 20 schoolchildren, has drawn attention to the shocking physical state of many of Italy's schools. 57% of the 10,800 state schools lack a certificate of stability.

Under 10% of Italy's schools are run by religious or private bodies. Private schools have parity with the state schools and are subject to the same standards. Six regions offer vouchers to subsidise children at private schools.

There are 12 state boarding schools (*collegi*) but boarding and private schools have no prestige in Italy. On the contrary, their alumni are often pitied or suspected of being retarded. The *scuola statale*, the state education system, is part of the national identity, for both rich and poor. The whole nation participates in the annual drama of the state exams every summer.

Implicit in the Italian state education system is the premise that school is supplementary to – and not a substitute for – the family. It is the family which must give children their main *educazione*. The word *educato* means well-brought up, well-mannered, as well as educated in the English sense. Parental back-up is vital – at home. At school – the teacher rules.

The Italian School System

The Italian school system is now to be organised as follows:

1. *Scuola d'Infanzia* (Infants School) otherwise known as *scuola materna* or *asilo*, lasts for three years starting from age 2½ to 3 and is optional, but attended by 95% of children. It typically keeps them from 8.30am to 5pm, feeds them two meals and puts them to bed after lunch. Parents normally contribute to food and transport. This frees mothers to work during term time. (For younger toddlers there is the *asilo nido* or nest, but this does not have full national coverage). The *scuola d'infanzia* is the same as a kindergarten, learning through play and social interaction under a *maestra*, for the whole day. It is extremely popular with children and an essential introduction into the system for expatriates.

- *Scuola primaria* (Primary School) lasts for five years starting from age 5½ to 6, and is compulsory.
- From class 1 a European language is introduced.
- Use of the computer is a priority.
- There are no state exams.

- *Scuola secondaria* (Secondary School) lasts for three years. Its main features are:
- Introduction of a second European language.
- Use of information technology.
- Career guidance (*orientamento*) for choice of next course.
- State exam – *esame statale* (at age 13-14) to complete the first level (*ciclo*) of education.

- The second level (*ciclo* or cycle) offers a choice between *liceo* schools and vocational schools, with the possibility of switching courses under qualified teachers guidance. Advanced information technology is prioritised. From the age of fifteen the following are the different learning approaches available:-
- full-time study
- alternating school and work, with work experience possibly abroad, in the real world, social, cultural and productive
- apprenticeship

- In the final year there is guidance (*orientamento*) for the choice of
- university, academy, superior vocational institute
- work and the professions

Liceo or High School lasts for five years, giving the choice of specialised schools of:-

- Art
- Human Sciences
- Languages
- Science
- Classics
- Economics
- Music
- Technology

For the first four years the special subject is balanced by other subjects to give a broad base. The fifth year is for in-depth study and career guidance for further studies. A State exam, *esame di stato* is taken at the end of the fifth year for university and third level entitlement, popularly known as the *maturità*. At least five subjects are compulsory.

Unacademic children can opt for three year technical or vocational courses at the age of 15, which are tailor-made according to region and the demands of the work place. New laws have revived the apprenticeship system on the German model for youngsters over 15, lasting from eighteen months to five years, at pay rates slightly less than the lowest regular wage, and with the supervision of a permanent tutor.

In Italian schools there is no streaming, no competition, no class marks, or orders. It is a contest between each student and the system: education by attrition rather than by encouragement. Unlike the American system – but more like the French system – children are not taught how to feel good about themselves. Teachers are stinting with their praise. Often this is difficult for children to cope with, and they can become depressed or even suicidal. However oral skills are encouraged. 35% of the state exam marks are *viva voce* (20% course work, 45% written). The result is that Italian educated children are notably eloquent.

Unruly classrooms, a growing phenomenon in developed countries (such as Japan) are now common in Italy, especially at the primary level. Shy quiet children can 'get a headache' from the noise. The average Italian pupil is, after all, a self-confident only child, indulged by parents, from a TV/consumer society, encouraged to be rumbustious from kindergarten level and increasingly precocious.

International Schools

International schools tend to be regarded as the best option for the children of expatriates who do not expect to remain in Italy in the long-term, or who want their children to have the option of attending university in their home country. Different schools within the category of International School offer UK, German, French, Japanese, Swedish, Spanish, and US curricula. Though international schools can be seen to isolate children from the communities in which they live, most International Schools admit students from many nationalities, including that of the host country, and students are given the chance to study the local language in a way suitable for non-native speakers. There are numerous schools in Italy that are possible options for expatriates, the majority of which are of high quality and offer a continuous style of education for transient expatriate children.

They also offer easier access to UK and North American higher education and
ensure that the level of English (or German, French or other language) of the
expatriate child remains at native level.

English medium schools in Milan:

The American School of Milan: Via Marx 14, 20090 Noverasco di Opera, Milano;
☎02 530 0001; fax 02 5760 6274; www.asmilan.org. Ages three 18.

International School of Milan: Via Caccialepori 22, 20148, Milan, Italy; ☎02 487
08076; fax 02 487 03644; www.ism-ac.it. Ages three to 19.

Sir James Henderson British School of Milan: Via Pisano Dossi 16, 20134, Milan;
☎02 264 13332/13310; fax 02 264 13515). Ages three to 18.

Rome:

Ambrit School: Via Filippo Tajani 50, 00149 Rome; ☎06 559 5301/5; fax 06 559
5309; www.ambrit-rome.com. Ages three to 14.

American Overseas School of Rome: Vica Cassia 811, 00189, Rome, Italy; ☎06
3326 4841; fax 06 3326 2608; www.aosr.org. Ages three to 18.

Castelli International School: 13 Via Degli Scozzesi, 00046 Grottaferrata, Rome;
tel/fax 06 943 15779. Ages five to 14 years.

Greenwood Garden School: Via Vito Sinisi 5, Rome 00189 (tel/fax 6 3326-6703).

International Academy of Rome: Via di Grottarossa 295, 00189 Rome (☎06 3326
6071). Ages three to 14.

Kendale Primary International School: Via Gradoli 86, Tombe di Nerone, 00189
Rome (tel/fax 06 366 7608). Ages 3 to 10.

Marymount International School: Via di Villa Lauchli 180, 00191 Rome (☎06
3630 1742; fax 06 3630 1738. Roman Catholic school. Ages three to 19.

New School: Via della Camiluccia 669, 00135 Rome; ☎06 329 4269; fax 06 329
7546). Ages: three to 18 years.

Notre Dame International School: Via Aurelia 796, 00165 Rome (☎06 680 8801;
fax 680 6051). Ages 10-18.

Rome International School: Viale Romania 32, Parioli (off Piazza Ungheria, Rome;
☎06 844 82650; fax 06 844 82651. Ages three to 18 years.

Southlands English School: Via Teleclide 20, Casal Palocco, 00124 Rome; ☎06
505 3922; fax 06 509 17192). Ages three to 14 years.

St Francis International School: Via Massimi 164 (Balduina) Rome; ☎06 353
41328; fax 06 353 48719. Ages three to 14. American system.

St George's English School: Via Cassia KM 16, 00123 Rome; ☎06 3790141/23;
fax 06 3792490). Ages three to 18.

St Stephen's School: Via Aventina 3, 00153 Rome; ☎06 575 0605; fax 06 574
1941. Ages: 13 to 19.

Other Cities:

American International School of Florence: Via del Carota 23/35, 50012 Bagno a Ripoli, Florence; ☎055 640033; fax 55 644226. Ages 2[ha] to 19.

American International School in Genoa: Via Quarto 13/C 16148 Genoa; ☎010 386528; fax 010 398700). Ages three to 14.

Anglo-Italian School Montessori Division: Viale Della Liberazione, Comando NATO, 90125, Bagnoli, Naples; ☎081 721 2266; fax 081 570 6587.

European School: Via Montello 118, 21100 Varese; ☎0332 806111; fax 332 806202. Ages four to 18. Waiting list of 2 years and the school generally only takes children of EU employees.

International School of Naples: Viale della Liberazione, 1 H.Q. AFSouth Post, Bldg 'A', 80125 Bagnoli, Napoli; ☎081-721 20 37; fax 081-762 84 29. Ages three to 18.

International School of Trieste: Via Conconello 16, Opicina, 34100 Trieste; ☎040 211452). Ages three to 18.

International School of Turin (American Cultural Association School of Turin): Vicolo Tiziano 10, 10024 Moncalieri; ☎011 645967; fax 011 643298). Ages three to 18.

International School of Modena: Via Silvio Pellico 9, Fiorano, 41042, Modena, Italy; ☎0536 832904; fax 0536 911189.

United World College of the Adriatic: Via Trieste 29, 34013 Duino (Trieste); ☎040-3739111; fax 040-3739225. Takes boarding students aged 16 to study for the pre-university IB diploma. Entry is exclusively by scholarship.

Italian Universities

Italian Universities have also been reorganised in the new reforms – more autonomy and diversification and encouragement of research, and a system of credits, and scholarships.

The degrees are as follows:

- *laurea di primo livello* or triennale after three years (general).
- *laurea di secondo livello* or *specialistica* after five years (specialised).
- *master,* very specialised, often tailor-made and sponsored by industry.

In a recent Censis survey the best universities in Italy, divided into five categories, were as follows:

Superlicei (up to ten thousand students): Reggio Calabria, Viterbo (Tuscia Lazio),
Camerino (Le Marche).

Small Universities (between ten to twenty thousand students): Trento (Trentino/

Alto Adige), Siena (Tuscany), Venice (Veneto) Cà Foscari.

Medium Universities (between twenty and forty thousand students): Calabria (Cosenza), Parma (Emilia Romagna), Pavia (Lombardy).

Mega Universities (over forty thousand students): Padua (Veneto), Bologna (Emilia Romagna), Turin (Piedmont).

Polytechnics (Universities with only two faculties: Engineering and Architecture),
Turin (Piedmont), Milan (Lombardy), Bari (Puglia).

Italian universities still retain medieval *Goliardic* traditions and other quirks. Trento gives free bicycles to its students. Its sociology faculty horrified the right wing press in November 2002 by mounting a photographic exhibition glorifying its past – 1968 – as a hotbed of revolution (it spawned the Red Brigades). The University of Calabria (Cosenza) has now taken over the baton of the revolutionary movement with its *disobbedienti* (the disobedients) arrested en masse in the same month.

HEALTH

In common with other systems under state control in Italy, the state medical system costs the government (i.e. the taxpayer) a fortune yet many hospitals are depressing places and with their lack of bathing and feeding facilities and general condition are in a far worse state than British ones.

Italy produces more medics than any other European country. Some of these are theoretical graduates who may never have seen a surgical procedure or even a corpse! Practical experience is usually gained by becoming the acolyte of a consultant (*primario*) and trailing them on their ward rounds. Despite the erratic standard of Italian medical training, there are many excellent doctors, especially in private clinics. Italy has a clutch of world-renowned specialists including a Nobel prize winner (Daniel Bovet), and a singing heart surgeon with a string of hit records (Enzo Jannacci). Simultaneously with some of the best doctors in Europe Italy possesses some of the most appalling hospitals, where treatment is irregular, care haphazard and facilities inadequate. That said, hospitals in the north are generally very good. However, there are usually long delays in receiving diagnostic tests, which can have severe implications when patients turn out to have serious diseases. If you use the state system you may have to wait weeks. However, the doctor treating you has the power to stamp your request for tests as most urgent, in which case you could go to the top of the list.

Many Italian residents, both nationals and expatriates, have private health insurance (see below) in case they need basic care, let alone long-term, expensive hospitalisation. Note that a list of local national health centres and hospitals is available from your local health authority (*Azienda Sanità Locale/Unità Sanitarie Locali*) in Italy; also most local embassies or consulates should be able to provide a list of English-speaking (private) doctors in your region.

When purchasing private healthcare it is essential to read the small print to ensure that the coverage is as complete as possible and covers all your possible future requirements – exclusions can be extensive. Paul Wolf of Innovative Benefits Solutions (www.ibencon.com) says, 'there are no bargains out there, you get what you pay for'.

The E111

It is essential that anyone resident or domiciled in the UK who intends to move permanently to Italy register their change of address with International Services, Inland Revenue National Insurance Contributions Office (Newcastle upon Tyne NE98 1ZZ: ☎0845-915 4811 from the UK or +44-191 225 4811 from overseas; fax 0845-915 7800 inside the UK or +44-191 225 7800 from overseas) before leaving the country. They will then be sent the paperwork required to obtain an E111 (allow one month for processing), which entitles all EU nationals whether they are tourists or working abroad to medical treatment by the national health service in any EU/EEA member country. Details are available on the Inland Revenue Website www.inlandrevenue.gov.uk/nic/intserv/osc.htm. The E111 is valid for twelve months, and is renewable on the proviso that the applicant still makes their UK National Insurance contributions.

Although the E111 covers emergency hospital treatment while abroad it does not include the cost for prescribed medicines, specialist examinations, X-rays, laboratory tests and physiotherapy or dental treatment. Consequently, private insurance should still be taken out for the required period, as this will provide financial protection against medical treatment costs which are not regarded as emergencies and which are not covered by the E111.

For those who are not moving to Italy full-time, an E111 can be obtained from the Post Office. E111 forms issued by European countries other than the UK expire after one year and this can lead to problems having an UK E111 accepted around Europe if it has been issued more than 12 months previously. To avoid this potential problem replacements can be issued by the International Services office listed above.

Using the Health Service

Anyone who makes social security payments in the EU, who receives an EU state pension, is unemployed, or under the age of 18 is entitled to the benefits of medical treatment on the Italian state health service (*Servizio Sanitario Nazionale*) free of charge. These include free hospital accommodation and medical treatment and up to 90% of the cost of prescription medicines; a contribution (*il ticket*) of

10% is required from the patient. Social security payments, which account for approximately 8% of a worker's gross income, are deducted from the employee's gross salary by the employer.

Obtaining a National Health Number. Any foreigner who has become a resident and who wishes to receive treatment under the Italian state system is obliged to register with and obtain a national health number from the local *Unità Sanitaria Locale* (a.k.a. USL). You will need to produce your *permesso di soggiorno* and a letter from your employer which states that you are working for him or her. Self-employed or freelance workers should first register with the INPS in Piazza Augusto Imperatore 32, Rome, where they will be given the necessary documentation to take to the local ASL office together with their *permesso di soggiorno*. ASL addresses can be found in the *Tuttocittà,* a supplement that comes with Italian telephone directories, or alternatively in the local newspaper.

Registering with a Doctor. Once you are registered with the *Unità Sanitaria Locale*, the next step is to register with *un medico mutualistico* (general practitioner). The system of free treatment is known as *la mutua.* Outpatients are normally treated at a *studio medico* or *ambulatorio* (surgery). A private clinic is *una clinica private.*

Some of the better hospitals are in Rome:

Policlinico Universitario: Largo Agostino Gemeli 8, Rome 00168 (☎+39 06 30151; www.ntweb.rm.unicatt.it/gemeli

Rome American Hospital: via Emilio Longoni 69, Rome 00155 (☎+39 06 22551; fax +39 06 2285062).

Salvator Mundi International Hospital: Viale delle Mure Giaconlensi 67, Rome 00152; +39 06 588 961; www.smih.pen.net

Fatebenefratelli: (Via Cassia 600).

In Milan:

Ospedale Maggiore di Milano Policlinico (via Francesco Sforza 32, Milan).

American International Medical Clinic: Via Mercalli 11, Milan 20122; ☎+39 02 5831 9808; fax +39 02 5831 6605; e-mail wfreilich@iht.it

Ospedale San Raffaele: Via Olgettina 60, Milan 20132; +39 02 264 31; www.sanraffaele.org

Local advice should always be taken from other expats as certain doctors and hospitals will be better set up to meet the needs of expatriates.

Emergencies

If you are involved in or at the site of a serious accident then get to the nearest phone box and dial 113, which will put you through to the emergency services; ask for an *ambulanza* (ambulance). Less serious injuries should be treated at the casualty (*pronto soccorso*) ward at the nearest hospital. Alternatively, most major railway stations and airports have first-aid stations with qualified doctors on hand – many of these first aid stations are reputed to be more effective than the hospitals.

In the event of minor ailments, aches and pains it may well be worth avoiding the chaos of the state hospitals and applying directly to your local chemist (*farmacia*). Chemists are generally extremely well qualified in Italy, and will probably be able to prescribe something for you. The *farmacie* are usually open all night in larger towns and cities and if the one you end up at is closed, there should be a list displayed on the door that lists which chemists in the area are open that night.

Sickness and Invalidity Benefit

Any EU citizen who is moving to Italy permanently and who claims sickness or invalidity benefit in their home country is entitled to continue claiming this benefit once in Italy. To claim either benefit, you must be physically incapable of all work, however, the interpretation of 'physically incapable' varies beyond literal truth. If the claimant has been paying National Insurance contributions in the UK for two tax years (this may be less depending on his or her level of income) then he or she is eligible to claim weekly sickness benefit. After receiving sickness benefit for 28 weeks, you are entitled to invalidity benefit.

Anyone currently receiving either form of benefit should inform their local branch of the Department of Work and Pensions that they are moving to Italy. They will then send your forms to the Overseas Branch of the DWP who will ensure that a monthly sterling cheque is sent either to your new address or direct to your bank account. The only conditions involved are that all claimants submit themselves to a medical examination, either in Italy or the UK, on request.

Italian sickness benefit for workers *(operai)* and salaried staff (*impiegati*) in commerce and industry is paid partly by the employer and partly by the state national sickness fund (INPS). Salaried staff get 100 per cent of their salary (at the employer's cost) for up to six months. For manual workers the amount is dependent on their labour contract and the length of service

Private Medical Insurance

In contrast with the lack of organisation in the public sector, the private sector of the health service is amazingly well organised. However, it is also expensive; charges at private hospitals and clinics are a minimum of £150 (US$210) per day for a room, so private health insurance is a must. If you currently hold a private health insurance policy for the country in which you are currently resident, you may find that the company will switch this for European cover once you are in Italy. However, with the increase in insurance companies offering this type of cover, it is worth shopping around to find the best cover for you and your family. If you have not organised insurance cover before leaving home you can organise it from Italy just as easily.

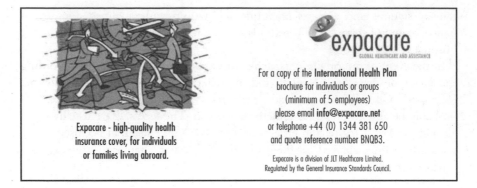
Useful Addresses

BUPA (British United Provident Association): 15 Bloomsbury Way, London WC1A 2BA; ☎020-7656 2000; fax 020-7656 2728. Aimed mostly at UK nationals.

BUPA International: www.bupa-international.com for non-UK Europeans and north Americans living and working around the world.

Expacare Insurance Services: Columbia Centre, Market Street, Bracknell, Berkshire RG12 1JG; ☎01344-381650; fax 01344-381690; e-mail info@expacare.net; www.expacare.net.

Innovative Benefits Consultants Ltd.: 40 Homer Street, London W1H 1HL, UK; tel/fax 0870-737 9000 ext 6129 (Paul Wolf). In New York ☎212 328 3030 ext 5854; info@ibencon.com; www.ibencon.com.

Private Patients Plan: PPP Healthcare Group plc, Vale Road, Tunbridge Wells Kent TN1 2PL; ☎01892-512345).

United Healthcare: BUPA partner providing services for North Americans.

Worldwide Travel Insurance: ASA Inc. USA; ☎1-602 968 0440.

SHOPPING

Italy excels in design and manufacturing. It produces exquisite objects of desire for discerning consumers, and Milan is the style capital of the world. No wonder that Americans, from the home of the shopping mall, flock to Italy for a very superior fix of retail therapy. Busloads of Japanese are also disgorged daily at the Prada factory outlet in Levane (Arezzo). Whether it is shoes in Vigevano, handbags in Naples, painted crockery at Deruta, glass at Merano, jewellery in Arezzo or Ferrari cars in Maranello, Italy tempts the consumer with the best quality products that the globe can offer. Every large town has at least one shopping centre (*centro commerciale*), which is up to the best European or American standards of quality and design. The *Ipercoop* Co-op chain now dominates the scene. It is a mutual co-operative society which sells everything from white goods (made in Pordenone), to bread baked fresh on the spot in wood-fired ovens. Preference is given to local products and goods sourced in Italy under strict ecological control. *Superal, Conad, Esselunga, Upim, Standa, Despar* are names of other chains, and *Auchan* from France has partnered *La Rinascente* of Milan to carve a large niche in the north.

The Small Shops. Back in the ancient city centres the local townsfolk (*borghesia*) maintain a tradition of dazzling small shops and boutiques which are more alluring than anything in Bond Street or Fifth Avenue: *Fendi, Furla, Valentino, Gucci, Versace*, big names or no names – Via Montenapoleone in Milan, Via Condotti in Rome, Via Tornabuoni in Florence, the Rialto in Venice, the covered arcades of Bologna – all cities have shopping streets (*corsi*) which attract discreet hordes of opulent shoppers and gourmets. At the lower end of the social scale weekly or permanent street markets under awnings supply the needs of locals and tourists alike in towns and cities throughout Italy.

THE COUNTERFEIT INDUSTRY

Alongside the production of genuine articles, there is a huge sweatshop counterfeit industry producing cut-price designer-label goods and pirate CD's etc. seemingly identical with the original, which are sold in the markets, or in the streets by platoons of '*vu cumprà*' Senagalese pedlars, who respond to ferocious haggling in any language, '*Vu cumprà?*', their nickname, means 'Wanna buy?'

Everyday Shopping

At a daily level, shops for basic needs, *negozi di prima necessità* – are to be found in every village or town quarter *rione*.

- **Food shops** (*alimentari*) are an area in which Italians thrive throughout the world. A slicing machine will dominate the counter for salamis, hams and cold cuts. Most produce and wine will be seasonal, and rolls, *panini* or sandwiches can be ordered expressly, put on the scales, and paid for by weight.
- **Papershop** (*edicola*) sells papers, magazines, stationery.
- **Tobacconist** (*il tabacchaio,* or *la tabaccheria* is marked with a big T sign which stands for *tabacchi* (tobaccos) which is what the English also call the shop. Tobacco is no longer a state monopoly but only T-licensed shops can sell it through some complicated distribution deal with the Italian Federation of Tobacconists. As a state monopoly outlet the *tabacchaio/tabaccheria/tabacchi* is also the still the place for postage stamps, official forms, bus tickets and salt. Salt is also sold in supermarkets.
- **Chemist's shop** (*farmacia*) dispenses medical advice as well as medicines, but does not handle photographic products.
- **Houseware shop** (*casalinghi*) sells anything for the house from electric blankets to dustpans.
- **Gift shop** (*articoli da regalo*) sells souvenirs, crockery, cutlery etc, beautifully

packaged.

- **The draper** (*merceria*) or haberdashery is fast disappearing from the scene.
- **A laundry** is a *lavanderia*.
- **A dry cleaner** is a *lavanderia a secco*.
- **A barber** is a *barbiere* where the men talk.
- **A hairdresser** is a *parruchiera* where the women talk.
- **A butcher** is a *macelleria* which supplies locally sourced meat.
- **A fishmonger** is a *pescheria*, for fresh fish from the coast,
- **A upholsterer** is a *tappezzeria* for cushions and curtains,
- **A picture framer** is a *cornicaio*,
- **A bookshop** is a *libreria*
- **A shoe shop** is a *calzoleria*
- **A bakery** is a *panificio* where you can order cakes and bread at all hours,
- **A perfume shop** is a *profumeria*,
- Other shops are tailor *sartoria*, paints and DIY *mesticheria* (Tuscany), delicatessen *pizzicheria*.

Most shops are open from 8.30am to 7.30pm and close for three hours or more at 1pm for lunch. They are closed by law for one day in the week.

Most villages have a weekly vegetable stall *fruttivendolo* and fish van *pescivendolo*.

Bargains. The following publications are guides to bargain shopping in Italy and worth looking at: The bargain finder *Lo Scoprioccasioni,* 6th edition 2003 is published by Editoriale Shopping Italia S.r.l. In addition, the outlet guide *La Guida agli Spacci* by Marina Martorana is published by Sperling Paper Backs.

MEDIA

Newspapers

It is estimated that 60% of Italian families buy a daily newspaper. There is no real equivalent of the most popular British tabloids and US supermarket newspapers, and only the down market papers, e.g. *Il Messaggero* carry horoscopes, cartoons or fun features.

The most widely consumed Italian dailies are *Il Corriere della Sera* (Milan) and *La Repubblica* (Rome), both of which have circulations around the half million mark. *La Stampa* (Turin) follows with just over four hundred thousand . *Il Giornale* and *Il Messaggero* trail in with less than two hundred thousand.

La Repubblica, is a liberal publication and tends to create the most controversy and excitement: everyday it is crammed with dense and penetrating commentaries, exhaustive graphs, statistics and diagrams. By contrast, the conservative *La Stampa* tends to back whichever government is in power at the time; however is respected for its high intellectual content and its highbrow book section. *Corriere della Sera* is authoritative and conservative. In the five most widely read newspapers above, articles on social issues are comparatively rare.

The two main financial dailies – *Il Sole/24 Or* and *Italia Oggi*, – are reasonably extensive in their coverage. The three sports dailies are *Corriere dello Sport*, *Gazzetta dello Sport* and *Tuttosport*. The regional newspapers, which focus on national news but include several pages of local news and comment, are particularly popular and widely read in Italy.

SOME IMPORTANT ITALIAN REGIONAL NEWSPAPERS

Il Gazzettino (www.gazzettino.it) Venice.

La Nazione (www.lanazione.it) Florence (Socialist)

Il Mattino (www.ilmattino.it) Naples (Christian Democrat)

Il Messagero (www.ilmessagero.it) Rome (Communist).

Il Resto del Carlino (www.ilrestodelcarlino.it) Bologna.

L'Ora in Palermo; at the forefront of anti-Mafia movement in the media environs of Sicily.

Libertà (www.liberta.it). Piacenza/Milano area.

Il Tempo (www.iltempo.it) Rome. Traditionally conservative.

La Gazzetta del Mezzogiorno (Bari)

L'Unione Sarda (www.unionesarda.it) Sardinia.

Il Piccolo (www.ilpiccolo.it). Trieste.

There are no separate Sunday papers as such in Italy; instead all of the national dailies print on Sunday and then have a day off on Monday. A comprehensive listing of all Italian newspapers can be found on the website www.ciao-italy.com/categories/newspapers.htm.

The International Herald Tribune (6 bis rue des Graviers, 92521 Neuilly, Cedex Paris; ☎ +33-1 41 43 92 61; fax +33-1 41 43 92 10; subs@iht.com; www.iht.com), is published in Paris in conjunction with the *New York Times* and *Washington Post*. It is available in Italy at newsagents or by subscription in Italy from 800-780 040, in the UK from 0800-4 448 7827 and in America from 800-8822884.

English Language Publications. The English-language magazine, *Italy*, (via M. Mercati 51, 00197 Rome; ☎06 322 1441, fax 06 322 3869) is full of useful articles on culture, politics, entertainment and general interest and is available by subscription from the above address. Another possibility is the expatriate website *The Informer* (www.informer.it), formerly published monthly but now totally online, that contains a variety of both useful and interesting articles ranging from tax and money matters to general interest. *The Informer* also has electronic newsletters and extensive archives of information available online to its subscribers. Those interested in taking out a subscription should sign up online at www.informer.it. Also useful is *The Survival Guide to Milan*, available from the *The Informer*.

There are two other fortnightly English-language papers published in Rome: *Wanted in Rome* (www.wantedinrome.com) sold on news-stands and in some bookshops, and *Metropolitan*. There is also the *International Spectator,* a quarterly publication, and *Rome Elite*.

The *English Yellow Pages* (via Belisario 4/B, 00187 Rome; ☎06-4740861; fax 06-4744516; www.intoitaly.it) updated annually, will be invaluable to any new arrival in Italy. The directory contains listings for English-speaking professionals, businesses, organisations and services in Rome, Florence, Bologna, Naples, Genoa and Milan and is available at international bookstores and from news-stands. The online version also has listings for Palermo and Catania. For a free listing, contact the above address. Free classified ads can also be posted on the website. Also from the same publisher is the *English White Pages*, an alphabetical directory of English-speakers living in Italy.

Television

The great majority of Italy's hundreds of channels are crammed with rubbishy quiz shows and low quality sitcoms and soaps and the general standard was described in a recent article in the London *Financial Times FT Weekend section* as 'My Italian TV hell.' The same article went on 'studio TV has replaced Parliament, and soft porn has replaced news.'

The three state-run channels, RAI 1, RAI2 and RAI3 manage to provide a higher quality programming and command higher viewing levels. RAI3 tends to show more cultural programmes than the others. In a recent comparison of Italian TV with the state radio and television networks of Germany the UK and France, RAI television did rather well. For example, the comparison with the BBC:

Comparison	RAI	BBC
Bigger audience share	47%	38%
Lower annual fee	93.80 euros	173.57 euros
Fewer employees	9,780	26, 880
More TV networks	3	2
Audience share compared with 1992	+1%	-6%

The important independent television channels are Italia 1, Canale 5 and Rete 4: these collectively account for about 45% of Italian viewing. Although Rete 4 is thought to be more highbrow than the other two, none of them offer really serious news coverage although Canale 5 has been attempting to give greater emphasis to documentaries and news.

In recent years there has been something of a public crusade in Italy against the probable dangers of certain types of television on the psychophysical development of children and younger viewers. The result was a watershed of

10.30pm for X-rated movies and other violent/sexually explicit programming. Italy was also a pioneer of the so-called 'violence chip', a piece of technology designed to filter out violent programmes on television when children are watching.

When shipping personal belongings to Italy it is worth remembering that Italian TV and videos operate on the PAL-BG system. The UK operates PAL-I, the USA and Canada operates NTSC and France operates MESECAM. TVs of one system do not correctly work with another (you can get black and white instead of colour, or have no sound). However, multi-system TVs and videos that play all systems types are freely available in Italy – in fact, many TVs and videos now sold in Europe are multi-system.

Expatriates can find watching local television channels not as relaxing as those they are used to, due to the concentration required to follow a foreign language. Thanks to satellite and cable technology it is now possible to receive a huge variety of international channels via satellite, including BBC World (free to air), BBC Prime (subscription only), CCNI (free to air), CNBC, The Disney Channel and other good quality English language channels throughout Europe. There are also many other channels available in the numerous European languages, plus the languages of the immigrant population – Arabic, Urdu, Hindi, etc. Local satellite suppliers can offer the best solution as not all areas are connected to cable networks and satellite dishes are not allowed in certain protected areas.

Radio

The Italian radio network was deregulated in 1976, the same year as television, with the result that the airwaves are crammed with a diverse range of obscure stations; over two and a half thousand of them. However, the three main radio channels are Radio 1, 2, and 3. The first two feature light music and entertainment while Radio 3 is similar to the UK equivalent, broadcasting serious discussion programmes and classical music. Finally there are Radio 1 and 2 rock stations which, although technically part of RAI, are on separate wavelengths. The accumulated audience for rock stations is immense (12½ million listeners). The total audience for radio nation-wide is estimated at 35 million. However, there are so many stations that this audience is hopelessly fragmented and some local stations are estimated to have no more than a few dozen listeners.

As with television, the main radio channels are all under the wing of a powerful sponsor who consequently has a substantial influence over the station's output.

BBC World Service. A monthly publication *BBC On Air,* which gives details of schedules plus advice and information about BBC World Service radio and BBC Prime and BBC World Television, is available on subscription (£20 annually) from BBC On Air, Room 310NW, Bush House, London WC2B 4PH (☎020-

7557 22875 (answer phone); fax 020-7240 4899); www.bbconair.co.uk.

Voice of America. For details of Voice of America programmes, contact VOA, Washington, D.C. 20547; ☎1-202 619 2358. Details of programmes and frequencies are also online at www.voa.org.

CRIME

Organised Crime

Organised crime in Italy is a veritable state within a state. Based in the South its tentacles spread throughout Italy – and abroad. It is nicknamed the octopus – *la piovra*. The *Mafia* or *Cosa Nostra* in Sicily is bigger, more calculating, and structured than the more chaotic and opportunistic outfits in the toe and heel and ankle of Italy: the *Camorra* in Campania, the *Ndrangheta* in Calabria and the *Sacra Corona Unita* in Puglia. Brave magistrates and policemen have struggled to quell the phenomenon. General della Chiesa of the police *carabinieri* was assassinated by the *Mafia* in 1982 and Giovanni Falcone and Paolo Borsellino ten years later, these latter two heroic magistrates now commemorated in the name of Palermo's international airport.

Despite the best efforts of the police and judiciary, crime unfortunately continues to pay. In 2001 it yielded over 16 billion euros in protection money, 5 billion euros from drugs, the same from cigarettes, and 51 million euros from kidnappings. Prostitution, loan-sharking, illegal immigration, building scams, markets, the commercialisation of Padre Pio – any lucrative field is fair game. The clans or *cosche* and their bosses or godfathers (*padrini*) have armies of young men at their bidding, arsenals of weaponry and sophisticated computer technology. They wield political power and gain collusion from local borough councils right up to the Senate in Rome. They command blocks of votes on their home turf which have been crucial to the electoral success of *La Casa delle Libertà*, prime minister Berlusconi's ruling coalition. The mafia have moved upwards into white collar crime – laundering money through banks and running legitimate businesses with the proceeds. Murder and the conspiracy of silence (*omertà*) are the means by which they retain power and respect. Excellent cadavers (*cadaveri eccellenti)* is the name given to their illustrious victims. Young boys of exceptional criminal daring and cunning are talent-spotted and recruited, and women have a powerful educational role inculcating the Mafia ethos into their boys.

The state minimises the problem although spending massively to contain it: 50 million euros a year for the protection of witnesses alone. It is beginning to achieve some results. In 2001 over 360 mafia fugitives were captured and 2,600 suspects prosecuted. In 2002 the state attacked the mafia's financial empire, confiscating villas, offices and a factory near Palermo worth 500 million euros, belonging to the bosses Buscemi and Catalano, which judges ruled were part of the Mafia's illegally gained wealth. Numerous bosses are in prison, including the infamous Totò Riina, but the superboss Bernardo Provenzano, on the run thirty years, is still in hiding as a *latitante* (fugitive).

Foreign visitors can console themselves that they are not the targets of organised crime, and they can be blissfully unaware of its existence. The local population of the supposedly crime-ridden south, in a survey by Demos for the *Repubblica* newspaper, were more than three times more worried by unemployment (48.2%) than by crime (14%). (In the industrial North-East the figures were 8.6% for unemployment and 20.5% for crime.) The spate of confessions by repentant mafia members (*pentiti*) starting with Tommaso Busceta in 1984, who spilt the beans with perfect recall on the arcanest areas of *mafioso* activities, could have been the turning of the tide – or a change in tack; the mafia mind is always two steps ahead of its adversaries. It remains to be seen whether heartfelt appeals by glamorous – and repentant – Camorra and Mafia bosses to young boys not to go into crime, combined with the new strategic educational reforms aimed specifically at 15-18 year old males, will succeed in reducing the twin evils of unemployment and organised crime.

According to the UK government's travel advice, major crime is not a problem in Italy but petty crime is, and the Italian Government tells its citizens that petty theft is rife in big cities and tourist sites (mainly Rome, Naples and Florence), on trains and buses, in museums and autostrade filling stations and in campsites; thieves and pickpockets operate on foot or moped. Danger spots are: Naples city centre and station area, Rome's public transport services connecting the station with the Vatican, and Palermo in Sicily. In these areas the only way to be sure of not being robbed are to adopt draconian measures:

- ○ refrain from wearing jewellery and watches.
- ○ don't carry cameras or videocameras.
- ○ keep car doors locked while driving in cities.
- ○ don't carry large sums of cash.
- ○ keep credit cards and cheque books separate and secure.

Microcriminalità as the Italians call petty crime has been eliminated in central Bari for example by patrolling Carabinieri, and they are also working on central Naples. But gangs of juvenile pickpockets, called *slavi* or slavs, from former Yugoslavia, have always been a problem at places like Rome's Termini station, and the infiltration of Albanian criminals throughout Italy has been an alarming result of the Balkan troubles of the 1990's. Ruthless operators, compared with whom the homegrown *mafiosi* are gentlemen, Albanians have been carving out territories throughout Italy involving drugs, cigarettes, prostitution, carjacking, burglaries. Italian businessmen driving top of the range German cars have been mugged at autostrada filling stations and their cars made to vanish without trace, presumably to the Balkans. In peaceful country areas villas have been ransacked

‥ and antique furniture taken away in pantechnicons.

‥e so-called white slave trade – mainly prostitutes from the former Yugoslavia and USSR – is run by Albanian pimps and competes for territory with a black slave trade. 60,000 prostitutes mostly from the Benin region of Nigeria ply the leafy lanes of il Bel Paese, masterminded from Africa. Shocked by this phenomenon the Italian government has set up a free charter flight service to fly the girls home where charitable homes have been set up to take care of them. A law is currently on its way (2003) through parliament to make visible prostitutes illegal, and it has been proposed to re-open state supervised brothels – abolished by a woman senator called Merlin in 1947. Italians seem to be fairly laid back about, and tolerant of, the trade, although sixty Nigerian girls were found murdered in 2001.

Some rural areas, however, in places like Umbria, Tuscany, the Marches, Emilia Romagna, Piemonte, Friuli, Molite, where the old local cultures prevail, are nearly crime free. You are told that the only crimes there are committed by outsiders. In places like Buonconvento (Tuscany) you can confidently predict, still, that a wallet lost in the street will be handed in to the local police station (the Carabinieri) with its money intact.

To put crime into perspective, Italy is no more hazardous than, say, England. To many visitors the streets of London are more threatening than the streets of Rome. The Costas of Spain – or the South Coast of England – may well contain more criminals per square kilometre than the Rivieras of Italy. Most of Italy is populated by polite law-abiding citizens belonging to extended families whose lives revolve around clearly defined routines.

The chaotic youthful drunkenness (and hooliganism), which has spread to the old market towns of rural England has no parallel in Italy – yet. Foreigners are made welcome, and most expatriates find the countryside and the way of life idyllic. You should take precautions against crime in Italy, certainly, but no different from the precautions you would take in your own country.

LEARNING THE LANGUAGE

If you don't speak Italian you are forced to rely on the expatriate community for your survival; few Italians speak English. Learning Italian can be a rewarding and therapeutic experience. Most Italians are flattered if you make an attempt to speak it. They will encourage you in your efforts; and it is a beautiful language to learn.

Standard Italian evolved from Tuscan, the language of Dante (*la lingua di Dante*.) It was forged by the poets Dante and Petrarch in the Middle Ages, and consolidated by writers like Alessandro Manzoni in the nineteenth century. Manzoni's novel *The Betrothed* (*I Promessi Sposi*), familiar to generations of Italian schoolchildren, was set on the shores of Lake Como, but instead of speaking the Comasco dialect the characters were made to speak in Tuscan. Manzoni washed his language in the river Arno 'rewriting' the book in 1840. In 1861 only 2.5% of Italians spoke standard Italian, in 1955 the figure was 34%, in 1988 it was 86%. By 1995, 93.1% of Italians were speaking standard Italian, 48.7% were bilingual dialect Italian speakers and only 6.9% spoke in dialect alone. Television has accelerated the standardisation of the language, especially among young people, sometimes to the dismay of their elders. In Milan recently some old locals in a trattoria were moved to tears by a group of very young people at the next table speaking and singing songs in their old dialect. The youngsters came from Ticino in neighbouring Switzerland where the dialect still survived. Nowadays a teenager from Naples and a teenager from Como, whose grandparents would not have understood each other, speak the same standard Italian. This is the language for foreigners to learn.

Learning Italian Before You Go

Part-time Courses. Part-time courses are ideal for those with domestic or professional commitments and are cheaper than the language courses offered by commercial organisations such as Berlitz, Inlingua, etc. Local colleges of education and community or adult studies centres are the best option as they often run day and evening courses in a wide and amazing variety of subjects. The courses cater for a variety of standards, ranging from beginners who want to learn Italian for next year's holiday or for general interest, to those who wish to take an exam leading to a qualification at the end of the course. Italian cultural organisations also offer courses and sometimes lessons can be arranged through the Embassy in countries where there is no formal Italian cultural organisation.

Intensive Language Courses with International Organisations. One real advantage of an international organisation is that it offers language courses which, begun in your home country, can be completed on arrival in Italy. Each course is specifically tailored to the individual's own requirements as far as the language level and course intensity is concerned and the cost of the courses varies enormously depending on these factors. Further information is available from the addresses below:

The Berlitz School of Languages: 2nd Floor, Lincoln House, 296-302 High Holbourn, London WC1V 7JH; ☎020-7611-9640; fax 020-7611 9656: Berlitz USA – 40 West 51st Street, New York City, NY 10020, USA; ☎212 765 1001; fax 212 307 5336; www.berlitz.com for international centres.

inlingua School of Languages: Quality Cobden Hotel, 166, Hagley Road, Birmingham B16 9NZ; tel/fax 0121-455 6677; www.inlingua.com; for information about US inlingua schools visit www.inlingua.com/usa.html.

Linguarama: New London Bridge House, Floor 12a, 25 London Bridge Street, London SE1 9ST; ☎020-7939 3200; fax 020-7939 3230; www.linguarama.com.

Self-Study Courses. For those who prefer to combine reciting verb endings with cooking the dinner or repeating sentence formations while walking the dog, then self-study is the most suitable option and has the advantage of being portable to Italy where you can continue to learn while practising total immersion in the language amongst the locals. Various well-known organisations produce whole series of workbooks, CDs, audiocassettes and videos for learning a wide range of foreign languages. The BBC has a wide range of teach yourself Italian books from phrase books, to course books with cassettes. Other courses are available from Berlitz and Linguaphone. Sample self-study courses are listed below:

Buongiorno Italia! Coursebook, £10.99 (plus three cassettes at £6.99 each). This combination of texts and recordings from the BBC focuses heavily on such aspects of everyday, conversational Italian as finding the way, shopping and understanding numbers and prices. The textbook, teacher's notes and cassettes can all be purchased individually from the BBC online shop: www.bbcshop.com.

Hugo: In Three Months Italian Course Book, £5.95. 253 page book, without cassette or CD Rom; www.hugo.com.

Italianissimo, also from the BBC, has courses ranging in price from £6.99, through to a full course at £42.99. Further details on all BBC courses can be obtained online at: www.bbcshop.com.

Italian for Dummies, US$24.99, including CD Rom. Based on the well-known Berlitz courses.

In addition, Linguaphone (Carlton Plaza, 111 Upper Richmond Street, London SW15 2TJ; 020-8333 4898; fax 020-8333 4897; www.linguaphone.com) have courses which range from Italian for tourists at £12.99, beginner courses that aim to teach a new language in twelve weeks (from £49.99) to complete course leading to fluency in Italian at £299.90.

Online bookstores such as www.amazon.com, www.amazon.co.uk and www.bn.com have a wide range of courses at discounted prices on their North American, European and other regional sites.

For those who want to maintain or improve their fluency in Italian *Acquerello Italiano* audio magazine is ideal for anyone interested in Italian language and culture. *Acquerello Italiano* is an hour-long programme on audiocassette with news, features and interviews from Italy. Rather than teaching you to order meals or book a hotel room, the programme is aimed at helping you expand and update your vocabulary. The cassette comes with a magazine that has transcripts, glossary and copious background explanatory notes. There are optional study supplements also available. For six editions annually the subscription is £69

(US$99), the study supplements are an additional £18 (US$30) from *Aquerello Italiano*, UK ☎0117- 929 2318; fax 0117-929 2426; USA ☎1-800 824 0829; www.acquerello-italiano.com or www.champs-elysees.com/aihome.php3).

Learning Italian in Italy. The most famous Italian language schools are at Perugia and Siena universities, at the British Institute in Florence and at the Scuola Leonardo da Vinci in Florence, Rome and Siena. But all major Italian cities have schools of Italian.

A typical university course in Italian e.g. at the University of Trento, costs 400 euros (about $400), for outsiders for 50 hours of lessons in total.

The first step in learning Italian is to understand that it is phonetic: the words are pronounced exactly as they are spelt. Once you have mastered the phonetic rules listed below, you can make yourself understood, immediately, by learning a few key phrases and idioms, of which a few examples are also listed.

To acquire the sound and the cadence of the language it is worth listening to Italian radio or TV. Quiz programmes are particularly educational in that they show words and their spelling on screen.

Essential Phonetics

The Italian alphabet is pronounced as follows: 'a' (ah), 'b' (bee), 'c' (tchee), 'd' (dee), 'e' (eh), 'f' (ehf-fey), 'g' (jee), 'h' (ak-ka), 'i' (ee), 'j' (ee loongo = *i lungo* or long i), 'k' (kahp-pah, 'l'(ell-ley), 'm' (em-mey), 'n' (en-ney), 'o' (oh), 'p' (pee), 'q' (koo), 'r' (ehr-rey), 's' (ess-sey), 't' (tee), 'u' (oo), 'v' (voo), ('w' is *doppio v* (dop-pyo voo), 'x' (eeks), 'y' (*ipsilon* = eepseelon), 'z' (zeta = dzeh-tah).

Vowels. must all be distinctly enunciated, never slurred or diphthongised as in English.

'a' sounds a in father	e.g. *padre* (pah-dray) = father
'e' has two sounds	open as in whey e.g. *pésca* = fishing,
	closed as in whet e.g. *pèsca* = peach
'i' sounds as in machine	e.g. *bambino* (bambeeno) = child
'o' has two sounds	open as in 'got' e.g. *uomo* (waw-mo) = man,
closed as in goat	e.g. *limone* (lee-moan-ey) = lemon
'u' sounds as in rule	e.g. *uno* (oo-noh) = one,
except before vowels when it sounds like	
the unstressed u in quit	e.g. *buono* (bwaw-noh) = good.

Diphthongs. In Italian, these are formed automatically by giving the full phonetic value to each successive vowel,

e.g. *Ciao!*	Chee-a-oh-(chow)	hi!
Vai!	va-ee-(vye)	go!

Consonants. Pronounced as they are in English but without any aspiration (except in demotic Tuscan – supposedly – from the Etruscan), and they are never swallowed or glottalised.

'c': has two sounds: before 'a, o, u' and 'h' like 'c' in car e.g. *caro* (kah-roh) = dear and *chiave* (kyah-vey) = key. Before 'e' and 'i', like ch in church e.g. *cena* (chey-na) = dinner.

'g' : has two sounds: before a, o, u and 'h' it is like 'g' in go, before 'e' and 'i' it is like 'j' in jump e.g. *gusto* (goose-toe) = taste, *gente* (jen-tey) = people, *ghetto* (get-toe) = ghetto.

'h': is never pronounced in Italian e.g. *ho* (oh) = I have.

'r': is *always* sounded with a distinct trill e.g. *carne* (carr-ney) = meat. This 'R' sound is more like the Scots 'R' than the West country or north American R. It can change the meaning of the word if you drop it e.g. *carne* = meat, *cane* (kah-ney) = dog.

's': has two sounds: 's' as in so, and 's' as in rose e.g. *presto* = quick and *rosa* (raw-zah) = rose.

'z': has two sounds: 'ts' as in hats, and 'dz' as in heads, e.g. *zio* (tsee-oh) = uncle, *zappa* (dzahp-pa) = hoe.

'ch': has the sound of 'k' as in kettle e.g. *bruschetta* (bruce-ket-ta) = toast..

'gh': has the sound of 'g' as in go e.g. *traghetto* (trag-et-toe) = ferry.

'gl': has the sound of 'lli' in million e.g. *piglio* (pee-lli-oh) = take.

'gn': has the sound of 'ny' in canyon, e.g. *bagno* (ba-nyo) = bath ,

'ng': sounds like 'ngg' as in hunger e.g. *lungo* (loong-goh) = long.

'sc': has two sounds. Before a, o, and u it sounds like 'sc' in scar, before e and i it has the sound of 'sh' in she e.g. *scusa* (skoo-za) = excuse, *scena* (sheh-na) = scene.

DOUBLE CONSONANTS

Note: all double consonants in standard Italian are fully sounded:

e.g. the 'tt' *in brutto* (ugly) is pronounced as in hat-trick

the 'cc' in *pacco* (package) is pronounced as in book-case

the 'll' in *bella* (beautiful) is pronounced as in male lamb

and so on with all the consonants.

Note: the meaning can change if you fail to sound the double consonant e.g. *penna* = pen; *pena* = pain.

SOME USEFUL PHRASES AND IDIOMS

Buongiorno, buona sera, buona notte,	good day, good evening, good night.	*Mi piace…*	I like.
Come sta?	(formal) how are you?	*Da morire*	to die for.
Come stai?	(familiar) how are you?	*Permesso? Posso?*	May I?
Non c'è male	not too bad.	*Scusi*	excuse me.
Molto bene	very well.	*Complimenti!*	Congratulations!
Tutto bene	all well.	*Grazie*	thank you.
pronto!	hello! (on the phone) literally = ready!	*Prego*	don't mention it, you're welcome.
a domani	till tomorrow.	*Guardi!*	look!
Ciao!	hi! or bye! (informal)	*Guarda*	(familiar) look!
salve	formal version of ciao.	*Che bella!*	How beautiful!
arrivederci!	see you!	*Che brutta!*	How ugly!
ieri	yesterday.	*Certo!*	sure!
presto – tardi	early, late.	*Senta!*	hey listen!
quanto?, quando?	how much? when?	*ascóltami*	listen to me (familiar)
dove? qui	where? here.	*è vero?*	is it true?
non lo so	I don't know.	*mi raccommando*	I urge you.
non si sa mai	one never knows.	*dai!*	go on!
un giorno sì, un giorno no	every other day, literally one day yes, one day no.	*vai!*	go! come off it!
a che ora parte? arriva?	what time does it leave? arrive?	*via!*	away!
La strada, il pullman, it treno per Firenze	The road, the bus, the train to Florence.	*un sacco di soldi*	loads (literally, a sack) of money.
Che ore sono?	what time is it?	*Buone cose!*	all the best! (literally, good things).
Che ora è?	what time is it?	*Lasciamo perdere!*	forget it! (literally, let's lose it!).

Sono le tre	It is three o'clock.	il mondo è paese	the world is like a village.i.e. things are the same everywhere.
Come si chiama questo?	What's this called?	Molto fumo e poco arrosto!	(lit. a lot of smoke and not much roast; i.e. much ado about nothing.
Questo, quello	this, that.	Buon lavoro!	Enjoy your work!
Adesso, allora	now, then.	Buona giornata!	Have a nice day!
Ora	now.	Buon proseguimento!	Carry on, and all the best.
Quanto costa?	how much does it cost?	Che diàmine! Per carità!	What on earth...!For goodness sake![
Magari!	if only!		

GENDER IN ITALIAN LANGUAGE

A distinction is made in Italian between masculine and feminine – in the ending of nouns and adjectives – feminine – a, masculine – o, thus *Brava!* well done! (of a girl), *Bravo!* well done! (of a boy). Girls especially must remember to make adjectives agree with their gender: thus *sono contenta* not *sono contento* (I am happy) when they are talking about themselves. Exceptions: some words of Greek origin ending in -a are masculine such as: *il poeta*, *il problema*, etc.

It is a good idea to learn *by rote* the alphabet, the numerals, the days of the week, the months of the year, the colours, and so on. Study the dictionary or an Italian language textbook and *Buon divertimento!* (Enjoy yourself!).

Body Language
Italians are famous for their expressive body language and gestures (bunched fingers, the wagging forefinger etc.). These are an integral part of any language and can only be learnt by personal observation and mimicry. The degree of gesticulation, closeness and body contact increase the further south you go, as you move from Northern European to Mediterranean norms of tolerance.

Familiarity
Italian retains certain polite forms such as the distinction between *Lei* and *Tu* (= you in the singular), *Lei* literally means She. The plural is *Loro*, which literally means they or them. It is the equivalent of English waiter-speak. 'Would the gentlemen like a drink?' meaning 'Do you want a drink?' The third person is used to avoid the familiarity of speaking directly with the second person. *Darsi del Lei* – (to use the *Lei* form) means not be on first-name terms with, which is *darsi del Tu*. *Tu* is used with children, colleagues, work mates, fellow students, relations

and patronisingly with servants. When in doubt use *Lei*, or wait for the native speaker to shift to *Tu*. Italians generally prefer to be reserved and courteous and do not have the same compulsion to be on first-name terms as some English-speaking people have.

ADDRESSING AND SIGNING LETTERS

The Envelope. On the envelope the polite form is : *Gentile Signore/Dottore Mario Rossi,*
which is abbreviated to: *Gent.Sig./dott. Mario Rossi*. Often abbreviated superlatives are used, such as: *Gentma dott.ssa Mario Bianchi* for *Gentilissima dottoressa Maria Bianchi*; (= very gentle) or *Preg. mo sig. Bruno Giordani* (= highly esteemed) for *Pregiatissimo signore Bruno Giordani;* or *Chiar. mo prof. Ezio Landi* for *Chiarissimo professore Ezio Landi,*
(*Chiarissimo* = very illustrious is only used for university professors).
Then the address:
via Nazionale, 23
53031 Buonconvento (Si).

NOTE

Put the postcode before the town name (CAP = *Codice di avviamento postale*), followed by the abbreviation of the province in brackets).
If it is confidential write, *riservata-personale;* c/o or *presso* is used for 'care of'.
'For whom it may concern' is *a chi di competenza*.
The sender's address must be written on the back of the envelope: *Mittente*: (= sender:-).
In many business and personal letters polite titles can be ignored.

Beginning The Letter. You begin the letter with the recipient's address on the top and the date below it, either in the short form (03.04.03) or preferably in the full form (3 aprile 2003).
Then you start with:
Caro...(masc.), or *Cara*... (fem.)   Dear... (followed by name).
Carissimo... (masc), or *Carissima*...(fem.)   Dearest ... (followed by name).
or just bluntly *Oggetto*   Subject
or more politely: *Gentile Signor Rossi,*...
or more formally: *Egregio Signor Fabbri,*

Signing Off. You end the letter with: *Cari*, or *Cordiali saluti* (dear or warm greetings), or more familiarly with: *Baci* (kisses) or *abbracci* (hugs) which can be *cari* or *affettuosi*. Thus: *affettuosi saluti* (affectionate greetings).
Distinti saluti (respectful greetings) is a cold formal ending which is normally

qualified by a polite preceding phrase such as: *'in attesa di un Vostro gradito riscontro'* (awaiting your kind reply). More formal and grovelling are the endings *con ossequio* and *con osservanza* (with deference, compliance), and finally, if you want to affirm your trustworthiness: *In fede* (in faith).

E-mail. Italian E-mail 'netiquette' follows the American example: Cut out all formality and get straight to the point as if you were speaking. *Oggetto:-* (= Subject....). The neutral greeting *salve* (hail!) and ending *saluti* are permissible. The use of capital letters means you are shouting.

ITALIAN FORMULA FOR SPELLING OUT NAMES ETC.

When Italians have to spell out names etc. the following alphabet mainly of town names is universally used. This alphabet is indispensable for foreigners and must be learnt.

a = Ancóna	b = Bari	c = Como
d = Domodóssola	e = Èmpoli	f = Firenze
g = Génova	h = Hotel	i = Ímola
j = Jesolo (ee-yeh-so-lo)	k =Kursaal	l = Livorno
m = Milano	n = Nàpoli	0 = Òtranto
p = Palermo	q = Quarto	r = Roma
s = Savona	t = Torino	u = Údine (oó-di-neh)
v = Venezia	w = Washington	x = (pronounced ee ks)
y = York (or Ipsilon)	z = Zara	

SUMMARY OF HOUSING

Compared with a 27% decrease in the Italian stock market since 1999 real estate has gone up by up to 24.7%. No other form of investment has done so well.

How Property Prices are Calculated. There are many different types of property on the market including those needing renovation, completely restored, apartments and new houses and developments. The price quoted in the table (*Summary of Housing*) pertains to the area of the buildings only, for example an apartment of 80m2 (square metres) at €1,000 per m2 = €80,000. The price per square metre does not include any land, swimming pool or tennis court that may be a part of the property. The price of the land on which the property sits (this does not apply to apartments) is determined by its position, for example if you own a property on or near the coast, you can expect to pay more than you would for a property in the hills with very rough (rocky) terrain. You can see examples of this difference in the 'properties for sale' section at the end of every region in *Chapter 3*.

The largest Italian estate agency, Gabetti has 500 offices nationwide (www.gabetti.it). Gabetti suggest using the following information to calculate property prices in 2004, 2005 and beyond.

O New or restored homes rise by 7.68% per annum.
O Partially restored homes rise by 7.48% per annum.
O Properties for renovation rise by 8.66% per annum.

Please note that these predictions are only a guide, subject to geopolitical fluctuations.

Sources of Information. The information/figures in the *Summary of Housing* are extracted from a twice-yearly supplement (*Osservatorio Immobilare*), part of the Milan-based financial newspaper *Ii Sole 24 Ore*. Nearly all the daily Italian newspapers carry a property section at least once a week. All you need in order to buy any property magazine etc. is to say *Immobiliare* (property) to the newsagent and he will show you everything available.

There are also publications in England with Italian properties for sale, including *Italy* magazine, *UK World of Property* and *International Homes*. The equivalent publications in Italy are:- *Case e Casale* and *Ville e Casali*.

Property Exhibitions. It is a good idea to be on the lookout for property exhibitions held in different venues around the UK. At the moment these exhibitions centre on properties in France and Spain but often Italy is included with other European countries. At these exhibitions you can meet experts, financial advisors and solicitors etc. who can advise you and you have the opportunity to see what is available and the cost. For more information on exhibitions: www.tsnn.co.uk or www.internatio nalpropertyshow.com.

Useful Websites. If you are looking for something different and would like to purchase a property in the Venice area or on the small islands off the coast of Italy you can log on to www.vladi-private-islands.de. Other sites which list property prices include:

www.nomisna.it. This is a Bologna based research team who do real estate research.

www.real-estate-european-union.com

www.italian-realestate.com

SUMMARY OF PRICES

Price per square metre e.g. 1,600 euros per sq.mt.

Region	Province	Comune	Maximum price (€)	Minimum price (€)
Piedmont	Asti	Nizza-monferrato	1,600	620
	Torino	Rosta	2,200	1,200
Lombardy	Bergamo	Albino	1,807	1,240
	Como	Cernobbio	2,500	1,200
	Cremona	Casalmaggiore	1,100	470
Valle D'Aosta	Aosta	Prè Saint Didier	2,500	1,200
Trento Alto Adige	Trento	Riva del Garda	2,500	1,300
	Bolzano	Centro	4,130	-
Veneto	Verona	Torri del Benaco	2,480	1,600
	Vicenza	San Felice	1,750	1,100
Fruili Venezia Giulia	Pordenone	Cordenons	1,343	826
	Trieste	Rozzol	2,300	1,200
Liguria	Genova	Rapallo-Porto	2,690	1,970
	La Spezia	Cinque Terre	4,000	1,600
Emilia-Romagna	Bologna	Bazzano	2.065	1,400
	Ferrara	Porto Ganbaldi	1,850	1,500
	Forli	Savignano	1,807	930
	Ravenna	Lugo	1,650	1,050
	Rimini	Riccione-Terme	3,400	2,500
Tuscany	Florence	Scandicci	3,200	2,100
	Arezzo	Sansepolcro	2,200	1,000
	Grosseto	Massa Marittima	1,549	620
	Livorno	Cecina	3,100	1,200
	Siena	Camollia (citta) (city)	4,000	2,000
Umbria	Perugia	Citta'di Castello	2,066	878
Marche	Ancona	Senigallia	2,852	1,291
	Pesaro	Fano	2,170	1,395
Lazio	Roma	Genzano	2,000	1,260
	Viterbo	Montalto di Castro	1,032	610
Abruzzo	L'Aquila	Roccaraso	2,580	1,700
	Pescara	Montesilvano	1,550	930
Molise	Campobasso	Tennoli	1,800	900
Campania	Naples	Forio d'Ischia	2,350	1,600
	Benevento	Telese	1,100	600
	Salerno	Vietri sul Mare	2,300	1,500
Puglia	Bari	Barletta	2,060	1,340
	Brindisi	Fasano di Brindisi	1,290	600
	Foggia	Vieste	1,800	1,000
	Lecce	Nardo	878	465
Basilicata	Potenza	Venosa	980	550
	Matera	Policoro	1,100	600
Calabria	Cosenza	Castrolibero	930	671
Sicily	Palermo	Monreale	1,446	930
	Catania	Gravina	1,446	775
	Siracusa	Augusta	1,500	550
Sardinia	Cagliari	Assemini	1,140	750
	Oristano	San Nicola	1,136	671
	Sassari	Alghero	1,549	723

Source: *Osservatorio Immobilare (Il Sole 24 Ore)* 2003

PUBLIC HOLIDAYS

Note that on Italian national holidays (*feste*) offices, shops, banks, post offices and schools are all closed. Whether museums, parks, etc, are closed will vary from region to region:

PUBLIC HOLIDAYS	
1 January	New Year's Day; *Capodanno*
6 January	Epiphany; *La Befana*
Easter Monday	*Pasquetta*
25 April	Liberation Day; *Anniversario della Liberazione*
1 May	Labour Day; *primo maggio*
15 August	Assumption; *Ferragosto*
1 November	All Saints'; *Ognissanti*
8 December	Immaculate Conception; *L'Immacolata Concezione*
25 December	Christmas Day; *Natale*
26 December	Boxing Day; *Santo Stefano*

City Festival Days. All cities. major and minor towns have a day to honour their own local patron saints. Shops and offices usually remain open on these days. Consult the tourist board in your area for information.

CONVERSION CHART

LENGTH (NB 12inches = 1 foot, 10 mm = 1 cm, 100 cm = 1 metre)

inches	1	2	3	4	5	6	9	12	
cm	2.5	5	7.5	10	12.5	15.2	23	30	

cm	1	2	3	5	10	20	25	50	75	100
inches	0.4	0.8	1.2	2	4	8	10	20	30	39

WEIGHT (NB 14lb = 1 stone, 2240 lb = 1 ton, 1,000 kg = 1 metric tonne)

lb	1	2	3	5	10	14	44	100	2246
kg	0.45	0.9	1.4	2.3	4.5	6.4	20	45	1016

kg	1	2	3	5	10	25	50	100	1000
lb	2.2	4.4	6.6	11	22	55	110	220	2204

DISTANCE

mile	1	5	10	20	30	40	50	75	100	150
km	1.6	8	16	32	48	64	80	120	161	241

km	1	5	10	20	30	40	50	100	150	200
mile	0.6	3.1	6.2	12	19	25	31	62	93	124

VOLUME

1 litre = 0.2 UK gallons   1 UK gallon = 4.5 litres
1 litre = 0.26 US gallons   1 US gallon = 3.8 litres

CLOTHES

UK	8	10	12	14	16	18	20
Europe	36	38	40	42	44	46	48
USA	6	8	10	12	14	18	

SHOES

UK	3	4	5	6	7	8	9	10	11
Europe	36	37	38	39	40	41/42	43	44	45
USA	2.5	3.3	4.5	5.5	6.5	7.5	8.5	9.5	10.5

RESIDENCE AND ENTRY REGULATIONS

CHAPTER SUMMARY

O Non-Italians planning to stay in Italy for over 30 days must apply for a *permesso di soggiorno* (permit to stay) even if they are from another EU country

O Those not from EU countries must apply for a *permesso di soggiorno* and a work visa before they enter Italy.

O All those planning to take up employment – including EU nationals – also need to obtain a *libretto di lavoro* (worker registration card) from the town hall; this will be held by your employer.

O Once you have the *permesso di soggiorno* and have moved into an Italian address you should obtain a residence permit (*certificato di residenza*): this is not compulsory for EU nationals, but has several uses and is proof that you have settled in Italy.

O All Italian residents, whether native or foreign, must carry an identity card (*Carta d 'Identità*) with them at all times.

O Italy is currently tightening its immigration laws to combat a rising flood of illegal immigrants (*clandestini*) from eastern Europe and Africa.

THE SCHENGEN ACCORD

Before discussing the visa regulations for Italy, it is important to understand the implications of the Schengen Accord. The introduction of new immigration laws (see below) and the extra vigilance at vulnerable border areas in Italy is not unrelated to the Schengen Accord – introduced in Italy in October 1997. At the time of writing there are fifteen countries in the Schengen group: Austria, Belgium, Denmark, Finland, France, Germany, Greece, Iceland, Italy, Luxembourg, Netherlands, Norway, Portugal, Spain and Sweden. The United Kingdom and Ireland, who have limited border controls between their two countries, have declined to participate in the Accord because they (especially the UK) believe that they are the final targets of most illegal immigrants and so wish to maintain border controls.

The Schengen countries have generally eliminated passport and baggage controls except for general airport and airline safety in the airports of their countries. In some cases this has meant modification of existing airports like the Malpensa 2000 airport in Milan to accommodate increased traffic. It is now possible to travel around much of Europe and only be aware that a border has been crossed when the street signs change language and car number plates change style.

The main fear of other Schengen countries, particularly France and Germany, has been that illegal immigrants will still find it easier to enter Italy, which has 8,000 miles of coastline, than other countries and will then pass through Italy to the other European countries. The Schengen agreement has been suspended once and temporary border controls implemented because of fears of a sudden major increase in illegal immigrants from Italy.

The Schengen agreement also allows nationals of countries from outside the EU to enter a member country through the normal passport controls on a visa issued by that country and then move around the Schengen Accord countries freely without further passport checks. To counteract possible abuse by the criminal fraternity and those who have been deported from one country and try to return through another, the member countries came up with the 'Schengen Information System' (SIS). This will connect Consulates and Embassies worldwide to a centralised data bank in Strasbourg where the names and details of all known criminals will be stored. Apart from at Embassies and Consulates, the information can be accessed from terminals at first points of entry to the Schengen Area. Under the protection of personal data regulations, private citizens are allowed to check information relating to them that is stored in the system.

VISA INFORMATION

All Nationalities

For stays of longer than 90 days all nationalities of visitor require a *permesso di soggiorno* (permit to stay), which must be applied for within eight days of arrival. EU nationals whose passports will not be stamped on arrival will not have to worry quite so much about this timescale as non-EU visitors whose visas will be checked and their passport stamped at the port of entry. With the Schengen Accord in place, passports of non-EU nationals will only be checked when they first enter Schengen area and the Italian authorities may use this date when calculating the 90 days.

Citizens of the following countries do not require visas for Schengen area countries when visiting for business or tourism, though technically they need to register for the residency permit (*permesso di soggiorno*) within eight days of arrival in Italy: Andorra, Argentina, Australia, Brazil, Canada, Chile, Cyprus, Czech Republic, Ecuador, Estonia, Hungary, Israel, Japan, Latvia, Lichtenstein, Lithuania, Malta, Mexico, Monaco, New Zealand, Paraguay, Poland, San Marino, Singapore, Slovakia, Slovenia, South Korea, Switzerland, USA, Uruguay,

Vatican City.

Citizens of the following countries do not require visas when entering Italy for business or tourism for 90 days or less: Bolivia, Bulgaria, Costa Rica, Croatia, El Salvador, Guatemala, Honduras, Malaysia, Nicaragua, Panama, Venezuela.

Up to date visa information can be found on the Italian Embassy in Washington website (www.italyemb.org), though visa applications must be made to the consular office whose jurisdiction covers the region or country in which the applicant lives (see end of this chapter for contact details).

Applications for all visas must be made in person and the length of time that the application takes to be processed ranges from twenty-four hours to five weeks. It is usually best to assume the longer timescale to ensure your visa arrives in time for your departure, especially during the busy summer months. The visa itself currently costs about US$30.

European Union Nationals

In theory the creation of the European Union is supposed to mean that European Union nationals can live and work anywhere they want inside the European Union borders. However, there is still a lot of red tape for those who wish to relocate within it for a long-term stay and obtain a residence permit that entitles them to public services as if they were a local national. Although all EU nationals are entitled to live and work in Italy, the bureaucratic rigmarole involved with taking up residence there can be complex and time consuming. The regulations concerning residence permits are dealt with in detail below and, in theory, the procedure for obtaining them should be the same everywhere in the country. In practice there may well be differences depending on the *comune* in which you are living and your particular circumstances. The main thing to bear in mind is that Italy is excessively bureaucratic and the bureaucracy is as much a bugbear for the Italians themselves as it is for foreigners.

Non-European Union Nationals

For non-European Union nationals the process is much more involved. For a start, a non-EU national must apply for their work visa and visitors visa before they enter Italy. For some nationalities it is also necessary to apply for and receive the visas through the Italian embassy in their home country, though it will often be possible to apply for a visa in the area where you are permanently resident. For long-term expatriates this usually means that they can apply for their visa in the country where they are currently living, especially if they have a residence permit or other official documentation to prove they live there full time. It is also necessary to have employment before applying for the visas. Work permits for non-EU nationals will be issued only to people outside Italy, and only for jobs where the provincial Office of the Ministry of Labour is satisfied that no Italian can do the job.

Work Permits. The Italian employer must apply for an *Autorizzazione al Lavoro* which must then be presented by prospective employee at the Italian Embassy in the applicant 's home country or place of residence. In recent years large numbers of non-EU citizens have been given work permits, mainly because of the skills shortage in the north created by the booming economy in the area. Skilled workers, especially in electronics and other high-tech industries, and those looking for work in an area where a skill such as native English ability or a skill only possible to obtain on another country is necessary will be most likely to secure a work permit. It is not possible to convert a tourist visa to an employment visa inside Italy – i.e. tourists must leave the country, apply for a work permit and then return once they have it. For those who want to try and work illegally, renewal of a tourist visa is possible, but not guaranteed. Proof of funds and a good reason for the extension (other than a nice job) are essential if one is to be obtained.

PERMESSO DI SOGGIORNO

EU Nationals: EU nationals who arrive in Italy without a job, but hoping to find one, must apply at the police station for *a Ricevuta di Segnalazione di Soggiorno*, which entitles them to stay for up to three months looking for a job. The only document required to obtain *Ricevuta di Segnalazione di Soggiorno* is a passport. In order to obtain a *Permesso di Soggiorno* the *Ricevuta* together with a letter from an employer confirming employment must be back to the police station.

EU nationals who arrive in Italy with a job already arranged must apply at the *questura*, or the police station in smaller towns, for their *Permesso di Soggiorno* (sometimes also known as a *Carte di Soggiorno*), within eight days of arrival. Reports vary as to how long it takes for the *Permesso di Soggiorno* to be issued, but three months is the official delay.

Requirements for the *permesso di soggiorno* may vary. In many cases you will be required to produce proof of financial solvency, of having some kind of income and be able to name your intended profession while in Italy, if this is relevant. The soggiorno is free of charge and issued initially for three months and then either every two years or five years. Note that failure to renew the document can result in a substantial fine. Renewals are made through the *comune*, or the *questura* in large towns and cities. The *Permesso di Soggiorno* has to be renewed every five years, no matter how long you live in Italy. All renewals must be made on special document paper, *carta bollata*, which can be purchased from most tobacconists (*tabaccherie*). Depending on your status, the *permesso di soggiorno* will have a different suffix, for example: employee, student, tourist, student, spouse, foreign spouse of an Italian, etc.

Non-EU Nationals. All non-EU nationals intending to live in the country must have received the necessary visas before arrival. Within eight days of their arrival they need to apply for their *permesso di soggiorno* to the *questura*, or the police station in smaller towns.

All Nationalities: When making an application for *permesso di soggiorno* it is advisable to take every document required at the time of application to make a return visit unnecessary, or worse, prevent having to repeat the entire process of waiting and aggravation. The list below is a guide to what many people have been requested to present, though the list should be checked at the office you will apply to as local requirements may vary, especially between EU and non-EU nationals.

- A valid passport. Most countries require your passport to be valid for six months or more beyond your intended stay and Italy is no exception. A photocopy of the relevant information pages, including your visa, will also be required.
- Up to four black and white passport sized photos.
- A tax stamp (*marca da bollo*) of the correct value (check what is required at the local *questura*).
- For employees, a letter of employment is necessary.
- For the self-employed, proof of registration with the Chamber of Commerce and VAT certificate (or exemption) is required.
- For students a letter from their institution is required.
- For retired/non-working people proof of financial resources is needed.
- Proof of health insurance or coverage by social security system of Italy or another country.
- Marriage/divorce certificate.
- Passports of children to be included on the *permesso di soggiorno*, if the children are not on the parents ' passport, plus the birth certificates of the children.

It is necessary to have notarised translations of certain documents and have others provided in Italian – check with the office where the application will be made for current requirements. Official translations of the marriage, divorce and birth certificates, as well as the letter of employment in Italian will probably be required. Translations should be done by an official translator and enquiries should be made at an Italian Embassy or at the *questura* where an application is to be made.

Worker Registration Card/Libretto di Lavoro

Many employees, including EU citizens, are also required to apply for a worker registration card (*libretto di lavoro*). This is obtained after the *Permesso di Soggiorno*, at the town hall (*municipio*). The *libretto di lavoro* is valid for ten years and once obtained will be held by the employer. During any periods of unemployment it will be kept by the equivalent of the job centre (*Ufficio di Collocamento*).

CERTIFICATO DI RESIDENZA

Once you have obtained a *permesso di soggiorno* and moved into your new Italian home, you will find it to your advantage to apply for a residence certificate, *certificato di residenza*. For non-EU citizens it is mandatory and should be applied for within 20 days of receipt of the *permesso di soggiorno*. Applications should be made at the Vital Statistics Bureau (*Anagrafe*) of the *Comune*.

Advantages of the *Residenza*. The *certificato di residenza* entitles the holder to many vital privileges. The *residenza* is also proof that you are no longer resident in another country and can have tax advantages for UK citizens and other nationalities who need to demonstrate that they are living abroad. The *residenza* also enables the holder to numerous other benefits, e.g. to ship your personal effects to Italy, apply for a driving licence, open a bank account, claim health care and send children to local schools. The number of certificates which you are required to obtain once in Italy for other, more obscure reasons, will vary greatly depending largely on the commune in question and on the nature of the local *maresciallo* (head of the commune).

The *comune* of Rome has a web page that lists, in English, the current application requirements for a residence permit: www.comune.roma.it/info_cittadino/schede/stranieri/inglese/ss_im_ps.htm

Entering to Start a Business
EU Nationals. Those EU nationals who wish to enter Italy to start up a business are free to do so and no prior authorisation is required. Anyone in this category should apply for a *permesso di soggiorno* in just the way described above. However, if you have received a *permesso* as an employee it is necessary to have it amended to reflect your change in circumstances. Proven experience of three years in the field of the intended business and registration with the Chamber of Commerce is necessary as is obtaining a VAT number, or an exemption. Registration with the Chamber of Commerce is relatively simple, though obtaining the tax papers can be more difficult and many expatriates employ a specialist company to help them through the process. Starting work before completing the registration process is not recommended as it is technically against the law and can lead to fines and confiscation of equipment. There are a number of incentive programmes available in Italy that include low-interest loans and tax rebates.

Non-European Union Nationals: For those without right of abode in the EU who wish to enter and start a business a visa is necessary. Proof of qualifications to start a business in Italy may be required. To obtain the visa it may be necessary to obtain documentation from Italian organisations in Italy (e.g. Chamber of Commerce), sometimes it is necessary to obtain the documentation from the local of office in the area where the business will be located. Advice should be sought from an Italian Embassy and other Italian oriented trade organisations.

Entering with Retirement Status

Anyone intending to retire to Italy must be able to show proof of funds with which to support themselves in order to obtain their *permesso di soggiorno*. Depending on nationality, the residence permit must be renewed at varying intervals from one to five years and continuing proof of funds must be provided each time. Non-EU nationals must also furnish proof of health insurance that covers them in Italy.

The Carta d 'Identità

All residents, native and foreign, are required to carry an identity card (*Carta d 'Identità*) with them at all times. This is a regulation that the majority of Italians comply with, without feeling that it is any kind of infringement of their personal liberty. Outside of the UK, most European countries require people to carry some form of identity at all times, as do the majority of countries around the world – the premise being that if you have nothing to hide why should you worry if the police want to know who you are. Permanent residents are issued with an identity card that includes the holder 's nationality and passport number. The card should be bought from the *comune*. However, only Italian nationals can use their Italian identity card as a travel document in lieu of their passport.

Registering with the Embassy

Expatriates are advised to register with their embassy or consulate in Italy – US, Canadian and British offices are listed below. This registration enables the Embassy to keep their nationals up to date with any information they need to be aware of and also enables the Embassy to trace individuals in the event of an emergency. Consulates can also help with information regarding their nationals' status overseas and advise with any diplomatic or passport problems. They may also be able to help in an emergency such as the unfortunate event of the death of a relative. However, the Consulates do not function as a source of general help and advice, nor act as an employment bureau and they make this quite obvious in response to any such appeals. Some embassies run social clubs for their nationals and the nationals of friendly countries may be allowed to join too. Apart from being a good place to meet fellow nationals and other expatriates, these social clubs can be useful places to network for employment and business opportunities.

Italian Citizenship

Residency is not synonymous with citizenship and those who wish to be adopted as a citizen of Italy may find that they have some difficulty in doing so. There are however various ways to gain Italian citizenship, some of which are easier to complete than others, these include:

- By descent (if one or more parent or grandparent were Italian).
- By marriage to an Italian, after six months of residency in Italy or three years

of marriage.

O Through residency of more than two years in Italy (see www.escapeartist.com/ efan/living_in_italy.htm or www.lainet.com for the story of a US national trying to obtain Italian citizenship).

However, for EU nationals it should be no inconvenience to retain your current nationality, as you will have most of the rights, and also obligations, of an Italian national – expatriates can even vote in local elections. However, non-Italian males resident in Italy are not liable to perform military service (*il servizio militare*) – probably something most people would want to avoid anyway. From 2005 compulsory National Service will finish and Italy will have an entirely voluntary armed forces.

Immigration

Italy is currently tightening its immigration laws in an effort to restrict the flood of immigrants (legal and illegal) from Eastern Europe, particularly Albania but the numbers from North Africa and the sub-Sahara are also causing concern. These immigrants form Italy 's 'underclass' and are the main pillar of Italy 's flourishing black economy. The *clandestini* as they are known work without being registered, so apart from being able to pay lower wages, their employers save up to 50% of their usual labour costs as there are no social security or holiday benefit payments to be made. Although the official immigration figure for Italy currently stands at around a million, the true figure is probably double that. To combat this problem, immigration legislation has been introduced, visa controls are being imposed and large numbers of police and military units have been deployed along the country 's massive land frontiers and coastline in a concerted effort to repel the swelling ranks of Italy 's illegal immigrants. Most recently there has been an influx of Kurdish refugees from Turkey and Iraq. Areas where vigilance has been especially concentrated are Sicily, Calabria and Puglia in the south and Friuli in the north.

The problems of illegal immigration are not limited to the sheer numbers involved, but also include organised crime. Either the illegal immigrants end up working for the Mafia or, as in the case of Albanians, they turn out to be more deadly than the local Mafia whom they have managed to intimidate and supplant in northern cities like Milan.

One of the new Immigration Laws enables the Italian state to deport any *clandestino* found guilty of committing a crime on Italian territory. The same applies if they are found to have a previous criminal record, or they refuse to produce proper identification. If a *clandestino* is unable to produce identification, he or she can be held at a detention centre for a maximum of 30 days while identification is being sought.

On a number of occasions Italy has allowed *clandestini* already living in the country without valid documents to apply for their situation to be regularised. If they can show good reason why they should be allowed to stay, they are almost always allowed to do so.

Sources of Information

Before getting too far into planning any move to Italy all and every piece of information should be checked and double checked – including information in this book. Italian Embassies and Consulates in whose jurisdiction you live and your own Embassy in Italy are the best places to get information, though they might not always respond quickly.

Inhabitants of Rome, its province or region, who are floundering helplessly in a sea of incomprehensible bureaucracy can call an emergency telephone line (06-884 8484). The helpline dispenses invaluable advice on where to go, what you will need to take with you and what the cost is of all of the *certificati* and *permessi* which you now find you need. This is a free public service known as Socialtel provided by a a combination of local government, university, trade union and the telephone company and formed in response to the numerous calls incited by the Italian bureaucratic system. The helpline also provides helpful advice about finding work in Italy and information about medical treatment.

Useful Addresses

Italian Embassies and Consulates in the United Kingdom:

Italian Embassy: 14 Three Kings Yard, Davies Street, London W1Y 2EH; ☎020-7312 2200; fax 020-7499 2283; www.embitaly.org.uk.

Italian Consulate General: 38 Eaton Place, London SW1; ☎020-7235 9371.

Italian Consulate General: Rodwell Tower, 111 Piccadilly, Manchester M1 2HY; ☎0161- 236 9024. Easier to get through to than the London Consulate. For latest regulations send a request and a stamped addressed envelope to the Visa Department.

Italian Consulate General: 32 Melville Street, Edinburgh EH3 7HW; ☎0131-226 3631; 0131-220 3695.

Italian Vice Consulate: 7-9 Greyfriars, Bedford MK40 1HJ; ☎01234-356647. Operates 9.30am-12.30pm Monday to Friday.

Italian Embassies and Consulates in the United States of America:

Italian Embassy: 3000 Whitehaven Street NW, Washington DC 20008; ☎202-612-4400; fax 202-518-2154; www.italyemb.org.

Italian Consul General: 690 Park Avenue, New York, NY 10021, USA; ☎737-9100 or 439-8600; www.italyconsulnyc.org.

Italian Consul: 2590 Webster Street, angolo Broadway, San Francisco; ☎415-931 49224/5/6; visa enquiries visa@italcons-sf.org; www.italcons-sf.org.

Italian Consul: Boston ☎www.italconsboston.org.

Italian Consul: www.italconschicago.org.

Other Italian Embassies and Consulates:

Italian Embassy: 21st Floor, 275 Slater Street, Ottawa, Ontario, KIP 5H9; ☎613-232240; fax 613-233 1484; www.italyincanada.com.

Italian Consul General: 136 Beverley Street, Toronto (ON) M5T 1Y5, Canada; ☎416-977 1566; fax 416-977 1119; www.italconsulate.org.

Embassy of Italy: 12 Grey Street, Deakin A.C.T. 2600, Australia, ☎621-6273 3333; fax 612-6273 4233; www.ambitalia.org.au.

Embassy of Italy: 63 Northumberland Road, Dublin, Eire; ☎031-6601744; fax 031- 6682759; http://homepage.eircom.net/italianembassy/

British Embassies and Consulates in Italy:

British Embassy: Via XX Settembre 80a (Porta Pia), 00187 Rome; ☎064-220 0001 (8am-1pm & 2-4pm); www.britain.it.

British Consulate General: via S. Paolo 7, 20121 Milano; ☎02 723001; fax 02-864 65081.

British Consulate: Viale Colombo 160, 09045 Quartu SF, Cagliari, Sardinia; ☎070-828628; fax 070-862293.

British Consulate: Palazzo Castelbarco, Lungarno Corsini 2, 50123 Firenze; ☎055- 284133; fax 055-219112.

British Consulate: Piazza della Vittoria 15/16, Third Floor, Genoa; ☎10-564833; fax 10-5531516.

British Consulate-General: Via dei Mille 40, 80121 Napoli; ☎081-423 8911; fax 081-422 434.

British Consulate: via Saluzzo 60, 10125 Torino; ☎011-650 9202; fax 011-669 6982.

British Consulate: Vicolo delle Ville 16, 34124 Trieste; ☎040-764752.

British Consulate: Accademia Dorsoduro 1051, 30123 Venezia; ☎041-522 7207; fax 041-522 2617.

Other Consulates are listed on the UK Embassy website www.britain.it.

United States Embassies and Consulates in Italy:

Embassy of the United States of America: via Vittorio Venetto 119/A, 00187 Roma; ☎06-467 1; fax 06-4882 672 or 06-4674 2356; www.usembassy.it.

US Consulate General: Lungarno Vespucci, 38, 50123 Firenze; ☎055-239 8276; 055-284 088.

US Consulate General: Via Principe Amedeo, 2/10 – 20121 Milano; ☎02-290 351; fax 02-2900 1165.

US Consulate General: Piazza della Repubblica – 80122 Napoli; ☎081-5838 111; fax 081-7611 869.

American Embassy to the Holy See: via dell Terme Deciane 26, 00162 Rome; ☎06-

4674 3428; fax 06-575 8346.

Canadian Embassy and Consul in Italy:
Canadian Embassy: Consular Section, Via Zara, 30, 00198 Rome; ☎06-445 981; fax 06-445 98 912; www.canada.it.
Canadian Consulate General: Consular Section, Via Vittor Pisani,19, 20124 Milan; ☎02-67581; fax 02-6758 3900.

Part II

LOCATION, LOCATION...

WHERE TO FIND YOUR IDEAL HOME

WHERE TO FIND YOUR IDEAL HOME

CHAPTER SUMMARY

O Historical and regional differences are an intrinsic part of life in Italy.

    O It is important to understand the character of an Italian region and its people before choosing which one will be most congenial to you.

O Among the regions of Italy, there are several well-known locations, which have attracted foreigners for generations. These are expensive and crowded, but comfortingly familiar.

O The smallest regions are in the north: Liguria and Valle d'Aosta.

    O the former is one of the most densely populated regions and the latter is the least populated area of Italy.

O Some regions have many abandoned hamlets include Valle d'Aosta and Campania.

O A saturation point might have been reached in the regions of Tuscany, Umbria and Le Marche, where the supply of suitable rural houses has nearly dried up.

    O Town houses and apartments in these regions are however still available and reasonably priced; and some foreign residents say they are more convenient.

O The up-and-coming regions are Abruzzo and Molise.

O Properties in Sardinia are likely to be a good investment.

O The South and Sicily have a different mindset to the North and the Centre. Here swagger and respect for power are king.

    O The south is changing with the younger generation injecting new vitality into thriving resorts, frequented mostly by Italians at present.

O Foreigners should beware of buying in Sicily as they may be asked to pay for 'fire insurance'. It is an offer you should not try to refuse.

OVERVIEW

If you had the choice of anywhere in the world, where would you go to live? Our immediate ancestors, if they had to go abroad, were normally posted somewhere without any choice in the matter. We now have a bewildering range of options to consider, as good members of our consumer society. Where on earth would we choose? If we choose Italy, we do so because it is politically stable, with a good climate, lovely people, good food, plenty of culture etc. It is an attractive country. Perhaps we have enjoyed holidays there, or we have friends or relations there. But where in Italy? Are we thinking of a second home to which we might eventually retire?

The following section on the regions of Italy, will give a picture, in depth, region by region, concentrating not only on the geography but also on the people, the local heroes, the culture, the food and wine, and the history.

It is important to whet your curiosity about the history of any location, to delve into the *genius loci* (spirit of the place). Benedetto Croce (1866-1952), an Italian philosopher, maintained that the character of a people was entirely the result of their history and nothing but their history. Italy more than anywhere is history personified. Italians themselves are keen on their local history. Most towns have a local group called the *Pro Loco* (for the place). Not for them the Anglo-Saxon view that 'history is bunk' (Henry Ford), or the mindless neophilia of British governments which has robbed Britain of some her local county identities.

Quite the opposite tendency is at work in Italy. Regional identity, and autonomy is respected and guaranteed by constitution. Historical differences are celebrated and it is good for you, as an outsider, to become aware of the nuances.

On the surface, Italy is united. The standard official language, the road signs, the uniforms of the *carabinieri,* the ubiquitous smell of espresso coffee and two-stroke exhaust fumes; all of these shout ITALY, but underneath there are fascinating variations in the behaviour and look of the people which can be explained by a study of history. For example, you are sitting on a beach near Gaeta in the south of Lazio, and you notice an invasion of small, vivacious people, quite unlike the locals. Who are they? They are from Naples just down the coast; big city cockneys perhaps, compared to whom your Gaeta friends are country yokels. But this alone cannot explain the huge difference between them. Study their history, and you can imagine that the crowd from Naples are Greeks, and the Gaeta people are Volscians (the ancient inhabitants of the area).

Some regions are more homogeneous than others. Tuscany for example, which was once a country in its own right. Others are disparate, like Campania, where the Neapolitans again, are quite different from the people of Benevento. Other regions, such as Veneto, have been cut off from their historical partners; Brescia and Bergamo are in Lombardy, but you can see the influence of Venice in the architecture and hear it in the speech.

Everywhere there is a difference between the mountain people and the coastal people, between the highlander and lowlander. Which ones are going to be most congenial to you? It does not follow that the hill country people are all going to be sterling yeomen like the *contadini* (country people) of Tuscany, Umbria and the Marches. The same kind of terrain in Sicily and Calabria produces bandits and outlaws. In Sardinia, a mountainous area called Barbagia (cognate with barbarian) is still a refuge for rebels which dates back to Roman times. Lowland areas which have enjoyed traffic and commerce for centuries are more welcoming to foreigners than the hilltowns.

Among the regions of Italy, there are several well-known locations, which have been tried and tested for centuries and which have always been popular with foreign residents. These are:

- **The Ligurian Riviera:** regarded as an extension of the French Riviera, which was colonised by the English in the nineteenth century, originally as a winter resort.
- The cities of **Rome**, **Florence**, **Naples** and **Venice.**
- **The Northern Lakes:** Como, Garda, Maggiore etc.
- **Asolo** in the Veneto hills and the Euganean hills (near Padua), associated with poets and writers.
- **Islands:** Ischia and Capri off the coast of Campagnia. The island of Elba off Tuscany.
- **Taormina** in Sicily.
- **Grado**, near Trieste in Friuli — the Mediterranean watering-hole of the Austro-Hungarian Empire.

Such places as these will be expensive and overcrowded, but reassuringly familiar.

Other regions which have become congenial to both English-speaking and German-speaking residents within the last forty years are: Tuscany, Umbria and Le Marche (The Marches). These are full of happy valleys of expatriates, mostly living or vacationing in converted farmhouses, in idyllic countryside, in symbiosis with salt-of-the-earth Tuscan, Umbrian or Marchigiano neighbours. But pleas have been heard from Umbria: a saturation point might have been reached: no more British people please. This is the reaction of the already ensconced British colony; but as we will see, the supply of suitable houses has practically dried up anyway. So you could try Abruzzo and Molise, which have the same old-fashioned charm of Umbria and the Marches, but have not been 'discovered.'

Or, if you still want to be in Tuscany or Umbria — you can forget the countryside and opt for a town house or apartment. These are still comparatively cheap. In the *Case Histories* at the end of this book, you can read about the perpetual inconvenience of driving long distances when you live in the country (see *Frank Lee*) and the relief and pleasure of town life and public transport (see *Charles Butterno*).

Further afield, if you like mountains, you have the magnificent range of the

Dolomites, which straddle the regions of Trentino Alto-Adige and Veneto, enjoying sunny winters and wet summers. They are much frequented by Italians, who might dream of driving to Scotland or the North Pole in the summer, but actually prefer the Tyrolean ambience on their own doorstep.

Another option that beckons strongly is the island of Sardinia. This has the same Mediterranean feel of Majorca or the Spanish Costas, but without the crowds. It has to come first on any list of desirable Italian locations. The island has not yet been spoilt by indiscriminate development; it retains the image of the Costa Smeralda (Emerald Coast), of rich and beautiful people, crystal clear sea, and colourful folklore. Glossy magazines often contain articles of splendid seaside houses in Sardinia, sometimes belonging to professional footballers. Such properties are still available at reasonable prices. Sardinia is well-served by cheap flights; it is no longer the preserve of the super rich.

Finally, your intrepid and pioneering house-hunter has the choice of moving to the southern part of Italy or to Sicily. These regions are not bland and anodyne and predictably European, like the north and centre of Italy. You are confronted by a radically different mindset, which is stereotypically Italian to the prejudiced Anglo-Saxon eye. Power and swagger are respected here, and organised crime can still be a problem. This is the part of Italy, which produced the bulk of Italian immigrants to the USA, Australia and Britain...since the 1890s; at first those migrants were despised , but they are now admired as upholders of the healthy, Mediterranean diet and praised for their flair and gusto; their women are portrayed as feisty and enterprising. The name of Versace springs to mind as an example.

It is remarkable how radically the image of the Southern Italian immigrant has changed in the last few years, and indeed a transformation is happening in their country of origin. Young resourceful southerners are bringing the ancient *Magna Graecia* back to life. *Magna Graecia* (greater Greece) is the Latin name still used for the southern Italian coast which was colonised by the Greeks from the eighth century BC. Their flourishing colonies produced great philosophers (Pythagoras, Archimedes) and poets such as Theocritus who, invented the idyll. Calabria, Basilicata, Puglia and Campania are the regions of *Magna Graecia*.

Over the centuries their idyllic towns were degraded by wars, malaria and deforestation – much of it by commercial Piedmontese tree fellers in the nineteenth century. Malaria was blitzed by DDT, by the Americans after the Second World War, but since then uncontrolled illegal building development has defaced much of the coastline throughout Sicily and southern Italy.

But a new awareness of the environment has coincided with the advent of the internet. The tide has turned, and splendid thriving resorts are growing throughout the regions of the South, which attract mainly Italian visitors at the moment, but could easily appeal to a more international clientele, who might have the imagination and the enthusiasm to re-invent the idylls of the old poets.

THE NORTH-WEST

PIEDMONT

Capital: Turin (30 metres above sea level)
Area sq.km: 25,395; *Population:* 4,166,442
Foreign visitors: 3,194,653; *Italian visitors:* 4,021,984
Climate:

Mean	Summer temp.	Winter temp.	Ann. Rainfall	Days of rain
12.3C	21C	7.2C	893mm	146

Airports: Turin: Caselle International airport, Cuneo airport
Unesco world heritage sites: 1997: Residences of the Royal House of Savoy
National parks: Gran Paradiso/Val Grande

Geography and Climate

Piedmont gets its name from its position at the 'foot of the mountains'. It is surrounded by Alpine ranges with famous skiing resorts such as Sestrière, Bardonecchia and Limone Piemonte. The regional capital, Turin, is a city of baroque art and architecture; it has the second most important Egyptian museum in the world after Cairo. As well as having a wide spread of industries Piedmont is also famous for its wine production and gastronomy (especially the white truffle).

Piedmont borders with France to the West (the Maritime Alps and the Cottian Alps), with the Valle d'Aosta to the north-west (the Graian Alps), with Switzerland to the north (the Pennine and Lepontine Alps), with Lombardy to the east, with Emilia-Romagna to the south-east, and with Liguria (the Ligurian Apennines) to the south. It is 43.2% mountainous, 30.3% hilly and 26.5% plain.

The highest peaks in the region are Gran Paradiso (4,061m) in the Graian Alps and Monte Rosa (4,633m) in the Pennine Alps. These massifs descend into morainal amphitheatres, in the districts of Rivoli and Ivrea, and sporadic hills, in the districts of Vercelli and Novara. There is a clear contrast between the encircling mountains and the plain, which can be divided into two areas, the upper plain at the foot of the Maritime Alps (the towns of Cuneo, Mondovì and Saluzzo) and the lower plain round the cities of Novara and Vercelli.

Turin, the capital, is situated in the centre of the region, on the river Po, at the extreme western end of the Po valley or plain. Its hinterland to the east is Rivoli and the valley of Susa, on the road to the ski resort of Bardonecchia and Sestrière and to the department of Savoy in France, via Modane or the Fréjus tunnel. The hills of Canavese north of Turin were favoured by mediæval aristocrats, who built ten castles there. The local town, Castellamonte, specialises in the manufacture of ceramic stoves. The road leads on up to the Gran Paradiso nature park.

The other provinces in Piedmont after Turin, in a clockwise direction are:

○ **Biella,** pre-eminent for its wool and textiles since ancient times, and proud to be a province since 1996;

○ **Verbania** on the western shore of Lake Maggiore, which includes Stresa and Pallanza (where Captain Neil McEacharn created the fabulous gardens of the Villa Taranto in the 1930s). The mild microclimate and the beautiful steep lakeside setting have made this a favourite retirement spot for centuries. There is another lake, Orta, 10 km to the west of Lake Maggiore, which is equally romantic and less crowded.

○ **Novara,** in the Po valley, near Milan, rich in manufacturing industries (such as bathroom fittings).

○ **Vercelli** – the 'rice capital', paddy fields and superb Gothic architecture.

○ **Alessandria,** a hub for road and rail communications; this province includes the spa resort of Acqui Terme, the town of Valenza, famous for its goldsmiths and jewellers, and Ovada, a wine and truffle area .

○ **Asti** – the most attractive hilly vineyard area famous for wine and truffles, with hill towns like Canelli, Nizza, Monferrato and Cocconato.

○ **Cuneo** – the breathtaking gateway into the Maritime Alps, full of art and gastronomy, with summer and winter resorts. Among its towns are Alba, the capital of the white truffle, also known for its wines, and mediæval Mondovì.

Climate
The climate of Piedmont is continental with extremes of temperatures. Winters are cold and foggy, summers hot and sultry, cooler in the hills and mountains. There is high rainfall in spring and autumn, especially in the lakes and mountains.

People
'*Piemontesi finti cortesi*' – 'fake polite Piedmontese' is the rest of Italy's opinion of the Piedmontese character. For a long time there was a royal court in Piedmont which supported an aristocracy and a bourgeoisie, which became accustomed to court ceremonials and rituals – hence the *cortesi*. In the late nineteenth century the whole of Italy was run by Piedmontese bureaucrats and officers, even when the capital of Italy moved from Turin to Florence and then to Rome. The Piedmont official came across as honest but haughty.

Dialects
The Piedmontese dialect is spoken by all classes and age groups in Piedmont. The other indigenous languages are Franco-Provençal in four (Valsoana) valleys and Occitan in five valleys (Limone), whilst a German dialect is spoken in the upper valley of the Sesia, called Walser – a twelfth century settlement from the Valais

Regions & Major Cities of Italy

in Switzerland – still surviving and protected. They have been self-sufficient for eight centuries.

Films and Books

For a flavour of Piedmont the 1948 film 'Bitter Rice' (*Riso Amaro*) by Giuseppe di Santis starring Anna Magnani gives a picture of life in the rice fields. *The Italian Job* (1969) with Michael Caine also stars the city of Turin and the Piedmontese mountain roads.

As for writers, Primo Levi (1919 – 1987) (*If This is a Man* 1947) is one of the major voices of the twentieth century, whilst Cesare Pavese (1908 – 1950) dwells on urban themes and a city, Turin, which he adored. The hills of Le Langhe where he was born are the background of his *House in the Hills* and *The Job of Living*.

La Stampa, an Italian national daily newspaper printed in Turin keeps alive the tradition of Piedmontese seriousness and integrity.

HISTORY

The original inhabitants of Piedmont were Ligurians who interbred with Celtic settlers in about the fifth century BC. One of their clans, The Taurinians, made Turin their capital, which was destroyed by Hannibal in 218 BC. Julius Caesar made Turin a Roman base in 29 BC as a gateway to further Gaul. The Dukes of Savoy dominated the region from 1280, confirmed Turin as capital and built an impregnable citadel there in 1564. The Savoys continued to build for the next few centuries, creating a great baroque city and a series of palaces around Turin, (Palazzo Madema, Stupinigi, Superga), masterminded by Sicilian architect Filippo Juvarra (1678-1736); the duke of Savoy was also the king of Sicily at that time.

In the eighteenth century the court of the Savoys in Turin vyed with Versailles, and Turin became known as 'Little Paris'. In the nineteenth century an elegant intellectual café life was centred on Turin and the Piedmontese enjoyed a short period as 'masters of the universe', with King Victor Emmanuel II and Count Camillo Bensour de Cavour playing a leading role in the unification of Italy in 1860. Turin was capital of the new kingdom of Italy (1861-1864). Piedmont led Italy's industrial revolution before the first world war (the Fiat automobile factory was founded in 1899) and was in the forefront of the Italian economic miracle after the second world war in the 1950s and 1960s again spearheaded by Fiat. The huge influx of southern Italian workmen and their families, topped by new waves of immigrants, particularly from North Africa, at the end of the twentieth century transformed the region, and especially, Turin into a multi-ethnic megacity, with the associated problems of crime and racial tension.

The severe floods of October 2000 and the crisis of the Fiat empire in 2002 have been offset by Turin's successful bid to host the 2006 winter Olympics. The region is inventing a new identity for itself as a leader in the New Economy. There are already the makings of a silicone valley at Ivrea, where Olivetti is the headquarters of an information technology empire. The focus is also on the environment, with particular emphasis on the region's heritage and its 'wine and food' traditions. The organisational infrastructure and the allurements are in place for a new revival: no better time than now to invest in property anywhere in the region.

Food and Wine

Food. Piedmont's gastronomy attracts visitors from as far away as Japan, who come to the truffle fairs of Alba. The cuisine throughout the area has become a refined amalgam of the bland aristocratic and the crude peasant flavours of the past.

There is also a variety of excellent cheeses: *Gorgonzola* from Novara, *Robiola* from Alba, *Toma* from Valsesia, *Bra* from Villa Franca – all flavoursome soft cheeses. Castelmagno, a hard cheese ('the best in the world'); several varieties of goat's cheese and many more, every bit as good as the French cheeses over the border.

Wine. The wines of Piedmont are among the best in the world. Of the reds, Barolo and Barbaresco, made from the Nebbiolo grape are the best known, but the Grignolin is good and the fizzy black Barbera has a tremendous following and is beginning to shake off its down market reputation. Dolcetto d'Alba is another great wine from a local grape variety, of the whites the Asti Spumante – is commercially inseparable from the Christmas Panettone, the Moscato bianco is a popular Muscat, and the Cortese di Gave excellent with fish.

> *Andova Regno 'l vin,*
> *A-i regna nen ël silensi.*
> Where wine is king
> there is no room for silence. *(Piedmontese Proverb)*

Typical Properties for Sale

Piedmont is a modern region with lots of high-tech companies. The house prices in Piedmont are moderate and you can buy a town house for as little as 600 euros per square metre in the smaller towns. Property prices at the ski resorts are climbing due to extensive modernisation. The architecture of the region is varied. In mountain areas there are stone houses with slate or stone tiled roofs. The Langhe area is reasonably priced. Any farmhouse in the hills in this region can grow wine, and many expatriates are tempted to go into the business of wine production. At the time of press, Piedmont Properties was offering several wine estates for sale. To buy a trophy vineyard, which is already successful is of course another matter. Passion, enthusiasm and money will overcome most obstacles!

Alta Langa: a detached house, completely restored and set in 24,000 square metres of land. Ground floor 'taverna' basement area made into living space – cellar, 2 garages and bread oven. First floor living room, kitchen, bathroom. Second floor 2 bedrooms. **Price:** €176.000,00

Near Asti: two old houses in a beautiful hillside location. The properties are old and in need of restoration. 1.5 hectares of Barbera D.O.C. Vineyard. **Price:** €500.000,00

Santo Stefano: large medieval stone house (*rustico*) with 2 hectares of land with outstanding views. **Price:** €250.000,00

Cuneo: a large villa and farmhouse in the hills near Cuneo with panoramic views. The whole property in 17 hectares of land is fully fenced. **Price:** €650.000,00

Agents for this region: www.casedicampagna.com; www.smith.gcb.demon.co.uk; www.casatravella.com; www.colletta.it (modernised ancient hamlet north of Genoa – apartments).

LOMBARDY

Capital: Milan (221 metres above sea level)
Area sq.km: 23,861; *Population:* 8,922,463
Foreign visitors: 3,194,653; *Italian visitors:* 4,021,984
Climate:

Mean	Summer temp.	Winter temp.	Ann. Rainfall	Days of rain
12.7C	21.8C	6.6C	1,191mm	80

Airports: Milan-Linate, Milan-Malpensa. Use also Bergamo airport.
Unesco world heritage sites: 1979 Rock Drawings in Valcamonica, 1980 Church, Dominican Convent of Santa Maria, Delle Grazie with *The Last Supper* by Leonardo Da Vinci, 1995 Crespi d'Adda.
National parks: Stelvio Val Grande

Geography and Climate

Lombardy covers the Po Valley and the middle of the Italian Alps, bordering Switzerland to the north, Emilia Romagna to the south, Piedmont to the west and Trentino Alto-Adige and Veneto to the east. It is the most densely populated Region (372 inhabitants per square km) especially the province of Milan, which has a fourteenth of the country's entire population and a density of 1,442 inhabitants per square km. 47% of the region is plain, 40.6% mountainous and 12.4% hilly.

The mountains and lakes, and their towns, from east to west are: Varese on Lake Maggiore, Campione on Lake Lugano (an Italian enclave with a casino), Como, Brunate, Lecco and Bellagio on Lake Como, The Lago d'Iseo is a lake east of Bergamo in the Franciacorta wine area. East of Brescia is Lake Garda with its towns of Salò, Desenzano, Sirmione and Limone. To the north-east are the Orobian Alps and the town of Sondrio in the valley of the river Adda and the Valtellina wine area. Further up is the resort of Bormio and the Tonale pass through to the Stelvio national park. North of Milan are the Brianza hills and in the south are the provinces of Pavia, Cremona and Mantua.

The fertile plain of the Po is heavily cultivated by large scale agribusiness – a lot of rice, wheat and maize, grazing forage, livestock and dairy industry, and vineyards in the Oltrepò Pavese (Pavia), Valtellina and Franciacorta.

Industrially and commercially Milan and its hinterland is the capital of Italy: textiles, manufacturing, engineering, petrochemicals, food and furniture (Brianza), shoes and leather (Vigevano). Rust belt areas like Sesto San Giovanni have been replaced by massive retail parks throughout the region. Milan has a bourse (stock exchange), is the headquarters of several financial institutions and is recognised as the design capital of the world, with an important Trade Fair facility. Bergamo and Brescia are rich entrepreneurial industrial provinces. Brescia is a world leader in the manufacture of firearms.

Climate. The climate of Lombardy is continental, hot and muggy in the summer, cold and foggy in winter. But the lakes enjoy a mild microclimate where lemons and olives thrive. The mountains, Bormio and Stelvio provide good snow, suitable for summer skiing.

History

The oldest evidence of humans in the region are the stone carvings in Valcamonica (6,000 BC) of which a rose emblem has been taken as the symbol of the region. Milan was founded by Celts, conquered by Rome in 222 BC, became capital of the empire in AD 282 and a religious centre under St Ambrose in the fourth century, was invaded by the eponymous Lombards in the sixth century, whose capital was Pavia, stood up to the Emperor Frederick Barbarossa in the thirteenth century, flowered between the fourteenth and sixteenth centuries with the Visconti and Sforzas in Milan and the Gonzagas in Mantua, who sponsored works by Leonardo da Vinci and Bramante. The Duomo of Milan, the Charterhouse of Pavia, the ducal palace at Vigevano, and Bergamo Alto are monuments to that age. The Lombards have left their name in the English language: 'Lumber' is pawnbrokers goods taken by Lombard pawnbrokers, 'Millinery' is what Milan was manufacturing, along with fine steel armour in the Middle Ages.

In the seventeenth century Lombardy came under the Spanish and suffered from the plague in 1630 – the subject of Alessandro Manzoni's novel '*I Promessi*

Sposi'. Under the Bourbon Austrian rule a civilised café intelligentsia developed in Milan in the eighteenth century. Lombardy played a leading part in the Risorgimento of 1860 in the creation of fascism after the First World War, and it was in the forefront of the Italian economic miracle after the Second World War.

The lake towns are much sought after by Italians, and Varese and Como are popular with expatriates because of their Mediterranean microclimate; there are superb gardens in the area. The mountains of Sondrio, the Valtellina and parts of the provinces of Brescia and Bergamo are thinly populated and cheap. The lake Garda area is attracting settlers from Britain because of its lifestyle possibilites – sports are well catered for. The lake is ideal for windsurfing, it is a paradise for children; schools and hospitals are good. There are ski-resorts nearby and golf courses at hand, and the food and wine are of course exquisite.

Mantua is a Renaissance gem, so was Cremona once; but a century of industry and pollution has degraded the area. The pollution and smog is pervasive especially in the winter. If you are driving here with children you will soon be reminded that this is the 'poo' valley because of the smell. Much of this is to do with the processing of the pig. The presence of Lake Garda to the north of this area is fortunate. It is a well-deserved lung for the hardworking population of the valley.

People

Milan was the main target for terrorist action in the 'years of lead' (*annia di piombo*) in the 1970s, and its magistrates and courts were the protagonists of the clean hands (*mani pulite*) campaign of the 1990's. Greater Milan – the province of Milan is now a teeming megacity of 3.8 million inhabitants nearly 5% of whom are immigrants. 35% of these are from Asia, 33% from Africa, Filipino domestics, Egyptians in catering and Chinese entrepreneurs are noticeable groups, while recent immigration has been dominated by Albanians, Ecuadorians and Romanians. The 'new economy' is buzzing with hundreds of thousands of *pendolari* or commuters using the *metro* and other public transport, every day immigrants are being absorbed into the system despite the protests of the *Lega Nord*.

Food and Wine

Gastronomically, Italy's Slow Food movement (see *Living in Italy, Food and Drink*) is at home here. Fish and sea food, both sea and lake, are very popular. Local specialities are: Bresaola a cured cold beef from Valtellina; risotto alla Milanese made with saffron, flavoured with sage and rosemary; brasato, slow stewed beef, and ossobuco marrow filled shin of veal, for which a pinch of lemon zest and rosemary is the magic ingredient. Also on the menu are Milanese cutlets, minestrone a thick vegetable soup, polenta (maize porridge served with game and stews, *lesso misto* comprised of boiled meats with green sauce, pheasant with grapes, pigeons with lemon, veal with marsala wine, baked spinach (*spinaci in tortino*), stuffed courgettes (*zucchine ripiene*), potato and onion pie (*pasticcio di patate*). Cheeses are Gorgonzola, Grana Padena, Stracchino. Sweets are mascarpone cream and syllabub, concoctions with names like *Barbajada* (with chocolate) and *Rossumada*.

Wine. Barbera from the Oltrepò Pavase, from the Valtellina and Franciacorta near Brescia.

> *El riss ch'el nass in l'acqua*
> *El voeur mori in del vin*
> Rice is born in water
> and likes to die in wine. *(Lombardy proverb)*

Typical Properties for Sale

Milan is the country's financial powerhouse and one of the most important commercial and fashion centres of Europe. If you are in this region it is most likely that you will have been posted here for your job in which case you will need to find an apartment in the centre of Milan if you can, in preference to a suburb. You will equally be looking for a place to go at weekends, or as an investment, typically near the lakes. There is much foreign demand for property in and near Milan.

Prices in the centre are prohibitive. However foreigners have purchased 10% of the houses on the market in this region in 2002. Apartments in Milan cost 6,000 euros per square metre. Around Lake Como, there are only apartments available. At Cremona there is a music school so a good investment might be a property in the city centre. The areas east of Milan e.g. Brescia are much cheaper.

Milan. In a quality modern building, a bright corner dwelling of 240 square metres. Large lounge, studio, 4 bedrooms, kitchen, 3 bathrooms, large terrace with beautiful view. **Price:** €408.000,00.

Como: A residence 3km from the Milan Como motorway. 20 minutes from Milan and Malpensa. High quality finish. 5 bedrooms en suite. Large entertaining rooms. 2 garages. swimming pool. Maximum privacy. **Price:** €1.800.000,00.

Varese. Dominating its surroundings with panoramic views, a short distance from Lake Como and city centre. A functional modern villa with spacious and comfortable interiors, well finished on two living floors plus basement. 3,000 square metres of fenced and planted land. **Price:** €1.300.000,00

Cernobbio. In a fine residential hill area in a 19th century villa a 150 square metres attic apartment. Recently renovated. Spectacular views. Living room with fireplace, 2 bedrooms, 2 bathrooms, 2 car places. **Price:** €300.000,00

Agents for this area: www.vilacingfo.com, www.ibossi.com, www.italian-network.it, www.leemans.com.

LIGURIA

Capital: Genoa (3 metres above sea level)
Area sq.km: 5,421; *Population:* 1,560,748
Foreign visitors: 1,157,096; *Italian visitors:* 2,344,064
Climate:

Mean	Summer temp.	Winter temp.	Ann. Rainfall	Days of rain
16.6C	24.5C	9.2C	1,057mm	101

Airports: Genoa, Cristoforo Columbo International Airport; also Nice in France.
Unesco World Heritage Sites: 1997 Portovenere, Cinque Terre including the islands of Palmaria, Tino and Tinetto.
National Park: Cinque Terre.

Geography

Liguria is one of the smallest regions and is often referred to as the Italian Riviera. The littoral region of Liguria is 65% mountainous and 35% hill zone. It lies between the mountains and the Ligurian Sea (*Mar Ligure*) and is backed by the Maritime Alps (*Alpi Marittime*) and the Ligurian Appennines (*Appennino Ligure*). Its coast is divided into the harsh and steep eastern riviera (*Riviera di Levante*) from Genoa to La Spezia, and the more open landscapes of the western part (*Riviera di Ponente*) which has many sandy beaches and small seaside resorts, and towns including Ventimiglia, San Remo, Imperia and Savona. Liguria reaches from the border with France to the west, to Tuscany and Emilia Romagna in the east. To the north is Piedmont.

The terrain is not suitable for animal-rearing as the amount of pasture is so restricted. Vegetables, flowers and fruit trees flourish, especially in the lower zones along the coast or at the ends of valleys, while olives, vines and cereals grow on the steeper middle zone. The zones above 500 metres are heavily wooded (52.3% of the region is woodland).

With the decline of heavy industry, the main commercial activity is tourism, especially on the coast where the population triples during July and August. The famously smart resort of Portofino lies east of Genoa. Other established resorts include Bordighera, Sanremo, Alassio, Finale Ligure, Nervi, Santa Margherita and Rapallo. The Cinque Terre national park is the end strip of the Riviera di Levante.

The chief city of the region is also Italy's largest port, Genoa (*Genova*) which sprawls along the coast for 25 km and inland for 15km up the valleys of the rivers Polcevera and Bisagno. It is a place of great diversity which reflects its maritime and artistic heritage from being the birthplace of Christopher Columbus to attracting artists of the calibre of Rubens and Van Dyck in its heyday. Buildings include a Royal Palace, historic churches and fisherman's houses.

The region has four provinces: Genoa, Imperia, La Spezia and Savona.

The Climate

Most of Liguria has a particularly mild climate thanks to the protective mountains against which it nestles. The littoral is more temperate than much of the Mediterranean. It has mild winters and summers less parched than much of Italy. Rainfall can be pretty hefty in autumn and winter – up to 3000 mm in some parts.

History

Inhabited since the Palaeolithic period, Liguria became an administrative department under the Romans from the second century AD until the fifth century. Open to invasion from the Barbarians and Lombardians, and later in the Middle Ages, the Normans and Saracens who were engaged in the Crusades, Liguria was subject to many influences reflected today, especially in the cookery of the region. Owing to the lack of agricultural space, Ligurians developed other sources of commerce, notably oil mills and pasta factories during the increasingly industrial period of the eighteenth and nineteenth centuries. The city of Genoa (founded by the Romans as *Genua*) became a great maritime republic in the 13th century. This republic fell to Napoleonic invasion in 1796 and was divided up into units by the French. In 1815 after Napoleon's defeat, Liguria became part of the Kindom of Savoia and Sardinia and was known as the Duchy of Genova. In 1861 it was incorporated into a united Italy.

The People

Although Liguria is one of the smallest regions it has the highest population density in Italy (303 inhabitants per sq.m) after Campania and Lombardy. Although not one of the richest regions, the people of Liguria have one of the longest life expectancies in Italy and the area has a large population of older people. 90% of the people live along the coast, especially the western part, and two-fifths of the population lives in Genoa.

Genoa has many incomers from the south, and neighbouring Italian regions, but the typical Ligurian physical type is distinctively small-waisted, with slightly swarthy skin, black hair and a small head. Supposedly, many Ligurians are of Greek origin.

Ligurians, particularly the Genovese have a reputation similar to the Scots (i.e. that they are mean). In both cases this is probably unjustified, however the Ligurians are known for a particular kind of thriftiness related to their ability to utilise every bit of nature's bounty (see *Food* below).

There is a Ligurian dialect spoken throughout the region, which is part of the Italo-Celtic dialect group of northern Italy.

Food and Wine

Food. Having a dense population in a small area has shaped the regional cuisine which includes almost anything edible from the land or sea. Ligurian cooking is typified by a range of humble ingredients that add up to a tasty whole. For instance *una ventresca di vitello piena* (stuffed calf stomach) doesn't sound appealing but the stuffing is made up of vegetables including *cima* (turnip) widely used in Liguria, other vegetables, ricotta cheese, pistachio, cheese, tongue and other things. The stomach is sewn up before being baked in the oven.

Wild plants grow particularly well thanks to abundant rainfall. Borage (a blue-flowered herb) is still widely used as a substitute for spinach in pasta fillings. *Insalatina alla genovese* is a way to use leftover meat, fish or sausage cubed and spiced with capers and a mixture of vegetables flavoured with a salad dressing. Recipes from the land include trofie pasta with pesto, *farinata* – delicate genovese tripe flavoured with mushrooms and pine kernels, *pansotti* – stuffing made with oven-cooked vegetables and nut sauce and *zuppa di ceci* (chick pea soup).

Basil and garlic also predominate in Ligurian cooking, perhaps no more so than in *pesto alla genovese*. The pesto dressing which contains basil, pine kernels, garlic and matured cheese should be made with a pestle and mortar (from which it takes its name) but is now more likely to be prepared with a blender. Pesto is strongly linked to Liguria and in particular Genoa, where the recipe has been known for centuries.

Traditional sweet fare includes *torta di riso* (rice cake) made with rosewater and sugar.

Wine. Its limited arable land space means that Liguria has a small wine production most of which is concentrated along the Riviera Ligure di Ponente. The nature of the terrain produces some original wines. North of La Spezia in the Cinque Terre fishing villages, vines are grown on steep inaccessible terraces where they have been planted since antiquity.

DOC whites include Pigato Riviera di Ponente, Bianchetta Genovese, Vermentino and Cinque Terre. DOC reds include Valpolcevera Rosso, Rossese di Dolceacqua and Sciacchetrà. Pigato is strongly recommended. There are other locally produced wines, which are good with local food and have to be drunk young.

> *A chi no ghe piaxe o vin,*
> *O segnô o ghe leve l'aegua*
> Anyone who doesn't like wine,
> O Lord, don't let him have water. *(Ligurian proverb)*

Typical Properties for Sale

Second homes are big business in Liguria. Its popularity with tourists means that property prices are high and increasing by more than the Italian average (up 6.5% in 2002). However, if you want a South of France lifestyle you will find property in Liguria is still better value than that of the chic resorts of France . However, note that the prices depend in part on the resort. Some of the most expensive are around Levanto thanks to gigantic waves, which make it an all year resort for surfing. San Remo is also expensive. In the main centres, the ports of Genoa and La Spezia, there is a lot of choice of apartments in modern buildings. Districts of Savona are undergoing restoration and properties bought there may turn out to be a good investment.

Better value can be found in the hills where ruins, houses and apartments can be found in the villages. Try to pick a village that is getting popular like Moltedo or Dolcedo (near Imperia), otherwise you will have difficulty selling on if you need to.

Location	Type	Description	Price
San Lorenzo al Mare, near historic buildings and shops	Flat in a new development	2 bedrooms, kitchen, bathroom, terrace, sea view	€145.000,00
Moltedo village	House	3 bedrooms, roof terrace, sea view	€90.000,00
Genoa city	Villa 650 sq.m	2 storeys. Master apartment with frescoed ceilings. Spacious reception room. Apartment for caretaker with utility rooms. Garage. Garden with lawn and vehicle entrance.	€1.300 000
Coletta di Castelbianco Italy's first cyber village 6km to coast	Completely restored abandoned village	1 bedroom apartments.	€165.000,00 €250 p.a. for broadband internet. €1,600 service charge.
Rapallo resort	Condominium	Spacious apartment with hall, kitchen, lounge, 3 bedrooms, 3 bathrooms, balcony and terrace with view of Tigullio bay. Covered car space.	€135.000,00

Agents for this region. www.villecasali.com; www.brianfrench.com; www.gabettionline.it; www.italy-riviera-realestate.com; www.casatravella.com

VALLE D'AOSTA

Capital: Aosta (583 metres above sea level)
Area sq.km: 3,263; *Population:*   119,356
Foreign visitors: 203,969; *Italian visitors:* 568,054
Climate:

Mean	Summer temp.	Winter temp.
10C	20.5C	0.8C

Airports: nearest Milan and Turin.
National park: Gran Paradiso

Geography and Climate

The Valle d'Aosta is the smallest and most thinly populated region in the Italian Republic, bordering with Switzerland (north) and France (west) and Piedmont (east and south). It became an autonomous region with special statute in 1948.

It is entirely mountainous, extending across the Graian and Pennine Alps. The head of the Valley is closed by Mont Blanc, the highest peak in Europe (4,810m), and by glaciers feeding the sources of the River Dora Baltea. To the south is the Gran Paradiso massif (4,061m) and to the north is the Monte Rosa group (4,633m), which is the north-east boundary of the region. The river Dora Baltea runs along the main valley, with smaller side valleys such as: to the left Valpelline, Valtournenche, Val d'Ayas, Valle del Lys; to the right, Valgrisenche, Val di Rhêmes, Valsavarenche and Valle di Cogne. There are 220 glaciers, the biggest of which are the Miage (1,100 hectares), Lys (1,070 hectares) and Brenva (750 hectares). These are favoured by the great height of the mountains and the wet Atlantic winds bringing snow.

[emThere are many small alpine lakes. The climate is affected by the high altitude, averaging 8°C at Courmayeur below Mont Blanc, 10°C at Aosta in mid-valley, and 12°C at St. Vincent lower down. Abundant precipitations in autumn and winter provide good snow for the ski resorts.

The valley up to 1,100m has vines, fruit trees and woodland with sycamore, beech, birch, hazel, elm and alder. Up to 2,200m beechwoods give way to larch, fir and pine, with hardier alpine shrubs such as rhododendron, alpine alder and juniper towards the summit, and alpine flora such as gentians, buttercups, campanulas, mountain vanilla, anemones and edelweiss.

The fauna is typical of mountain areas including ibex and chamois; rarer species are ermine, ptarmigan, golden eagle and raven. About one sixth of the area is covered by the Gran Paradiso national park, the first Italian national park, donated by King Victor Emmanuel II in 1922, who gave his own hunting reserve to the nation. About a thousand protected rare species of plants are preserved in the Paradisia Botanical Garden at Cogne.

There is a great production of wine and of Fontina the typical regional cheese. There are iron (Aosta) and textile (Châtillon) industries, facilitated by hydro-electric power (Cogne). There are craft industries, in wood and marble, and a casino at St Vincent (one of four casinos in Italy), which has a considerable role in the regional finance.

Commerce and finance are concentrated on **Aosta** (583m), the regional capital, lying on the important Mont Blanc tunnel arterial through route, is in an attractive position on the crossroads for France and Switzerland, encircled by the Alps. It was founded by the Romans in 25BC on a previous Salasso tribal settlement and called Augusta Praetoria. It passed through the hands of Goths, Lombards, and Franks. In the eleventh century it came into the possession of the Savoy family (from St. Maurienne in Savoy) and shared its destiny. There are impressive Roman remains in the town.

There is a railway line up the valley from Turin to Mont Blanc.

The salient features of the Valle d'Aosta are:

- The Mont Blanc tunnel – opened in 1965. It was closed in 1999 after a truck caught fire in the tunnel and 39 people died. It reopened three years later to restricted traffic and environmentalist protests.
- Courmayeur and the Mont Blanc mountain. This fine resort is open summer and winter,
- The Matterhorn mountain – the southern approach at Cervino and Brevil, is within the region, still popular with skiers and climbers.
- The Gran Paradiso National Park
- The St. Vincent Casino, which also has a thermal spa, in the lower valley.
- 70 castles, of which Sarre, St. Pierre and Sarriod la Tour are worth a visit.
- Aosta (altitude 583m)

People

The population is concentrated in the valleys. The mountain areas have become depopulated since the nineteenth century, except for the major tourist centres in the lateral valleys. Tourism has replaced poor mountain agriculture.

The official languages are French and Italian although the local population normally speak a provençal patois. In the Lys valley a German mountain dialect, Walser, survives from the thirteenth century, when settlers descended here from Valais. Their traditions and language are proudly preserved in the upper valley and at Issime.

Food and Wine

Food. It is the food and wine, which are one of the greatest attractions of the Valle d'Aosta. A *valdostana* is a breadcrumbed veal chop fried then covered with slices of ham and fontina cheese and baked in the oven for seven minutes. This tangy local cheese is the basis of many of their dishes, such as the melted cheese fondue, and of most soups. Each village has its own soup – whether onion, leeks, cabbage, pumpkin combined with toasted black bread and melted cheese. Soup is the 'national' dish. Boiled meats are a speciality as are polenta, salt-beef, ratatouille style vegetables, mountain game such as braised ibex with polenta, trout in wine, nettle omelette, spinach with fontina, mint fritters and strawberry compote.

Wine. The wines, which are produced from picturesque mountainside vineyards, some, in the lee of Mont Blanc, reputed to be the highest in Europe, are exquisite. French and Piedmontese grape varieties are used, but the most intriguing wines are produced from the earliest known indigenous grapes such as Cornalin and Petit Rouge, with a wild rose bouquet. Torrette superior and Nus Rouge are DOC wines with these varieties and there are several others. There is an annual wine festival at Nus in May.

With the winter Olympics booked for 2006 for Turin, property in the Valle d'Aosta is a good investment in 2003. It is rentable summer and winter, in an extremely accessible area, within one or two hours drive of the major cities of Turin, Milan and Geneva.

Sobra le table, santé durable
Sober table, lasting health *(Valle d'Aosta proverb)*

Typical Properties for Sale
The property market here has gone up nearly 10% in the last couple of years. The centre of Aosta has been modernised. The architecture is Medieval and Roman and for renovation properties at 516 euros per square metre you could find a bargain. There are houses available in the hills near the city. There are many ski-resorts with lots of chalets built from stone with heavy stone slab roofs. There are properties for sale in the centre of the region along the Dora Baltea River, the houses here are timber-panelled cottages with slate roofs and the prices are moderate becoming more expensive the nearer you get to a ski-resort.

Saint Pierre: A beautiful unrestored property about 320 square metres plus outhouses of about 45 square metres and land to the east of about 400 square metres. **Price:** €150.000,00.

Roisan: recently restored small detached house (140 square metres). It has 3 stories with a big cellar and a small garden. It is situated in a tranquil area, a perfect holiday home. **Price:** €150.000,00.

Valsavarenche: semi-detached renovated house on two floors. Has 3 bedrooms, 2 bathrooms, large living-room. Private garden with barbecue. The house is furnished. **Price:** €120.000,00.

Antey Saint Andre: right next to the ski lift up to Chamois. 4 independent flats with their own heating in a totally renovated period house i.e. stone slab roof and stone walls. 47 square metres. **Price:** € 88.000,00.

Agent for this region: www.immobiliare-la-tout.com.

THE NORTH-EAST

TRENTINO ALTO ADIGE

Capital: Trento (187 metres above sea level)
Area sq.km: 13,607; *Population:* 937,107
Foreign visitors: 3,595,650; *Italian visitors:* 3,094,179
Climate:

Summer temp.	Winter temp.	Ann. Rainfall
28C	0C	724mm

Airports: Nearest: Venice-Treviso, Verona, Brescia, Forli
National park: Stelvio

Geography and Climate

This is the most northerly region of Italy, bordering Switzerland to the northwest, Austria to the north, Lombardy to the south-west and Veneto to the east and southeast. It has been an autonomous region with special statute since 1948, consisting of the two autonomous provinces of Bolzano and Trento, which take it in turns to be regional capital every two years. Trentino means the territory of the ancient city of Trent or Trento. Alto Adige means Upper Adige (a river), a name adopted after World War I to replace the German Süd Tirol (South Tyrol). The area is mostly mountainous with the lowest population density in Italy after the Valle d'Aosta.

The mountains are known as the Dolomitic Alps (or the Dolomites) named after the French soldier and geologist Déodat de Dolomieu who analysed the rocks here in Napoleon's day. The mountains of the north are the Ortles group (3,899m) near Bormio which join with Venoste, Breonie and Aurine Alps spreading eastwards. To the south is the Vale of Merano and the Rolle Pass and the Alto Adige plateau of gentle hills contrasting with the rugged mountains of the north and the spectacular peaks to the south such as the Marmolada (3,342m) and the Brenta (3,150m).

Climate. Widely varying microclimates are the result of this flow of mountains and valleys. A section of Lake Garda – at Riva del Garda – within the regional boundary and other protected hollows such as Bolzano and Merano have mild climates, while the higher mountains have cold, dry winters, and wet breezy summers. Rainfall varies from high in the south and southwest to much lower in the wide sheltered valleys.

604,000 hectares of woodland in the region account for 44% of the territory. Oak and chestnut gives way at higher altitudes to beech, spruce, larch and pine. Interesting plants include germander, glacier crowfoot and martagon lily. Lake Garda and the sunny hollows of Bolzano and Merano are the habitat of Mediterranean plants, laurel, rosemary and lavender etc. Deer and ibex are found in the Stelvio National Park shared with Lombardy.

One of the greatest characteristics of the Dolomites is the near-vertical walls hundreds of metres high, such as the Sella on the Marmolada, the Pale di San Martino, the Torri del Vaiolet and Campanile Basso di Brenta. Victorian writers, artists and climbers were the first to discover the beauties of these thrilling mountains, Josiah Gilbert and G.C. Churchill were reminded of Gustav Doré's illustrations of Hell in their book *The Dolomite Mountains* (Longman 1864).

Languages. The province of Trento is almost entirely Italian speaking with Venetian and Lombard dialects. Small pockets of the Rhaeto (Romanche or Ladin) language survive in Val Gardena, Val Badia and Val Pusteria. it is a protected language, taught in schools.

The standard of living is above the national average. The main cereal grown is rye. Flourishing dairy and livestock, and apple production, combined with vine growing, added to massive timber and hydroelectric industries, give a picture of health and prosperity even without the tourist industry which buzzes at all seasons.

The region is the obligatory corridor between the Mediterranean and central Europe. It has a superb rail and motorway system linking Verona with the Italian – Austrian Brenner pass. For sports, summer and winter, the Valgardena is the jewel of the Dolomites with the skiing villages of Selva Gardena, Sante Cristina and Ortisei offering excellent pistes in the winter, beautiful hiking paths in the summer and a lively aprés-ski scene. Several resorts are high enough for summer skiing. The numerous lakes and torrents are well equipped for water sports and white water rafting. Pony trekking, tennis, golf and mountain biking are all catered for. There are bright folk costumes and brass bands. The Gardena music festival in July and August is only one of many in the region. There are famous health farms – of Austro-Hungarian grandeur – in the resorts of Merano and Bressanone.

Architects and planners have made few mistakes in this region: the style of modern buildings is in a homogeneous continuum with the old traditions. The powerful Tyrolean Culture, based on the traditions of carpentry and wood carving, not to mention the Tyrolean spatterdash finish, copied throughout the world, is at home right here, demanding to be followed.

If you are buying a house in this region it is wise to be aware of Radon gas. Consult with your *geometra* and refer to the Bolzano province environment website (www.provincia.bz.it). Radon is a radioactive gas which causes lung cancer, liable to occur on some granite, porfido, gravel or tufa substrates, for which there is an 'at risk' map on the website.

Bolzano (altitude 250m population: 97,524) is a Tyrolean German speaking town. Bolzano airport has flights to Rome, Naples, Cagliari, Olbia, and Lamezia Terme). It has a new university founded in 1997.

Trento (altitude 194m, population 106,073) is a great Renaissance Italian town with imposing buildings and a famous university. Local heroes are: Ötzi, a Bronze Age mummified man discovered in a glacier at Similaun on the Austrian border, now in the museum at Bolzano; and Rheinhold Messner, born at Vilnöss in 1948, one of the greatest mountaineers of all time, who climbed Everest without oxygen in 1978 and Nanga Parbat.

History

Historically, because of this strategic position, the region has shuffled between Austria and Italy ever since the Lombard and Frankish Dukes were absorbed by the Bishopric of Trent as part of the Holy Roman Empire. In the sixteenth century the Council of Trent redefined the Roman Catholic Church in reaction to the Protestant reformation, with repercussions which are still felt today. In 1802 the region was secularised by the French Revolutionary army and then taken over by the Austro-Hungarian Empire. The imperial resorts of Riva del Garda and Merano retain the atmosphere of that time.

The Italian speaking people of Trento fought to be 'redeemed' by the newly-united kingdom of Italy in 1860, achieving this objective in 1919, by the treaty of St. Germain, thanks to Italy having been on the winning side in World War I. Mussolini's regime in the 1930s brutally Italianised the area by voluntary expatriations to Hitler's Germany of German speakers, name-changing and the imposition of the Italian gendarmerie. But in 1946 the Italians were on the winning side, again, against their previous allies and the De Gasperi – Gruber agreement was drawn up (in English) in Paris, safeguarding the rights of the German minority. A long series of terrorist bombings by the Südtirolerfolkspartei led to an intervention at the United Nations by the Austrian Chancellor Bruno Kreisky. A new package of measures was ratified in 1971, protecting bilingualism for both German and Ladino speakers, and establishing proportionality for public jobs, housing and other benefits. These arrangements are constantly under review.

You will not fail to notice that the people of Bolzano prefer to speak German;

they will communicate in Italian, but are increasingly only too happy to speak in English. Their food and wine are superb. Tyrolean cosiness and Italian flair combine to make this one of Italy's most delectable regions, most appreciated by Italians themselves, who flock here winter and summer.

People

The population of Bolzano is ethnically and linguistically subdivided into three groups: 66.4% German, 29.4% Italian, 4.2% Rhaeto Romanic. One third of the inhabitants live in small mountain communities. The Bolzano countryside is more flourishing than the Trentino, thanks to the different laws of inheritance and farm ownership (the *maso chiuso*), meaning that land cannot be split up but must pass in its entirety to the eldest son; hence large family-run farms and less population drift. There is a considerable flow of workers from the south of Italy and the Veneto region attracted by the jobs available in hotels and tourist resorts.

Food and Wine

Food. The cuisine is a triumph of smoked meats, sauerkraut and potatoes, unforgettable soups, game brilliantly accompanied by bilberries or plums, meat strudels and fresh mountain trout *au bleu*. The breads, based on the staple of rye, come in all shapes and sizes from an extremely serious bakery culture, and the pastries vie with those of Vienna.

Wine. Bolzano and Trentino vineyards have built on an ancient tradition, with a massive commercial production of Chardonnays, Merlots and Cabernets and, Pinot Noirs; on home ground it is worth looking for their native Terlaner or Meranese di Collina. There are breweries too, such as Fürst in Merano, as good as any in Germany.

> *Pam e vin e zoca,*
> *lassa pur ch'el fioca.*
> Bread, wine and logs;
> Let the snowflakes fall. *(Trentino proverb)*

Typical Properties for Sale

This region has a low population density and there is a definite Austrian flavour. The architecture is baroque with painted façades. Lots of large wood and stone chalets and fine estates and castles (*castelli*). Properties are in high demand and the mountains are popular. These are affordable properties in the south of the region – the wooden house (*maso*) built on a rock foundation which has shingled roofing and costing 1,500 euros per square metre The property market rose by 8.6% in 2002. Bolzano has attracted many immigrants and they tend to buy properties near the station.

Trento. Property unfinished. 150 square metres 3 bedroom house with garage and a large garden. **Price:** € 93.000,00.

Near Trento. A new 2 bedroom apartment of 95 square metres with 80 square metres of garden. **Price:** €180.000,00.

Bressanone. Two floor flat with kitchen, 2 bedrooms, large attic. Terrace. Garage and cellar. **Price:** € 140.000,00.

Bolzano. Two-storey terrace house with basement, 3 bedrooms, 2 bathrooms, living room, garage, cellar. Laundry, large kitchen, balcony and garden facing south and view over fields. **Price:** €335.000,00.

Agents for this region: www.studiocitta.it, www.ilsole24ore.com.

VENETO

Capital: Venice (0 metres above sea level)
Area sq.km: 18,391; *Population:* 4,490,586
Foreign visitors: 7,154,387; *Italian visitors:*   4,339,393
Climate:

Mean	Summer temp.	Winter temp.	Ann. Rainfall	Days of rain
16.3C	22.6C	4.9C	428mm	95

Airports: Venice: Brescia, Marco Polo, Treviso, Forlì.
Unesco world heritage sites: 1987 Venice and its lagoon, 1994 City of Vicenza, Palladian villas of the Veneto, 1997 Botanical garden (Orto Botanico) Padua, 2000 City of Verona.
National parks: Dolomiti Bellunesi.

Geography and Climate

The region of Veneto is in the north-east of Italy bordering on Austria to the north, Trentino Alto Adige to the west, Lombardy to the south and west, Emilia Romagna to the south, Friuli-Venezia Giulia and the Adriatic sea to the east. It is 56.4% plain, 29.2% mountainous and 14.4% hilly. There are seven provinces in the region:-

The province of **Belluno** in the north is mountainous (the Dolomites). The highest peak is the Marmolada (3,342m), which is near Italy's most fashionable winter resort, Cortina d'Ampezzo. Belluno (population 34,946) is a charming small city with ancient Venetian architecture, high-tech modern industry (eye wear) and tourism.

The province of **Padua**, west of Venice, is flat except for the Euganean hills

(603m) south of its capital Padua (population 203,350). Padua has a fine city centre, an ancient university, and a smart thermal spa resort at Abano Terme, and quite a lot of industry.

The province of **Rovigo** south of Venice is completely flat, its southern border being the river Po, its coastline delta country, and its northern boundary – the river Adige. This area is also called *Polesine.*

The province of **Treviso**, just north of Venice, is mostly hilly, rising to Monte Grappa (1,775m) in the west, and Monte Cesen (1,570m) in the north-west – beyond the vineyards of Valdobbiadene. Asolo is a resort hilltown with a glorious past, and the pretty hills of Conegliano Veneto are the home of Prosecco wine. Treviso itself (population 79,875) is an elegant country town, which has become a bustling industrial centre (the headquarters of Benetton, Sisley etc).

The province of **Venice** is on the coastal plain with a large unique lagoon area, the world famous city of canals (population 366,181) a heavily industrialised hinterland at Mestre, and several seaside resorts on the Adriatic: Jesolo, Eraclea, Caorle and Bibione. Bibione has extra-hot thermal springs (51C) and a fine marina.

The province of **Verona**, in the west of the region, is flat and fertile in the south, mountainous in the north (Monte Lessini, 2,259m) and bordered by the hilly shores of Lake Garda to the west, which is also great wine and oil country (Bardolino, Valpolicella). The city of Verona (population 243,474) on the edge of the plain is a thriving combination of industry, agriculture and tourism, which also offers the world's best open air operas and horseshows.

The province of **Vicenza,** east of Verona, contains the uplands of Asiago (1,001m) in the north, and the Lessini hills in the west. The city of Vicenza (population 106,069) is in a plain flanked by the Monti Berici hills (444m) to its south.

The transport system – rail, road, and air is excellent. Industries are favoured by the excellent communications infrastructure, which offers direct arterial links with Austria and Germany, Central Italy, the Balkans, Switzerland and France. Heavy traffic and industrial development is confined to the spacious Po plain, leaving the hilly and mountainous districts, with their historic towns, as desirable locations for recreational living.

History

Veneto takes its name from the Indo-European tribe, the Veneti, which intermarried with Ligurians in the Euganean hills in about 1000 BC. 'Ven' means 'shining' or 'noble' and is cognate with a tribe of the same name, which founded the Vendée in western France.

From the seventh century BC the town of Adria, which is now in the province of Rovigo south of Venice, was a thriving Greek seaport, which gave its name to the Adriatic sea. Although over-run by Gauls this region was never a threat to the expansion of the Roman Empire, into which it was absorbed, as the tenth province with the name of Venetia. Verona, Vicenza and Padua were Roman cities, which produced such people as Livy (59 BC-AD 17) and Vitruvius (70-25 BC), respectively the greatest historian and the greatest architect of ancient Rome.

The barbarian invasions (Attila the Hun in AD 452 and the Lombards in AD 569) caused an influx of refugees to the lagoon islands of north of Adria, led by their bishops. The first doge (Venetian for duke) was elected in AD 729, based in Malamocco on the Lido. Venice itself grew spontaneously, founded by no-one, starting in AD 810 at Rivo Alto (Rialto).

The Venetian empire began in 1000 with the capture of Dalmatia; Constantinople and much of the eastern Mediterranean was added in 1204. Venice became a Mediterranean superpower, eclipsing Genoa and Pisa, opening out, thanks to its strategic position, to the lucrative spice trade of the east. Marco Polo (1254-1324) was a Venetian who toured as far as China.

By 1484 Venice had annexed all its inland neighbours: Treviso, Padua, Vicenza, Friuli, Ravenna, Brescia, Bergamo, Polesine etc. Ruled by a powerful art-loving oligarchy, Venice was a leading player in the flowering of the Renaissance. The Manuzio brothers (c. 1500) set up their Aldine press there, producing glorious typography and scholarship, while Venetian painters of that age have immortal names like Carpaccio (1460-1525), Giorgione (1477-1510), Titian (1490-1576) and Tintoretto (1518-94). Venetian aristocrats commissioned Andrea Palladio (1508-80) to build their summer retreats on the banks of the Brenta which are still the acme of elegance.

In World War I the region was the scene of Italy's greatest military victory, and loss of life, on the Piave river (1918). Venice was spared destruction in World War II and now receives attention of millions upon millions of tourists. It has sunk 23 centimetres in the last 100 years. Millions of dollars of international and Italian money has been earmarked to 'save Venice', but the proposed tidal barrages are yet to be built.

People

Until the 1950's Veneto was a poor region suffering from emigration to the boom towns of Turin and Milan. This situation has been reversed for successive decades, and the region is now buzzing with successful small businesses: gold in Vicenza, glass in Murano, textiles in Schio and Valdagno, clothing and furniture at Treviso, ceramics and grappa at Bassano, footwear on the Brenta.

The health service in Veneto is excellent, but school leavers are less qualified here than the national average. *Val più la pratica che la grammatica* (the practical is better than the grammatical) is a favourite Veneto saying. Newspaper readership, TV viewing, and the crime rate are low. There are more church marriages and fewer divorces than in any other region. There is a strong smallholding tradition;

Another favourite saying is *chi no ga' orto ne' porco, porta el muso storto* (having no vegetable patch and no pig can put a man's nose out of joint). Part-time farming by industrial workers is a relevant factor in the economy.

Food and Wine

Food. From its sea to its mountains Veneto has a huge range of gastronomic delights to offer. The climate is perfect for rice such as *vialone nano* grown near Verona and an infinite variety of risotto is cooked: with mussels (*con peoci*), with squid and its ink (*nero*), with red radicchio (*con radicchio rosso*), with baby peas (*risi e bisi*) and with any other of the superb vegetables that these enthusiastic gardeners produce. (or fish, or game, or frogs, or mushrooms). Pasta is often homemade – *pasta e fasioi* is a mixture of pasta and broad beans. *Bigoli* noodles are a speciality of Vicenza.

But the people of Veneto are archetypal *polentoni* or polenta eaters. It has been their staple diet ever since maize was introduced in 1603. Polenta is either mashed as a vehicle for gravy, as in *Polenta e oséi* (polenta and fowls) or it is fried in strips for savoury toppings for starters.

Wine and Other Liquor. Veneto wines are excellent. Sparkling whites such as Prosecco (like champagne) and Verduzzo (for dessert) are consumed in great quantities, from Treviso province. Lake Garda produces Lugana, excellent with fish. Verona has Soave, Valpolicella and Bardolino which are mostly gulping wines rather than sipping wines.

This is a region with a drinking culture from the rugby players of Rovigo, who drink beer by the litre, to the grappa downing *Alpini* veterans of Bassano. These are men who are serious about their drinking. The quality of the local grappa is consequently excellent, and the Nardini distilleries at Bassano are probably the finest in Italy, having been established there for more than two hundred years.

> *Magna quel ca t'ga e tasi quel ca t'sa.*
> Eat up and shut up. *(Veneto proverb)*

Typical Properties for Sale

Veneto is a rich region with Venice at its heart with its wonderful architecture including palazzi built of pink Istrian stone. In Venice properties are very expensive e.g. 6,000 euros per square metre and sold with clauses to do with their preservation in a conservation area. However, Treviso, Verona and Vicenza have villas for sale many of them in the Palladio style at 2,000 euros per square metre. There are about five thousand Veneto villas (*ville Venete*) built between the fifteenth and the nineteenth centuries of which 1,400 are declared of historical and monumental interest. Villas were built in great numbers in the sixteenth century as a result of hisorical events e.g. wars against Turkey and Spanish competition in the cereals trade and the Venetian government was forced to promote inland agricultural production, so, basically the villas are grand Palladian farmhouses. There are popular resorts on the east side of Lake Garda e.g. Sirmione, where foreigners own apartments and villas and new buyers are trickling into the area. The winter resort of Cortina D'Ampezzo has a high population of foreigners.

Jesolo Lido. In the heart of a pinewood only 300m from the sea, an elegant furnished house with independent entrance and garden. Spacious lounge and kitchen on ground floor, 2 bedrooms and bathroom on the first floor. Swimming pool in the 5,000 square metres condominium park. **Price:** €470.000,00.

Venice Lido. An apartment in a small complex with swimming pool. The ground floor has a large storeroom and two rooms with a balcony and a garden of 70 square metres. The house is 200 square metres. From the first floor balcony/terrace there are panoramic views. **Price:** €450.000,00.

Rossano Veneto. A small town bordering on Treviso, 18 km from Bassano del Grappa and 30 km from Vicenza. The apartments are part of a new development with 2-3 bedrooms, bathrooms, finished to the highest standard. **Price:** € 130.000,00.

Verona. A small rustic cottage made of stone. The house is in a good position in need of some renovation, and has a mature garden. It is near the town of Peschiera and 2km from Lake Garda. **Price:** €285,000,00.

Agents for this region: www.collinepiacentine.it, www.ronchiato.it.

FRIULI-VENEZIA-GIULIA

Capital: Trieste (20 Metres above sea level)
Area sq.km: 7,855; *Population:* 1,183,000 (ave. density 151 per sq.km).
Foreign visitors per year: 757,557; *Italian visitors per year:* 962,277
Climate:

Mean	Summer temp.	Winter temp.	Ann. Rainfall	Days of rain
16C	24.1C	5.6C	873mm	137

Airport: Trieste: Ronchi dei Legionari International Airport
Unesco World Heritage Sites: 1998 Archaeological Area and the Patriarchal Basilica of Aquileia

Geography

Occupying the northeastern extremity of Italy, Friuli-Venezia-Giulia is bordered by Austria to the north, Slovenia to the east, the Veneto region to the west and the Adriatic Sea to the south. It is split into a mountainous northern part and the Venetian plain in south. The region is divided into four administrative provinces, two are Giulian (Trieste and Gorizia) and two are Friulian (Udine and Pordenone). In 1976 a large area of Friuli was struck by a severe earthquake. There were two shocks, which produced a trail of devastation amongst the 117 *comunes* of the Udine and Pordenone provinces.

Mountains. 43% of Friuli-Venezia-Giulia is mountainous and these mountains include the *Alpi Carniche* and *Alpi Giulie* (Carnic and Julian Alps). The southern part of region is characterised by hills and slopes, and is the wine and fruit-growing area. About 19% of Friuli-Venezia Giulia is hill zone. The hill region contains hundreds of castles and fortifications as befits a frontier land. As with remote mountainous regions in general, it is quite poor and under-populated.

The Flat South. 38% of Friuli-Venezia-Giulia occupies the Adriatic basin which consists of plains (*Pianura Veneta*) in which Venice is located (in the adjacent region of Veneto). The south is fairly well off and industrial; Udine, Trieste, Muggia and Montefalcone are important industrial cities combining ship construction, textiles and chemical production. Tourism is highly developed in the Adriatic seaside towns of Lignano and Grado, popular since the 1890s when the Austro-Hungarian nobility watered there. Grado is especially popular with families and over 50s and is attached to the mainland by a four-mile causeway. Both Lignano and Grado are situated on a lagoon.

Climate. Like the landscape the climate is divided into two parts; a severe Alpine climate to the north and a milder one in the Venetian plain. Trieste has its own extreme winter climate of bitterly cold and fierce north-eastern winds (the *bora*). Rainfall is abundant.

History
Before being incorporated into the unified Italy in 1866, this region was part of the Austro-Hungarian Empire, which made the disputed city of Trieste its access to the Mediterranean. After World War Two, Trieste and Gorizia became part of the new Italian region. Nowadays Trieste contains communities of various ethnic and religious backgrounds including Jewish and Greek Orthodox. Because of it's particular ethnic diversity Friuli-Venezia-Giulia is one of Italy's five special status autonomous regions.

People
The majority of the people of Friuli-Venezia-Giulia live in the plains and on the coast. The large provinces of Udine and Pordenone are historically populated

by the Fruiliani whose language (known locally as *furlan*), is spoken by about half a million people. Fruilian or *furlan* is related to Ladin and Romansch. The population of the Gorizia and Trieste provinces includes minorities of Slovenes (distributed mainly in the Natisone and Val Resia valleys). About three-quarters of a million people speak Slovenian. German-speakers live along the northern borders around Tarvisio, Sauris and Timau. The people of the region have the reputation of being serious, diligent, law-abiding, cultured, tranquil and warm without the excitable volubility of their more southern countrymen and women.

Food/Wine

Wine. Viticulture has been practised in Friuli-Venezia-Giulia for over two thousand years. The impact of wine-growing culturally and economically has been apparent since Roman times. In the sixteenth century the governor of Venice banned the removal of vines which he said provided the city of Udine and all of Friuli with 'its main strength and sustenance.' There are about 35 varieties of vines and of those about one third are native. The controlled Origin Denomination (DOC) wine areas are Annia, Aquileia, Carso, Collio, Colli Orientali del Friuli, Friuli Isonzo, Friuli Grave, Latisana and Ramandolo. The majority of wine production is white. Particularly renowned varieties include Tocai, Pinot Bianco, Pinot Grigio, Chardonnay and Sauvignon. Sweet wines include Picolit and Verduzzo. Reds are mainly Cabernet Franc and Merlot. Current wisdom claims that wine in general, especially when red, is medically beneficial. Certain wines from this region have a reputation for being especially good for you: reds from Terrano and Refosco and whites from Malvasia in the Carso region are said to derive their therapeutic qualities from the high mineral content of the soil.

Producers of top quality Friulian wines include Gravner, Jerman and Mario Schioppetto.

Food. Friuli's most famous product is probably *prosciutto di San Daniele,* exquisite air-cured raw ham from the town of San Daniele. The brand is origin controlled (DOP) and comes from livestock reared exclusively on approved farms from ten regions of northern Italy. Other meats worthy of note include sausages and smoked ham of Sauris.

The regional cheese is *montasio* whose methods of production go back to the Middle Ages when it was made by monks. Montasio, made from pasteurised cows' milk, is a full-fat, semi-hard cheese with small holes. It can be eaten fresh or aged. The aged variety can be used for grating. The production area includes the whole of Friuli-Venezia-Giulia. If you want to try something different, *formaggio asino* (asses milk cheese) from Spilimbergo is another regional speciality.

The recipes of Friuli include many soups whose ingredients include vegetables, cereals, red beans (*fasûj*). Also, an unusual type of pasta – envelopes called *cjalçons* that have savoury or sweet fillings including spinach, raisins, brandy, cinnamon, mint, chocolate and potato. Breads include those made from rye and pumpkin flour.

The Adriatic coast unsurprisingly favours seafood dishes. Grado has its own sea chowder (*boreto alla graisana*). Risottos are made with fish or sometimes even frogs.

Cuisine in Trieste is heavily influenced by eastern Europe. *Gulasch*, and minced pork and beef 'burgers' called *cevàpici* are popular as well as sauerkraut. Sweet pastries and strudels are Austrian and eastern and include rolls filled with nuts, raisins, candied fruit, pine nuts and cinnamon.

An excellent informative cookery book *La Terra Fortunata: The Splendid Food and Wine of Friuli Venezia Giulia* by Fred Plotkin (ISBN 076790611X) will tell you all you need to know about the food, history and culture of the region in addition to the many recipies and wine suggestions.

> *'Formaio a merenda xe oro,*
> *A pranso xe argento,*
> *A çena el xe piombo'*
> Cheese at breakfast is gold,
> At lunch, silver
> At dinner, lead.
> *(Friuli Proverb)*

Typical Properties for Sale

The varied cultural influences of Friuli-Venezia-Giula and the climate have shaped the types of architecture: slate-roofed, stone chalets in the mountains, neoclassical and art nouveau style in Trieste, Venetian in the towns. The city of Udine, came out top in an Italian poll on the best place to live. If you want something really different you can buy a fisherman's house built of reeds with a conical roof. These are good for letting. The property market in this region jumped by 8% in the first half of 2002. Property is reasonably priced and apartments in towns should be considered.

Location	Type	Description	Price
Trieste	Modern Apartment 2nd Floor, 105 sq.m.	4 rooms + bath & kitchen. 2 balconies. Parking. Quiet area. Small wood infront.	€145.000,00
Pordenone near centre	Villa 240 sq.m. Villa and land together cover 2000 sq.m.	8 rooms + bath & kitchen. Underfloor central heating. Cellar and double garage.	€300.000,00
Montagna, Faedis	12,000 sq.m. land	A wood plus a stone ruin. Plot has access and possible to restore ruin.	€12.000,00

Trieste	Roof-top apartment in a prestigious palazzo 260 sq.m	Sea view. Terraces. Cellar and Garage with the property	€125.000,00
Pineta	New terraced house 200sq.m.	four storeys, garage, cellar, 3 bathrooms, 4 terraces garden and sea views	€222.000,00

Agents for this region: www.casainrete.com,www.italiannetwork.com.

EMILIA ROMAGNA

Capital: Bologna (38 metres above sea level)
Area sq.km: 22,124; *Population:* 3,960,549
*Foreign visitors:*1,868,005; *Italian visitors:* 5,577,463
Climate:

Mean	Summer temp.	Winter temp.	Ann. Rainfall	Days of rain
17.7C	25C	5.8C	351mm	86

Airports: there are three: Bologna Marconi, Forlì and Rimini.
Unesco World Heritage Sites: 1995 Ferrara City of Renaissance – Po Delta, 1996 Early Christian Monuments of Ravenna, 1997 Cathedral Torre Civica, Piazza Grande, Modena.
National parks: Appennino Tosco – Emiliano, Monte Falterona Campigna & Foreste Casentinesi.

Geography and Climate

The sixth largest region bordering with Piedmont and Liguria to the west, Lombardy to the north and north-west, Veneto to the north east, the Adriatic Sea to the east, the Marches and the Republic of San Marino to the south east, and Tuscany to the south. It is 47.8% plain, 27.1% hilly and 25.1% mountainous.

Here the wide, fertile alluvial plain of the Po Valley and the Romagnola plain is bordered along the south west by the mountain range of the Tusco-Emilian Apennines of which the highest peaks are Monte Cimone (2,165m) and Monte Cusna (2,121m) south of Modena. The once extensive forests now only cover 17.2% of the area, mostly in the Casentino range bordering Tuscany. Remnants of beautiful umbrella pine forests are to be found at Ravenna and Cervia. Original swamps and wetlands in the Po Delta have been preserved in the Comacchio Valley – a nature reserve north of Ravenna. But the rest of this flat terrain has been extensively irrigated and cultivated for thousands of years. There are interesting chalk formations round Bologna, the 'Gessi Bolognesi' with grottoes and valleys and some rare plants.

Except for the river Po, which flows along the northern boundary of the region

– all the other rivers which come down from the Apennines or into the Adriatic are torrential in the winter and dry in summer. There is as much as 3,000mm annual rainfall in the mountains. The climate of Emilia Romagna is sub-continental with cold winters and hot summers, moderated by sea breezes along the Adriatic. Fog is frequent on the plains in the winter.

The mountains are thinly populated, with a few modest winter-sports resorts (*Cerreto Laghi, Sestola*) and spas such as Porretta Terme and Salsomaggiore in the hills near Parma. The beaches of Romagna on the other hand are geared for mass tourism – mostly Italian, but a lot of Russians and eastern European visitors, particularly at Rimini. Cervia is the best yachting marina. There are wide sandy beaches in all the resorts: Milano Marittima, Cervia, Cesenatico, Bellaria, Rimini, Riccione, Cattolica, and the Ferrara and Ravenna beaches, which are packed with regimented deckchairs, umbrellas, beach bars, and famed for their own Romagna style of accordion dance music. In the off season it is possible to find a strip of wild empty beach at Cesenatico, but July and August are to be avoided because of overcrowding.

The population is dense along the axis of the Via Emilia – the old Roman road which goes through Piacenza, Parma, Reggio, Modena, Bologna, Imola, Faenza, Forlì, Cesena and Rimini. There is an excellent communications network: the autostrada del Sole: Milan – Bologna – Florence – Rome, which branches off to Padua and Rimini at Bologna. The Bologna railway junction is the hub of the Italian railway system.

Typical industries that thrive here are: clothing and knitwear (Carpi), Ceramic tiles (Sassuolo, Imola), pottery and 'Faience' (Faenza), chemicals (Ravenna, Ferrara,) engineering, agricultural machinery, racing cars (Maranello). There are thermonuclear power stations at Caorso (Piacenza) and deposits of natural gas at Cortemaggiore (Piacenza) and Ferrara and Ravenna.

All this activity leads to pollution and traffic problems. At Faenza and other towns odd and even number-plate days have been introduced to control the volume of traffic. The Bologna-Rimini motorway is always jammed at rush hour. Ravenna suffers from both air and water pollution.

Bologna is known as the city of the three T's – Towers, Teats and Tortellini (*Torri, Tette, e Tortellini*).

History

The Villanovans were prehistoric settlers here; then the Etruscan colonists of the seventh century (at Felsina) were pushed back south by Celtic invaders, and this region became part of Cisalpine Gaul. It fell to the Roman Empire under Augustus in the first century BC, who granted his war veterans tracts of land on the fertile plain, which hence became known as Romagna. Ravenna became the headquarters of the Adriatic fleet. Classe = classis (fleet) was the harbour, long since silted up. Later it was capital of the Western empire of Theodoric and the Ostrogoths, and of the Byzantines, and ultimately fell into the hands of the papacy. Noble families and city states flourished here in the Middle Ages: the Farneses at Parma and Piacenza, the Bentivoglios in Bologna and the Malatestas in Rimini. Bologna was the foremost university in Europe. Art and architecture flourished. To this day the cities of the Po valley are known as the 'Cities of Art', astonishingly rich in high culture. The *Teatro Regio* in Parma, opened in 1829, is one of the most demanding and important opera houses in the world. Giuseppe Verdi (1813-1901) is commemorated in nearby Busseto.

At the unification of Italy in 1860 Emilia (north-west) was separate from Romagna (south-east). The present combination dates from the constitution of 1948.

The People

There is a strong influx of immigrant labour throughout the region, mostly integrated and tolerated, despite political agitation by the *Lega nord Padania*. A general air of prosperity is enhanced by the large number of self-made men driving around in very fast cars in a happy combination of solidarity and opulence.

Romagna's most famous son, Benito Mussolini (1883-1945) was born in Predappio near Forlì. He typifies the character of the Romagnolo, described by Stendhal in 1819 as 'full of fire, passion, generosity and sometimes imprudence'. Although Mussolini became the incarnation of Fascism, he started his career as a socialist agitator, a typical Romagnolo.

Food and Wine

Food. This area has a rich and varied cuisine. Each town has its own speciality. Handmade pasta, with ragù (meat sauce, which includes nutmeg and chicken livers) or with rich broth; tagliatelle, cappelletti, passatelli (made with Parmesan cheese, breadcrumbs and eggs), lasagne; pasta and beans in Piacenza, fish risotto or frog soup in Ravenna, fritto misto – mixed fried meats in Reggio. Fired sole and squid at Rimini. Butter, (rather than olive oil), milk, Parmesan cheese, and bacon are basic ingredients. There is a great nostalgia for peasant traditions and a culture of the *magnêda* – the proper sit-down meal or blow-out. The Romagna people claim the Piadina or griddle bread and the *zuppa inglese* (custard trifle) as their own inventions. The region lives by, off, and for food.

Wines. Wines are bland to accompany the rich food – such as the fizzy Lambrusco di Sorbara. Reds are: Sangiovese, Cagnina di Romagna. Whites are: Trebbiano, Malvasia and Albana.

> *Un got e'fa ben, du I n'fa mêl.*
> *U t'sagàta un buchêl.*
> One drop is good for you, two won't harm,
> but a jug will wreck you. *(Romagna proverb.)*

Typical Properties for Sale
Emilia-Romagna known as the Flatlands is a region which extends towards the republic of San Marino. Prices of properties in Bologna, the capital and Europe's oldest university town went up by 5% in 2002. The region has beautiful villas but very few come onto the market and there are hardly any for renovation. Ravenna with its Byzantine mosaics, Rimini, Marittima and Riccione on the Adriatic coast are popular summer resorts for young Italians and foreigners who often own apartments along the coast. Historic town centres have a mixture of new buildings and period houses. The people in this region enjoy a high standard of living.

Novellano: Traditional stone barn with planning permission already given to convert into living accommodation. Novellano has magnificent views of Monte Penna, which at over 1,200 metres dominates the surrounding countryside. The barn is south facing and the stone is local. **Price:** approx. € 50.000,00.

Casa Stantini: A large traditional stone farmhouse in the hamlet of Stantini. Exceptional surroundings. The house is located within the hamlet. In need of renovation. **Price:** approx. € 85.000,00.

Between Rimini and Riccione: In the pleasant *Romagnola* countryside, a characteristic 2 storey eighteenth century farmhouse of 700 square metres. Partially restored, with small parsonage and 8 hectares of level land. Convenient for main roads. **Price:** €1.600.000,00.

Bagnacavallo (Ravenna): Palazzo Rusconi, apartments in town centre, 2

---

bedrooms, living room, kitchen, bathroom, balcony. Shared garden. **Price:** €108.455.00.

Bagnacavello: 1 mile from Bagnacavallo, 1950s house with garden. House 250 square metres of land. In need of restoration. **Price:** €250.000,00.

Agents for this region: www.lacasaemilia.com, www.gabimm.it, www.secondacasa.com.

CENTRAL ITALY (NORTHERN)

TUSCANY

Capital: Florence (38 metres above sea level)
Area sq.km: 22,997; *Population:* 3,460,835
Foreign visitors: 5,334,163; *Italian visitors:* 4,708,948
Climate:

Mean	Summer temp.	Winter temp.	Ann. Rainfall	Days of rain
16.9C	25.2C	6.7°C	813mm	154

Airports: Florence: Amerigo Vespucci international; also Pisa Galileo Galilei Airport
Unesco world heritage sites: 1982 Historic Centre of Florence, 1987 Piazza del Duomo (Pisa), 1990 Historic Centre of San Gimignano, 1995 Historic Centre of Siena, 1996 Pienza Historic Centre.
National parks: Appennino Tosco – Emiliano, Arcipelago Toscano: Monte Falterona, Campigna and Foreste Casentinesi.

Geography and Climate

Tuscany, the fifth largest region, is bordered by Liguria to the northwest, Emilia Romagna to the north, the Marches and Umbria to the east and Lazio to the southeast. To the west is the Tyrrhenian sea and the Tuscan archipelago including the islands of Elba, Capraia and Giglio. The Tusco-Emilian Apennines stretch along the north-east region, peaking at Pratomagno (1,592m) between Florence and Arezzo. In their lee, southwest is the upper valley of the river Arno (Valdarno superiore) and the Chianti mountains. The Apuan Alps (1,945m) lie parallel to the coast between Aulla and Pisa, whilst to the south are the Colline Metallifere (metal-bearing hills) west of Siena, and the Monte Amiata massif (1,738m) north of Grosseto.

Tuscany has 866,211 hectares of woodland, vast tracts of aromatic Mediterranean scrub (macchia), beautiful umbrella pinewoods, chestnut, ilex, arbutus, juniper, oak, Turkey oak and higher up beech, fir and alpine pastures. Outstanding nature reserves are in the Casentino, famed for its timber, and in the lower Maremma, in the Parco dell'Uccellina, where herds of wild Maremma oxen and horses still roam.

The population of Tuscany is heavily concentrated along the Tyrrhenian coastline between Carrara and Livorno, and in the lower Valdarno plain, where densities of 500 persons per sq. km. are recorded. This part of Tuscany is a sprawling industrious megacity, whilst the surrounding mountains and the less populated hills in the south are more rural and backward.

The road and rail networks are well-developed and overcrowded. There is a railway line down the coast, through Pisa and Grosseto, and down the middle through Florence and Arezzo. The spinal arterial *autostrada del sole* motorway, which connects the north and the south of Italy, is severely congested especially in the section between Florence and Bologna (tight curves and narrow lanes through tunnels).

If the traffic on the autostrada has reached saturation, so has Tuscany's major industry, which is, of course, tourism. Tuscany's massive heritage of architecture and art and its glorious countryside continue to attract millions of visitors, and to some tastes tourism has become a blight on her still beautiful cities. More than two hundred coach-loads of sightseers are disgorged daily, into the streets of Siena for nine months of the year, and Siena opens its heart to them. Smaller towns like San Gimignano have no other life left except for tourism (and a prison). Other towns that have sold their souls to the package tour are: Cortona, Montepuliciano, Montalcino, Pienza, Greve and Radda and any pretty hilltop town is sure to follow – even the centre of Lucca has become a tourist ghetto.

Two parallel universes have evolved here: the real world and the tourist world, which are parallel industries. The real world is populated by truck drivers and commercial travellers, schoolchildren and housewives, but mostly workers. Thus in San Quirico d'Orcia in southern Tuscany you will find the Albergo Garibaldi, a hotel, filling station and truck stop on the main road where one or two hardworking local women and a cook will be serving all comers; meanwhile round the corner more than one dedicated establishment, with imported labour, themed for tourists, will be serving food which is twice as expensive and half as good. Beware of being sucked into the tourist ghettoes in Tuscany. The real universe is better.

The same argument can be applied to the buying of property. Ruined farmhouses in Tuscany if available, are disproportionately expensive now, both to buy and to do up. €700,000 for a ruin is normal in 2003. Before you throw up your hands and go to Croatia or Poland, think of the advantages of Tuscany. A modest bolt hole in a central location, a flat in a village preferably with a garden, is all you might need.

Rural properties are still reasonably priced in the more remote areas such as the

Lunigiana, the Casentino, the Colline Metellifere, where sometimes you will hit on a village of charm or a colony of congenial compatriots to make up for the interminable driving up and down the tortuous mountain roads.

Chiantishire

'Chiantishire' is a journalistic expression invented in the 1970s to describe the perceived English colony which is supposed to have taken over Chianti. Chianti is a district in Tuscany between Siena and Florence. The historic Chianti League is strictly confined to the *comunes* of Greve, Radda and Gaiole. The Chianti Classico D.O.C. wine area adds the Comune of Castelnuovo Berardenga to the specified area.

The notion that large numbers of English people have populated this area is a myth which Italian magazines such as *Panorama* have latched on to. The truth is that only a few dozen English families have settled permanently in the area, including three or four writers and a lord or a celebrity or two. Even if more English people wanted to settle it would be physically impossible for them to do so, for the simple reason that there are not enough houses of the right type available for them. The limited stock of abandoned farmhouses suitable for conversion in 'Chiantishire' has already been exhausted. New buildings are not allowed except in designated areas and residential estates. Most of these are social housing or condominium apartment blocks, which are aimed at the local Italian market. No expatriate *Inglese* would dream of living in such accommodation. Even in a case where these new buildings command a good view, such as the terrace block in Vagliagli near Siena which overlooks the village, no foreign buyers are tempted to move in. The area has, however, become extremely popular with summer visitors with holiday homes of whom Germans and Americans outnumber the British. Greve Radda and Gaiole are crowded to bursting point during the summer. Castelnuovo Berardenga, previously undiscovered, is about to acquire a five star hotel in the Villa Chigi and a *centro storico* revamp in the piazza hitherto a car park. It, too, will certainly attract visitors.

The word *Chiantishire*, therefore, conveys mockery, but it is a misleading description of that particular part of Tuscany.

History

How did Tuscany acquire its distinctive culture? The Etruscans (see *History, Living in Italy* Chapter) were their ancestors. The area around Lucca was Gaulish; there was a strong Lombard and Frankish input at the land owning level with names like Ugurgieri della Berardenga ('my ancestors came here with Charlemagne'). Then came the rise of the independent city states, in conflict with each other and the *popolo minuto* literally 'little people' fighting for a share of power with the grandees. Siena was independent until 1555, with a long reputation of good government and civilised living (see Ambrogio Lorenzetti's frescoes in the town hall of Siena *the Allegory of Good and Bad Government* (1338). Lucca was independent for much longer and until Napoleon's day a republic, and both Siena and Lucca have the word *Libertas* (freedom) as their motto. Travellers from Michel de Montaigne to John Evelyn commented on the civility of the people. Then came the flowering of the Renaissance in which Tuscany, dominated by the Florence of the Medicis, was the motor of Europe. During all this time the bulk of the population, the *contadini*, although essentially serfs (i.e. they belonged to the land but the land didn't belong to them) developed a powerful co-operative hardworking culture of multi-family, or extended family households, who worked the land following routines which survive to this day.

The *capocchia* was the headman of the farmwork, the *massaia* was housewife in charge of the household; oxen to work the fields were stabled in the *stalla* on the ground floor, their breath heating the living quarters upstairs, which consisted of a large kitchen with a great hooded fireplace (*focolare*) and a sink (*acquaio*) and bedrooms (*camere*) leading into each other. A pigsty (*porcilaia*) outside, a bread oven (*forno*) attached to the house and an *aia* or paved threshing floor and a haybarn (*fienile*) completed the picture, and a shed (*capanna*). The self-sufficient life of these *contadini* – they made their own soap, wove their own cloth, made their own wine, oil, bread and pasta, killed their own pigs, continued until the 1950s when the system of *mezzadria* or sharing the crop with the landlord was abolished, and *contadini* flocked to the cities and factories and lived in apartments. But their culture still lives on.

People

It is not for the sightseeing or the countryside or even the weather, which can be fickle and harsh, it is the people. Compared with other parts of Italy and Europe the people of Tuscany are extraordinarily good-natured and polite. They have a reputation in the rest of Italy of being droll and laid back. Their favourite phrases are *'con calma'* and *'non c'è furia'* ('easy does it', 'there's no hurry'). It is part of their culture not to be inquisitive, the height of bad manners to be *'invadente'* or intrusive. They are conscious of personal space and always ask *'permesso'* (May I?) before crossing a threshold. To the southern Italians the Tuscans are regarded as cold and reserved and the Florentines, especially, are very difficult to become familiar with, even to their neighbours from Poggibonsi.

But this reserve and detachment combined with the good nature and lack of inquisitiveness makes life perfect for the expatriate. Whether you are black, white, gay or straight you will be tolerated with a good-natured lack of curiosity, which you will not find in the culture of the south of Italy, or Greece, or Croatia, where, since Homeric times all strangers have been subjected to a personal interrogation as a matter of accepted courtesy, and treated with suspicion until they proved themselves acceptable. It is no coincidence that the Italian ideologue of good manners was a Tuscan, Monsignor Della Casa who wrote *il Galateo* in about 1550, and whose estate in the Mugello near Florence has become a farmhouse country resort. (www.monsignore.com.).

Food and Wine

The *food and wine* varies throughout the region. In the Maremma the quality of the vegetables is sensational, probably because of the volcanic soil. Sometimes porcupine (*istrice*) is on the menu or wild asparagus. *Maremmani* is the name for the jumbo ravioli of the area, which also specialises in wild salad gathered in the fields. Da Michele in Saturnia (hot springs) is the Mecca of Maremma cooking. Up the coast the seafood is dominated by the Livorno style; *cacciucco* is a fish soup flavoured with tomatoes, garlic, olive oil and parsley. At Pisa the speciality is *ce'e* (blind things) masses of tiny elvers eaten like vermicelli; north to Lucca and the Garfagnana is the realm of the thick soup of *farro* (spelt) and beans. The Mecca here is the truckstop called La Rotonda at Altopascio off the *autostrada* between Lucca and Florence. In Florence the *Fiorentina* reigns supreme – the massive T-bone steak from the white Chianina breed of bullock. In Siena and Arezzo the food is simple, depending on the excellent quality of the ingredients – the flavour of the chicken or guinea fowl; a *contadino* speciality is courgette flowers fried in batter (*fiori di zucca*).

Wine. As for wine, you may choose between Chianti, Brunello di Montalcino and Montepulciano. The Grand Duke Leopoldo favoured the high rocky Chianti of the Castello di Ama. The whites in this region are disappointing. But the olive oil? Chianti is the best.

> '*Chi paga prima, secca la vigna*'
> Pay before time, wither the vine.
> (i.e. don't pay before you have done the job) (*Tuscan proverb*)

Typical Properties for Sale

Over the last 30 years many foreigners have purchased properties especially in western and central Tuscany. Now, the derelict farmhouse in need of renovation there is extinct. Tuscany is expensive and strict regulations make it impossible to extend a small ruin. The architecture is 'rustic', stone built farmhouses with terracotta roofs. There are fortified hilltop towns with castles and towers e.g. Cortona and San Gimignano. There are many villas painted red or ochre, but their prices are exorbitant and only for the very rich. Properties are cheaper north of Lucca. The area of Garfagnana has been popular with the English over the last twenty years and there is more availablity in Lunigiano. Information on Tuscan property auctions – properties being sold by local authorities where they are located – can be found on www.italymag.co.uk.

Near Florence: Mugello: farmhouse partially restored on two levels 140 square metres. Ground floor consisting of storerooms. First floor has a living room, kitchen, 3 bedrooms, study, 2 bathrooms and loggia, total area of 180 square metres. The property is situated on 4 hectares and is 5 km from village of Vicchio. **Price:** €362.000,00.

Arezzo: A country house, not isolated but detached at the border of a small rural village, partially restored. Kitchen, lounge/dining room, studio, bathroom, laundry, 3 bedrooms and bathroom on first floor. Panoramic hill position. **Price:** €370.000,00

Sorano Toscana: Located in the 'Maremmana' country, recently renewed stone villa split into 3 different sized apartments each one with an independent access. Large private gardens. A good investment. **Price:** € 360.000,00.

Northern Tuscany: La Spezia: typical Italian villa with swimming pool split into 3 apartments situated in Aulla and 12km from the sea. Nearest airport is Pisa (about 45 minutes). The property is large, 480 square metres. There are 14 rooms, attractive well kept garden of 15,000 square metres, a barbecue, wood oven, central heating and cellar. **Price:** €413.166,00.

Agents for this region: www.spazioimmobiliare.com, www.caseemstici.it, www.dimore.com, casedimore@libero.it, annaredi@tin.it, www.re-network.com, www.TuscanPropertySales.com.

UMBRIA

Capital: PERUGIA (205 metres above sea level)
Area sq.km: 8,456; *Population:* 815,588
Foreign visitors: 615,673; *Italian visitors:* 1,334,451
Climate:

Mean	Summer temp.	Winter temp.	Ann. Rainfall
11.8C	30ºC	0C	796mm

Airports: Perugia
Unesco world heritage sites: 2000 Assisi. The Basilica of San Francesco and other Franciscan Sites
National park: Monti Sibillini

Geography and Climate

Umbria is in the middle of Italy, with no coastline, bordering with the Marches (Le Marche) to the north-east and east, Lazio to the south, and Tuscany to the west and north-west. It has the fourth lowest population of all the Italian regions. The density of the population is half the national average.

It consists of 29% mountains and 71% hills, split by the Valley of the Tiber and the Valle Umbra. To the west are the low and rounded pre-Apennine hills; to the east are the higher and steeper Apennine mountains. The highest peaks are east in the Sibillini mountains, Mount Maggio (1,416m) and Mount Subasio (1,290m).

The river Tiber flows southwards through Umbria joined by tributaries Nestare and Paglia, Chiascio and Nera, Topino and Velino. Lake Trasimeno on the Tuscan border is the fourth largest lake in Italy. Piediluco is another lake on the Lazio border.

The climate: prevalently Mediterranean: Mild winters and cool ventilated summers. In the mountains rainfall can exceed 1,400mm a year and the winters are harsh. A temperate microclimate surrounds Lake Trasimeno.

Umbria lives up to its description as 'the green heart of Italy' by virtue of its 260,000 hectares of woodland. 30.8% of the total surface. It has seven nature reserves:

○ **The Sibillini mountains**, shared with the Marches, whose slopes are dotted with watchtowers and castles, beautiful orchids, lilacs and fritillaries, and flowering meadows in the spring. In the Fiastrone valley is the *Grotta dei Frati*, an ancient hermitage. There are rare gentians and huge beech forests. *The Gola dell'Infernaccio* is a spectacular canyon.

○ **The park of Lake Trasimeno**. This includes the towns of Castiglione del Lago and Passignano, and three islands, one inhabited. Rich marsh vegetation, and wildlife, rare cormorants and raptors, survive here and the waters teem with carp, eel, tench, pike and perch.

○ **Tiber River Park** (Parco fluviale del Tevere). In the south, this goes down to the hydroelectric dams of Corbara and Alviano, past Todi towards Orvieto, through the 'Forello' ilex, hornbeam, heather and broom-clad gorge into the Vallone della Pasquarella valley, home to buzzards, sparrowhawks, kites, mallard, herons, and kingfishers, linking up with an old droving trail.

○ **Monte Cucco**, in the north east, is in the centre of the Umbra Valley, to which Assisi is the gateway; a mystical area associated with St Francis – Spello, Nocera Umbra and Gualdo Tadino are nearby towns.

- ○ **Colfiorito Park**. An upland plateau east of Perugia with wetland flora and fauna and the ruins of a Roman city, *Plestia*.
- ○ **The Nera river park** (Valnerina) to the east, with the reservoir of Piediluco, waterfalls, springs and gorges, and flourishing wildlife, including abundant trout and crayfish.

Another beautiful spot, mentioned by the poet Virgil: The waters of Clitumnus (Fonti del Clitunno) towards Spoleto.

By-passed by the arterial *autostrada del sole* and by the Florence – Chiusi – Rome main railway line, Umbria is an enclave of history preserved, a mystical home of saints and hermits, the birthplace of St. Benedict of Norcia, St. Francis of Assisi, of St. Clare and St. Rita. The gates of its medieval towns welcome pilgrims from everywhere. It is the most spiritual region of Italy.

History

In early times it was home to the palaeolithic pebble culture (to be seen in caves near Orvieto – *Le Tane del Diavolo*). In 1000 BC the area was invaded by a warlike Indo-European tribe called the Umbrians. Hemmed in by the Sabines in the southwest, the Picenes in the north-east and the Etruscans in the northwest the Umbrians were squeezed into the area around Amelia. The Romans defeated them at Sentinum in 295 BC and colonised their land, building a new road, the Via Flaminia, connecting the Po delta with the Adriatic coast; which gave future invaders an easy run into Rome. Roman baths and aqueducts are still to be seen at Amelia. The Umbrians adopted the Latin language and became loyal to Rome.

In the third and fourth centuries AD all the 21 cities of Umbria became early Christian bishoprics. The Roman empire lost control and barbarians poured in. Alaric, King of the Visigoths came down the Via Flaminia with his army and sacked Rome in 410. Theodoric, King of the Ostrogoths captured Spoleto in 488. The Ostrogoth general, Totila destroyed Assisi and Perugia. In turn the Ostrogoths were defeated at Gualdo Tadino by the Byzantine general Narses in 552. After a few years of peace the Lombard nation invaded the peninsula in 568. In the thirteenth century religious fervour gripped Umbria. Perugia became a university, Benedictine abbeys sprang up in Perugia, Montellabbate, Foligno and Subasio. The new mysticism produced St Francis of Assisi, who with St Clare created the Franciscan Order. Monasteries and convents of different orders proliferated, vying with each other for the beauty of their art and architecture. Assisi stands out for its church of Santa Maria degli Angeli, where St Francis died, with its frescoes by Giotto and Cimabue, sadly damaged by the earthquake of 1997.

In 1798-99 Napoleon's French revolutionary armies incorporated Umbria into their Roman Republic as the Department of Clitumnus and Trasimeno with Spoleto as capital. The Napoleonic empire fell in 1814 and Umbria reverted to the Papacy. In 1860 the Piedmontese general Fanti conquered Perugia for the new Kingdom of Italy. Unification brought a marked downturn to the lives of the people. High taxes and the *mezzadria* sharecropping system of agriculture benefited a few rich landlords at the expense of their hardworking tenants who struggled to survive. But there were no upheavals until the arrival of the Germans, followed by the heavy bombing by the allies, in the Second World War in 1943, which deeply scarred the artistic and cultural landscape.

It was only in the second half of the twentieth century that the southern part of the region saw any noteworthy industrial development – a firearms and steel-working plant at Terni and a chemical works at Narni. Light industries expanded around Perugia such as clothing, confectionery and metal work, whilst a cluster of ceramic craft industries made Deruta world famous.

People

Umbrians today still display the old fashioned virtues of family solidarity and hard work of their grandparents who were brought up in the tough school of the *mezzadria* system. The region is full of hotels, factories and enterprises, which are monuments to the entrepreneurial talents of Umbrian peasants who emigrated in the 1950s, mostly to Rome, and returned with money to invest. The ones who stayed, such as the potters of Deruta, maintained their crafts, which are still being handed on from father to son. They seem to have a distinctive, inherited artistic flair, and a co-operation, or a division of labour, between the sexes and a politeness, which contrasts with the regions further south.

Food and Wine

Food. *Cucina povera* (poor man's food) is the style in Umbria. 'Eat little, eat well, and eat often' is an Umbrian proverb: monastic simplicity and quality, with an emphasis on roast meats, particularly wood pigeon and game, for which the traditional sauce is made from red wine, olive oil, sage leaves, capers, garlic, rosemary, salt, pepper – and anchovy. *Porchetta* (roast piglet) here is recognised as the best in Italy, as is the *norcineria* (sausages and salami products) of particular refinement from Norcia, which also specialises in black truffles. Cannelloni for special occasions, *cappelletti* (stuffed pasta 'little hats') from Gubbio, lentils from Castelluccio, wild asparagus spaghetti, pasta with hare sauce (*pappardelle alla lepre*), bacon and marjoram flavoured spaghetti from Spoleto, truffle-flavoured pasta everywhere. As for fish, roast eel, and chunks of pike are an acquired taste, but the queen of Lake Trasimeno is stuffed carp 'porchetta' style (*Regina in porchetta*); wild fennel, garlic, rosemary, salt, pepper lemon and olive oil provide the flavour. Umbrian oil is superbly delicate made mostly from Moraiolo and Frantoio olives with a touch of Leccino, and invariably local.

Wine. The wine is just as local as the food and is best ordered by the pint (*quartino*); the local grape varieties to look for are Grechetto, Sagrantino and Corniolo. Orvieto white has achieved international fame.

Chi vuol vedere il medicu da la finestra
Beva del vino dopo la minestra.
To keep the doctor from your door:
No wine till after the soup, be sure. *(Umbrian proverb)*

Typical Properties for Sale

The stock of abandoned farm houses in Umbria has been steadily bought up over the past quarter century, mostly by English speaking buyers, aided by efficient compatriot restorers such as John Tunstill (e-mail properties@tunstill.it; www.p ropertiesumbria.com) and Umbertide in particular is well served by an English speaking infrastructure. The Trasimeno area is also popular – the lake is superb for sailing and water sports, there are Dutch and German colonies and an idyllic atmosphere, reflected in the price of the rare properties that come on the market. Città di Castello in the north of Umbria is worth investigating as is Orvieto to the south.

The property market increased by 8% in 2002. This is the greenest region of Italy. Perugia the capital is good for property investment because of the language school and university which means good renting possibilities. In the south of the region at Terni you can find hundred-year-old properties for sale for 516 euros per square metre. The property market is good and many foreigners are buying property here as an alternative to Tuscany. Near Lake Trasimeno and in Umbertide detached properties are scarce and buyers are now looking at apartments in condominiums, which have been constructed from deserted hamlets and large abbeys.

Lake Trasimeno. 10 km south of Lake Trasimeno in a panoramic hillside setting. Part of a restored house comprising 120 square metres, accommodation with several outbuildings and land of 2.5 hectares. **Price:** €160.000,00.

Monte Lagello. The medieval castle of Monte Lagello is situated between Perugia and Todi with a beautiful view over fields, olive trees and woodlands. 5 apartments available within the village, every apartment has its own entrance and most of them have a private garden or terrace. The properties also include a shared car parking area and a swimming pool, a caretaker and 24 hour security. **Price:** €200.000,00.

Perugia. An apartment in the heart of old Perugia beautifully restored. Arches, vaulted ceilings and old terracotta floors, sitting room with sofa bed, kitchen and bathroom. Windows with view of cathedral. **Price:** € 103.500,00.

Prato. A 3-storey farm cottage on a hillside in a small village. The farm cottage is in need of full restoration. There is also another cottage which has been restored and a barn which has a new roof. There is a garden with some mature trees. The property is 6km from Monterchi, home of the Madonna del Parto. **Price:** €100.000,00.

Agents for this region: www.propertiesumbria.com, www.greenumbria.com, www.gabimm.it,www.casait.it, www.UmbriaPropertySales.com.

LE MARCHE

Capital: Ancona (5 metres above sea level)
Area sq.km: 9,694; *Population:* 1,463,868
Foreign visitors: 363,586; *Italian visitors:* 1,620,453
Climate:

Summer	Winter	Ann.
temp.	temp.	Rainfall
27C	1C	1,157mm

Airports: Ancona, Falconara
Unesco world heritage sites: 1998 Historic Centre of Urbino
National park: Monti Sibillini: Gran Sasso-Monti della Laga

Geography and Climate

The region of the Marches in central Italy borders on Emilia-Romagna and the Republic of San Marino to the North, Tuscany, Umbria and Lazio to the west, Abruzzo to the south and the Adriatic sea to the east. It is 68.8% hilly and 31.2% mountainous. Mount Vettore (2,476m), part of the Sibillini range on the Umbrian border, is the highest mountain.

The 116 km of the Adriatic coast is for long stretches a ribbon of narrow sandy beach (at Fano and Sinigallia), punctuated by the occasional rocky outcrop such as Monte San Bartolo (Pesaro) which has steep cliffs and pebble beaches. Monte Conero (Ancona), and Grottammare (Ascoli Piceno).

Upvalley locations seem remote and landlocked. Socialising expatriates get used to long drives on winding roads. But the coast has excellent communications: The arterial Bologna – Taranto autostrada relieves the flow on the shore road along the Adriatic. A projected *superstrada* linking the Adriatic with the Tyrrhenian sea has reached the level of Urbino. Ancona has direct intercity rail links with Bologna and Rome as well as an international airport.

One sixth of the population is engaged in agriculture. The people of the Marches, *Marchigiani*, are attached to their smallholdings and often conduct small craft businesses such as pottery, carpentry, wrought iron and basketwork. Important crops are wheat, sugar beet, cauliflower and table olives. There are thousands of hectares of vineyards. Fisheries are well developed, especially mussel farming. The entrepreneurial and economical skills of the Marchigiani have led to the creation of many small successful businesses in footwear, textiles, paper (Fabriano – a long tradition), musical instruments (Castelfidardo), mechanical engineering (Pesaro – Benelli motorbikes), and boat building (Ancona). There are petrochemical works at Falconara (Ancona). Levels of pollution are low.

Climate. The climate varies considerably in this region. Along the coast it is drier and more temperate than in the hills, where it is wetter and windy. Rainfall can be as much as 2000mm a year. Winds, predominantly from the east and north-east can be tiresome.

The Adriatic coast attracts tourists and yachtsmen with its charming seaports. Fano (population 56,000) dates back to the Roman temple (Fanum) to the goddess Fortuna on the Flaminian Way, which reached the coast here; it is a quiet, old-fashioned town. The hilltown of Grottammare, colonised by Picenians in the ninth century BC, by Italian aristocrats in the seventeenth century AD and developed as a resort in the 1930s is proud of the palm and orange trees which grow on its mild seashore plain. San Benedetto del Tronto (Ascoli Piceno) is dedicated to boat building as well as tourism, and Sirolo (Ancona) is one of the most enchanting resorts in Italy with its beaches and crags in the lee of Mount Conero, where conditions are excellent for windsurfing.

The Sibillini mountains on the Umbrian border (Ascoli Piceno) offer a combination of modern skiing facilities and ancient mediaeval towns; Sarnano, Ussita, Frontignano del Tronto, Forca Canapina and Castelsantangelo sul Nera. Cross country skiing has become a favoured pastime here.

The upland pastures and other inland rural areas – only eight hours drive from Munich – are full of idyllic second homes belonging to Germans. The British are also in evidence – a veritable colony now – pioneered by refugees from Tuscany in the 1970s. But the secret came out and property prices went up alarmingly in the 2000s.

History

Each city has an individual history, Ancona for example was a Greek foundation whilst Ascoli Piceno was founded by the Picenians. Rome conquered the area in the third century. The emperor Trajan made Ancona one of the biggest naval harbours in the Mediterranean, and a thousand years later it was used for shipping crusader armies to the Holy Land. The Sienese pope Pius II died here on his abortive crusade of 1464.

The Goths, Lombards and Byzantines overran the area in the dark ages. The Franks donated it to the Papacy, but for centuries church control was nominal. The great Hohenstaufen emperor Frederick II was born in a tent in Jesi in 1194. In the Middle Ages the region suffered from the internecine conflict between Guelphs (for the Pope) and Ghibellines (for the emperor).

The city of Urbino was dominated by the Montefeltro family between 1155 and 1508. Their court was in the mainstream of the culture of Renaissance Italy, producing great artists, such as Raphael (1483-1520), and the ideologue of courtly behaviour Baldassar Castiglione (1478-1529) whose treatise *Il Cortigiano* (the Courtier) became a self-help manual throughout renaissance Europe. Castiglione glorified the Court of Federico the duke of Montefeltro (1422-1482) and he had this to say of Urbino:

> *Although located in a mountainous region less pleasant than some we may have seen, it is favoured by heaven in that the country is exceedingly fertile and rich in the fruits of the earth. And besides the pure and health giving air of the region all things necessary for human life are to be found here in great abundance.*

People
The people of the Marches became employed by the Papal states as tax collectors, and to this day they retain a reputation for parsimoniousness. They are quietly spoken, serious and hardworking, cherished as neighbours by the many expatriates who have second homes in the region. A southern Italian writer, Angelo Agozzino, describes them as:

> *Full of polite hospitality, with a deep sense of solidarity – which spreads to all aspects of life: their respect for nature, their attachment to old traditions and culture, their constant readiness to listen and evaluate what people have to say, without preconceptions – these are civilised qualities which will greet anyone who has the good fortune to visit this region and get to know its people.*

Food and Wine
Food. In the Marches there is a strong tradition of self-sufficiency with regard to wine, oil and vegetables. People still keep and slaughter their own pigs for home cured hams and salami. Sheep's cheese is made and often flavoured with thyme, or matured in caves. Truffles black, white and grey are sold in the market of Aqualunga (Pesaro). Ascoli Piceno is the home of the *Ascolana* the large olive, which is stuffed and fried in batter (like a Scotch egg). *Vincisgrassi* is their bestknown pasta dish; like lasagne without the tomatoes. Stuffings (*ripieni*) are a speciality of the region, especially for pigeon and rabbit, incorporating truffles, salami, raw ham and Marsala wine as some of their ingredients. Stuffed and baked artichokes, called *Scarcilfuli a l'abréa*, combine oil, wine, garlic, parsley and breadcrumbs. Squid and sole are similarly stuffed, whilst the Pesaro way of cooking red mullet is to use raw ham and sage leaves. Mussels are baked in the half shell with breadcrumbs, olive oil and parsley. The fish soup (*brodetto*) and the fried fish (*frittura di pesce*) are celebrated. Given the superb pasturage of the region, the quality of the meat is so good that the meat consumption here is the highest in Italy: Mixed grilled meats *alla brace*

(cooked on embers) are unrivalled.

Among the sweets there is the sweet ravioli of Ascoli Piceno and Ancona called *caciuni*, and a rice pudding with candied fruits and chocolate chips called *Bostrengo* for Christmas.

Wine. As for wine the Marches produce the exquisite dry white wines of the Castelli di Jesi and Matelica vineyards using their indigenous Verdicchio grape. Whilst their reds are mostly based on the Montepulciano and Sangiovese grape.

> *Quannu lu corpo sta vè*
> *L'anema no scappa.*
> When the body is well
> the soul won't escape.*(Marchigiano proverb)*

Typical Properties for Sale

You can find property bargains here, from hilltop castles to small apartments. Local architecture is white stone farmhouses and cottages. The villages are attractive and interesting. Here you can buy an inexpensive apartment on the coast. Property in rural areas is very cheap but access roads can be a problem. Monse is popular with foreign buyers as it is on the coast and the communications are good. The Marche is a popular region with buyers who are enchanted by the friendly people and the beautiful landscape.

Monte Vicone: traditional brick-built farmhouse in isolated position near the town of Monte Vicone, not far from Fermo. 2 floors with stables downstairs, six rooms upstairs. There is a well. Approximately 1,000 square metres of land. **Price:** € 90.000,00.

Montelpare: In the Fermo region a neat stone house on a hillside in need of renovation due to fire damage. House west facing – breathtaking views. Approximately 2,500 square metres of land. House measures 100 square metres per floor and is on two floors. **Price:** € 75.000,00.

Ancona: Senigallia: old country house rebuilt 1996 set in a panoramic position surrounded by park of 10,000 sq. m. The house enjoys views of the sea and the rolling landscape. House is on 3 floors and measures 550 square metres. The house has a large living room and dining room with seventeenth century fireplaces. The first floor has 3 double bedrooms, two of which are en suite. The second floor an attic, studio with two storage rooms. The house has new windows with antique style grills. There are two covered verandas at 35 square metres each. **Price:** €800.000,00.

CENTRAL ITALY (SOUTHERN)

LAZIO

Capital: Rome (35 metres above sea level)
Area sq.km: 17,207; *Population:* 4,976,184
Foreign visitors: 5,449,270; *Italian visitors:* 4,268,931
Climate:

Mean	Summer temp.	Winter temp.	Ann. Rainfall	Days of rain
18.1C	25.4C	11.8C	482mm	142

Airports: Rome: Ciampino, Rome: Fiumicino
Unesco world heritage sites: 1999 Villa Adriana (Tivoli), 2001 Villa d'Este (Tivoli)
National parks: Abruzzo, Lazio and Molise, Circeo

Geography and Climate

The region of Lazio is on the Tyrrhenian side of central Italy, bordering on Tuscany, Umbria and Le Marche to the north, Abruzzo and Molise to the east, and Campania to the south. it is 53.9% hilly, 29.1% mountainous, 20% plain and dominated by Italy's capital city and conurbation of Rome. It has five provinces: Rome, Viterbo, Rieti, Frosinone and Latina.

The coastal strip, north to south, is called the **Maremma** (a continuation of the Tuscan Maremma) as far as Tarquinia. After the interruption of the Tolfa hills (616m) and the Linaro promontory, near the seaport of Civitavecchia, the flatlands are called the Agro Romano – or the Roman Campagna – which is the site of Rome's international airport, Fiumicino, and of ancient Rome's silted up seaport, Ostia, at the mouth of the river Tiber. Southeast of this, near Latina, are the Pontine marshes, once swampy and malarial, but reclaimed over the centuries and finally drained in the 1930s. Continuing down the coast Monte Circeo (541m) and the hills of the Circeo national park form the headland which stands between the ancient coastal towns of Anzio and Terracina. The naval harbour and bay of Gaeta complete the extreme south of the region. The islands of Ponza, which belong to Lazio lie off this coast.

Except for the rocky capes of Linaro, Circeo and Gaeta the 310 kilometres of Lazio coastline are mostly sandy:- long stretches are hideously disfigured by rampant twentieth century building. Only a few sections remain unspoilt:- the nature reserve and bird sanctuary of Macchiatonda on the coast between Ladispoli and Santa Marinella south of the Tolfa hills and the nature reserve of Tor Caldara near Anzio, the Circeo national park, and the coastal lakes of Fogliano, Sabaudia and Fondi.

The best resorts for yachtsmen are Tarquinia, the island Ponza, San Felice Circeo, Sperlonga, and the island of Ventotene. The best beaches are near Pescia Romana, Montalto di Castro, Ladispoli, Ostia, Tor Caldara, Nero's grotto near Anzio, Nettuno, Sperlonga and Gaeta.

Inland Lazio is hilly, the province of **Viterbo,** (known as Tuscia in recognition of its Etruscan origins) contains two volcanic mountain ranges, the Volsinian and Ciminian (1,053m), with huge craters, which hold Lake Bolsena and Lake Vico. In the north of the province of Rome, Lake Bracciano is a similar crater in the Sabatini hills. South of Rome are the Alban hills (956m) and Lake Albano, an area rich in history and legend, full of castles and vineyards (Castel Gandolfo, Frascati).

North east of Rome is the province of **Rieti** and the Sabine hills. The city of Rieti (elevation 406m) is in the upland valley of the river Velino. West of Rieti in the Apennines is the Mountain of Terminello (2,213m), the ski resort of the Romans.

The province of **Frosinone** east of Rome called Ciociaria, a rugged and hilly terrain with the Mainarde Alps (Monte Cairo 1,669m), in which the famous Abbey of Monte Cassino, rebuilt after its destruction in the war, stands sentinel.

The province of **Latina** south east of Rome is partly reclaimed marshland (the Pontine marshes) and partly mountains. The Ausonian range (1,090m) is north of Terracina and the Aurunci mountains are north of Gaeta sheltering these seaside towns from the *tramontana* wind.

The Bay of Gaeta has been a favourite resort since Roman times because of its exceptional climate. On its shores are Gaeta, Formia, Scauro and Minturno. Gaeta is the headquarters of the US Sixth fleet. English-speaking infrastructures, schools, shops, clubs have consequently developed in this delightful region. Formia is an ancient seaport, originally Greek, with ferry services to the islands of Ponza and Santo Stefano.

The climate. The weather in Lazio is, as we have seen, almost ideal in favoured coastal regions. In the hills and mountains there are greater extremes and more rainfall, particularly in the cold zones facing north.

Rome: 73% of the working population is employed in the services sector, Rome being the headquarters of public administration, banking, tourism, journalism and the media. There are large numbers of *statali* (state employees), often pensioned off young and with second jobs on the side: *Roma Ladrona* 'thieving Rome', in the opinion of the people of northern Italy. The Romans themselves are proud to joke that '*A Milano si lavora, a Roma si frega*' (in Milan one works, in Rome one steals).

Rome is above all the centre of the Italian communications network. It is the home not only of the government of Italy but also of the Vatican, a massive multinational, a state within a state. It therefore contains two sets of embassies from most nations in the world. It is a magnet for pilgrims and tourists, and crowded at all times of the year.

The centre of Rome is barred to traffic in certain areas, outside which, within the circle of the ring road (*il raccordo anulare*) is a nightmare of traffic jams, which are even worse than those of Paris. As a result, many Italians find Rome far too confusing for comfort (*troppo confusionaria*) and not 'liveable' (*poco vivibile*).

History

For the history of Lazio, see the history of Italy. Rome expanded inexorably, absorbing its neighbouring tribes, from the day of its foundation (on April 21, 753 BC). The city was rebuilt in marble by the emperor Augustus in the first century BC. It was sacked by Alaric in AD 410 and fell into insignificance in the Dark Ages. The Roman forum became known as a cow field (*campo vaccino*) and the marble statuary was crushed wholesale for the production of lime in lime kilns. But Rome rose to glory again, with the Church, as *caput mundi*, the head of the world, and all roads still lead to Rome.

The territory of Lazio is densely covered with ecclesiastical institutions, particularly Benedictine abbeys, which survived Saracen raids of the sixteenth century, the Napoleonic suppression of the late eighteenth century and the ravages of the Second World War.

When Rome became the capital of Italy in 1871 it underwent a huge building development; the English writer A.E.W. Symonds complained about the ugly yellow modern buildings. The same buildings now, after their Millennium facelift, present a mellow, antique ochre appearance, festooned with greenery.

People

And yet the glamour and appeal of the place has attracted thousands of foreigners who are delighted to live in Rome permanently, from aesthetes and intellectuals who favour the posher areas of Parioli and Piazza Navona to the *extracomunitari* or foreign workers who gravitate to the main railway station, the *Stazione Termini*, and the seedier suburbs.

Diplomats, ecclesiastics, journalists, academics, film makers – all produce a lively social and cultural scene in Rome, which is leisurely and cosmopolitan. They are joined by scores of Italian landowners and aristocrats, who feel more at home in the metropolis than on their rural estates. Immigrants, mostly from the Philippines, provide the service, and the local colour is provided by the indigenous Roman population, the *Romanacci*, who are loud, vulgar and humorous, personified by the late lamented comic actor Alberto Sordi (1920-2003).

The country areas outside Rome enjoy a higher standard of living than the national average. The Alban hills south of Rome are particularly opulent, (Frascati). The hilly Ciociaria district in Frosinone province east of Rome seems to be very much the spiritual heartland of the great city, having produced, since antiquity, Rome's most eloquent orator, Cicero, her best satirist, Juvenal, at least two saints, including St Thomas Aquinas, and six popes. In the twentieth century the film director Vittorio de Sica and the actors Nino Manfredi and Marcello Mastroianni (of *La Dolce Vita*) were Ciociaria-born giants of charm and humour in the world of films. The Ciociaria district proudly preserves its culture and folklore, reflected in the name of its website, literally 'ancient mind', (www.menteantica.it). Live folk music and culinary traditions, are upheld in well-kept small towns such as Atina and nature reserves such as Lake Posta Fibrena, near Sora, which features an annual sub-aqua display, wine festival and accordion championships.

The people in the province of Viterbo in northern Lazio, on the other hand, are quite different from the metropolitan Romans. Their district is called Tuscia, and the physical resemblance between the modern inhabitants and the ancient Etruscans featured in the tomb frescoes at Tarquinia is uncanny.

Outside the ancient Papal city of Viterbo, Tuscia is characterised by wide open country and sleepy ochre-coloured towns such as Tuscania, Vetralla and Canino, where people still sit and chat on their doorsteps in the balmy evenings.

Lake Bolsena is surrounded by lush and fertile country and eight charming villages. The town of Bolsena has a lively and friendly square with a resort atmosphere. On the northern approach to the lake, San Lorenzo Nuovo is an unusual eighteenth century architectural gem: a hexagon on a crossroads on the via Cassia.

Food and Wine

Food. Roman eating houses, *osterie* and *trattorie*, have always been well patronised by all classes. They are human theatre, at their most characteristic in the working man's Trastevere area, and in the cool hills of the Castelli. 'The more you spend the less well you eat' is the rule ('*più se spenne e pejo se magna*').

Classic dishes are *supplì* (fried rice balls), *stracciatella* a delicate broth with beaten eggs and semolina, simple spaghettis such as *alla carbonara* (egg, bacon, and grated pecorino), and *con aglio, olio e peperoncino* (with garlic, olive oil and chillis). For the meat course, lamb reigns supreme: *garafalata di agnello* (lamb spiced with cloves), *abbacchio alla Romana* – baby lamb baked with garlic, white wine, chopped rosemary and ham, and potatoes. For vegetables: Jewish-style artichokes (*carciofi alla giudia*), are round tender Romanesco artichokes immersed in boiling oil so that the outer leaves become crisp and open up into the shape of a flower. The Jewish ghetto in Rome, where there were once thirteen synagogues, also inspired the deep-fired *fritto misto*, and certain pastries. As for salads, the Romans invented the *pinzimonio* raw vegetable dip, and the *misticanza* mixed wild salad such as rocket. Lettuce is still as popular as it was with the legionaries of ancient Rome.

For fresh fish the Lazio coast offers the rich catches of Gaeta, especially lobsters and crayfish grilled on charcoal, or bream (*orata*) baked with the celebrated Gaeta olives, oil and white wine, followed perhaps by chestnut ice-cream.

In Tuscia (*Viterbo*) a distinctive peasant cuisine has become conscious of its Etruscan origins: thick vegetable soups with grains and beans, wood-grilled meats dressed with olive oil, lentils from Onano, strawberries from Nemi; and eels from Lake Bolsena perhaps washed down with a *fiasco* of Montefiascone. Chopped herbs including thyme, savory, parsley are much used, and a sharp-tasting truffle called *scorzone*.

The province of Rieti is also truffle country. The Sabine hills offer aromatic goat's cheese (*marzolina*) and *ricotta* (whey), and boiled meats (*fregnacce*). The province of Frosinone (Ciociaria) is not dissimilar, with the addition of unusual dried meats (*coppiette ciociare*) and smoked pecorino cheese.

Local chefs have built on these traditions with exquisite inventions such as 'basil, ricotta and mushroom soup', 'quail paté with juniper', and partridge with honey and cinnamon'.

Wine. The wines of Lazio are predominantly white: Frascati of the Castelli Romani, in the Alban hills, Montefiascone, celebrated by Est! Est! Est! The uncommercial local wines are light and drinkable (Cerveteri, Nettuno etc.) and the best native red is from the Ciociaria hills: Cesanese del Piglio, which comes in dry, sweet and fizzy versions. Good Cabernets and Merlots are produced for modern palates, but the people of Lazio have always favoured sweeter *abboccato* wines for social drinking.

> *Chi se vò imparà a magnà*
> *da li preti bisogna che va.*
> If you want to learn how to eat well
> you must go to the priests' house.*(Roman proverb)*

Typical Properties for Sale

The capital Rome has the largest number of foreign residents after Milan. There are plenty of schools, associations etc. for foreigners. It is difficult to find a reasonably priced house. The region has fortified hilltop towns and seaside resorts. Towns like Viterbo have medieval houses and the prices are low. In the centre you can buy an apartment for 620 euros per square metre for renovation. The architecture in Lazio is varied, tall narrow houses built of grey stone and tufa rock in the towns. Many villas on the outskirts are large and some have been split into apartments for sale. Frosinone is a good place for property investment as the town has a new university campus and the '*centro storico* is being modernised.

Monalto di Castro is a good seaside town near the Etruscan tombs. At Latina there are houses for sale on the sea front. They are old buildings and have exposed wooden beams and terraces.

Bolsena: Modern garden apartment within 150 metres of lake Bolsena and close to all the town's amenities. Accommodation: living room, double bedroom, bathroom, large store cupboard, small paved garden with awning. **Price:** € 65.000,00.

Zagarolo: East of Rome. Stone hut 60 sq. m. for complete renovation, set in a cultivated vineyard of 6,000 square metres. **Price:** €57.000,00.

Rocca Priora: a few km outside Rome, Villa Paola, a new villa in a perfect location to enjoy the peace and tranquillity of the countryside. 2,000 square metres of beautiful garden (enough room for a pool). Immaculate condition. 3 bedrooms, 2 bathrooms. Spacious garage in basement. **Price:** € 400.000,00.

Rome: Colle Romito: Renovated house consisting of 110 square metres. 3 bedrooms, laundry, kitchen, 3 bathrooms. Private garden 500 square metres with swimming pool 10 x 5. Near transport. Schools, sports facilities. **Price:** €158.760,00.

Agents for this region: www.fingertiphomes.com, www.europropertynet.com.

ABRUZZO

Capital: L'Aquila (721 metres above sea level)
Area sq.km: 10,798; *Population:* 1,244,226
Foreign visitors: 161,876 ; *Italian visitors:* 1,099,803
Climate:

Mean	Summer temp.	Winter temp.	Ann. Rainfall	Days of rain
17.4C	25C	7C	635mm	128

Airports: Pescara
Unesco world heritage sites: Gran Sasso-Monti Della Laga, Abruzzo, Lazio & Molise, Majella

Geography and Climate

Abruzzo, in the middle of the peninsula, borders with Le Marche to the north (the river Tronto), Lazio to the west, Molise to the south (the river Trigno) and the Adriatic sea, 129 km of coastline, to the east. It is 65.1% mountainous and 34.9%

hilly, and one of the least populated regions in Italy. The peak of the Gran Sasso d'Italia massif (2,912m) is the highest in the Apennines. Of the four provinces, L'Aquila, inland, is completely mountainous, Chieti is hilly, whilst Pescara and Teramo are half hilly and half mountainous. A third of the whole region is protected by national or regional park or nature reserve status.

On the coast, Mediterranean scrub has been largely replaced by crops, olive groves and vineyards, interspersed with ilex, flowering ash and black hornbeam. In the mountains two thirds of the vegetation is thick forest, chestnut, beech, oak, ilex, birch and black pine. Among the carefully preserved wild animals there are 100 Marsican bears, 400 Abruzzo chamois, wolves, otters, wild cats, martens, red deer and roe deer. There are golden eagles, eagle owls and goshawks, and a host of beautiful wild flowers. At Torino di Sangro on the coast there is an impressive protected ilex forest, and classic pinewoods on the dunes of Pineto.

Winter sports have transformed many of the upland towns and villages, and there are 22 skiing resorts, mainly in l'Aquila province, but some on the Teramo side of the Gran Sasso and Maiella mountains.

The coastline is varied; broad sandy beaches and well-tended resorts, with night life, at Alba Adriatica and Pineto ('the pearl of the Abruzzo Riviera') give way further south to rockier small beaches at Rocca San Giovanni, and sand dunes at Punta Penna and Vasto, with areas off the beaten track rich in wildlife including the occasional sea turtle.

San Giovanni in Venere is the site of an imposing Benedictine Abbey, where ancient fishing contraptions called *travocchi* are still in use. It is a recommended location for holidays or retirement – a few minutes from the lively seaport town of Pescara, from a golf and country club (at Miglianico), from beaches, ski resorts, autostradas, an international airport, and a direct rail link with Rome and Bologna.

Agriculture in the Fucino and Sulmona valleys supplies the Rome market (100km away) with vegetables. There are ancient sheep-droving connections (*tratture*) between Abruzzo and the winter pastures of the *Agro Romano* of Rome and the *Tavoliere* of Puglia. Fisheries (Pescara), mollusc farming and floriculture are other thriving activities. Industries are developing in Abruzzo encouraged by the recently improved communications such as the Pescara – Rome and the Teramo – Rome autostradas and the 10km tunnel under the Gran Sasso mountain, added to the Bologna – Bari coastal autostrada and the international airport at Pescara.

Tourism, both summer and winter, has benefited from this excellent communications infrastructure. As well as the attraction of the great national parks an astonishing amount of genuine antiquity and folklore has survived the depopulation of the last century. There are 99 legendary castles surrounding L'Aquila, and on the coast ruined lookout towers still guard against the Turks and the Saracens.

Climate. The climate of Abruzzo – on the eastern side of the Apennines towards the sea is temperate and dry compared with the cool wet highlands to the west, where rainfall often exceeds 1,700 mm per year and temperatures average less than 12°C. There is heavy snowfall in the mountains, and even a small glacier, the Calderone, in the shadow of the Gran Sasso. North-east winds predominate.

History

The Picenians were here first. Their most famous relic is the stone statue of the warrior of Capestrano at Chieti. They and the other Italic tribes, Praetutians, Equians, Marsians and Vestinians were subdued by the Romans in the fourth century BC and bloodily suppressed when they revolted in 90 BC. Roman settlements included Sulmona, the birthplace (43 BC) of the poet Ovid, and Amiteanum near L'Aquila, the birthplace (86 BC) of the historian Sallust. Lanciano, Vasto, Penne, Atri and Teramo are also full of Roman remains. In the brief Napoleonic period the region was divided into Abruzzo Ulteriore I (Teramo), Abruzzo Ulteriore II (L'Aquila) and Abruzzo Citeriore (Chieti), hence the persistence of the plural usage, *Abruzzi*. Pescara was made a province in 1927.

People

As well as Sallust and Ovid, Abruzzo is associated with the popular preacher and patron saint of advertising, St Bernardino, of Siena, who spent the last part of his life wandering in the mountains of Abruzzo where he died in 1441. The father of the English pre-Raphaelite poet and painter Dante Gabriel Rossetti was an Abruzzo man (an exiled education minister of the Napoleonic regime). Gabriele D'Annunzio, the flamboyant Italian poet and military hero was born in Pescara in 1863; he had a strong sentimental attachment to the landscape of his childhood, and his poetry, such as *La Pioggia nel Pineto* (Rain in the Pinewood) has rich and sensual associations.

The great historian and philosopher Benedetto Corce (1886-1952) was born at Pescasseroli, (L'Aquila), an ancient town which is now a charming resort in the heart of the National Park of Abruzzo. The writer, Ignazio Silone (1900-1978), came from Pescina (l'Aquila). An exile from fascism he was the authentic voice of the south, 'a socialist without a party and a Christian without a church', whose novel *Fontamara* (1933) describes the plight of illiterate peasants whose families have lived in isolated communities for centuries, confronted by the institutionalised corruption of the landlord class and the horrors of fascism.

Food and Wine

Food. The region has produced these illustrious intellects; it also boasts the highest life expectancy rates in Italy, and L'Aquila has a distinguished Rugby club. But it is in the field of gastromony that Italians recognise in Abruzzo a foodies' paradise. The best machine-made pasta in the world is made by Fili De Cecco, of the quaint Adriatic village of Fara San Martino. Handmade pastas are of course the norm in the local cuisine, such as ravioli and pancakes (*scripelle*) baked with spinach and béchamel sauce. *Timballi* – savoury pasta or rice baked in moulds are said to have been introduced by a Breton deserter from Napoleon's army. Seasonal feasting is also a powerful tradition in Abruzzo. The Gargantuan *Panarda* of the first of May is a meal in which there are seven dishes to a course and you are not allowed to shirk a dish. *Virtù* is a traditional soup consisting of seven types of pulse, seven fresh legumes, seven fresh vegetables, seven of fresh meat, seven of pasta, seven of spices all cooked for seven hours. The lentils of Capracotta are the best in Italy outside of Umbria. *Farro* (spelt) an ancient Roman wheat grain, is also grown here and used in soups.

A good variety of fish is supplied by the Adriatic sea: fish soup, *brodetto*, has local variations. In Pescara the different kinds of fish are put into the soup at different times; in Vasto they are all put in at once, the essential flavouring being olive oil, garlic, and chillies – here called *diavolilli* (little devils). There is less use of tomatoes here than in other regions. On the Chieti coast *scapece* (universal throughout the Mediterranean) is a speciality of fish dusted in flour, fried in oil, and then steeped in vinegar with a flavouring of saffron from Navelli.

Boned and stuffed fowl, rabbit, kid, mutton, turkey and suckling pig are food stall favourites. Pig's blood and chocolate are combined into a black pudding (*sanguinaccio*). *Cif e Ciaf* is the name of a dish of pork chops and bacon pan fried with chillies. Stuffed and baked vegetables (*ripieni*) are popular and include peppers, tomatoes, artichokes and eggplant. Potatoes are baked in the embers. Truffles are much used. Nettles, asparagus and even turnip tops are lovingly picked in the wild, and the red garlic of Sulmona has been known for centuries for its curative properties.

The sweets in Abruzzo are also local (and seasonal), with special concoctions for Easter and Christmas, such as *calgiunitti*, literally little cushions of pastry stuffed with jam, chick peas, candied fruit, pine seeds and chopped walnuts.

Wine. The choice of wine is simple: red is Montepulciano d'Abruzzo, white is Trebbiano d'Abruzzo. There is also a Cerasuolo from Chieti – a rosé version of Montepulciano d'Abruzzo.

Matrmônij' e mmaccurune
Ha da ji' calle calle
Marriage and macaroni
Should be taken hot hot.*(Abruzzo proverb)*

Typical Properties for Sale

The region is not popular with foreigners. The houses are built using local stone in a traditional style with small windows and terracotta tiles. They are built in groups, L'Aquila, the capital is a university town and has many old buildings and stone palazzi. Farms in the hills are divided into small plots. In Abruzzo you can find entire abandoned towns (ghost towns) for sale.

L'Aquila. One of four apartments situated in a villa in the hamlet of Elfi, 3 minutes from the centre of L'Aquila 190 square metres. **Price:** €133.000,00.

Pescara. Farmhouse with 5 acres of land, in need of restoration. 20 minutes inland from Adriatic coast. **Price:** €400.000,00.

Villa Marazzi. Fontecchio. A section of a villa situated in the historical centre of Fontecchio, an attractive and characteristic village in the picturesque valley of Abruzzo and 25km from the capital L'Aquila. It is easily reached from Rome and Pescara each 90 minutes away. **Price:** € 90.000,00

Agents for this region: www.cercarcasa.it, www.incasa.it.

MOLISE

Region: Molise
Capital: Campobasso
Area sq.km: 4,438; *Population:* 316,548
Foreign visitors: 16,522; *Italian visitors:* 168,063
Climate:

Summer	Winter	Ann.
temp.	temp.	Rainfall
26C	1C	628mm.

Airport: Pescara
National parks: Abruzzo, Lazio and Molise.

Geography and Climate

Molise is 55% mountainous, with a 38 km stretch of Adriatic coastline, bordering with Abruzzo to the north, Lazio to the west, Campania to the south and Puglia to the south-east. The Apennines divide Molise into isolated mountains and a chaotic array of hills, which create a state of isolation and make communications difficult. The highest peak is Monte Miletto (2,050m) near Bojano on the border with Campania. There are half a dozen nature reserves inland, such as the Casacalenda bird sanctuary, and the Collemeluccio and the Montedimezzo reserves, where the golden oriole and various owls and birds of prey share space with wolves, polecats and other fauna. There are several rivers, which are greatly affected by fluctuations in seasonal rainfall, heaviest in spring and autumn, longer lasting in winter, peaking in November and at its lowest in July. Inland the weather is extreme with up to 2,500mm annual rainfall. The coastal area is milder and drier.

Agriculture is a major activity, often at subsistence levels. The most common crops are wheat, broad beans and potatoes. Vineyards and olive groves flourish between the foothills and the sea. Traditional sheep farming and flock droving is practised, Ancient crafts survive such as knife forging in Frosolone, lacemaking in Isernia and bellfounding in Agnone. There is only one real industrialised area, near Termoli on the coast (furniture, engineering, textiles, building materials, processed foods etc) and tourism is undeveloped.

The Italian tourist board is urging people to visit Molise before it becomes fashionable. It has mountains with winter sports – and speleology – at Campitello Matese, archaeology and Roman remains at Sepino and Isernia, but for many the most attractive area will be the benign foothills by the sea, the wide sandy dunes and the old droving trails (*tratturi*). Campomarino, Casacalenda, Guglionesi, Santa Crocedi, Magliano, Petacciato Larino and Termoli are names to conjure with. The coastal plain, once extensive marshland, has been drained and built on since the nineteenth century, but the original environment still remains on the banks of the river Biferno with its tamarisk woods, canebrakes and clumps of Aleppo pine. The beach at Campomarino, where this river flows into the sea is surrounded by pinewoods and dunes covered with couch grass, heather and cistus. These beaches are still wild – crowded in July and August – but delightful in the off-season.

Termoli is the only sea port, from which ferries ply to the three Tremiti islands 25km offshore, once a Benedictine monastery, then a Bourbon prison, now a magical resort for yachtsmen and divers, in the limpid blue waters of the Adriatic.

Back in the uplands – not far from the Benedictine Abbey of Monte Cassino across the regional border – is the ancient town of Venafro, whose heyday was in Roman times. It has an amphitheatre, and a cathedral, spontaneously added to over the ages, with fabulous Baroque marble altars and interesting frescoes painted between the fourteenth and eighteenth centuries. The surrounding foothills luxuriate with olives and vines.

Another truly magical spot is Pietrabbondante – the highest ancient settlement in Italy – at 1,000m – an important Samnite sanctuary, on the beech-covered slopes of Mount Caraceno – where there are also the remains of a Roman theatre. Agnone too, is a charming hilltown, full of craftsmen's shops and bell foundries.

Campobasso is the regional capital, with its historic purlieus and fifteenth century Montforte castle. Isernia is the second city and provincial capital high up between the rivers Carpino and Sordo, full of ancient remains, a fountain, an abbey and a hermitage of St Cosmos and St Damian built on the site of the pagan temple of Priapus.

The Molise dialect is similar to that of northern Puglia. There are linguistic enclaves of Albanian in the province of Campobasso.

History

Molise is the site of the most ancient human remains found in Italy, 730,000 years old, *homo erectus Aeserniensis*, discovered in Isernia in 1979, where there is now a wonderful archaeological museum. In the fifth century BC this was in the territory of the Samnites, who fought three epic wars against their Roman neighbours, and ended up as part of the Province of Sabina et Samnium. In the dark ages the area was overrun by Goths, Byzantines, Lombards, Saracens and Normans – It was feudalised, and acquired its name from Hugh II of Mulhouse who died in 1168. In 1221, under the Holy Roman Emperor Frederick II, it became a province of the Kingdom of Naples. It attracted gypsy and Slav immigrants, and a colony of Albanians in the fifteenth century, who came under the control of alternating Angevin and Aragonese overlords.

In the Second World War the Campobasso area was devastated by ferocious warfare between Allied and German troops, which was ended by the Allied landings at Termoli in 1943. In 1963 Molise was divorced from Abruzzo and became a separate region, albeit one of the smallest and most backward in Italy. Massive and continual emigration in the twentieth century has led to thriving colonies of Molisani in Canada and the USA and South America, many of whom come back to visit their old home towns.

The earthquakes in 2002 which killed 26 children and three adults in San Giuliano di Puglia drew the attention of the world to the stoical character of the people – and to the danger of ignoring anti-seismic building codes. Molise's most famous personality, Antonio di Pietro, the crusading Milan magistrate of the 1990's 'clean hands' (*mani pulite*) campaign epitomises the stern integrity which lies at the heart of this old-fashioned region.

Food/Wine

Food. The food in Molise is genuine, old-fashioned and local; the region abounds in romantic rustic eating places, particularly the town of Guglionesi which has two first class restaurants including *Ribo* (contrada Malecoste 7) offers exceptional traditional Molisano dishes.

Typical regional dishes include:

- *Calcioni*: fried ravioli stuffed with minced ham, ricotta and provolone cheese.
- *Fruffella*: thick vegetable soup enriched with diced bacon, garlic and chilli pepper.
- *Macche*: baked polenta slices interspersed with sausage or bacon.
- *Mappatelle*: pancakes stuffed with spaghetti, bacon and pecorino, au

gratin.

○ *Mucische*: sun-dried and lightly smoked mutton, sliced thin with olive oil and chillis.

○ *Taccozze*: pasta squares dressed with ricotta and tomato sauce.

Trout is baked stuffed with capers, olives and chopped parsley, covered with breadcrumbs and sprinkled with oil.

Rabbit is boned, chopped into chunks, wrapped in ham, interspersed with pieces of sausage and bay leaves on a skewer, and cooked on a charcoal fire, or in the oven.

A typical Molise Christmas *dolce* (sweet) is ravioli – stuffed with blended chestnuts, honey roasted almonds, bitter chocolate, candied citron, vanilla and cinnamon, and fried in boiling oil.

Wine. For these savoury foods you need a good Montepulciano di Molise or Aglianico red.

Fa chiù meracule 'na votta de vin
che 'na chiesa de sante
A barrel of wine works more miracles
than a churchful of saints. *(Molise proverb)*

Typical Properties For Sale

Molise is in an earthquake zone, a fact, which has deterred many prospective buyers. Indeed, many towns have been completely rebuilt several times. The architectural style is largely rustic. There are farmhouses on the plains, abandoned monasteries in the hills and castles hidden in the mountain forests. A good investment is a typical 3-4 room house for renting out in the university town of Isernia. 100-year-old properties are easy to come by costing about 300 euros per square metre. Apartments in the *centro storico* (historic centre) of the towns are popular and there are a large number of houses on the market. Property in Molise costs less than some other regions and local and immigrant labour is cheap.

Location	Type	Description	Price
Roccaraso- Capracotta Close to skiing locality of Abruzzo and Molise	Small village house 250 sq.m	In need of renovation. Quiet location.	€150.000,00
Isernia, Cerro al Volturno Medieval town centre	Apartment 260 sq.m with garage. Plus garden 100 sq.m	10 rooms, 2 bathrooms and 5 balconies. Can be divided and sold as 2 lots.	€155.000,00

Campobasso Castelmauro In the hills; 8 km from Guardiafiera Lake; 40 km from sea.	Large, solid red house. 800 sq.m	Needs renovating. 22 rooms. Possibility of a regional grant for reconstruction. Buy as a residence or business. Has planning permission for restaurant or bed and breakfast	€200.000,00

Agents for this region: www.oliva.com; www.casainrete.com.

SARDINIA

SARDINIA

Capital: Cagliari (1 metre above sea level)
Area sq.km: 24,090; *Population:* 1,599,511
Foreign visitors: 41,9117; *Italian visitors:* 1,302,997
Climate:

Mean	Summer temp. 30C	Winter temp. 6C	Ann. Rainfall 585mm	Days of rain 65

Airports: Cagliari (Elmas), Olbia (Costa Smeralda) and Alghero (Fertilia).
Unesco world heritage site: the Nuragic village of the Val di Noto
National Parks: La Maddalena/Asinara, Gennargentu e Golfo di Orosei

Geography

Sardinia is the second largest island in the Mediterranean, 12 km from Corsica to the north, 120km from Tuscany to the north-east and 185 km from North Africa to the south. It has 1,849 km of coastline and very deep coastal waters, high rocky cliffs running straight for miles, often ending in promontories and surrounded by islands. Inland are ponds, marshes and extended barren hills. The north-west and north-east coastlines are jagged and impassable for long sections. The geology is palaeozoic going back 300 million years; rocky uplands predominate of granite, schist, trachyte, basalt, sandstone and limestone peaks between 300 metres and 1000 metres above sea level. The highest mountain, Gennargentu (1834m) is in the middle of the island and is part of the 40 km Marghine chain, which spreads towards the north. The valleys are deep and there is not much flat ground except for the great plain of Campidano, which extends across the south (the Gulf of Cagliari) for about 100km up to the Gulf of Oristano.

Tracts of virgin forest have survived totalling one sixth of the whole surface of the island, about 485,000 hectares, mostly of ilex, oak and chestnut, and carob. In the south, the forest of Gutturu Mannu is the largest forest in the Mediterranean area.

The central wilderness of Iglesiente teems with wildlife, Sardinian breeds of deer, wildcat, goats, sparrows and partridges. Pink flamingos flock to the salt marshes at the Stagno di Molentartguis near Cagliari. Sardinia is the home of the macchia (Mediterranean scrub); cistus, broom, heather, mastic, lentiscus, arbutus and wild olive and cork woods.

Climate

The climate is generally mild, influenced by the masses of air flowing from the Atlantic, Africa and the Arctic. The weather is fair – 300 days of bright sunshine in the year, the rest rain, falling mainly in the autumn and winter with occasional showers in the spring.

The island is well ventilated – the northwest wind, the *maestrale*, dominates, fresh and bracing in the winter, cooling and drying in the summer. Less frequent is the scirocco, from the south, the *levante* on the east, and the *ponente* on the west coast.

History

Prehistory of the Bronze and Iron Age 1500-500BC is very much in evidence. Curious stone towers called *nuraghi*, perhaps once castles or forts, are scattered all over Sardinia – seven thousand of them. These are predated by strange caves dug out of the ground near Alghero. The island was raided for its mineral resources and timber by the Myceneans, Cypriots, Phoenicians, and occupied by Carthage (500-238BC). Exploitation continued under the Romans who slaughtered 12,000 islanders in 177BC – and built roads, which still survive. When the Roman Empire weakened, Sardinia fell prey to invaders including Vandals and Byzantines, and in the ninth century the Arabs took to raiding the coasts forcing the people to move inland where they formed four autonomous *giudicati* (jurisdictions): Arborea, Cagliari, Gallura and Torres. In the thirteenth century the mainland republics of Genoa and Pisa moved in to stake their claims. Sardinia's own warrior queen, Eleonora d'Aborea started a resistance, which kept her fiefdom Arborea independent until 1478, when the Spanish took the whole island. The kingdom of Aragon and Castile reigned until the eighteenth century, when Austria owned Sardinia briefly (1708-1718) ceding it to the house of Savoy at the Treaty of London (1718). Sardinia retained an internal and repressive feudal autonomy until 1847, when it was united with the central government of Piedmont, becoming part of the Kingdom of Italy in 1861. Sardinia is one of five autonomous regions under special statute, of the Republic of Italy with four provinces Cagliari (the capital), Sassari, Nuoro and Orestano.

The People

As a result of centuries of neglect and harsh feudal oppression, Sardinia has retained a unique archaic culture. Old folk in the hinterland still wear traditional costumes and the folk music and singing thrives spontaneously – villages do not need to revive any folklore for the tourists, it is such a powerful part of their living culture. Their speech is not so much a dialect as a language in its own right with archaic Latin features such as *kentum* for a hundred and *flumen* for a river. In the Alghero region an archaic form of Catalan is still spoken and sung by 15,000 people.

Food and Wine

Food. Wild and archaic too is the Sardinian style of cookery – rooted perhaps in the ancient Nuraghic civilisation – the preparation of roasts of pork, lamb or kid is almost a religious ritual. Wild boar is cooked in a pot over a bonfire. Hybrid influences have come by sea from Phoenicians, Carthaginians, the Spanish and Byzantines such as *fregula* (cous-cous), crisp bread (*pane carasau*) and nougat (*torrone*). Pecorino sheep's cheese reigns supreme; famous dishes are *porceddu* (spit-roasted pork with myrtle), *culingiones* (stuffed pasta), *malloreddus* (dumplings), seafoods like lobster with vernaccia wine, *bottarga* made from mullet roe, cured tuna *(tonnina)*, meatballs called *bombas*, baked artichokes and aubergines. Saffron is grown and used.

The influx of Italian tourists has increased the number of refined restaurants, but the traditions are just as proudly preserved in the humble trattorias.

Wine. Sardinian wine owes much to the Aragonese, who imported their grape varieties: Vermentino white in Sassari, Cannonau red (grenache) in Nuoro, Carignano in Sulcis, Girò in Cagliari – and Malvasia. Each district has its own cuisine and its own wine.

The Property Buyers' Perspective

At the moment Sardinia is regarded as a place to visit by the yacht-borne super rich who have a fabulous enclave on the Costa Smeralda in the north east. This development was the brainchild of the Aga Khan who has since sold out to a consortium. Private beaches accessible only from the sea, completely unpolluted water, a wild hinterland and an irresistible seafood cuisine, lure more than one million Italians to Sardinia every summer. A property anywhere near a beach or a village would be an extremely good investment – easy to rent in summer and delightful to live in during the winter – bright sun and bracing winds – but above all, local people of great warmth and passion – a deep culture at the local folklore level, and also at the museum and archaeological level.

The English have a long tradition in Sardinia. DH Lawrence is revered for his flattering comments in *Sea and Sardinia*, Garibaldi had English neighbours on his island of Caprera, Mr. and Mrs Collins, from whom he had bought his corner of it. The Englishman's goats and pigs helped themselves to Garibaldi's potatoes and cabbages. The General responded by building a stone wall right across the island from west to east along his border. Years later in 1864, after Mr. Collins had died, a number of Garibaldi's wealthy admirers in England purchased the southern half of the island and presented it to their hero. To this day English people still own islands in Sardinia. A favourite area is Alghero in the north west which has an airport served by Ryanair. Gallura, Sassari and Bosa are full of properties to snap up and agents to sell them.

Drawbacks and myths. Sardinia is an earthquake-free zone, but there are drawbacks and myths to look out for:

O **Water shortages.** 1995-2000 were emergency years. Be ruthless in ensuring the adequacy of your water supply.

O **Radon gas.** The granite substrata provides favourable conditions for this cancer hazard. Make precautionary checks with a *geometra* (surveyor) if you are building or renovating.

O **Kidnapping.** The Barbagia and the impenetrable Gennargentu mountains were the traditional haven for outlaws and shepherds, who could hide their captives for months in the pathless wilderness, fruitlessly pursued by the Carabinieri. Sometimes Sardinian convicts were called in from the mainland prisons to negotiate. Italian businessmen were the target for this rare phenomenon, which probably ended with the last century. But ostentatious displays of wealth can always attract criminal interest.

O **Political demonstrations.** The Sardinian Action Party (*Partito Sardo d'Azione*) strongly resent the extensive NATO presence on the island. Beware of volatile stand-offs, on this and other issues.

Getting to Sardinia. There are frequent ATI, Meridiana and Air Sardinia flights from Italian mainland airports to Cagliari, Olbia and Fertilia (for Alghero and Sassari). The sea ferries are cheaper from Italy, Sicily, Tunis, Corsica and France run by Navarma, Tirrenia, Trenitalia and Sardinia Ferries. For high season bookings for the summer have to be made two or three months in advance.

International flights combined with car rental are now extremely well catered for, making Sardinia an easy and attractive destination for international travellers.

The Regional Giunta of Sardinia is tourist friendly and image conscious. In 1999 they changed the island flag, previously a St. George's Cross with four blindfolded blackamoors heads facing left to a St. George's Cross with four suntanned European heads wearing bandannas facing right. But appearances are not everything.

Bentre piena cantat,
et non camija bianca.
It's the full belly that sings,
and not the white shirt. *(Sardinian proverb)*

Typical Properties for Sale

Foreigners buy property in Sardinia for the spectacular views on this sparsely populated but fantastically beautiful island. The beaches are also a big attraction as they have fine white sand and at resorts like Santa Margherita di Pula, property is very expensive. In the north east there are villas, marinas and golf courses; this area is the playground of the rich and prices in this area and other attractive coastal areas are four times higher than in the towns inland. There are a variety of properties for sale but most of the architecture is simple: stone houses painted white, with terracotta roofs.

Location	Type	Description	Price
I Coppi near Alghero	Two apartments	Set in olive groves on hillside. Could be converted into one house with five-bedrooms	€220.000,00
La Rossa 15 minutes from Alghero airport and about 4 miles to coast	New villa	4 bedrooms, 3 reception rooms and kitchen. Surrounded by terraces and garden with fruit, olive and oak trees. Room for pool	€400.000,00
S. Teresa di Gallura close to Rena Biana beach and town centre.	First floor town apartment	2 double bedrooms, bathroom, living-room with kitchenette and terrace. Needs modernisation.	€100.000,00
Near Bosa 5 minutes from the coast (Costa Verde)	Building plot	Planning permission for a 160sq m villa with 3000 sq.m of land. Sea views.	€125.000,00
Near marina (Isola Rossa)	Luxury apartments	1 or 2 bedrooms. 300 metres to private resort beach	€125.000,00

Agents for this region: www.brianfrench.com, www.casealsole.com, www.casatravella.com, www.porto-cervo-realestate.com, www.fpdsavills.co.uk.

THE SOUTH AND SICILY

CAMPANIA

Capital: NAPLES (5 metres above sea level)
Area sq.km: 13,595; *Population:* 5,652,492
Foreign visitors: 1,801,052; *Italian visitors:* 2,765,317
Climate:

Mean	Summer temp.	Winter temp.	Ann. Rainfall
18.1C	25.4C	7.9C	790mm

Airports: Salerno airport and Naples – Capodichino airport.

Unesco world heritage sites: 1995 Historic Centre of Naples, 1997 18th Century Royal Palace at Caserta, the aqueduct of Vanvitelli and the San Leucio complex, 1997 archaeological areas of Pompei, Herculaneum and Torre Annunziata, 1997 Costiera Amalfitana.

National parks: Vesuvio, Cilento and Valle di Diano

Geography and Climate

Lying on the Tyrrhenian sea between the Bay of Gaeta and the Gulf of Policastro, Campania is a mainly maritime region with its capital, Naples, the hub of communication lines between the south and the centre of Italy. It borders Lazio to the north-west, Molise to the north, Puglia to the north-east and Basilicata to the south. It is 50.6% hilly, 34.6% mountainous, 14.5% plain and has the highest density of population in Italy.

The mountainous interior, with its cities of Benevento and earthquake ravaged Avellino, contrasts with the fertile plain north of Naples, where Capua and Caserta show signs of past wealth. The Vesuvian coastline south east of Naples leads through Sorrento to the steep Amalfi coast and the city of Salerno which is the gateway eastward to Eboli and the uplands of the Lucanian Apennines, and southwards to the coastal plain of Sele flavoured by ancient Greek settlers and still dominated by the fabulous temples of Paestum in the lee of the Cilento mountains, which extend to the Gulf of Policastro. This is the most favoured area of the region, with its combination of beaches, climate and unspoilt hill country.

The rivers Garigliano, on the northern boundary, the Volturno coming down past Capua and the Sele north of Paestum are springfed rivers with a smooth constant flow. Twenty per cent of the region is still woodland with chestnuts and beech dominating in mountain areas.

Herds of buffalo are reared extensively – particularly in the area once known as the Terra di Lavoro (capital Caserta). Authentic unpasteurised buffalo mozzarella is a product of great international importance. The buffalo is an ancient draught beast – originally from India – at home in the swamps and marshes of this region, its milk is twice as nutritious as cow's milk and the mozzarella industry is now extremely hygienic, computerised and high-tec.

There are concentrations of factories around Naples, Sarno and Salerno, which have a pollution problem, as have the agglomerations of Pomigliano d'Arco, Casoria, Castellamare di Stabia, Pozzuoli, Torre Annunziata, San Giovannia Taduccio, Nocera Inferiore, Pagani and Battipaglia.

Climate. The climate is extraordinarily mild along the coast, with fairly wet winters and occasional storms in the summer. Inland the weather is harsher and more continental. In general the fertile volcanic soil and the frost free winters are perfect for citrus fruits, bougainvilleas and tropical creepers, and roses bloom all year at Paestum.

History

Settlers have been attracted here since antiquity. Cumae, just north of the present Pozzuoli, was the first ancient Greek settlement in Magna Graecia in the eighth century BC, where Greeks and Etruscans did business. The sibyl in her cave at Cumae was a real oracle, mentioned by the poet Virgil. Under the Romans this area was known as Campania Felix (Happy Campania). This was where Tiberius had his villa, on the isle of Capri, and where Maecenas gave Virgil a rural retreat. Roman life is preserved dramatically in the ruins of Herculaneum and Pompeii – destroyed by the eruption of Vesuvius in AD 63. At Capua there was a famous school for gladiators.

After the fall of the Roman empire Campania came under the influence of Byzantium but retained a certain amount of autonomy and flourished. From AD 839 the republic of Amalfi enjoyed three centuries of glory as a seapower of fabulous wealth, overcoming the Saracens, but succumbing to the Normans and the Pisans, and, finally, to plague and earthquake.

In 1735 the Bourbon Charles III of Spain took over the Kingdom of Naples and presided over a period of enlightment. He built the opera house, the Teatro San Carlo, in 1737. The City of Naples became the last stop on the grand tour, and was colonised by British artists and grandees. With a population of three hundred thousand it was not only the liveliest but also the biggest city in Italy. British Ambassador Sir William Hamilton and his wife Lady Emma were later residents, and Naples was the scene of Emma Hamilton's first meeting with Captain Horatio Nelson in 1793.

There was a brief Napoleonic interlude which ended with Joachin Murat as King of Naples 1808-1815. He was executed when he tried to regain the throne. During his reign the secret society of the Carbonari was born in Naples, a seditious organisation which appealed to the poets Byron and Shelley; it was absorbed into the Risorgimento, leading to the successful unification of Italy in 1860, when Campania, with the defeat of the Bourbon army, became part of the Kingdom of Italy.

To this day Campania is full of aristocrats and monarchists. It was the favourite refuge of White Russians after the Russian Revolution of 1917, and a popular haven for celebrities up to the present day.

The islands of Capri and Ischia, and the resorts of Ravello, Amalfi, Positano and Sorrento are associated with many famous names, from Gracie Fields to Graham Greene, from Rudolph Nureyev to Gore Vidal. A rich, aristocratic cosmopolitan society is very much alive in those idyllic locations – and owners are holding on to their treasured houses. It is easier to rent than to buy. Zig-zag roads past olives and carobs lead to fabulous villas with terraces overlooking the sea amid a riot of subtropical greenery.

In the Second World War Naples became infamous as a black market. Unemployment and rural depopulation combined with chaotic unplanned development, pollution and crime, represented by the *Camorra*, brought an image of degradation to the area in the post war years. But now there is a renaissance of hospitality, a rediscovery of past riches and a cleaning up, which is rightfully restoring Campania to its ancient glory.

People

A huge black economy thrives in this region. Sweatshops of all kinds produce leatherware, fashion garments and fake shiny objects, supplying markets and pedlars throughout Italy with their characteristic wares. Naples lives up to its reputation as a riot of illegal building, criminal activity and noisy street life. *Scugnizzi,* the traditional street urchins, still dart around, and tourists are warned not to leave their cars unguarded for an instant.

Campania is one of the few regions of Italy which has retained a powerful musical tradition, distinctively Neapolitan, deep rooted and popular, still building on the clichés of the past such as '*O sole mio*' and '*Funiculi funicula*'. The colourful, poetic Neapolitan dialect makes a magic combination with virtuoso mandolin play, not all of it just for tourists.

Food and Wine

Greek, Roman, Turkish, Spanish, French, Neapolitans are proud to have resisted all these foreign influences and to have retained a down-to-earth gastronomical fantasy of their own. They have given pizza to the world (it was the original urban fast-food sold by the portion in street stalls), and mozzarella and *pommarol* tomato sauce. During the Spanish occupation the Spanish soldiery would throw to the populace the entrails of their slaughtered cattle and then come back in the evening to eat the delicious soup that was on sale in the streets. Pizza, pasta and seafood: the Naples version of the Mediterranean diet has been exported throughout the world.

Wine. As for wine, Campania was famous for its vineyards since the Greeks. Greco di Tufo and Lacryma Christi were popular in the eighteenth century, from the Vesuvius region. Now inland vineyards at Avellino and Taurasi are competing with coastal producers in the Cilento. Indigenous grape varieties such as the Fiano and Capri (white) and the Aglianico and Piedirosso (red) are exceptionally good local wines.

Chi fatica magna
Chi nun fatica magna e beve.
A man who works, eats
A man who doesn't work eats *and* drinks. *(Neapolitan proverb.)*

Typical Properties for Sale

The region has many Roman sites and ruins. The area is one of natural beauty but impoverished, Capri, Ischia, Procida and Positano are expensive areas and there were only a few sales in 2002 because of the dearth of properties available. Houses with sea views are top of the buyer's list e.g. Amalfi. The market is enthusiastic and prices have risen 55% between 1998 and 2003. There are apartment blocks along the coast but they are shoddily built. The coastal areas are overpopulated. Further inland you can easily find half-abandoned villages for sale at very reasonable prices.

Salerno: Ogliastro Cilena. 200 square metres new, terraced house built 2002, set in a private park, a few minutes from the sea. Kitchen, living room, 6 bedrooms, 2 bathrooms – garage, cellar. 80 square metres of garden. **Price:** € 552.000,00.

Nr. Tolentino. Beautiful large property set on top of a hill. 500 square metres of living space, 12 hectares of land. Situated with good access to Tolentino. House made of stone and brick outbuildings. **Price:** €250.000,00.

Ravello: A 2-storey house with a flat terraced roof located on a hillside facing south towards the bay of Salerno. The house has five rooms and needs total renovation though the basic structure i.e. walls and roof are sound. **Price:** €156.000,00.

Agents for this region: www.unicasa-italy.co.uk, www.restorationitalia.com.

PUGLIA

Capital: Bari (1 metre above sea level)
Area sq.km: 19,362; *Population:* 3,983,487
Foreign visitors: 273,382 ; *Italian visitors:*   1,560,818
Climate:

Mean	Summer temp.	Winter temp.	Ann. Rainfall	Days of rain
19.7C	24.8C	8.2C	438mm	122

Airports: Bari: (Palese), Brindisi airport, Foggia airport

Unesco world heritage sites: 1996 Castel Del Monte, 1996 The Trulli of Alberobello
National parks: Gargano

Geography and Climate

The heel of Italy, Puglia is next to Campania and Basilicata (west) and Molise (north-west), with an Adriatic and an Ionian shoreline. It is the seventh largest region in Italy with an above average population density. It is 53.2% flat land, 45.3% hilly and 1.5% mountainous, mainly limestone.

It falls into five geographical regions from north to south:

The Gargano Promontory: very beautiful hills culminating in Monte Calvo (1,055m) with the remains of a magnificent forest of massive Aleppo pines, ilexes, Turkey oaks, beeches and yews. Its seaports of Rodi Garganico, Peschici, Vieste, Pugnochiuso, Mattinata and Manfredonia are on the Adriatic.

Coastal lakes: Lesina and Varano.

The Tavoliere plain (Foggia) with a low, sandy dune fringed coastline, between the Candelara and Ofante rivers, backed by the Capitanata Apennines which peak at the Monti della Daunia (1,152m). This is the largest plain in Italy after the Po Valley.

The Murge plateau which slopes down to Bari and the coast.

The Salento peninsula, south of the seaport of Taranto, with an amphitheatre of hills overlooking the Gulf of Taranto. Brindisi is a seaport on the Adriatic side. Otranto and Gallipoli are coastal towns on either side of Cape Leuca.

There are some caves, Grotte di Castellana near Bari, and salt flats (Saline di Margherita di Savoia) full of storks and waders and other marshland and shore birds.

A characteristic of the Puglia countryside is its emptiness – the farm workers live in towns. Agriculture is very important despite a shortage of water, partly solved by government irrigation systems. Olive oil and wine production is massive as is the production of tomatoes, lettuce, artichokes and fennel, carrots, aubergines, peppers, cabbage, wheat, maize, almonds and cherries. There are natural gas deposits (*Capitanata*) and bauxite and marble are quarried at Trani. Taranto has a steel industry, and is a naval base. At Brindisi, there are chemical works and other small industries, a ferry to Greece and an American military base. A coastal *autostrada* motorway, from Rimini, ends at Taranto. Lecce, in the middle of the Salento peninsula is at the end of a railway line from Milan.

Tourism is a major industry, Tourists visit the wide and sandy beaches, rocky caves, the charming ports like Gallipoli, and delightful inland towns: Lucera, Alberobello, with its extraordinary *trulli* (conical buildings) and Frederick II's beautiful Castel del Monte at Canosa. There are cathedrals, churches galore and Lecce is a gem of exuberant baroque architecture.

The centre of old Bari, previously a no-go area of *microcriminalità* (petty crime), has been cleaned up and transformed into a chic nocturnal paradise, with sea-front bars and restaurants. The Tremiti islands north of the Gargano are considered the pearls of the Adriatic. In the summer packed with Italians, they are best visited in the off season from Termoli in Molise (see *Molise*).

History

Puglia's fine harbours and fertile plains always made her vulnerable to invaders. In about 2000 BC there were Japygeans from the Balkans; today it is refugees from Albania. In the eighth century BC Greeks from Sparta founded Taranto, Gallipoli and Otranto. In 272 BC, after the defeat of Pyrrhus, the Romans took Taranto and made Brindisi their main port for Greece. Puglia enjoyed six centuries of Roman civilisation. After the fall of the Roman empire in 410 BC. Christian bishoprics friendly to Byzantium kept the candles burning against invading Herules, Goths and Lombards. The Arabs briefly occupied Taranto in AD 840 and Bari in AD 847. Two centuries of Byzantine rule were ended by the Norman invasion in 1056. Splendid cathedrals (Bari, Taranto, Otranto, Canosa) and Benedictine abbeys belong to this flourishing period of hybrid Romanesque – Byzantine – Arab culture. Puglia was the favourite region of Frederick II, who built the octagonal castle at Canosa (c.1240) and other fine buildings, but he started the war with the papacy which would be disastrous for Puglia for centuries. Puglia entered the Monarchy of united Italy in 1860 in a state of poverty and endemic criminality which was relieved by massive emigration. A group of humanitarian, socialist intellectuals pushed through energetic reforms, which gradually transformed the agriculture of the region, at the end of the nineteenth century. During the fascist regime after the first world war the University of Bari was inaugurated in 1925 and the Bari Trade Fair in 1930. The Italian fleet was destroyed by the British in Taranto harbour in World War II and in 1944 Bari hosted the first anti-fascist political congress leading to the creation of the Italian Republic. In the post war period Puglia benefited from huge subsidies from the *Cassa per il Mezzogiorno* for the building of industries such as the steel yards in Taranto ('cathedrals in the desert'). At the beginning of the twenty-first century Puglia's agriculture and tourism are thriving, and the environmentally conscious regional government is enthusiastically legislating to preserve and improve Puglia's glorious countryside and heritage. In 2003 you can still find a ruin to restore in the intensely romantic promontory conjured up by the title of Horace Walpole's gothick novel (*The Castle of Otranto*). In 2010 it will be too late.

As for the seaside if is hard to choose between the glorious beaches available. Zaiana north of Vieste attracts young party-lovers, while the town of Monopoli south of Bari has a lively nightlife. In general, Brindisi is to be avoided whilst the **Gargano Peninsula** is considered the most delectable place in the south of Italy.

People

Alberobello, Locorotondo, Martina Franca a Cisternino are jewels in the Valle d'Itria, the 'kingdom of the trulli', which has attracted musicians, scholars, political idealists and new age mystics, not to mention hippies. There is an Indian ashram, a Tibetan temple, and a yoga centre serving a happy expatriate community in this paradise.

As well as the nightlife, craftsmanship thrives in Puglia: papier mâché, weaving, pottery, stone carving, basket weaving, wrought iron, stained glass and painting etc. It is stimulating to see these traditions surviving so exuberantly in such a creative environment; a good place for an artist.

Food and Wine

Food. The cuisine of the region is naturally based on fish, like the Japanese, the Puglians love raw fish and their favourite starter is a plate of raw seafood: sardines, prawns and particularly, cuttlefish and squid. Other specialities are: mussels and potato soup, roasted oysters (dressed with oil, lemon, breadcrumbs, parsley, garlic and marjoram); and wild poppy soup with cauliflower, horseradish leaves, olives, raisins and walnuts. In Bari sea bream is cooked with white wine raisins and parsnips. Dry white wine is also used for baking lamb with peas – a typical Easter dish. Ragù, a thick meat sauce, is another 'monument to the cuisine of Puglia', to go with their superb handmade pastas and of course salads such as rocket, and vegetables, such as aubergines and fennel are part of the rich local produce. This is the home of the sun-dried tomato and virgin olive oil on an industrial scale. The wines are local and strong. *Terra d'Otranto, Bianco di Trani* are whites. *Castel del Monte Rosso* and *Rosata* is the best known red and rosé from the region. For dessert there are unusual nougats and pastries made with wine, honey, almonds, figs or cinnamon.

> *Parle a vigna e ddice*
> *'Sole e ssola sole'.*
> If the vine could speak it would say
> 'Sun, sun and only sun'. *(Puglian proverb)*

Typical Properties for Sale

Puglia is a peninsula and is known as the land of two seas. It is an industrial and wealthy region and foreigners are buying here; large properties with spectacular views. Gargano is home to many foreigners and property here is reasonable. Coastal properties are box shaped and whitewashed, and usually built in clusters. The village of Alberobello is entirely made of *trulli* – the whitewashed stone houses with a dark conical roof. The *trullo* is the emblem of the region, There are clusters of *trulli* and they are not expensive.

The port of Brindisi and Lecce are famous for baroque and romanesque architecture and it is possible to buy a 15th century Salentine baroque estate for a moderate amount – the property will consist of eight bedrooms, have olive groves and a working olive mill for €150,000 euros. There are isolated walled farmhouses (*masserie*) and both Italians and foreigners are flocking here to buy properties, and turn them into hotels and holiday villages.

There is a good range of restorable property available. But hurry while stocks last. Other buyers are not so much British as Italian. There is an absence of English-speaking entrepreneurs. A reliable supply of water is the main priority. Air-conditioning and, inland, a swimming-pool are essentials, especially if you want to rent out your house in the summer. It is an attractive region for young people and for socialising with Italian holidaymakers. It is also an earthquake-free zone.

Brindisi. Large new villa, 17 rooms, 4 bathrooms 660 square metres. 9,000 square metres of fenced garden, automatic gates, alarm and air-conditioning. It is 2 miles from the shops (San Vito) and 8 km from the sea (Ostuni). **Price:** €413.165,00.

Otranto. A fifteenth century fort, 600 square metres with an underground passage to the sea, private garden of 800 square metres and splendid views of the bay of Otranto.
Price: €414.999,00.

Lecce. Recently built apartments, 2 bedrooms en suite, kitchen, living room, terrace, 50 square metres. **Price:** € 175.000,00.

Leglie Messapica. A *trullo* for restoration in the village of *Leglie Messapica*, in northern Salento. Set in about an acre of gardens, the property is currently divided into 12 rooms. It is 25 km from Brindisi airport. **Price:** € 54.000,000.

Agents for this region: www.casaclick.it, www.oikos-immobiliare.it, www.trullinet.com.

BASILICATA

Capital: Potenza (819 metres above sea level)
Area sq.km: 9,992; *Population:* 595,727
Foreign visitors: 38,921; *Italian visitors:* 315,553
Climate:

Summer temp.	Winter temp.	Ann. Rainfall
20.5C	0.8C	588.7mm

Airports: Naples Capodichino

Unesco world heritage sites: 1993 I Sassi di Matera
National parks: Cilento and Vallo di Diano: Pollino

Geography and Climate

Basilicata is situated between Calabria and Puglia (Apulia) at the foot of the Italian peninsula. It is 47% mountain, 45% hilly and 8% plain. There are altitudes between 1,000m and 2,000m in the Vulture mountain range in the west, from which clay hills undulate towards the east, often topped by picturesque hill towns. Streams and rivers have worn deep gorges into the soft terrain, especially in the Matera district. The Murge landscape in the northeast of Matera is calcareous with dramatic canyons. In the southeast is a silted plain where rivers drain into the Ionian Sea with sandy beaches at Mataponto and Policoro (ancient Heraclea). In the west the mountains sweep steeply down to the gulf of Policastro and the narrow sandy beaches of Maratea.

The flora is typical Mediterranean maquis. The crags and landslides offer a superb nesting habitat for birds such as swifts, ravens, redstarts, kestrels and kites and a rare species of fishing eagle.

The rivers are torrential in winter and dry in summer. Several dams and reservoirs provide mains water, springs are frequent and there are hot springs, at S. Catalia (Bella), Bagni (Latronico) and Rapolla.

The Pollino mountain range to the south-west is noted for the rare pine *pino loricato*, wolves, serpentine green marble and spectacular wild flowers such as yellow gentian and white asphodel; Ferns grow in areas made acid by pasturage. Typical birds are the jackdaw and the black woodpecker. In the Sirino mountains to the west, near Lagonegro, bothies, farm houses, chapels and schools are to be found up to 1,000m among forests of oak, chestnut, beech, alder, hornbeam, white poplar and silver fir, with frequent jays and green woodpeckers. There are massive rock basins (*marmitte dei giganti*) and a three-hectare lake, Sirino, with superb trout and beautiful landscapes. Ski resorts with brand new lifts and facilities and superlative views 15 km from the sea are icing on the cake. There are other ski resorts at Viggieno and Monte Volturino towards Potenza.

Earthquakes affect this region. Potenza was devastated in 1980. There is a NW-SW faultline in the Vulture mountains, and a history of destruction and rebuilding over the centuries. The Lucanian Apennines, as these mountains are called, is the most sparsely inhabited area of Italy. There are splendid, silent beechwoods, spring and autumn cyclamens in red and pink; English-type landscape to the north, moonscape to the south – The *Christ stopped at Eboli* landscape of Carlo Levi, who was banished here by the fascist regime in the 1930's.

The weather is influenced by three seas and the mountainous terrain. Rainfall is irregular, heavy in winter and light in summer. Maximum rainfall is in the Lagonegro area subject to the Tyrrhenian Sea – between 2,000mm. and 3,435mm. per annum – the same as Amazonia. The lowest rainfall is on the Ionian Coast, and the lower valleys of the Basento and the Cavone rivers average 500mm. down to 22mm. registered at Pomarico, which is comparable to desert rainfall. The area is also affected by wind – particularly the *scirocco*.

History

Basilicata is in the general area once known as Lucania and the people here are called Lucanians. It was originally populated by the Lyki from Anatolia (Turkey) whilst the coast was colonised by Greeks from the eight century BC; ineffectually opposed by Oscan and Sabellian tribes from the interior. They were allies of Pyrrhus against Rome (defeated in 275 BC) and then got absorbed into the history of the Roman Empire. The Via Appia trunk road from Rome to Brindisium passed through the north of Basilicata and the poet Horace was born at the Roman staging post of Venosa in 65 BC. Byzantines, Lombards, Saracens and Normans, conquered the region. In the post-unification period Basilicata was rife with banditry and it became the object of parliamentary investigations, and special laws were enacted to improve the social and economic life by public works – the building of dams, roads and railways etc. In 1943 the Anglo-Americans liberated the region from fascism with the spontaneous support of the locals – particularly in Rionero and Matera.

Mountains and hills predominate in Basilicata, but it also boasts two superb stretches of seaside. You have the choice between the flat and fertile plain of Metaponto on the Ionian, or the Romantic craggy beaches of Maratea on the Tyrrhenian coast.

Bernalda is a fascinating medieval town inland from the Ionian shore, near the extraordinary Greek ruins of Metaponto, which is becoming a charming tourist area, good for sailing, gastronomy and *agriturismo*. A few miles south is the beach of Terzo Cavone, on the estuary of the Cavone river, in the comune of Scanzano Ionico (on the SS106 road), a huge expanse of fine golden sand full of friendly fishermen – shaded by pine forests with excellent *agriturismo* facilities in old farmhouses.

The finest beaches on the Tyrrhenian Coast are:

- Maratea – 30 km of cliffs sheltering caves, crags and solitary beaches accessible by trackways off the SS18 road between Sapri and Castrocucco,
- Cala Jannita – a long strand of dark sand South of the Ilicini nature park, next to three other enchanting beaches (off the SS18).
- Calaficarra, further south, for grottoes and stalactites.

Maratea is as beautiful as the Amalfi coast, but still unspoilt. It has very good fish restaurants, excellent hotel accommodation, miles of managed beaches, consistently pure and unpolluted seawater, and it is little known to foreigners. The rocky seabed is ideal for snorkelling and diving. Maratea is a charming medieval town.

People

Basilicata is one of the poorest regions in Italy. After massive emigration there are many more Lucanians living abroad than in Basilicata itself, mostly hardy frugal mountain folk who thrive as emigrants. Their most famous landmark – The Sassi of Matera, a town of cave dwellings, was inhabited until 1952 by a population of 15,000 who were evicted and re-housed.

Food and Wine

The inhabitants of the harsh mountainous hinterland have evolved their own style of frugal cooking and a hundred different ways of doing pasta, all decidedly savoury – red chillies are triumphant, hung up to dry in bunches on balconies. Their *caciocavallo* is a strong tasting hard cheese made from whole cows' milk. Their small wild tomatoes are an explosion of flavour – these and their wild mushrooms, sweet peppers, aubergines, beans, lentils, cardoons (related to the globe artichoke), and chicory are the basis of a predominantly vegetarian diet. Meat is a rare and precious ingredient, when you find it, it will be lamb, mutton or game, sometimes pork from the free range pigs which rootle in the mountains alongside the sheep. Meat is usually cut up with vegetables and combined with diced pecorino (sheeps' milk cheese), chopped salami and a single finely chopped chilli pepper and stewed slowly in a crock. The authentic accompaniment is rock hard bread and red Aglianico wine. Fish is usually combined with garlic, parsley, tomato and olive oil – often grouper (*cernia*) or hake (*merluzzo*). Fresh sardines are steeped in vinegar dusted with flour, fried and flavoured with a hot sauce of chopped garlic, parsley, chillies and mint. For dessert, fried ricotta ravioli is a speciality. As for wine with fish, chilled white Aglianico is supreme.

Convivial Lucanians love to share polenta heaped on a single board the size of half a table set in their midst.

> *Stu vinu ié bello eiè galanti*
> *a la salute di tutti quanti.*
> This is a fine and gallant wine,
> To the health of all of us that dine. *(A Lucanian toast.)*

Typical Properties for Sale

This region is one of the poorest yet the rugged mountains and the excellent resorts on the coast are attracting foreigners. Property prices are cheap here and you can get a bargain in one of the hill-top towns eg. Maratea. The government has poured massive resources into the south to fund immigration projects.

Typical Properties for Sale

Location	Type	Description	Price
Maratea Cersuta near the sea	Villa with 2,300 sq.m of land	1st floor: Large living room, kitchen, laundry and terrace. 2nd floor: 3 bedrooms and 3 bathrooms.	€516.000,00
Marina di Maratea	1940s semi-detached village house 100 sq.m and 2000 sq.m of land	Small. Needs renovating. 2 floors. 30 metres above sea level	€150.000,00
Potenza, near city centre, near the new university.	4th floor apartment with attic. 140 sq.m	Needs renovation. Seven rooms and two verandas.	€144.607,00
Laurenzana at 1000m altitude. 30 minutes from Pollino National Park	farmhouse 240 sq.m	Needs renovation. Is set in an orchard with an artesian well.	€60.000,00

Agents for this region: www.rustica.com; www.casainrete.com

CALABRIA

Capital: Catanzaro (15 metres above sea level)
Area sq.km: 15,080; *Population:* 1,993,274
Foreign visitors: 136,101; *Italian visitors:* 946,977
Climate:

	Summer temp.	Winter temp.	Ann. Rainfall
	30°C	6°C	682mm

Airports: Calabria: Reggio di Calabria and Lamezia Terme
Unesco world heritage sites: 1998 Cilento and Vallo di Diano National Park with the Archaeological sites of Paestum and Velia – Certosa di Padula.
National parks: Pollino: Aspromonte.

Geography and Climate

Calabria is the toe of the Italian peninsula bordering Basilicata to the north and stretching between the Tyrrhenian sea to the west and the Ionian sea to the east in the direction of Sicily, from which it is divided by the Straits of Messina. It is 41.8% mountainous 49.2% hilly and 9% plain.

To the north is the Pollino massif (2,267m) which merges southwards, via Castrovillari, into the Coastal Chain (Catena Costiera), on one side of which is the jagged coastline of the Tyrrhenian sea, on the other the inland valley of the river Crati (Vallo del Crati). The Crati flows north-eastward from Cosenza to the plain of Sybaris into the Bay of Taranto. To the east of Cosenza lies the Sila range of mountains: Sila Greca, Sila Grande (1,928m) and Sila Piccola, south of which, on the Tyrrhenian side is Lamezia Terme (Bay of St Eufemia) . A mountain range called Le Serre goes down to the toe, which is crowned by the mountains of Aspromonte (1,955m) in the lee of which Reggio di Calabria faces east over the Straits of Messina, and Locri faces the Ionian Sea to the east.

Flowing eastwards from the Sila range is the Neto river which drains into the Ionian sea north of Crotone. This estuary is a valuable, luxuriant wetlands area, still partly unexplored, a tangle of impenetrable growth and a haunt of endangered wildfowl which have miraculously survived their annual slaughter at the hands of local *cacciatori* (hunters). The Parco Nazionale della Calabria was set up in 1968 for the protection of this magnificent environment. North of Sybaris towards the Pollino range is San Lorenzo Bellizzi and the amazing Raganello gorges, where rare eagles nest, the Bifurto abyss 683m deep, and the Ninfe cave and sulphurous springs, famous since Roman times.

The climate: in the mountains it is continental; harsh extremes, and heavy rainfall, whilst on the coastal strips it is mild, dry and frost-free.

The whole of Calabria is an area of high seismic risk. Towns like Catanzaro were wrecked and rebuilt several times over the centuries. Reggio di Calabria was devastated in 1908 and rebuilt according to the strictest anti-seismic norms.

Agriculture is widely practised, often at a subsistence level, specialist crops being: olives, citrus fruits, wine grapes, sugar beet, potatoes, aubergines, tomatoes, onions, water melons, beans and peppers. The standard of living and the per capita income are the lowest in Italy. Industry is undeveloped despite state aid over the years.

The Tyrrhenian coast from Praia a Mare south to Paola is known as the 'Citrus Riviera' because of the perfume of citron blossom. Mandarin oranges and limes are grown commercially. The best beaches are: Praia a Mare, Isola di Cirella, Citadella del Capo, Scogli di Isca, breathtaking (*mozzafiato*). Further south is the internationally famous beach of Tropea which was a favourite royal resort in the days of the Bourbons.

Emigrants are coming back, a 'holiday atmosphere' is in the air. Cosenza university is a hub of youthful idealism. In the area of Locride (the ancient Greek city of Locris) the dream of living off tourism is coming true. The beach at Marina di Gioiosa Ionica is populated by aesthetes and gourmets, mostly Italian, who can buy locally made silk clothes, Attic vases, Bergamot perfume, 'grossa di Gerace' olive oil, rare 'bianco Greco' white wine, sun-dried tomatoes, sheep's cheese, and eat exquisite lamb cooked in a terracotta amphora. At Mammola nearby (population 3,000) there are 14 superb restaurants.

All these places are now accessible thanks to the opening up of Lamezia Terme airport to cheap flights and the improvements in the Salerno – Reggio di Calabria autostrada. Above all, there are signs that a new generation of environmentally conscious youthful entrepreneurs is gradually replacing the traditionally corrupt and insensitive developer class of the past. Tourism has become vibrant and exciting in this magnificent area dotted with tiny picturesque villages hugging the hills that slope down to the sea.

Calabria is the antithesis to the Tuscany or Umbria experience: most of the structures are new. The stone built farm if it exists, is seen as an earthquake risk. The property on offer is in new developments, specifically geared to tourism. It is unlikely that a family would emigrate to Calabria. The infrastructure – the schools, the hospitals do not inspire the same confidence as say, the infrastructure at Lake Garda. The mentality of the locals is more impenetrable and exotic. The heat, the ruins, the colours, the mountains, the wild Mediterranean , the warmth of the friendships once acquired, the ruthless intelligence – all these might inspire a creative writer or artist.

> Recently, Mr and Mrs Barclay, both advertising executives, sold a farmhouse in the Tuscan hills, after twenty years as a holiday home, and bought an apartment in a condominium near Lamezia Terme. They walk to the street market and to the fish restaurant; their shaded verandah overlooks the sea. They can swim in April and they can rent out their apartment in the heat of the summer to Italians. They are pleased with the move.

The other side of the coin in Calabria is the crime. Tourist are not affected. But you will notice it in certain areas: near Reggio. In Villa San Giovanni where the ferry terminal is, there were 47 killings in broad daylight in a three-and-a-half-month period in 1997. The Mafia meet the 'Ndrangheta. Gioiatauro up the coast is a horrendous place, according to Tim Watson a language teacher who was on holiday there in 2000. They always short-change you, testing you, to see whether you are *in gamba* (smart), a shocking and sinister place, he says. Certainly no place for a good-natured indolent individual who does not count his change.

History

An Italic tribe the Bruttians inhabited this area around 1000 BC. The coast was settled by Greeks in the eighth century BC. Croton was the birthplace of the mathematician Pythagoras (c582-c507 BC), and Sybaris – famous for its luxury – was destroyed by the Croton army in 510 BC. The Romans took over the whole region in 204 BC. In AD 410 Alaric, King of the Visigoths, died here after sacking Rome and is reputedly buried with his booty in the bed of the river Busento near Cosenza. Goths, Byzantines and Lombards, and more enduringly Saracens, overran the area until the Norman conquest in the middle of the eleventh century, after which it shared the history of the Kingdom of Sicily. Albanians fleeing from the Moslems settled in the fifteenth century and Piedmontese Protestants fleeing from the Inquisition colonised Guardia Piemontese in the sixteenth century. Garibaldi saw action here in his lightning tour of 1860 – and he was wounded and defeated at Aspromonte in an anti-papal engagement in 1862 – after which he was pardoned and allowed to retire.

Over a million Calabrians emigrated to Brazil, North America and Australia in the last two centuries. Bad communications within their home mountains have hindered progress. The brigandage of yesteryear is the organised crime of today.

There are three Calabrias each with their own subdialect: Cosenza, Catanzaro and Reggio. Archaic Albanian is still spoken in 34 villages, centred on Castrovillari. Franco-Provençal is spoken at Guardia Piemontese near Cosenza, and Attic Greek in Bova (Reggio Calabria). Standard Italian is universally understood and spoken.

People

Norman Douglas's book *Old Calabria* has been recently published in Italian and is regarded as an excellent guide to the ancient lore of the region. Norman Douglas makes an interesting distinction between the 'Bruttians of the mountains' and the 'Greek or Saracen strains of the coasts':

> *That these inhabitants of the Sila are Bruttians may be inferred from the superior position occupied by their women-folk, who are quite differently treated to those of the lowlands. There, all along the costs of South Italy, the cow-woman is still found, unkempt and uncivilised; there, the male is the exclusive bearer of culture. Such things are not seen among the Bruttians of the Sila any more than among the grave Latins or Samnites. These non-Hellenic races are, generally speaking, honest, dignified and incurious; they are bigoted, not to say fanatical; and their women are not exclusively beasts of burden, being better dressed, better looking, and often as intelligent as the men. They are the fruits of a female selection.*

Wine

The famous wines are: Cirò Rosato, Donnici Red.

Chi mangia de bon' ura
ccu nu pugnu scascia nu muru.
If you eat early you can knock down
a wall with your fist. *(Calabria proverb)*

Typical Properties for Sale

This region has a magnificent coastline with wide sandy beaches and small bays with summer homes,which are simple whitewashed houses with terracotta roof tiles.

Coastal properties especially at Tropea and Scalea are sought after and they are not cheap. Inland the houses of the mountains with their grey stone walls and slate roofs are more reasonable, however access to some parts can be difficult. The region is poor and tourism is an important industry, tourists are encouraged to look at properties in the hope that they will buy and make Calabria their home.

Lamezia Terme. An apartment 88 square metre, 2 bedrooms, 2 bathrooms, terrace and balcony all around. The apartment is located within walking distance of the sea. The location is semi-residential, close to restaurants, church, bakery and shopping centre. A major train station and the Lamezia Terme airport are both 10km away. **Price:** € 95.000,00.

Orsomarso. In the *centro storico* (old part) a mountain house with 6 rooms, 2 bathrooms, 110 square metres. The house has a balcony and a private garden. It also has a cellar and garage. **Price:** € 61.974,00.

Calabria: Tropea. A villa which is a converted convent on a cliff top overlooking the thirteenth century Santa Maria del'Isola, the crystal clear sea and the island of Stromboli in the distance. There is a large private terrace, four bedrooms, 2.5 bathrooms, huge living, dining rooms with spectacular views and a gourmet kitchen. Entrance is through a private courtyard with palm trees and a fountain. The property is near shops, and restaurants. (Price is negotiable). **Guide price:** €549.000,00.

Agents for this region: www.bingocasa.it, www.realestate.escapeartist.com.

SICILY

Capital: Palermo (5 metres above sea level)
Area sq.km: 25,708; *Population:* 4,866,202
Foreign visitors: 1,501406; *Italian visitors:* 2,456896
Climate:

Mean	Summer temp.	Winter temp.	Ann. Rainfall	Days of rain
22C	25.2C	11.8C	433mm	120

Airports: Palermo (Falcone Borsellino) and Catania (Fontanarossa)
Unesco world heritage sites: archaeological area of Agrigento, Villa Romana dei Casale, Isole Eolie (Aeolian Islands) and the late baroque towns of the Val di Noto (in south-eastern Sicily).

Geography

Geographically, Sicily is a series of broken hilly country in the middle with bare peaks and forested slopes; a chain of mountains along the north and a volcano, Etna, south of Messina in the east in the Catanian plain. Etna is the highest point of the island at 3,650 metres and is still active. The coastal areas can be divided into three, each coast with a different character and climate:

The Northern Shore, from Messina west to Palermo and Trapani, is steep and rocky with deep waters, good harbours and excellent fishing. There is a small fertile plan called Conca d'Oro near Palermo and much forestland on the mountain slopes with dry river beds. The weather tends to be harsh, sometimes windy, but it is a healthy climate.

The Eastern Shore, from Messina, south to Syracuse and Cape Passero. The Catanian plain, the best agricultural land in Sicily, is sheltered by mountains to the north and southwest. The climate is agreeable and there are excellent harbours and a good beach.

The Southern Shore, the south coast, has shallow waters, shifting sands, lakes, lagoons and marshes with a sultry climate. There are good orchards, olive groves and some pastures on an inland plateau 100 metres up. The southern shore suffers the scirocco wind.

The interior is thinly populated and mountainous, deforested and eroded over the centuries with sulphur mines. Caltanissetta (538 metres) and Enna (931 metres) are the cities in the middle.

The People

The Sicilians have a complicated history and it takes years to understand the complexity of their mentality. The interior of the island is under the micro control of the mafia, who enforce a viciously conservative murderous system (see *Crime, Living in Italy* chapter). They are said to be incredibly charming once you get to know them. The mafia (the name means hiding place in Arabic, not unlike Al Qaeda) are historically, heirs of the *gabelloti*, the rent collectors who were the middlemen between the land-owning aristocracy and the peasants. They belong to and are recruited from a few powerful families. The name Corleone springs to mind. The ordinary working folk are warm, hospitable and charming and the aristocrats are some of the most erudite and cultured people you can find in Europe, on a par with Giuseppe di Lampedusa, author of the most famous book on Sicily, *Il Gattopardo* (The Leopard). To get to know them at all levels, and to become accepted by them takes time. There are huge cultural differences, illustrated by the horror stories of British or Irish girls getting engaged to Sicilian men while on holiday, coming to live in Sicily and then having to escape from virtual imprisonment. But the 'men of honour' treat tourists well, and there are areas where their writ does not run, such as Syracuse and Noto. An excellent way to get to know the people is to stay in *agriturismos,* e.g. near Catania at Calatabiano, www.galimi.it, and in an old monastery near the Marina di Ragusa on the south coast where you can taste aristocratic cuisine, go parachuting or take a boat to Malta, www.eremodellagiubiliana.it.

Taormina was always popular with the English, especially bachelors, and it is still very beautiful. Noto is pleasant and Syracuse is recommended. The

Conca d'Oro near Palermo has stunning scenery. Sicily has 36 parks or nature reserves, including the Aeolian islands (Lipari, Vulcano, Salina, Panarea, Filicudi, Alicudi and Stromboli), which are very chic and highly sought after for romantic hideaways.

Climate

The weather in Sicily is delightful in spring. February, March and April are the best months to visit. It is agreeable to live there from October until the end of May, but the summer months are hot and dry, when air-conditioning is called for. Near the coast the climate is mild throughout the winter, the greatest rainfall being in November and December. The almond blossom is in full beauty in February and the *zagara* or lemon blossom reaches perfection in April. April and May are the best months for enjoying the interior and the Aeolian islands.

History

Sicily was the melting pot of the Mediterranean, for thousands of years bridging the east and the west. It was called Trinacria by the Greeks because of its three capes. The Romans nicknamed it *Triqueta* (triangle), symbolised by a head with two wings, three legs and three blades of wheat. Paolithic, neolithic and Bronze Age remains can be seen in the archaeological museum of Palermo. From around 1000 BC Sicily was colonised by Sicanians from Spain, Elymians from Asia Minor and Siculians from mainland Italy, who gave their name to the island. Phoenician traders from Lebanon opened depots there in about 800 BC. The first Greek colonies were founded by Chalcis and Megara in 735 BC, followed by Corinth, Syracuse and Crete, Gela and Catania soon after, each Greek home city sponsoring independent colonies whether Ionian or Doric. The island, especially the east was completely Hellenised by 500 BC. Syracuse became richer than Athens and was called the 'queen of all cities' by the poet Pindar (518-438 BC).

From then until the Middle Ages, Sicily was variously invaded by Vandals, Goths, Romans, Arabs, Normans and the French. In 1250 Charles of Anjou became the military dictator and king. At Easter in 1282, a slightly drunk gendarme at a church in Palermo importuned a young Sicilian woman whose husband responded by fatally stabbing him. This sparked a killing spree against the French throughout the island. The Sicilian word for chick peas, *ciceri,* unpronounceable to a Frenchman, was used as a shibboleth to winkle out the French for slaughter in this episode known to Sicilian history as the Sicilian Vespers. Garibaldi and his thousand men successfully invaded the island in 1860, and Sicily was united with the Kingdom of Italy by popular vote in the same year.

Poverty and hardship were the lot of the Sicilians well into the last century. There was mass emigration (900,000), mostly to America. The Great War, fascism and the Second World War did not help much but the arrival of the Americans in the Second World War revived the fortunes of the mafia which fascism had repressed. Sicily remains backward, not helped by the layoffs at the FIAT factory in Termini Imerese in 2002.

Sicily is one of Italy's five regions with Regional Autonomy by special statute.

Food and Wine

Food. Sicily's cuisine is an eclectic mix from all its foreign invasions: olives and bread from the Greeks, focaccia from the Romans, tangy cheeses from the Byzantines, citrus, rice and spices from the Arabs, salt cod from the Swabians, pastries from the Aragonese, and tomatoes and chocolate from the New World via the Spaniards. Sicily passed all these things on to Italy. Myriad pastas are imaginatively accompanied by sardines, aubergines, fried zucchini, ricotta cheese, squid, peppers, tuna and so on. Vegetables are presented in the form of *caponata* – diced and stewed, stuffed, and sweet and sour (*agrodolce*). Seafood is paramount, running riot in delicious variety: tuna steaks with breadcrumb and olive oil sauce, swordfish with olives and capers, couscous or other Arab accompaniments such as orange salad; of the meats, rabbit (from the Normans) and kid are popular, grilled or stewed with aromatic vegetables. Pastries and sweetmeats are fabulous in all regions, ice creams and the famous *cannoli* and *cassata* are without equal in Italy. Candied fruits, almond paste (marzipan), and prickly pear paste are magic ingredients.

Wine. Tasty wines accompany this exuberant food. Sicilian grapes such as Nero d'Avola provide good, strong dry reds, but it is the dessert wines of Sicily that are the most famous: Moscato from Lipari, Malvasia from Messina, and Zibibbo (Arab for grape) a delicious white liqueur wine. From the south-west, the Marsala wines developed English wines dynasties from Nelson's time, Woodhouse, Inghams and Florio.

A tavula si scordanu li trivuli
At table you forget your troubles (*Sicilian proverb*)

Typical Properties for Sale

Most towns are on the coast and the houses are grouped together. The island is architecturally rich: Roman, Byzantine, Islamic, baroque, all these styles are to be found in the buildings of the island. Much of the coastline of Sicily has been defaced by rogue building, the destruction of beautiful areas like Bagheria is a scandal. Most new houses have flat roofs and are badly constructed. Foreigners are wary of buying property because of the organised crime and links to the mafia. If you own an apartment or house, it is very likely that a man will ask you if you have fire insurance. You pay: you don't argue. Once you have understood this salient fact about Sicily, you can revel in her glorious folklore, climate, wildlife, food, history and people with equanimity; but make absolutely sure there is a water supply before you buy.

Location	Type	Description	Price
Piedmonte Etneo 45km Catania airport	Old wine estate. House 350 sq.m Garden 1,300 sq m.	3 bedrooms, 1 bathroom. Mature garden with palms and fruit trees.	€380.000,00
Palermo	Penthouse: floors 16 and 17 of apartment block. 220 sq m + 300 sq.m terrace	3 bedrooms and 3 bathrooms. Garden terrace with hanging garden. Views of the port and old town centre	€200.000,00
near Siracusa. 15 minutes to the town	Villa by the sea. Possible to divide into two dwellings	Ground floor: kitchen, living-room, bathroom, large veranda. 2nd floor: two bedrooms and bathroom and another very large room (160 sq.m). Garden is tree-lined and covers 1500sq.m.	€130.000,00

Agents for this region: www.nwwea.net, www.capital-residence co.uk, www.casainrete.com

Part III

THE PURCHASING PROCEDURE

FINANCE

FINDING PROPERTIES FOR SALE

WHAT TYPE OF PROPERTY TO BUY

RENTING A HOME IN ITALY

FEES, CONTRACTS & CONVEYANCING

BUYING FOREIGN CURRENCY FOR YOUR PROPERTY

If you're buying a property abroad for the first time, you've probably got enough to think about without worrying about exchange rates. You've found your dream home and secured the price of your property, and now all you have to do is look forward to your new life abroad. Right? Well, partly. Somewhere along the line you will have to change your pounds into euros, and that's where the dream can become a nightmare if you don't plan ahead. Whether you're buying a property outright or buying from plan in instalments, protecting yourself against exchange rate fluctuations can save you hundreds, if not thousands of pounds on the price of your new home.

Foreign Exchange markets are by nature extremely volatile and can be subject to dramatic movements over a very short space of time. In some ways it's all too easy to leave your currency exchange to the last minute and hope that the exchange rates fall in your favour. But if you don't take steps to protect your capital, you could find yourself paying a lot more than you bargained for.

As a matter of course, many people will approach their banks to sort out their currency, without realising that there are more cost-effective alternatives in the marketplace. There are a number of independent commercial foreign exchange brokers who can offer better rates and a more personal, tailored service. Their dealers will explain the various options open to you and keep you informed of any significant changes in the market. They will also guide you through every step of the transaction so that you are ultimately in control and able to make the most of your money.

If you're not still not convinced of how planning ahead can help you, take a look at the following example:

You've found your dream home and agreed the price of €200,000. When you signed your contract and paid your deposit in August 2002, the pound stood at 1.60. Just six months later when your next instalment was due, changes in the political and economic climate have caused the pound to weaken. You now only get 1.49 for your pound.

Agreed Price of Your New Home €200,000	Date	Rate	Cost in Pounds
	August 2002	1.60	**£125,000**
	February 2003	1.49	**£134,228**

In just 6 months the price of your home has **increased** by over **£9,000**.

Although changes in the economic climate may be beyond your control, protecting your capital against the effect of these changes isn't.

There are a number of options available to you:

- **Spot Transactions** are ideal for anyone who needs their currency straight away as the currency is purchased today at the current rate. However, if you have time to spare before your payments are due, it may be wiser to consider a Forward Transaction.
- **Forward Transactions** allow you to secure a rate for up to a year in advance to protect yourself against any movements in the market. A small deposit holds the rate until the balance becomes due when the currency contract matures.
- **Limit Orders** allow you to place an order in the market for a desired exchange rate. This has the advantage of protecting you against negative exchange movements whilst still allowing you to gain from a positive movement. Your request is entered into the system and an automatic currency purchase is triggered once the market hits your specified rate.

If you haven't had to deal with this kind of transaction before, this can all seem a little daunting. But that's where a reputable currency company can really come into its own. With specialists in the field ready to explain all the pitfalls and possibilities to you in layman's terms and guide you through each stage of the transaction, you can be sure that your currency solutions will be perfectly tailored to your needs.

Currencies Direct has been helping people to understand the overseas property markets since 1996. Specialising in providing foreign exchange solutions tailored to clients' individual financial situations, it offers a cost-effective and user-friendly alternative to the high-street banks.

With offices in the UK and Spain, Currencies Direct is always on hand to help you. For more information on how you can benefit from their commercial rates of exchange and friendly, professional service, call the Currencies Direct office in London on 020 7813 0332 or visit their website at www.currenciesdirect.com.

FINANCE

CHAPTER SUMMARY

O **Banks.** There are banks in Italy familiar with arranging mortgages on Italian property for foreigners.
  - O Some banks have special departments for Overseas buyers.
  - O Italian numbers are written with the comma and full-stop in opposite positions to the UK or USA, so ten thousand euros and 14 cents is written €10.000,14.
  - O In Italy it is a criminal offence to issue a dud cheque.

O **Mortgages.** Recent legislation in Italy allows any bank to offer mortgages.
  - O Mortgages in Italy are regulated to protect the consumer against excessive usury.
  - O For dilapidated property it is easier to buy it first and then get a mortgage for renovation.

O **Importing Currency:** You can save thousands of pounds by using the services of a currency dealer rather than going through a high street bank.

O **Taxes.** It is recommended that you enlist the services of a *commercialista* (accountant) as the Italian tax system is very confusing.
  - O Italian property is subject to a range of taxes.
  - O Property taxes are higher on a property that is not a principal residence.
  - O Italian property is taxed on a notional income, even if it is not earning a rental income.
  - O In 2001 Italy suspended Capital Gains tax and abolished inheritance and gift tax.
  - O The object of the above tax reform was to attract capital back to Italy.

O **Insurance.** Home insurance is very expensive in Italy because the crime rate is high in the cities.
  - O Expect to pay double for insurance in Italy compared with the UK and USA.

BANKS

Foreign Banks in Italy

The financing of a property purchase in Italy has never been easier. The property boom in Britain and Ireland has opened up opportunities for selling and remortgaging. Cash is available. Italian banks are competing with each other to lend money at historically low rates of interest. It is worth investigating the English speaking financial institutions which do the same in Italy. These are the Abbey National Bank and the Banca Woolwich.

The major UK high street Bank Abbey National Has an affiliated company in Italy, *Abbey National Mutui S.p.A.* This has been operating in Italy since 1989, specialising in tailor-made insurance linked mortgages, based in Milan, with branches in Turin, Bergamo, Udine, Padua, Bologna, Genoa, Florence, Pescara, Rome, Bari and Naples. It has an English speaking call centre, *Pronto Abbey*, tel.+39 02 667 29.1, +39 02 667 29. 356 and a foreign buyers area on its website www.abbeynational.it which is well worth consulting,

The Woolwich (www.bancawoolwich.it) – a subsidiary of Barclays Bank – has been growing rapidly in Italy for the last ten years, with branches in Milan, Turin, Bergamo, Brescia, Verona, Bologna, Genoa, Rome and Naples. It offers mortgages in association with policies by the Helvetia and Vittoria insurance companies and has also formed a partnership with the leading Italian real estate franchise company Gabetti. Paradoxically it is Gabetti and not the Woolwich that offers an English language website, www.gabetti.it.

Another international bank worth considering – and inclined to be Anglophone in that it is German – is the Deutsche Bank (www.deutschebank.it), which acquired the Morgan Grenfell Group in 1989 and has branches in London, Guildford, Edinburgh, Dublin, Sydney, Melbourne, Auckland and extensively in North America. It has been growing in Italy since 1977 and with over three hundred branches, is particularly strong in Lombardy, Liguria, Campania, and Puglia. It offers a full range of financial products and services: private and business banking, offshore banking, wealth management, investment funds, insurance, loans and mortgages, and a think-tank: DB Research.

To have an account in your own country with one of the above financial institutions could be advantageous for the purpose of cross-referencing and transferring funds, and also if you prefer your mortgage in your own currency. Much will depend on how conveniently their branches are located at either end.

Useful Addresses

Abbey National Mutui S.p.A: Via Nicolo Putignani, 137, 70122 Bari; ☎080-5237030; fax 08 05237094.

Abbey National Mutui S.p.A: Via Quarenghi, 36, 24122 Bergamo – (Bg); ☎03-5313130; fax 03 5313636.

Abbey National Mutui S.p.A: Via Marconi, 71, 40122 Bologna – (Bo); ☎05-14210028; fax 05 16390361.

Abbey National Mutui S.p.A: Viale G.Matteotti, 33, 50121 Firenze – (Fi); ☎055-5001514; fax 055 5001546.

Abbey National Mutui S.p.A: Via G.Fara 27, 20124 Milan; ☎02-6672906; fax 02-66729247.

Abbey National Mutui S.p.A. Ag. Milano 1, Via Dante 16. Milan; ☎02-86465193; fax 02-86465158.

Abbey National Mutui S.p.A: Via Medina 41/42, 80133 Napoli – (Na); ☎081-2520038; fax 081-5422124.

Abbey National Mutui S.p.A: Via Altinate, 8, 35139 Padova – (Pd); ☎04-98761380; fax 04-98761381.

Abbey National Mutui S.p.A: Ag. Roma 3, Via Cicerone 58, 00198 Rome; ☎06-328061; fax 06-3221536.

Abbey National Bank: Via Nizza 48, 00198 Rome; ☎06 841 3890; fax 06 841 3896. Via G. Fara 27, 20124 Milan; ☎02 66 7291; 02 66 981755.

Abbey National Mutui S.p.A: Via San Tommaso 24, 10121 Torino; ☎011-542000; fax 011-546110.

ABN Ambro Bank N.V.: Via Principessa Clotilde 7, 00196 Rome; ☎06 321 9600; fax 06 320 4851. Via Mengoni 4, 20121 Milan; ☎02 722671.

American Express Bank:, Piazza San Babila 3, 20122 Milan; ☎02 77901; fax 02 76002308.

Banca Woolwich SpA= Via Pantano 13, 20122 Milano; 20122 Milano; ☎02-584881; fax 02-58488511.

Banca Woolwich SpA: Milan Regional Office: Piazza della Repubblica 8, 20121 Milan; ☎02 290401; fax 02 290 40619.

Banca Woolwich Sp A: Via Angelo Maj, 10/L, 24121 Bergamo; ☎035 38371; fax 035 3837 359.

Banca Woolwich Sp A: Via Riva di Reno 37, 40122 Bologna; ☎051 29137 11; fax 051 29137 29.

Banca Woolwich: Via Fratelli Ugoni 8, 25126 Brescia; ☎030 29451; fax 030 2945 319.

Banca Woolwich Sp A: Piazza Dante 49/R, 16121 Genova; ☎010 57638 11; fax 010 57638 29.

Banca Woolwich Sp A: Via Vittorio Emanuele 43, angolo VS Brigida, 80133 Napoli; ☎081 7040 111; fax 081 7040678.

Banca Woolwich Sp A: Corso Cavour 31/A, 37121 Verona; ☎045 80648 10; fax 045 80648 77.

Banca Woolwich SpA: Via XX Settembre, 67, 10122 Torino; ☎011 5117 1; fax 011 5117 339.

Banque Nationale de Paris: Via Lazio 6, 00187 Rome; ☎06 4817041; 06 4818508. Via Meraavigli 4, 20123 Milan; ☎02 721241; fax 02 865 948.

Chase Manhattan Bank: Via M. Mercati 39, 00197 Rome; ☎06 844 361; fax 06
844 36220. Piazza Meda 1, 20121 Milan; ☎02 88951; 02 88952229.

Citibank: Via Bruxelles 61, 00198 Rome; ☎06 854 561. Foro Bonaparte 16,
20121 Milan; ☎02 85421.

Creditwest: Via Santa Margarita 7, Milan; ☎02-8813.

433969; www.credem.it.

National Westminster Bank: Via Turati 18 20121 Milan; ☎02 6251; fax 02
6572869.

Woolwich Europe Ltd:= 30 Erith Road, Bexley Heath, Kent DA7 6BP; ☎020-
8298 4771; fax 020-8298 5315.

Italian Banks

The governing body of Italian banks is the Banca d'Italia (Via Nazionale 91,
00184 Rome). The biggest bank is the Banca Nazionale di Lavoro which is state
owned and comes fifteenth in the league table of European banks. Other larger
national banks include: Credito Italiano, Banco di Roma, Banco di Napoli,
Banco di Sicilia and Banca Commerciale Italiana.

It is ironic that from the tenth to the fourteenth centuries parts of Italy, in
particular Venice and Lombardy, were responsible for some of the most innovative
banking practices in Europe. The Italians virtually brought banking to England
(hence Lombard Street in London) and then the rest of the world. Thus medieval
Italy was the pioneer of banking in the Western world. The word *bank* itself is of
Italian origin. Yet Italian banking now looks to the Anglo-Saxon countries for its
terminology and innovation. Italian banks have become noticeably quicker and less
bureaucratic in the last few years whilst retaining the element of personal contact
which has disappeared in Britain. Italian agriculture, manufacturing and export
industries have always depended, for their undeniable success, on the co-operation
of local agricultural *agricola*, people's *popolare* and savings *risparmio* banks. In return
these neighbourhood banks have pumped their profits into local infrastructures.

An example is the Monte dei Paschi, di Siena – founded in 1472 as a
pawnbroker – which now finances the upkeep of Siena's buildings, streets and
medieval pageantry. Local recognition and trust are still vitally important in
Italian banking. Banks are part of the social capital; they give you a sense of
belonging. You should therefore check out the local banks in your area and open
an account with whichever is the most convenient.

To open an account all you need is:

- Your passport
- Your *codice fiscale* (an Italian tax identity number based on a formula from
  your passport data, and obtainable at the local tax office *ufficio delle imposte
  dirette.*
- Money.

This will obtain you a *conto estero* (foreign, i.e. non-resident account), and, if required, a cheque book, *un blocchetto di assegni,* and a credit or a *Bancomat* card, *carta Bancomat.* You need to be an Italian resident to open a normal current account, *conto corrente,,* but this requirement is often waived, and you are treated as a local. An advantage of the *conto estero* is that you can keep it in pounds, dollars, or Swiss francs if you prefer.

In Italy it is a criminal offence to issue a dud cheque. For this reason it is a good policy to keep friendly with your bank manager; he or she may allow you to go into the red – rather than into a black list – should any of your cheques inadvertently overdraw your account. To cash a cheque the payee has to endorse it with his or her signature on the back; especially with tradesmen, very often you will be asked to pay someone with a cheque made out to yourself,*a me stesso/a, me medesimo/a* or *mio proprio,* and endorsed by yourself. This can then be exchanged for cash at a bank which trusts both parties. The correct figures and the signatures are important. With the euro the cents *centesimi* have to be shown as follows, even if they are zeros:

○ €300,00 (in figures: note the comma, which is normally pre-printed).
○ *trecento*/00 (in letters; note the forward slash).

The wording must be in Italian. Cheques for more than €10.329,14 (corresponding to twenty million lire) must be crossed with the words *non trasferibile* (non transferable) and the payee, *beneficiario,* must be named; as required by the anti-money laundering law, *la legge antiriciclaggio.* Note that the dot and comma in Italian numbers are the reverse of the English usage.

The Bancomat card enables you to pay bills and tolls, and to obtain cash, by dialling a PIN number directly on to the dial supplied by the shop, hotel, restaurant, petrol station, toll booth or cash machine. Debiting is instantaneous. You should not allow anyone to see the number you are dialling. The Bancomat card can also be used as an ordinary credit card. It has a monthly limit which can be renegotiated.

A vital function of a local bank is to pay your utility bills by standing order, *ordine permanente.* You simply take in your current utility bills, *bollette,* to get this set up.

Useful Addresses

Banca Nazione di Lavoro: Direzione Generale, Via Vittorio Veneto 119, 00187 Rome.

Banca Nazionale dell'Agricultura (BNA): Direzione Centrale, Via Salaria 231, 00199 Rome.

Credito Romagnola: Via Zamboni 20, 40126 Bologna.

Istituto Bancario San Paolo di Torino: Via della Stamperia 64, 00187 Rome; ☎06 85751; 06 857 52400. Piazza San Carlo 156, Turin; ☎011-5551.

Istituto Monte dei Paschi di Siena: U.S.I.E. Sett. Serv. V.le Toselli 60, Siena.

UK MORTGAGES

A number of people planning to buy second homes in Italy arrange loans in the UK – taking out a second mortgage on their UK property and then buying with cash in Italy. It is possible to approach UK banks and building societies for a sterling loan in this way. Note that this is different from approaching the subsidiaries of high street names such as Abbey National and Woolwich which are located in Italy and are in effect no different from Italian banks when dealt with in Italy.

The method of calculation for the amount you are borrowing, if you are borrowing in the UK, is at two and a half times, or three and a half, times your primary income plus any secondary income you may have, less any capital amount already borrowed on the mortgage. Sometimes the amount that may be borrowed is calculated at two and a half times joint income, less outstanding capital. Your credit history will also be checked to assess whether you will be able to manage increased mortgage payments. It is most usual for buyers to pay for their second home with a combination of savings and equity from re-mortgaging an existing property.

Naturally, the mortgage will be subject to a valuation on any UK property and you can expect to borrow, subject to equity, up to a maximum of 80% of the purchase price of the overseas property, (compared with the availability of 100% mortgages for UK properties). If you are going to take out a second mortgage with your existing mortgage lender then a second charge would be taken by the mortgage company. Note that some lending institutions charge a higher rate for a loan to cover a second property.

UK and Italian Mortgages

Re-mortgaging or taking out a mortgage in the UK could have some advantages as it may be easier to arrange, and you may be able to borrow more than you would in Italy. If your income is in sterling it may make better sense to have a mortgage in the UK. Interest rates are however also an important consideration. As interest rates change frequently, it is up to the buyer to check the current interest rates in both countries to see which is lower before deciding whether to take out a mortgage in the UK or Italy.

The value of the euro is another variable that may affect your decision where to take out a mortgage. If it rises in value, and if you have a mortgage in Italy and you are sending money from the UK to Italy, you could be losing money every time you do this.

ITALIAN MORTGAGES

A mortgage, *un mutuo,* is normally required to buy, build or renovate a property.

In principle you borrow from a bank against the security of your property; if you default on your agreed repayments the bank repossesses the property. Most financial institutions such as the Abbey National, the Woolwich and the Deutsche Bank mentioned above tailor the mortgage and offer a personalised package including insurance cover. Different banks have different rules and possibilities. The smaller banks offer straightforward loans, and the insurance is up to you. Recent legislation in Italy has allowed any bank to issue mortgages, subject to strict rules against excessive usury; to protect the consumer. Non-residents are treated with more caution than Italian residents. The following arrangements are typical:

Purpose of mortgage:	primary or secondary residence for purchase, renovation or completion, or for other stated purpose.
Types of repayment:	fixed, variable, mixed or capped rates, or interest only. (see below)
Sum available:	up to 80% of the value of the property – 60% for non-residents. NB. valuations are conservative.
Duration:	normally 5, 10, 15, 20 years but up to 25 or 30 years.
Age limit:	mortgage to expire at age 65, 70, 75, or as long as you are able.
Frequency of repayments:	Monthly, quarterly or biennially.
Setting up expenses:	typically 0.20% of the sum borrowed, but variable.
Valuation expenses:	typically €300, but variable, sometimes free.
Occasional expenses:	typically €1,29 for every communication or €1,00 for each repayment.
Insurance cover:	insurance is compulsory, in favour of the bank, against the risk of fire, lightning, gas explosions, possibly also against the risk of impact of vehicles or aircraft, 'socio-political events', 'atmospheric events' burst pipes etc. Insurance premium to be paid in a one-off *una tantum* payment. Premium typically 0.21% of value of property for 20 year contract. A life assurance policy guaranteeing repayment in the event of your death, accident, illness or loss of job is optional.
Penalties for early redemption:	typically between 0.5% and 3% of residual capital, depending on the timescale.
Penalties for late payment or default:	late payments, *vitardati pagamenti,* are defined as ones made 30-180 days after the due date. They incur the application of interest on arrears, *interessi di mora.* If you are more than seven times late with your repayments – not necessarily consecutively – the bank can repossess the property. The bank will also foreclose on you if you fail to make a repayment within 180 days of the due date.

Collateral guarantees required:	A first degree state-registered mortgage, *ipoteca di primogrado,* of the property. Some banks accept – in addition or as an alternative – a life insurance policy, stocks and bonds, and the transfer to them of rental contracts. A third person can also give a guarantee, *fideisussione.*
Conditions:	You might have to open an account in the mortgager's bank. Sometimes it is a condition that the property be a first home *primaria abitazione* or that it only be used for residential purposes.
Evidence of income:	bank guidelines require proof that your repayments are not more than 33% of your disposable income.

There is an excellent Italian website dedicated to mortgages and loans for instant competitive quotations online: www.mutuionline.it.. There are over 20 banks, mostly Italian (but including Abbey National and Deutsche Bank) to compare on the website. In January 2003, the bank coming up with the most competitive quotes was *San Paolo IMI* for a ten year mortgage with monthly repayments.

- fixed rate: 5.40%
- variable rate: 4.07%
- mixed rate: 4.70% – 4.15% initial 24 months
- mixed rate: 4.17% – 4.15% thereafter.

In order to consider your mortgage the bank will require the following documentation, which it will photocopy:

- The preliminary sale documents, the *compromesso* or *preliminare di vendita,* between you and the vendor of the property in question, or a land registry proof of your title.
- Your passport.
- Your Italian fiscal code number, *codice fiscale.*
- Your most recent tax returns (at least three).
- Your most recent bank statements (at least three months).
- Any other documents proving your income.

The bank will also require documentation on the property itself, which only your surveyor, *geometra,* can supply:

- *La provenienza del bene* – The provenance of the property.
- *Il certificato storico ventennale* – a twenty year retrospective certification of the property.

Non-residents may find it difficult to obtain a mortgage to buy a dilapidated or isolated rural property, but easier to buy it first and then obtain a mortgage for renovation.

The bank will normally require at least four weeks to process your application. The next step is to get the mortgage registered officially with a notary (*notaio*) who will require you and the representative of the bank to sign a deed in his presence, which he will then register against the title of the property in the local Land Registry, *L'ufficio del Registro*. You must set up the appointment with the notary well in advance, if necessary giving a power of attorney to a third party to sign on your behalf *una delega* or *procura speciale*. You, not the bank, have to pay the notary's fees which are at the notary's discretion .

What Kind of Mortgage?

Fixed rate	– if you want to be sure of the exact amounts and the end total, in advance, and if you foresee growing inflation.
Variable rate	– if you foresee a drop in inflation, have a medium to high income and like taking risks.
Mixed rate (renegotiable every 24 months)	– if you are unsure of the present state of the economy and want to have the option of adapting to more advantageous conditions in the future.
Capped rate	– if you want to keep to a flexible rate whilst limiting the risks, and at the same time retain the guarantee of a fixed rate without the extra costs.
Balanced rate	– if you have a feel for market movements and like to manipulate the balance between fixed and variable rates.
Interest only	– if you expect to be able to pay off the capital sporadically.

Banks sometimes offer cheap promotional introductory rates for a brief initial period (3-6 months).

Useful Contacts

Casa Travella: (www.casatravella.com) ☎01322-660988) is a property agent that may be able to give assistance with obtaining mortgages with some banks, for instance Banca Popolare di Sondrio in Como, or Banca di Toscana depending on the region and the branches.

Conti Financial Services: 204 Church Road, Hove, E Sussex BN3 2DJ; ☎0800-018 2811; fax 01273-321269. Conti have many years of experience arranging finance for clients (both UK and non-UK nationals) purchasing properties overseas as independent mortgage brokers.

Taxes on Mortgages

A single tax called an *imposta sostitutiva* of 0.25% is levied by the notary on the

delivery of the mortgage. It is so called because it is a substitute for the previous stamp duties and VAT taxes in force.

Tax Concessions on Mortgages

Interest payments on a mortgage for the purchase of a first home are deductible from the IRPEF tax (see below). The deduction is at the rate of 19% on a maximum sum of 3,615 euros, subject to certain conditions, and only if the property has become your principal residence within one year of purchase. There are also tax concessions on the expenses of renovation.

OFFSHORE MORTGAGES

Another option open to expatriates is to take out an offshore mortgage. For convenience and tax-free interest on their savings, expatriates often utilise offshore banking and financial services. Jersey, Guernsey and the Isle of Man are the prime offshore banking centres in Europe, along with Switzerland, Liechtenstein and Luxembourg for those with a lot of money. Banks in Jersey, Guernsey and the Isle of Man operate under UK banking rules and offer reliable and efficient banking and financial services, including Euro mortgages for buying property in Europe.

Offshore mortgages work slightly differently to standard mortgages and potential mortgagees should investigate them thoroughly before taking one on. Articles on offshore mortgages and details of providers can be found in expatriate magazines such as *FT Expat, Nexus* etc. Independent mortgage brokers who advertise in the expatriate magazines should also be able to advise you on offshore financial services.

IMPORTING CURRENCY

When buying property in Italy, you will, under normal circumstances have to pay in euros, the local currency. In the days of foreign exchange controls, before 1974, it was usual to take a suitcase full of pound notes over to Italy to pay for your property. Thanks to the Single Market, you can take as much cash as you like with you, but there is no advantage in doing so, and it is certainly risky. If you take more than €10,330 (about £6,000) in cash with you into Italy, you are required to declare it to customs. Taking a large amount of cash is not only risky, but you could be suspected of being a drugs dealer or terrorist by Italian customs if they find out.

Currency is nowadays normally sent using electronic transfer; the SWIFT system is the most well-known. There are charges involved at both ends so you need to know who is paying for them, and how much the receiving bank in Italy is likely to charge. The receiving bank should charge very little. The use of banker's drafts is not recommended as they are far too slow, and there is a risk of losing the draft.

Since the UK is not part of Euroland, anyone buying property abroad is confronted with the painful possibility that a percentage of their money is going to disappear into the coffers of a high street bank. Fortunately, this need not be the case, since a number of specialist companies have started up to lessen the financial penalty of the transaction.

A specialised company such as Currencies Direct (Hanover House, 73-74 High Holborn, London WC1V 6LR; ☎020-7813 0332; fax 020-7419 7753; wwww .currenciesdirect.com) can help in a number of way, by offering better exchange rates than banks, without charging commission, and giving you the possibility of 'forward buying' – agreeing on the rate that you will pay at a fixed date in the future – or with a limit order – waiting until the rate you want is reached. For those who prefer to know exactly how much money they have available for their property purchase, forward buying is the best solution, since you no longer worry about the movement of the pound against the euro working to your detriment. Payments can be made in one lump sum or on a regular basis. It is usual when building new property to pay in four instalments, so-called 'stage payments'.

There is a further possibility, which is to use the services of a law firm in the UK to transfer the money. They can hold the money for you until the exact time that you need it; they will use the services of a currency dealer themselves.

MAINTAINING UK AND/OR OFFSHORE ACCOUNTS AND TRUSTS

The majority of expatriates do not normally choose to transfer all their assets into their Italian bank account. There are sound reasons for this. Not only are bank charges very high in Italy, but one is liable to attract the grasping hands of the Italian tax authorities. The consensus seems to be that one should maintain an account outside of the country (either 'at home' or 'offshore' somewhere) and transfer the minimum funds needed as cash to Italy. Credit and/or debit cards linked to accounts outside the country can be used to make purchases in Italy and also have the advantage that it can take weeks for the charge to reach the account in question. If UK citizens do maintain accounts in the UK it is essential to inform the British tax authorities and the bank that they are resident abroad in order to prevent double taxation.

Offshore Banking

One of the financial advantages of being an expatriate is that you can invest money offshore in tax havens such as the Isle of Man, the Channel Islands and Gibraltar, thus accruing tax-free interest on your savings. Many such facilities are as flexible as UK high street banking and range from current accounts to long-term, high interest earning deposits. Mortgage facilities are also available (see above). Many of the banks that provide offshore facilities have reassuringly familiar names and include a number of building societies that have moved into this field since demutualising.

Useful Addresses

Abbey National: PO BOX 824, 237 Main Street, Gibraltar; ☎010 350 76090; fax; www.abbeynationaloffshore.com.

Alliance & Leicester International Ltd.: P.O.B. 226, 10-12 Prospect Hill, Douglas, Isle of Man IM99 1RY; ☎01624 663566; fax 01624 617286.

Barclays International Personal Banking: PO Box 784, Victoria Road, Georgetown, Jersey JE4 8ZS, Channel Islands; ☎01534 880 550; fax 01534 505 077; www.internationalbanking.barclays.com.

Brewin Dolphin Bell Lawrie Ltd. Stockbrokers: 5 Giltspur Street, London EC1A 9BD; ☎020-7246 1028; fax 020-7246 1093.

Bristol & West International: P.O.B. 611, High Street, St Peter Port, Guernsey, Channel Islands GY1 4NY; ☎01481-720609; fax 01481-711658; www.bristol-west.co.uk/bwi/.

FT Expat: Subscriptions, Oakfield House, 35 Perrymount Road, Haywards Heath, West Sussex RH16 3DH; England; ☎01444 445520; fax 01444 445599; www.ftexpat.com

Halifax International (Jersey Ltd): P.O.B. 664, Halifax House, 31-33 New Street, St. Helier, Jersey; ☎01534 59840; fax 01534 59280.

HSBC Bank International: P.O. Box 615, 28/34 Hill Street, St. Helier, Jersey JE4 5YD, Channel Islands; ☎01534 616111; fax 01534 616222; www1.offshore.hsbc.co.je.

Lloyds TSB Offshore Centre: P.O. Box 12, Douglas, Isle of Man, IM99 1SS; ☎01624 638104; fax 01624 638181; www.lloydstsb-offshore.com.

Nationwide Overseas Ltd: 45-51, Athol Street, Douglas, Isle of Man; ☎01624 663494.

Woolwich Guernsey Limited: P.O. Box 341, La Tonnelle House, Les Banques, St. Peter Port, Guernsey GY1 3UW; ☎01481 715735; fax 01481 715722.

ITALIAN TAXES

There are numerous taxes in Italy and so only the main ones that expatriates will be most likely to come across will be covered below. As the tax regulations change frequently it is worth checking frequently what the current situation is. Information is available on the internet though self-employed expatriates earning income in Italy are well advised to employ an accountant with experience of working with expatriates in order to avoid double taxation. You can spend up to 183 days a year in Italy and still be regarded by the tax authorities as resident in your home country. *The Informer*, an English language website (www.informer.it) for expatriates in Italy is a goldmine of advice on tax issues and goes into much more detail than is possible here. The taxes expatriates might incur are:

Imposta sui redetti delle persone fisiche **(IRPEF).** This is levied in a format most people are used to, i.e. it is a progressive tax that increases with the amount you earn. US citizens in particular are likely to consider the rates very high. However, Italians get a lot in return for their taxes in the form of pensions, health care and other social security benefits and the rates are not the highest in the EU. Tax rates begin at 23% and go up to 45% for high earners. Employees have the taxes deducted at source every month by their employer based on an estimate of the year's tax – any necessary adjustment will be made early in the following year. Self-employed workers operate under a complicated system whereby some taxes are paid at source and some in arrears – expert advice from an accountant is recommended.

Imposta regionale sulle attività produttive **(IRAP).** This is a corporate tax that is charged to every business no matter how small. The rate is decided by the region in which the business is located. IRAP also includes health contributions. It is a tax on services and goods produced, on the difference between the value realised after specified production costs (except labour costs) have been deducted. The basic rate of IRAP is around 4.25%, but as with ILOR there is a reduced agricultural rate (3%). The rate for banks, insurance companies and other financial services is approximately 5%. IRAP was once levied directly into the National Treasury but is now a regionally payable tax, so local rates can vary.

Imposta sui redditi delle persone giuridiche **(IRPEG).** This is a corporate tax levied on S.r.l. and S.p.A. type companies; not generally applicable to self-employed workers.

Imposta sul valore aggiunto **(IVA).** This is VAT (value added tax) and is levied on all sales, whether retail or wholesale, and even by consultants and other businesses who do not sell an actual product. There are three rates of 4%, 10% and 20%, the standard rate being 20%. Most foodstuffs are taxed at 10%. For other goods including most clothing, shoes, records, cassettes and certain alcoholic goods the rate is 20%.

Social security contributions. Whilst these are not really a tax, they amount to approximately 10% of income.

When trying to estimate your tax bill it should be borne in mind that a number of allowances are available that can be deducted from the taxable income and therefore reduce the amount of tax payable. Therefore, a married employee with a dependant spouse and two children in full-time education will pay much less tax than a single, childless employee. Housing allowances, education allowances, overseas living allowances and many of the other benefits that expatriates may enjoy are all counted as part of the income and their value will be taxed and added to the tax liability.

2003 INCOME TAX RATES (IRPEF)

Income	Tax rate
up to €15.000,00	23%
€15.000,00 to €29.000.00	29%
€29.000,00 to €32.600,00	31%
€32.600,00 to €70.000,00	39%
over €70.000,00	45%
Regional and municipal IRPEF vary according to the region and city of residence.	

ALLOWANCES IN EUROS FOR DEPENDANT SPOUSE AND CHILDREN FOR 2003-2004

Spouse

Total income up to €15.493,71	€546,18
€15.493,71 to €30.987.41	€546,18
€30.987,41 to €51.645,69	€496,60
Over €51.645,69	€422,23

Children

	Up to €51.645,69	Over €51.845,69
General Conditions		
For the first child	€303,68	€285,08
For each further child	€336,73	€285,08
If single parent – for the first child	same allowances as for spouse (see table above)	
Further deductions for each child under 3 years	€123,95	€123,95

Other allowances, up to a maximum of 19%, including medical expenses, life assurance, mortgage interest on property in Italy and limited university tuition fees can also be claimed in certain circumstances.

Other Taxes

Apart from the main taxes listed above there are a multitude of other taxes payable by those living in Italy, which include:

○ Rubbish disposal (*nettezza urbana*) and water rates (*acquedotto comunale*). Note that the first two listed above are based on the floor area of the property. House owners with their own independent water supply such as a well or spring are exempt from water rates. Note also that for second houses these charges are higher. This is to ensure that the better off pay more tax.

○ Car (or other motorised vehicle) tax.

○ TV licence fee.

Tax Evasion

Tax evasion in Italy is a popular topic of conversation and supposedly occurs on a grand scale, mainly amongst the self-employed. Though Italians reputedly do it, expatriates should consider the implications of doing it themselves and getting caught – being put in an Italian prison, deportation, the financial burden of playing catch-up with the tax authorities. It has been estimated by the tax inspectors' organisation, *Il Servizio Centrale degli Ispettori Tributari*, that 83% of the self-employed category declare an annual income of less than £4,000. The reason such modesty does not attract the attention of the *Guardia di Finanza*, (a.k.a. *i Finanzieri*, the tax police) is that they are often in on the fraud at the highest levels. It is probably a mark of their schizophrenia that from time to time, *i Finanzieri* feel obliged to indulge in advertising campaigns to remind the public and themselves that they are there to root out the culprits, and not to co-operate with them. However, despite the enormity of the problem facing them, the Finance Ministry has been making progress in catching tax evaders, especially as far as high income earners are concerned. *I Finanzieri* have proved more effective than might have been expected in pursuit of offenders. Foreigners become taxable as residents if they are working in Italy for 183 days or longer and technically all their worldwide income is taxable.

Deciding to pay one's taxes gives rise to its own set of problems, particularly if one is in business or self-employed, as the system is constantly being amended. Unfortunately, new taxes are often brought in without the old ones being cancelled. This induces a permanent state of chaos in the tax system so that it is extremely difficult to ascertain which taxes one is actually liable for. However, it is undoubtedly better to pay some taxes rather than none at all. It is probably unwise to proceed without the services of an accountant (*commercialista*) preferably obtained through personal recommendation.

To combat tax evasion that the authorities decide to investigate, but that they can not actually prove, they have devised a cunning, if arbitrary, scheme for assessment based on perceivable assets. For instance, yachts, expensive cars, estates and household staff are all deemed to represent, according to their size and quantity, a specific amount of income. Since Italians are born showoffs, there is little chance that they will resort to driving around in battered Lancias in order to conceal their assets and lower the likelihood of being hit with a hefty tax bill.

There are other peculiarities regarding the Italian tax system: unlike Britain where the tax office will chase you to fill in a tax form, in Italy it is up to the individual to present him or herself at the *Intendenza di Finanza* (local tax office) to fill in a standard tax form (known as a *modello unico 740*) and be given a *codice fiscale* (tax number). A *codice fiscale* is needed in order to work, and for various transactions such as property and car purchase, rentals and bill payments.

Owing to the fact that Italian personal taxation rates can be very steep at the higher levels it is advisable not to have all one's assets in Italy if one can avoid it. The alternatives, as already mentioned above, are to maintain offshore accounts or investments in such places as Luxembourg. Owing to the complexity of taxation it is strongly recommended that you take independent, expert financial advice before moving to Italy as well as after arrival. A list of such advisors in the UK can be obtained from the Financial Services Authority (25 The North Colonnade, Canary Wharf, London E14 5HS; ☎020-7676 1000; www.fsa.gov.uk).

The estimated amount of both income and business taxes are payable in two tranches in May and November. There are big fines for non-payment and under estimation of the amount due. Late payment is also penalised with fines.

Further information and advice can be obtained from:

British Chamber of Commerce in Italy: www.britchamitaly.com.

American Chamber of Commerce in Italy: www.amcham.it.

Penta Consulting, Business & Fiscal Advisor Firm; tax-law-firm@geocities.com; www.geocities.com/WallStreet/4019/.

Invest in Italy, Investor Advisor; http://investinitaly.com.

Studio di Consulenza Aziendale:, Accountant, Largo Augusto, 3 – 20122 Milano, Italy; tel. 02 796141; fax 02 796142; info@cosver.com; www.scaonline.it.

REAL ESTATE TAXES

The majority of those buying a house in Italy will have only two taxes to pay: the ICI and the IRPEF, for which you are well advised to consult a local accountant or *commercialista*. A *commercialista* is a qualified professional registered in the local *Albo dei Dottori Commercialisti* who will take care of all your taxes, for a fee. It is impossible to navigate the labyrinth of Italian taxes without the help of a *commercialista*.

The ICI is the *Imposta Comunale sugli Immobili*, or property tax, which is levied by the local borough council *comune*, and calculated according to their own criteria within minimum and maximum limits imposed by the state, and in proportion to the *valore catastale* or rateable value of the property. It is payable in two instalments – normally at the post office – in June and December. When you buy your property you – or your *commercialista* must report it to the *comune* in a *dichiarazione* ICI. It is an unpopular new tax, which seems cheap to foreigners, averaging about €1,000 per year per property, with a reduced rate for primary residences.

The IRPEF tax is the *Imposta sul Reddito delle Persone Fisiche*, literally tax on the income of physical, as opposed to juridical, persons i.e. income tax, levied at between 23% and 45% at the time of writing. Whether you are resident or non-resident, your property is regarded by the state as having a *rendita catastale*, literally a land registry (notional) income, which is taxable, even though it is yielding no actual rent. For details of IRPEF on earned income see *Italian Taxes* section above.

All habitable property must be registered in the urban building register, *catasto edilizio urbano,* which gives it a rateable value. IRPEF is payable in two instalments, June and November, the form required for it is :*modello di pagamento unificato* F.24. For more see details of IRPEF see the *Tax* section above. Both ICI and IRPEF are payable on-line. The IRPEF is under the control of the Revenue Ministry, *Ministero delle Entrate,* who have as enforcement officers not only the Tax Police, *Guardia di Finanza,* but also the *Carabinieri.*

Taxes due on the purchase and registry of property. Registry Tax *L'imposta del registro* of 3% of the purchase price of the property. Note that it is 7% if the property is a second home or the buyer is not resident in the municipality where the property is located which is often the case with a foreign purchaser.
For registering the preliminary contract of sale (optional) i.e. the *compromesso* or *contratto preliminare di compravendita*: €129,11; which is deductible from 0.5% levied on the deposit money or earnest *caparra confirmatoria* – subject to minor variations.
For registering the property on completion of the sale: principal residence €129,11 otherwise 1% of the declared value.

VAT on property bought from a builder or Cooperative. If you buy a property from a builder or a Cooperative Housing Association you have to pay:
1. 4% VAT if the property is going to be the buyer's main residence and he/she is resident in the same municipality where the property is located; or if the buyer is going to obtain residence in that municipality within 18 months of the date of purchase.
2. 10% VAT in all other cases (e.g. second home; if the buyer is not resident in the municipality where the property is located as is often the case with foreign purchasers).

REMOVAL OF INHERITANCE AND CAPITAL GAINS TAXES

What you lose on the swings you gain on the roundabouts: the Berlusconi government has 'suppressed' the capital gains tax, (the old INVIM), abolished the inheritance and gift tax, and there is no such thing as a wealth tax. One object of these cuts was to attract capital back to Italy, but there is no cause for rejoicing –
The capital gains tax on the sale of property might have been abolished but the IRPEF tax will still regard the profit on the property as income, *plusvalenza* if it is not the primary residence, and the abolition of inheritance tax does not affect

non-Italians: Italian law regards property owned in Italy by foreigners as subject to the inheritance taxes of their home country – that is the country in which they are domiciled. Italian residence alone is not enough for them to benefit from the Italian inheritance regime.

MOVING TO ITALY

Procedure for UK Residents. The situation is reasonably straightforward if you are moving permanently abroad. You should inform the UK Inspector of Taxes at the office you usually deal with of your departure and they will send you a P85 form to complete. The UK tax office will usually require certain proof that you are leaving the UK, and hence their jurisdiction, for good. Evidence of having sold a house in the UK and having rented or bought one in Italy is normally sufficient. You can continue to own property in the UK without being considered resident, but you will have to pay UK taxes on any income from the property.

If you are leaving your UK company to work for an Italian one then the P45 form given you by your UK employer and evidence of employment in Italy should be sufficient. You may be eligible for a tax refund in respect of the period up to your departure in which case it will be necessary to complete an income tax return for income and gains from the previous 5th April to your departure date. It may be advisable to seek professional advice when completing your P85; this form is used to determine your residence status and hence your UK tax liability. You should not fill it in if you are only going abroad for a short time. Once the Inland Revenue are satisfied that you are no longer resident or domiciled in the UK, they will close your file and not expect any more UK income tax to be paid.

If you are moving abroad temporarily, then other conditions apply. You are not liable for UK taxes if you work for a foreign employer on a full-time contract and remain abroad for a whole tax year (6 April to 5 April) as long as you spend less than 183 days in a year, or 91 days a year averaged out over a four-year period, in the UK. If you are considered a UK resident and have earned money working abroad then taxes paid abroad are not deductible. If you spend one part of a year working abroad and the rest in the UK you may still be considered non-resident for the part spend abroad, the so-called split tax year concession; this only applies to someone abroad for a lengthy period of time.

Italy has a double taxation agreement with the UK, which makes it possible to offset tax paid in one country against tax paid in another. While the rules are complex, essentially, so long as you work for an Italian employer and are paid in Italy then you should not have to pay UK taxes, as long as you meet residency conditions outlined above. For further information see the Inland Revenue publications IR20 *Residents and non-residents, Liability to tax in the United Kingdom* which can be found on the website www.inlandrevenue.gov.uk. Booklets IR138, IR139 and IR140 are also worth reading; these can be obtained from your tax office or from *The Centre for Non-Residents (CNR):* St. John's House,

Merton Road, Bootle Merseyside L69 9BB; ☎0151-472 6196; fax 0151-472 6392; www.inlandrevenue.gov.uk/cnr.

Procedure for US Citizens. The US Internal Revenue Service (IRS) expects US citizens and resident aliens living abroad to file tax returns every year. Such persons will continue to be liable for US taxes on worldwide income until they have become permanent residents of another country and severed their ties with the USA. If you earn less than a certain amount abroad in one tax year then you do not need to file a tax return. The amount 2002 was $7,200 for a single person; other rates apply for pensioners, married persons heads of household etc.

Fortunately, the USA has a double taxation agreement with Italy so you should not have to pay taxes twice on the same income. In order to benefit from the double taxation agreement you need to fulfil one of two residence tests: either you have been a bona fide resident of another country for an entire tax year, which is the same as the calendar year in the case of the USA, or you have been physically present in another country for 330 days during a period of 12 months which can begin at any time of the year. Once you qualify under the bona fide residence or physical presence tests then any further time you spend working abroad can also be used to diminish you tax liability.

As regards foreign income, the main deduction for US citizens is the 'Foreign Earned Income Exclusion', by which you do not pay US taxes on the first $80,000 of money earned abroad (as of 2002; the amount has in recent times gone up by $2,000 every year). Investment income, capital gains etc. are unearned income. If you earn in excess of the limit taxes paid on income in Italy can still be used to reduce your liability for US taxes either in the form of an exclusion or a credit, depending on which is more advantageous. The same will apply to Italian taxes paid on US income.

The rules for US taxpayers abroad are explained very clearly in the IRS booklet: *Tax Guide for US Citizens and Resident Aliens Abroad,* known as Publication 54, which can be downloaded from the internet on www.irs.gov. The US tax return has to be sent to the IRS, Philadelphia, PA 19255-0207; ☎215-516-2000.

INSURANCE

Italy has a bad reputation for petty crime – burglary, pickpocketing and theft. However, this is much worse in the cities than in country areas and villagers often leave their homes unlocked. The rates of crime detection are appalling – less than 10% of burglaries are solved. As a result, insurance premiums are high and because it is expensive to insure house contents, most Italians do not bother. Foreign residents from Britain will find that insurance quotes from Italian firms are at least double what they would expect to pay in the UK and North America – Turin and Milan, two of the most likely destinations for expatriate workers, also have some of the highest premiums in Italy. Italian insurance companies are also notoriously slow about settling claims.

Some English owners and permanent residents find it easier to insure their properties in Britain, particularly for the provision against loss of rent and for properties left unoccupied. SAGA provides cover for owners over 50 www.saga.uk. Schofields (www.schofields.ltd.uk) are specialised holiday home insurers with Lloyds' connections.

To protect their houses from burglary it is normal and advisable in Italy for ground floor windows to be protected by grilles, and shutters reinforced by iron bars and latches etc.

Most mortgages include a house insurance policy, and estate agents sometimes offer house and contents insurance at competitive rates to their clients and it is worth asking them about this. For owners of second homes, an alternative to an Italian insurer is to use a British company such as those listed below, who will insure rural properties in Italy. Annual rates vary depending on the extent of the cover but are roughly £4 per £1,000 of the house value and £9 per £1,000 of the contents value. It is important to note that if you are moving to the earthquake zone, most insurance policies exclude earthquake damage.

Owing to the expense of insuring city apartments, it is prudent to take anti-burglar precautions – multiple locks and bars on ground floor windows are two of the absolute basic requirements and an obvious deterrent to any prospective burglar.

Useful Addresses – UK based Insurers

Barlow Redford & Co: 71a High Street, Harpenden, Herts AL5 2SL, England; ☎01582-761129; fax 01582-462380.

Copeland Insurance: Roy Thomas (Managing Director), 230 Portland Road, London SE25 4SL; ☎020- 8656 8435); fax 020-8655 1271; service@andr ewcopeland.co.uk; www.andrewcopeland.co.uk. Provides insurance for both holiday homes and permanent residents.

John Holman: Broadway House, 1-7 The Broadway, Wickford, Essex SS11 7AQ; ☎01268-730733; fax 01268-730490. Has overseas house-insurance designed for owners of property in Europe (expatriate and holiday homes).

O'Halloran and Co: St James Terrace, 84 Newland, Lincoln LN1 1YA, England; 01522-537491; fax 01522-540 442; tpo@ohal.org. Will arrange cover for holiday homes in Europe.

Property Insurance Abroad: P O Box 150, Rugby CV22 5BR, England; ☎01788-550294; fax 01788-562579. Will provide a free quote.

Woodham Group Ltd.:= 1 Goldsworth Road, Woking, Surrey GU21 1JX, England; ☎0800-163180; www.woodhamgroup.com. Insurance Consultants linked to John Holman (above).

Italian Insurance Companies

Italian insurance companies generally cover the following risks:

- Public liability *responsabilità civile*
- Fire and material damage
- Water damage
- Broken glass
- 'Atmospheric events'
- Investigation of the damage

Agencies vary considerably in the guarantees they offer and in their interpretation of them.

Be careful to note whether your valuation of the property is index-linked in the contract (*indicizzata*).

The contract is based on the information you give which is generally as follows:

- Year of construction of the building,
- Use of the rooms: living, working, storing, etc,
- State of upkeep of the building.

The value of the house is based on the cost of rebuilding it from new including plumbing, wiring and heating, but excluding the value of the site. The local college of builders usually provides their updated formulae to calculate his figure. You are allowed by law, to ask the insurer for an independent estimater.In the event of an accident you must inform the insurer in writing within the terms of the contract – usually three days. The contents and furniture are included in a comprehensive policy if you are permanently resident in a house at a reasonable rate, but if the house is a holiday home, or left empty for long periods, the Italian premiums asked on furniture are prohibitively high – as much as 7% of the value. This reflects the fear of burglary.

In 2003 annual insurance premiums for holiday houses in rural Tuscany by the Reale Mutua insurance company were between €200 and €500. A separate policy on a swimming pool was €153. Reale Mutua, (founded in 1827), is the largest mutual insurance society in Italy with 356 branches, tradition, innovation, banking, www.realemutua.it. In some rural areas an old-fashioned tally-man or insurance agent still operates, calling on householders and issuing reminders in person, from Reale Mutua.

FINDING PROPERTIES FOR SALE

CHAPTER SUMMARY

- Italy has 20 regions in which you can search for property.
  - In theory, you can live anywhere in Italy but practicalities and proximity of facilities usually play a large part in property choices.
- It is easier to find an English-speaking agent in the popular areas like Tuscany and Umbria.
  - Le Marche is getting very popular.
- **Estate Agents.** Increasingly Italian estate agents are learning English to cope with the demand from English-speakers.
  - Italian estate agents have to be qualified and possess indemnity insurance.
  - Estate agents charge a fee for viewing properties after a crack down on time wasters wanting a free tour of the countryside.
  - Estate agents in Italy advertise a great deal of property on the internet.
  - Remember that estate agents need to get rid of remote hovels, as well as prime property.
- **Local Contacts.** Websites are not usually the best places to find property to buy.
  - Making local contacts in your chosen area is likely to pay off in your search.
  - Locals who can help include *geometres* (surveyors), builder's merchants, bank personnel and even the barber.
  - Old-fashioned communities may have a *mediatore* a kind of facilitator who has a good memory for what property is likely to be for sale.
  - The mediatore is in the process of being formalised into a profession by younger people.

Italy is divided into 20 regions and these are divided into 95 provinces. *There are five regions with special autonomy:-* Valle d'Aosta, Trentino-Alto-Adige, Fruili-Venezia-Giulia, Sardinia, Sicily, *and 15 with ordinary autonomy:*

Piedmont, Lombardy, Veneto, Liguria, Emilia-Romagna, Tuscany, Umbria, Marche, Lazio, Abruzzo, Molise, Campania, Puglia, Basilicata, Calabria.

Each region governs itself but the general electoral system remains under State law. The widely varying historical development has meant that strong regional differences persist in Italy, so it can be a difficult task to choose which region is for you. Moving to Italy requires a lot of thought so that you locate to the right region. The exodus to the Mediterranean is part of the hedonistic revolution which has glorified the Mediterranean diet and the perceived lifestyle which is part of our advertising imagery i.e. Granny and Grandpa eating salads and olive oil and dancing and swimming at 'the fountain of youth'. Many purchases in Italy are probably romantic and spur of the moment decisions which might land you with a romantic ruin which could mean years of restoration. There are many factors to influence your choice i.e. proximity to shops, schools for children, health care, transport system, climate, is the area prone to flooding, earthquakes etc., location of airports and a friendly community. If you are going to buy a *casale* (farmhouse) in the middle of the countryside you might find some roads to it inaccessible without a 4x4 vehicle.

For working expatriates, those who have been posted to a certain region for employment purposes; the north of the country is most likely to be their destination, especially Milan and Bologna, or in the south, Rome or possibly Naples. There is no disputing that Italy has glorious scenery, an impressive cultural heritage, and a relaxed lifestyle. In theory it is of course possible to live anywhere in the country but in reality it depends on the considerations mentioned above and of course your ability to speak Italian (or the availability of English-speaking estate agents and other expatriates to socialise with) your budget limitations and the prospect of living in an earthquake zone. Another consideration is the resale value of your property. At some point in time you may want to consider this. Is the area fashionable? Does the area have all the facilities to attract buyers?

Choosing a location means checking out all these criteria:

- Shopping: If you live in the country, your access to shops will be very limited. At best there will be a small shop (*alimentari*) that sells all the basic foodstuffs like, bread, eggs, cold meats, cheeses, canned goods and a selection of cleaning materials. The *alimentari* will often be a bar and tobacconist too. Some of these shops have a delivery van, which is stocked up once a week and driven to areas where there are no shops for miles. If you can't get to the shop, it comes to you, though the prices will be high for this convenience shopping. The food is always fresh and home-grown, fruit and vegetables, free range eggs, olive oil and wine are readily available from the van. If you live near a town or village there is always a plentiful supply of supermarkets (*supermercato*) i.e. co-op, and often a weekly market selling everything from fresh fruit to socks. A fishmonger (*pescivendolo*) can be found at the market and many drive to outlying hamlets at least once a week. The very large cities have enormous retail parks (*centri commerciali*) where the large supermarkets e.g. *ipercoop* have absolutely everything you want.

O Schools: If you are moving to Italy and have children of school age – then it is a priority that you locate near schools or if a few miles away and there is no school bus provided ensure you have reliable transport and well maintained roads so that you can cope with all weather conditions.

O Health care: Thirty years ago when expatriates reached 70 they would return to Britain because of the health care. It is important to check out where the nearest hospital is. Some regions have better hospitals and medical care facilities. The Southern Regions e.g. Calabria are not as good as say Lombardy in the north. Finding and registering with a local doctor (some speak English) especially if you have young children or an illness which needs monitoring, then healthcare should be a priority. See chapter on Health.

O Climate: If you want to bask in hot sunshine then you should look to the southern regions of Italy including Sardinia and Sicily, but make sure you have air-conditioning as the temperatures reach 30 degrees Celsius or more, and it's just too hot for many, so it is worth considering purchasing a property further north at Lake Garda or Friuli where the summer temperatures are three or four degrees lower.

O Transport: If you have a job that requires international travel then close vicinity to an airport is vital. If you live near Volterra, or further south in the Maremma area of either Lazio or Tuscany you will need a car to get to a railway station, bus depots or airports. Regions in the north such as Lombardy, Veneto and Liguria have better connections because of a larger infrastructure network. The south and Sicily except for areas near airports e.g. Brindisi, Naples – are difficult to access and as a result are not so attractive.

Another factor which may affect your decision is whether you need English-speaking back up, or want to go native? If you feel you need English-speaking backup, find a location where there are colonies of English speakers. Remember this is not like Spain or France where English-speaking infrastructures have been set up in several areas. In Italy it is useful to go to an area where there are other English speakers e.g. Umbria, Tuscany, and the Marche. The sort of people who are attracted to Italy might be kindred spirits and easy to befriend.

POPULAR LOCATIONS

Over the past three decades Italy has been the dream destination of thousands of Europeans, Americans and Australians who have a passion for Italian culture and the landscape. Umbria and Tuscany have been popular with overseas house buyers for so long because of their rural, peaceful and civilised charm creating an idealised form of England. Cortona, a hill town in South-east Tuscany is attracting a lot of Americans since the success of the book *Under a Tuscan Sun* (1996) by Frances Mayes, which has been made into a film. This is sure to attract more house-buyers. It is probably easier to find an English-speaking estate agent in these areas. Apart from Umbria and Tuscany there are other parts of Italy where the aesthetic attractions are equally as good; these include Le Marche. English people have been steadily emigrating to Le Marche as their first choice (instead of Tuscany) and attracted a colony of English-speaking people who, in certain areas now outnumber Germans whose traditional terrain this has been. There are a few English-speaking people with houses around the Lakes and the Ligurian Riviera but these parts are expensive and overcrowded. Today's expatriates are attracted to the countryside and especially the hills where property is cheaper, for example, the vineyards of Piedmont. Further south; Sardinia is becoming very sought after. The property prices are reasonable and there is a variety of places available to rival the Costas of Spain and Portugal.

When you have researched by reading (see *Where to Find Your Ideal Home – Regions*) and actually living in the region that interests you and when you have more or less decided what sort of property you want, then, the next step is to find an estate agent.

ESTATE AGENTS

A percentage of property sales in Italy are private in order to avoid paying agents' fees. However, estate agents (*agenzie immobiliari*) or other agents (*mediatori*) handle all other sales and you, as a purchaser, can be assured of quality of service and peace of mind throughout all the transactions. There are a large variety of estate agents to choose from and most are listed and advertise a huge selection of properties on the internet. Checking adverts on websites does not necessarily mean that you will find the best properties. There are other, possibly more fruitful methods like approaching contacts in your chosen area. Often, the best contacts are:

- *Geometras*
- Builders' merchants
- Bank personnel
- The local barber who hears it on the grapevine!

In old-fashioned rural communities, a tradition sometimes survives of a dealer/mediator (*mediatore*) or (*sensale*) whose function in the community is to provide a market place for houses and land. He has kept up his reputation and trust by a lifetime of discretion and honesty. The *mediatore* has a good memory, he seldom has a written description of the property which he has been entrusted with, but a vivid verbal one. In order to communicate with this archaic survivor you or a friend should have knowledge of the local dialect. Nowadays, a properly qualified younger generation, are taking over this business.

There are also amateur estate agents in the expatriate community who make it their business to seek out the desirable properties in their area in response to the ever-growing demand . You might think all the best houses have been sold but there is still a chance of an occasional gem cropping up.

Finding an Estate Agent

If you want to deal with an estate agent in your area look in the local Yellow Pages (*pagine gialle*) under estate agents (*Agenzie Immobiliari*). There is also an increasing number of estate agents who have premises located in high streets of towns and cities. More and more Italian estate agents now speak English and are used to dealing with foreigners; but you might feel happier using an agent from your own country located in Italy and you can find these in the English Yellow Pages (EYP). Whoever you choose, make sure you know what sort of property you are looking for and it is a good idea to have a rough idea of the market value as foreigners are generally perceived to be rich and so can easily pay too much.

English estate agents specialising in Italian properties are likely to be based in Italy. The Federation of Overseas Property Developers and Consultants – FOPDAC (3rd Floor, 95 Aldwych, London, WC2B 4JF) (www.fopdac.com; e-mail info@fopdac.com) is an association of English speaking agents, lawyers and other specialists in the property field who work with people looking to buy European property; companies must meet very strict criteria for membership.

Italian estate agents have to be professionally qualified and licensed and they are required to hold an indemnity insurance. They must also be registered (law introduced in February 1989) with the local Chamber of Commerce (*camera di Commercio*) and have a certificate issued by the local *comune* as proof of registration. An agent should also be registered with the Association of Real Estate Agents (AICI, Via Nerinos, 20123 Milan), the Italian Federation of Professional Estate Agents (FIAIP, Via Monte Zebio, 30, 00195 Rome; www,fiaip.it) or the Italian Federation of Mediators and Agents (FIMAA) (www.fimaa.it).

In city environments and resort areas estate agents are becoming more commonplace and it is worth visiting them methodically with a check list of what you are looking for. Make a note of everything and take photographs, all details and the date. Italian agents have grown wary of time wasters (*perditempo*) tourists who want a free tour of the countryside e.g. 'Dolly Duke who cruised around the country for two weeks in an obliging *mediatore's* Mercedes Benz without the remotest intention of buying; although by her appearance she was a woman of substance'. Italians have now grown wise to this practice and charge a fee for viewing properties. The fee is anything from €50 for an afternoon.

There is a specialised service from a company called Restoration Italia (www.re

storationitalia.com). For a specified fee (see website) they offer:

- ⟡ A comprehensive property search that details every aspect of the property.
- ⟡ Property procurement. With their team of professionals – you will be guided through the purchasing process and helped to find a lawyer (*notaio*).
- ⟡ Restoration services. Restore your home to your specifications.

This company deals with your registered Italian estate agents and together the purchase/restoration is completed with ease. The only drawback is that you the purchaser are on the sidelines like a spectator rather than the main protagonist. Restoration Italia is for someone who knows what he wants and is happy to hand over the planning and organisation to a third party.

 Remember, a lot of estate agents are trying to get rid of a lot of rubbish including some remote and distant hovels and you should check everything for yourself before eliminating them and that usually means looking at the property. Beware of con men (*imbroglioni*), who may well be of your own nationality, who will take a down payment or deposit to secure a property for you and then disappear. Always bring in a trusty professional and a *geometra* to double-check on the validity of the proposed sale.

Reliable Estate Agents

The Italian Federation of Professional Estate Agents (FIAIP) have printed a profile of a serious professional estate agent. How do you recognise a good agent?

- ⟡ He behaves like a professional at all stages.
- ⟡ He works with official documentation registered in the Chamber of Commerce.
- ⟡ He specifies clearly whether he is the principal or the intermediary. If it is his own house he is selling, he does not ask the buyer for commission.
- ⟡ He specifies in his written agency agreement the exact commission he will charge and that it will be on the actual price obtained and not on the declared price.
- ⟡ He does not ask for a higher commission on selling in the event of his getting a higher price than the agreed one.
- ⟡ He indicates clearly in the agency agreement whether he is to be refunded for any expenses for advertising or for any other extras.
- ⟡ In the case of an exclusive and irrevocable agency contract he will tell you what privileges you are allowed, such as freedom from having to pay expenses, a list of potential buyers and the official land documentation.
- ⟡ He refrains from inserting a tacit renewal clause in the agreement – or if there is one, he gives a reasonable short time within which to cancel the agreement.

○ He never pockets for his own use any sums of money he has received as a deposit from the buyer. He puts the deposit in the vendor's name and pays the vendor the balance immediately after he has completed the searches to guarantee the absence of liens and mortgages.

Respected agencies in Italy include *Gabetti* (www.gabetti.it), *Tecnocasa* (www.tecnocasa.it) and *Grimaldi* (www.grimaldi.net).These large agencies have regional offices throughout Italy but there are many agencies, which only specialise in one area or at the most four or five. A list of all registered estate agencies in Italy can be obtained from: FAIAP (www.faiap.it).

Looking at Properties

So you have found a property or properties that have aroused your interest. Here are some guidelines about how to proceed with the viewing process:

○ Before departing from home make sure the property you are interested in is still on the market.
○ Make a note of the property reference number.
○ Make an appointment to view the property.

In Italy you are nearly always shown around by the agent – because houses are lived in or often difficult to find.

○ If you can't keep an appointment you should contact the agent.
○ Investigate properties on arrival in Italy – in case you want to look at them again before departure.
○ View as many properties as you can.
○ Take photographs.
○ Make a note of a property's advantages/disadvantages. Measurements – etc.
○ Mark properties on a map in case you want to return.

Amateur Estate Agents

Sometimes amateur agents are better at conducting a discreet negotiation than the professional estate agent who advertises. For example, a rich American entrepreneur looking for a villa in Tuscany asked someone who had set themselves up as an amateur agent, to find him a villa. The owner of a villa met the agent socially and mentioned that he was considering selling his property, which included a villa. Within six weeks the deal was completed.

A lot of Italians want to sell their property but want to do it discreetly as they don't want a lot of people to know. As a result properties never reach estate agents, so it is worth enquiring if you see houses in need of renovation or ruins on farmland. Make enquiries about the ownership and track down the owner and if you are not fluent take a local interpreter with you and impress on the owner that you are the principal and not an agent and you want to negotiate (*trattative privata*). This could result in you getting a good property and the farmer retaining his.

On the other hand, it is more likely that the landowner is so happy to know his property is sought after and therefore of a high market value, that he will not sell. However, usually, everything has a price! If you make an agreement you must get a *geometra* to carry out any searches etc. before any money changes hands, see chapter on *Fees, Contracts and Costs*.

Useful Addresses
Estate agents in the UK & FOPDAC:

Brian A. French and Associates: ☎ 0870-7301910; fax 0870-7301911; e-mail loui se.talbot@brianfrench.com; www.brianfrench.com: Italian office 075-9600024 or mobile 340-341 5667 (Mr Steve Emmett). Offers one of the widest range of areas of any of the British agents including Tuscany, Umbria, Le Marche, Abruzzo and Calabria.

La Casa Emilia: 11 Westfield Avenue, Beverley, East Yorkshire HU17 7HA; ☎01482-679251;   e-mail   info@lacasaemilia.com;   www.lacasemilia.com. Specialists in Emilia Romagna, with properties ranging from luxury villas to traditional stone farmhouses.

Casa Travella; 01322-660988; fax 01322-667206; e-mail casa@travella.f9.co.uk; www.casatravella.com; Has agents mainly in Northern and Central Italy but will help locate contacts for all other regions and will help with relocation, restoration, etc.

Chalcross: 18 Market Place, Chalfont St. Peter, Bucks SL9 9EA; ☎01753-886335; fax 01753-886336. Will search for requested property on request, through an agent in Italy. Mostly searches for property for sale, particularly around Lucca in Tuscany. Contact: Kenneth Arton.

Eurovillas: 36 East Street, Coggeshall, Essex CO6 1SH; ☎ 01787-479191. In business for 30-40 years, they are a letting agency for the Lake Garda area and Tuscany around Lucca. They can also provide purchasing contacts in these areas and can rent accommodation from which to carry out a reconnaissance of likely properties to purchase.

Hello Italy: Woodstock, Forest Road, East Horsley, Surrey KT24 5ES, England; ☎01483-284011; fax 01483-285264; www.helloit.co.uk. Letting agent for northern Tuscany (about 30 minutes from the Ligurian coast). Can provide introductions to purchasing contacts in the area, help with restoration and building and sales after care. Many clients who buy have subsequently used Hello Italy as a letting agent.

Knight Frank: Head Office, 20 Hanover Square, London W1S 1HZ, ☎020-7629 8171; e-mail info@knightfrank.com; www.knightfrank.com an international agency with associates in Tuscany and North America (*Grub & Ellis*; 800-877-9066; www.grubb-ellis.com; with offices across America). North American clients can approach the London office of Knight Frank direct.

Piedmont Properties: Angelika Smith-Aichbichler; ☎01344-624096; www.piedmont.co.uk; info@piedmont.co.uk. Specialises in marketing villas and vineyards in the Monferrato and Langhe regions of southern Piedmont (south and west of Asti).

English-speaking estate agents in Italy:

In addition to the estate agents' addresses listed below, there are agents' websites in *Where to Find Your Ideal Home* at the end of each individual region's description, online agencies can be found via websites such as www.findaproperty.com and www.accommodation.com.

Barga Estate Agents: Piazza Angelio 15, 55051 Barga, tel/fax 0583-710275; e-mail info@barga-estateagents.com; www.barga-estateagents.com.

Consulenze Immobili Marche: Michael Sattler, Cascernia, 62032 Camerino; ☎+39 335 836 7630; fax +39 0737 630551; e-mail ctolkmitt@marcheproperty.com. Specialises in property in Le Marche.

House Around: Via Pesaro 16, 65121 Pescara; ☎+39 085 421 7301; e-mail enquiries@HouseAroundItaly.com. Helps non-Italian speakers buy property in Abruzzo.

John Tunstill: 61, via Cortonese, Calzolaro 06019, Pg; ☎+39 075 930 2428; e-mail properties@tunstill.it; www.properties.umbria.com. Specialises in developing properties for sale in the Upper Tiber valley of Umbria.

THE INTERNET

Another source of property for sale is the Internet where many properties are advertised. A search using any of the major search engines such www.google.com and www.dogpile.com will find numerous online agencies. There is also the Shop Cases section on the home page of Yahoo! Italia where property in most regions is advertised.

For information online about living in Italy you can access www.intoitaly.it. This website is especially for English-speakers. The Italian Embassy and tourist authority also supply the would-be immigrant with information on www.emit.it.

Some internet sites for property:

www.italyhousescont.com
www.turchi.it
www.casalieville.com
www.portocervoonline.com

www.restorationitalia.com
www.ideeresidenziali.it
www.lacasa.de
www.globalmart.co.uk

www.fiaip.it

www.tuscandream.com

www.real-estate-europeanunion.com

www.italian-realestate.com

www.casa.it

www.grimaldi.net

www.relocationagents.com

www.tuscany-on-thames.com

www.escapeartist.com

www.goitaly.com

www.gabetti.it

www.fimaa.it

ADVERTS

Italian newspapers and magazines include many homes for sale and often contain supplements dedicated to properties for sale, at least once a week. A glossary of terms that appear in such adverts is given at the end of this section.

Additionally there are magazines available for buyers in English e.g.

- *World of Property* (outbound@aol.com)
- *International Homes* (www.international-homes.com)
- *Homes Overseas* (www.homesoverseas.co.uk)
- *Italy* (www.italymag.co.uk)

Italy also produces real estate magazines:

- *Casa per Casa* (www.casapercasa.it)
- *Dimore-homes* (www.dimore.com)
- *Cerca Casa* (www.cercasa.it)
- *Ville & Casali*

PROPERTY EXHIBITIONS

There are an increasing number of property exhibitions organised in the UK, some by Outbound Publishing of Britain. Exhibitions give prospective buyers a chance to collect details of properties that are for sale and make useful contacts. You can also talk to the expert lawyers and estate agents that take stands at these exhibitions. Sometimes there are seminars dealing with different aspects of buying a house e.g. arranging a mortgage etc. At present, the majority of property exhibitions deal with France or Spain. However, Italy is increasing in popularity as a place to buy property and more Italian property exhibitions are likely. Exhibitions usually last for two days but more often they are at weekends. Exhibitions are advertised in magazines such as Homes Overseas and World of Property. If you want to know when and where the next exhibition is to take place you can log onto: www.tsn.co,.uk or www.internationalpropertyshow.com.

GLOSSARY FOR ITALIAN PROPERTY ADVERTS

Interior features:

Angolo cottura – cooking corner

Bagno – bathroom

Cantina – cellar

Camera – bedroom

Cucina – kitchen

Doccia – shower

Locale – room

Ripostiglio – storeroom

Riscaldamento – central heating

Servizi – kitchen, bathroom

Stanza – room

Sala – hall

Salotto – parlour

Tinello – living/dining room

Exterior features:

Cancello – gate

Cortile – courtyard

Campo da tennis – tennis court

Cotto – terracotta

Cemento – cement

Di pietra – of stone

Da restaurare – to be restored

Frutteto – orchard

Forno – bread oven

Giardino – garden

Infissi – collectively, doors and windows.

Legno – wood

Legnaia – woodstore

Piscine – swimming pool

Orto – garden (vegetable plot)

Restaurare – restore

Pozzo – well

Stufa – stove

Resede di terreno – plot of land attached to property

Tettola – canopy (tiled)

Tetto – roof

WHAT TYPE OF PROPERTY TO BUY

CHAPTER SUMMARY

O The majority of Italian homes are of a very high standard.

O Italy's historic town centres are usually residential districts where you can buy restored houses and apartments popular with all ages.

O Farmhouses are the most popular buy for foreigners.

O Italians prefer an apartment by the sea or a house in the mountains as a second home.

O **Planning.** Anyone buying an Italian farmhouse has to re-register it for 'urban' (as opposed to rural) use before renovation can legally begin.

   O Any change of usage from rural to urban has to be done through a *geometra* (surveyor).

O Abandoned hamlets found mainly in the south, or in remote mountain regions of the north, can be the ultimate restoration project.

   O Restored hamlets can be turned into accommodation to let out.

O **Condominiums.** Condominiums are minutely regulated by Italian law.

O For people working in a large Italian city, living in a block of flats with friendly Italian neighbours is probably preferable to living in a condominium full of foreigners or your own countrymen.

O *Comunione.* If entering into shared-ownership (*comunione*), it is essential to make a clear written agreement covering yourself against every conceivable eventuality.

O **Co-operative.** Buying as a co-operative means you have to have a minimum of nine members.

   O A co-operative is useful for groups with a communal interest like artists, craftsmen, small traders etc. where a community spirit is paramount.

How Italians Live

To understand the Italian property market and the availability of different types of accommodation it is necessary to understand how Italians live and the sort of homes they prefer. In the last 50 years there has been a raising of standards in Italian homes and these are now the envy of many European countries.

A high proportion of Italian families live in apartment blocks, many of which were built in the 1960s and 70s. Even when children move out of the parental apartment, usually to get married, they will voluntarily take a flat in the same block as their parents and continue to live as part of an extended family. As a result of the way Italians live, irremediably bonded in tight family units, bachelor apartments or single accommodation (i.e. small flats) can be extremely difficult to find.

Italian apartments are not very large and usually there are three bedrooms at most. However, this is not the case in Naples where there is a great deal of overcrowding resulting from poverty and an acute housing shortage. Many families in Naples live in large, single-room apartments in the notorious slums (*i bassi*) of that city.

Unlike the old city centres in other European countries, Italy's town centres, usually the old part (*centro storico*), are still thriving residential districts. The old cities are living cities with the residents living and working in the centre. The houses have been upgraded and improved and are popular with all ages of the community. Many buildings such as cinemas and inner city factories have been converted into luxury living accommodation as opposed to offices.

In Italy, the areas outside the centre are known as *il semicentro*, where most of the purpose-built apartment blocks are located. The suburbs (*la periferia*) are where the least well off generally live, although new housing estates with detached homes and gardens are appearing – Silvio Berlusconi made a fortune in some of the first such property developments in Italy.

Council accommodation (*le case popolari*) experienced an upsurge after 1964 when Law 167 was passed requiring local *comunes* to provide social housing for 40%-70% of the housing requirement of their area. As a result, there has been widespread building of these estates in recent times. The architecture and the quality of the building materials has improved since the boom years of the 1950s and 60s and today the estates are as good as those in the private sector. The estates built in central and northern Italy are on brownfield or valley sites, which do not impinge on the natural landscape. In the south and Sicily planners (or lack of them) are not as conscientious and a blind eye is often turned to illegal housing developments.

About 78% of Italian families are owner-occupiers, one of the highest rates in Europe. However, rich Italians looking for a second or holiday home in their own country rarely go for the type of rustic property favoured by foreigners. Italians are more likely to buy or rent a luxury seaside flat or a house in the mountains.

TYPES OF PROPERTY – GLOSSARY

Appartamento	apartment
Agriturismo	bed and breakfast on a working farm
Annesse	outbuilding
Attico	attic
Bilocale	apartment with 2 rooms
Box	garage
Casa	house or home general term
Casa canonica	priest's house, usually next to a church
Casa bifamiliare	semi-detached house
Casa padronale	landlord's mansion
Casale	farmhouse or small hamlet
Casetta	small house
Castello	castle
Capanna	barn
Cascina	farmhouse
Casa Colonica	farmhouse
Casolare	house in the country
Dependance	outhouse (granny flat)
Fienale	hay barn
Fattoria	working farm
Monolocale	studio apartment (one room)
Masseria	huge farming estate in the south
Mansarda	loft conversion
Maso	farm in Alto-Adige region (ancient Celtic word for home)
Palazzo	used to refer to any large building including blocks of flats.
Porcilaia/porcile	pigsty
Podere	farm (small holding)
Rustico	rustic property, usually in need of modernisation
Rudere	ruin
Stalla	stable
Terratetto	semi-detached house
Torre	tower
Trullo	stone house with conical roof (regional, Puglia)
Vilette a schiera	terraced house
Vigneto/Vigna	vineyard

APARTMENTS

Modern Apartments

Most modern *appartamenti* are constructed using a concrete frame, which is filled in with blocks. The majority of newer apartments were built in three decades from the 1950s. Buying apartments in city centres or by the coast is popular with foreigners. Internally, the walls are plastered and floors are *terrazzo* (tiled), with tiles made from marble and cement mixed, or ceramic, or marble. Some apartments come with fitted wardrobes in the bedroom and there will be bathroom porcelain plus the kitchen sink. All other furnishings and appliances have to be bought by the new owner.

Old Apartments

Nineteenth century and older apartments tend to have high ceilings beamed and often the walls and ceilings are elaborately decorated. The can be a range of materials including terracotta tiling and wood. Sometime tiles have been covered with marble. The stairs, sills and window frames are m of stone, marble or travertine (a light-coloured rock). Externally, the buildings are made of brick, often with peeling stucco. The problem with older buildings is that the fixtures, fittings, plumbing etc may be old fashioned. However, this appeals to some buyers.

RURAL PROPERTIES

Farmhouses (Casali)

Farmhouses in rural settings are the most popular buy with foreigners. The typical rural farmhouse of 60 years ago or more had the living quarters on the first floor and the animals were stabled on the ground floor. It was usual to climb outside stone steps to the first floor and enter into a very large kitchen with a hooded fireplace where the cooking would be done. The hearth and fireplace were a very important focal point for the family as it provided heat, meals, and a place for them to gather and sit. The bedrooms would be off this main living room. One of the advantages of having the cattle stabled below was that the rising heat from their bodies kept the chill off the bedrooms above. A typical farmhouse also has very thick stone walls to keep cool in summer and the cold out in winter. In the north of Italy where temperatures drop much lower, double-glazing is essential these days. Typically, rural farmhouses had an outside bread/pizza oven (*forno a legna*).

Property buyers should note that such farmhouses are classified as rural buildings and need to be registered for change of use to 'urban' otherwise renovation is illegal. It is as well to consider the implications of this when deciding what type of property to buy.

In planning matters the difference between a rural and an urban house is important:

A Rural Building. farmhouses, pigsties, outbuildings and the land have no value separate from the land. The property will be registered with a plan showing the land and buildings available, but there will be no interior details.

An Urban Building. An urban house (or apartment) is registered with a plan of the interior that has all the internal measurements.

Change of Usage. Any request for a change of usage from agricultural to urban (i.e. to a dwelling for people), is made through a *geometra* (surveyor) who will provide detailed drawings of any proposed improvements e.g. to convert former stables into a kitchen or the *capanna* (outbuilding) into a flat for renting out. The geometra will obtain the permission from the *comune* and then register with *il nuovo castasto* (land registry) who will ratify the permission to change from rural to urban use. Renovations can only start after permission is obtained.

Village Houses

Buying an old house in the historic centre (*centro storico*) of a small town or village can mean acquiring an architecturally and historically interesting (and possibly listed) building. The downside of living in an ancient dwelling is that it will probably need major renovation work. A modern property needs far less attention and will only need basic redecorating. Modern floors of marble or travertino, or sometimes parquet are very easy to care for.

What you will get in an old village house is probably a built-in bread oven (*il forno*) or a fireplace (or both) and probably a storehouse as well. These attractive features are not usually part of modern houses. Note that in villages any new housing is likely to be social housing (*case popolari*) under law 167.

Living in a village house has more advantages than living in a remote one:
- It is connected to a mains sewer
- It is connected to mains gas and electricity
- It has a reliable water supply
- It is close to public transport (buses and trains)
- The shops are close by
- There is proximity to health care and schools
- Access to staff for cleaning and gardening

The disadvantages are relatively few. Some people might find a village noisy or object to the regular ringing of church bells. There could also be a large influx of tourists depending on where you are.

There is definitely a trend of buying houses in villages, especially amongst Americans who enjoy the social life of an Italian neighbourhood. At the moment prices are reasonable, for example a typical medieval building for sale at time of going to press, in the old part (*centro storico*) of a southern Tuscan hill town with beautiful views, is valued at approximately €400.000,00. For this you get 150 square metres of habitable space on the first floor and the same area on the ground floor. Two large wooden doors open up into the old olive mill and at the back of this are two sandstone caves, which go underneath the village war memorial. The living quarters have been renovated to provide two flats which retain the character of the building. From the flats you step up to large storerooms and through them to a terrace. There is also an orchard of 400 square metres. In the same area, a rural property would probably cost from €660.000,00.

Estates and Vineyards (Ville e Vigneti)

Very large estates created by the nobility are found in the country usually within 50km of a city. Villas of this type can date from the late Renaissance or the highly ornate and extravagant baroque period of the 17th and 18th centuries. A great many estates have vineyards and olive groves attached and still in production which could be useful as a way of helping to fund the costs of running such an estate. Estates are however likely to be a minority requirement for prospective property buyers.

Ghost Towns (Paesi Abbandonati)

Ghost towns, abandoned by the *contadini* (country people) seeking a better or less harsh life, are found mostly in the southern regions, or in the north at high altitude and a long way from a city. Comprising a cluster of buildings they can be an interesting proposition for a buyer who likes a challenge. Abandoned villages are the ultimate restoration project and can be turned into hotels or other living accommodation that can be rented out. In Liguria, a former ghost village, Coletta di Castellano, has been turned into Italy's first cyber village. The village was purchased by a consortium that also arranged for Telecom Italia to sponsor a fibre optic link so that Coletta is a working village. The buildings have been transformed into modern apartments and the internet access for all means that those moving there can run a business from home if they wish.

Castles and Monasteries (Castelli e Conventi)

Castles and monasteries can be converted and restored into living accommodation for private individuals buying as a consortium. A group of twelve Canadians did just this, buying an abbey in Umbria. They arranged a restoration done to the highest standards and when not staying there, the members rent it out very successfully, thus recovering some part of the vast cost of the restoration. Some monasteries on the market come complete with frescos, cloisters and inevitably, a church or chapel within the main buildings. These properties are part of Italy's enormous architectural heritage and it can be very satisfying to bring such properties back to life.

NEW HOUSES AND VILLAS

New houses may not have the charm or magic of older properties (or their crumbling walls and ancient plumbing), but they do have several advantages. Modern building standards ensure than new houses are very comfortable and built to a high specification. New houses are also well insulated and double-glazed; central-heating and air-conditioning are fitted as standard. New property is also covered by a ten-year guarantee (*responsibilità della ditta*), against any defects in the structure. Most services such as the central heating system, are also guaranteed for a limited period. The types of new houses available are either part of a development, usually coastal or on the outskirts of cities or towns. Such properties are normally built and sold by property developers. There is normally a show house on site so you can get a good idea of what you are buying. The fittings are usually luxurious, especially bathrooms, and kitchens can be built to your specifications. Floors can be marble, ceramic of a high quality timber such as iroko (a pale hardwood from Africa). When completed they are ready to move into (*chiavi in mano*).

BUYING A PLOT OF LAND

Some people dream of picking their ideal spot for a house, buying the land and having a house built from scratch just for them. If this is your intention, before you buy land you should make sure that there is planning permission for building, and check that the size of your intended building and the proposed design is legal. This is a job for a *geometra* (surveyor) who will check at the local town hall (*comune*). You may be thwarted by regulations governing scenic regions, which prohibit building. Plots are usually located in a zoned development area (*terreno edificabile*) on the outskirts of a town.

It is normally easier to look for a large parcel of land with a small stone building or ruin on it and apply for planning permission to change it into a residence.

Further information about geometras can be found in *Fees, Contracts and Costs*, and building details in *Building or Renovating*.

CONDOMINIUMS

Most Italians live in apartment blocks in which each apartment is privately owned but certain facilities and structures are shared – such as the foundations, the roof, the bearing walls, the stairs, the entrance, drains, sewers, wells, corridors, terraces, courtyards, porter's lodge, boiler room, heating, car park etc. This is called a *condominio* – (condominium) – a social urbanistic phenomenon which spread greatly in the second half of the twentieth century and had to be regulated by new sections in the Italian Civil Code (*Codice Civile* articles 1117-1139), and continues to be regulated by new precedents and judgements handed down by law courts throughout Italy.

Condominio is differentiated from *comunione*, which is a simple form of co-ownership whereby each owner has a share of a property in its totality. *Comunione*, co-ownership, was an established concept in Roman Law which described it as *mater controversiarum* (the mother of controversies). *Condominio* is a more virulent member of the same family – to judge by the litigation it generates in Italy. Be wary therefore of buying into a condominium, but if you have to, it is worth knowing how it is regulated and how you will have to participate.

The fellow-owners in a *condominio* must form a committee (*assemblea*), to meet at least once a year, to pay the common bills, to budget and plan for maintenance etc.

If there are more than four owners, the annual appointment of an administrator (*amministratore*) becomes compulsory. Normally there will also be a professional *commercialista*, to keep minutes, exact contributions, pay bills, count votes and render accounts in accordance with well-defined legal guidelines.

If there are more than ten owners in the complex, the *condominio* is required by law to formulate a set of rules (*il regolamento*) listing the facilities and their use, the division of expenses, imposing rules and fines etc. from where you can hang your washing to where you can park your car.

The ownership of the shared facilities and expenses of a *condominio* is proportionate to the value of each individual property. This is counted in *millesimi* or thousandths – a thousand being the value of the entire complex. – and set out on a chart called a *tabella millesimale*. The common expenses (caretaking, cleaning, heating etc.) are paid for in accordance with this proportion of *millesimi*, but for some things such as lifts the payment is in proportion to their use and central heating is usually calculated in *millesimi calore* (heating thousandths).

The decisions of the *assemblea* are made by 51% majority vote. The quorum of the ownership required for voting is normally 50%; for certain decisions it is two thirds of the ownership; for others – such as for major architectural changes – complete unanimity is required.

The *condominio*, therefore, is minutely regulated by Italian law. If you buy into one, and wish to fight your own corner, it is essential to have a good grasp of the language, and also to consult updated publications and guidelines on the subject such as *Condominio* by Paola Bertolotti (de Vecchi Editore) or the www.ilsole24ore/website. The best bet, however, is to delegate a *commercialista* to act on your behalf.

A *condominio* which has separate buildings as part of an estate is known as a *supercondominio*. Most joint-owned resort complexes come under this heading. In many areas of Umbria and Tuscany where the stock of small isolated houses has been exhausted and only hamlets or large barracks-like structures are left for developers to divide up, units in a *condominio* or a *supercondominio* are the only properties on offer, usually in a pre-developed state.

The advantages of a *condominio* or *supercondominio* are:

- ⭕ The organisation and infrastructure are supplied.
- ⭕ Instant neighbours are on hand for socialising.
- ⭕ The sharing of expenses and economies of scale mean proper car parks, tennis courts, swimming pools, fitness rooms, landscaping, staff etc. are available, which *could* be beyond your reach if you were on your own.
- ⭕ Greater security against burglars – possibly.

The disadvantages are:

- ⭕ The possible stress of constant negotiation and contact with fellow members.

- The committee meetings, and the other duties required by condominium rules.
- The rising expenses which cannot be controlled if you are in a minority.
- The difficulty of controlling the nuisance level of your neighbours or their tenants.
- The future problem of selling on the property; condominiums often develop a culture or an ethos which buyers might find it difficult to buy into: too German, too English, too snobbish, too down market, too fussy, too lax etc.

The standard Italian block of flats, with normally friendly neighbours, is a straightforward proposition, in which you will know what to expect. But a *supercondominio* full of foreigners – or of your own countrymen – could hold surprises beyond your control. In general you will need to be a good committee person, with communication, accountancy and political skills if you want to succeed in a condominium – the same skills as are required by members of the European Union, for example, which is a macro-condominium. If you are of an independent spirit or devoid of the requisite skill, a condominium is not the right place for you.

> Example of the legal micro-management of the *condominio*: – Article 1121 of the Civil Code permits condominium committees to reject requests for architectural changes, if these are deemed to be 'onerous or extravagant' (*gravosa o voluttuosa*).
>
> The court of Taranto on May 27, 1986 judged that 'Travertine cladding to the height of two metres and sixty-five centimetres was *not* an onerous and extravagant replacement of existing marble cladding'.

Before you buy into a condominium, the first thing to do, is to see the *amministratore* and check on the following:

- any possible debts owed to the condominium by your predecessor which you must pay;
- the exact rules of the condominium (*il regolamento*);
- your own possible requirements regarding such things as sub-letting, pets, TV aerials, parking space, barbecues etc;
- the details of your share of condominium expenses which are reckoned according to consumption, such as heating, water, garbage disposal etc. (*millesimi calore, millesimi acqua, millesimi immondizia*);
- the date of the compulsory annual general meeting.

The administrator of a condominium is obliged by law (*codice civile, articolo 1130*) to fulfil his duties with the 'diligence of a good father of a family!' He can call extraordinary meetings whenever necessary, providing he gives at least five days notice to all members. You, as a member, can call a meeting, providing you have the support of at least one other condominium member, and that your combined share in the condominium is at least one sixth (i.e. not less than 166.66 *millesimi*).

The *condominio* is a tightly regulated institution. Many Italians are inured to endless pettifogging litigation to do with their *condominio*. Tact and caution are advised before entering into one.

SHARED OWNERSHIP

Comunione
Caution is also called for when entering into co-ownership of a property – or *comunione*.

If you are married and buying a property the notary registering the deed will want to know whether you are in joint ownership with your spouse (*in regime di comunione dei beni*) or separate (*...di separazione dei beni*). This is a distinction, which English common law does not make, unless you have made a pre-nuptial agreement. Italian law assumes you are *in comunione dei beni* with your spouse unless you state otherwise.

If you are friends sharing, be prepared to risk the end of your friendship. Follow the advice of the Italian proverb, 'clear agreements, long friendship' (*patti chiari, amicizia lunga*). Make a written agreement covering yourselves against any conceivable eventuality. The pitfalls to guard against are:

- unequal sharing of the use of the property,
- unequal sharing of expenses,
- unequal recognition of works done,
- unequal sharing of rents,
- the consequences of eventual marriage of a co-owner, bringing a new personality into the equation and a possible hostile take-over,
- the consequences of an eventual divorce or bankruptcy of one of the co-owners, which might require the sell-out of a share; how do you evaluate this? Answer: You take the average of three independent valuations.

EXAMPLES OF SHARED OWNERSHIP

- Two couples of old friends from England, The Browns and the Smiths, young families with children, themselves friends since childhood, shared in the purchase of a small house in a village in southern Tuscany which they took it in turns to live in. They fell out over petty disagreements and now no longer speak to each other. According to

> Mrs Brown 'From day one you want to have an agreement no matter how close your friendship is'.
> ◐ Two other couples, from Germany, bought a house as a holiday home, and made a written agreement, to the effect that couple A get the choice of dates one year and couple B the next year, strictly for themselves; they never rent. They are still friends.

The Cooperativa

The concept of the Cooperative is enshrined in the Italian Constitution (Article 45),

'The Republic recognises the social function of cooperation in the sense of mutuality without any goals of private speculation … The law provides for the safeguarding and development of craftsmanship (*artigianato*)'.

A *Cooperativa* is a legal entity which can be formed by a minimum of nine partners. As such it can buy and sell property in its own right. Normally it is used by groups of craftsmen, small traders, hauliers, artists, musicians and such like, combining together in a spirit of mutual help.

BUYING IN THE NAME OF AN ITALIAN COMPANY

There are various business entities in Italy:

- ◐ Snc (*Società in nome collettivo*) a general partnership with unlimited liability;
- ◐ Sas (*Società in accomandita semplice*) a limited partnership with liability limited to capital invested;
- ◐ SapA (*Società in accomandita per Azioni*) a partnership in which the managing partners liability in unlimited;
- ◐ SpA (*Società per Azioni*), a limited liability company incorporated by public deed;
- ◐ SrL (*Società a responsabilità limitata*), a private company whose partners liability is limited to their share in it – ;

To buy a company or to set up a new one is a complicated business which requires the services of a *commercialista*. To buy a property in the name of a company, the notary will tell you what documents are required.

Buying in the name of a foreign company

For this process you will need to employ a notary. To set up an offshore or foreign company you will need *una procurs speciale* special power of attorney given by the directors of the company to you (the beneficiary) to buy the property. You will also need an *Apostille,* a document issued by a Channel Island company. Also The

Articles of Association and your passport data.

The main disadvantage of an offshore company is the often exorbitant annual fee required to keep it going; from £1,200 per year upwards.

The advantage of offshore anonymity for the purpose of tax avoidance is no longer relevant. Beneficiaries of property owned abroad in the name of offshore companies now have to declare themselves as such to the tax authorities thanks to Chancellor of the Exchequer Gordon Brown's dispositions in 2002.

TIMESHARE

Timesharing – *multi-proprietà* – whereby property is shared on the basis of the right to occupy it for designated times of the year has not caught on in Italy.

The European Union issues brochures warning about the dire consequences of signing a timeshare agreement. In Italy there is not much timeshare property available: sites such as www.bcomps.demon.co.uk and www.timeshare.com give lists of timeshare properties but these are relatively few compared to France and Spain. Instead of renting a room in an expensive hotel in Venice, you buy a share in a property that gives you the right to use the property for a certain number of weeks for the rest of your life. The catch is you never actually own anything, just the right to use it for a fixed period. There are disadvantages in owning a timeshare:

- you never own the property
- other people use the property for most of the year
- the property will never feel like yours
- it can be difficult to sell your share
- there may be possible substantial losses if you sell.

There are costs involved with timeshare: you can expect to pay £500 annually in management fees. The average timeshare costs from £3,000 – £12,000.

How Timeshares are Sold

The timeshare company will invite the interested buyer to a desirable location in their own country or even offer a free flight to a location near the timeshare property. You are taken/invited to a presentation where you are often given lunch and plied with drink. You are shown glossy brochures of the properties for sale and sometimes a free gift – the list of gifts ranges from a laptop computer to a crystal wine decanter.

The sales techniques are high pressure; you are bombarded with facts and told how lucky you are to have this chance and you must put a deposit down on the spot to make sure that the opportunity you are being offered doesn't slip away. Do not buy a timeshare until you have done proper research.

The property you are offered may not even be built and any photos on display may be misleading. If you sign up and pay a deposit on a new timeshare, beware, because the resale value will be much lower so it is better to consider buying timeshare from a timeshare owner. Always read the small print and ask plenty of questions, however a lot of deposits are non-returnable and the timeshare company if not bona fida could very well disappear with your money. Timeshare companies sometimes advertise in *Dalton's Weekly* and *Exchange & Mart.* You can access the Timeshare Consumer's Association (T.C.A.) web-site www.tcaforum.com for information. Dealers that resell timeshares should be members of the OTE Organization for Timeshare in Europe; see www.ote-info.com or www.timeshare.org.uk.

There is not a lot of public information on timeshare but there is a good book with all the pros and cons written by Michael Strauss and called *Timeshare Condominiums for the Beginner.*

BUYING A HOUSE UNDER CONSTRUCTION

Advantages and Disadvantages
Advantages:
- You can adapt the house/flat to your own taste and needs.
- New houses are better built technologically, better insulated, more spacious etc. than older properties.
- No rebuilding required for years.
- By law (*la garanzia postuma decennale*) the builders' insurance guarantees to repair any faults for ten years after construction.

Disadvantages:
- No guarantee of date of delivery.
- Advance payments are statistically much more at risk than in a private sale. The builder, for example, risks bankruptcy if he fails to sell a certain number of properties immediately.
- You have to be twice as cautious when you buy a house under construction than when you buy a built one.

Planning requirements
Before starting any building project planning permission has to be obtained, *le concessione edilizia,* from the *Comune,* in accordance with their *piano regolatore* or master plan. There is nothing to stop the sale of property *before* planning permission has been obtained, or while waiting for a change in the *piano regolatore.* This can take a long time and should be at the builder's risk.

Essential Enquiries
Who owns the land? Another check to be made: in the unlikely event of a

builder building on land which he does not own – the house belongs to the owner of the land.

Who is the developer?   Be careful not to confuse two or three different actors on the scene of a development: The first is the developer, or promoter of the scheme, who should own the land. The second is the building contractor. The third could be the agency that looks after the sale of the units.

It is the developer who is by far the most important of these. He is the legal counterpart of the buyer. You need to have a lot of trust in him. It is not difficult to check out his trustworthiness: Has he been on the scene for years? Has his company a large capital fund? or is he financing himself as he goes along?

If it is a recently created company, perhaps a S.r.l. with a capital of €5,000 (the minimum is €10,000) it is better to tread carefully.

The Specification (Capitolato)

Many developers favour rather terse specifications. Others use the technique of blinding with science. Don't hesitate to seek an explanation from the vendor of anything you do not understand in the *capitolato*. Building terminology is a jargon, which even its initiates find hard to understand. If in doubt get the help of a *geometra*, with an interpreter if necessary.

The Contract and Payments (stadi di avanzamento)

Scrutinise the contract with great care. Look out for clauses to do with revising the prices, or that are vague about delivery times. Stage payments (*stadi di avanzamento*) should be as small and frequent as possible and linked with the progress of the work.

Don't trust a developer who asks for too many, or too big, stage payments at the beginning of the job, or who asks for payment by post-dated cheque or *cambiale*, which you should never give. Always withhold a percentage (at least 10%) for payment on transfer of title (*rogito*) (not on hand over of keys).

RENTING A HOME IN ITALY

CHAPTER SUMMARY

O Renting different kinds of properties in Italy is a good way to find out what type of property you want to buy.

O Renting is also a good way to get to know a region and make contacts with the locals before you decide to move there.

O Many people who rent an Italian property progress to buying their own.

O Italians sometimes prefer to let to foreigners as the strict rental laws of Italy favour the tenant, but they do not apply to non-residents.

O For short-term rentals there is a lot of choice.

O For long-term rentals longer than three months, the low season (November-March) is best as you should be able to negotiate a lower monthly rate (as opposed to a high weekly one).

O For most rentals you have to pay a deposit, refundable only when you hand over the property in the same condition as you found it.

O Agents' fees range from a month's rent for a short let, to 20-30% of the rental for a year's lease.

O Most prospective tenants have to provide proof of income such as a bank statement or pay-slips.

O Expatriate communities' websites carry adverts for rentals.

O Tenants have to obtain an annual safety certificate for heating boilers and gas heaters at their own expense.

O As an alternative to renting, short-term accommodation can be found in hostels, monasteries, hotels and *Agriturismos* (farm B&B).

WHY RENT?

If you are thinking of buying a property in Italy, renting reduces the possibility of making a wrong decision, which could mean years with a property you do not like. If you have not decided on a region, you could plan to rent properties over several months in the regions that appeal to you. The value of renting in your chosen region(s) is that you can find out first hand what they are like. It allows you to become familiar with the region, the amenities and most importantly, the local people. You can also check out following:

- Is the climate bearable in summer?
- Is the winter climate pleasant?
- What are the best locations, within the region, during winter?
- Which parts of the region are convenient for connections to roads and airports?
- How easy is it to get telecommunications connections?
- How far away is the coast/skiing area?

Many people who rent first in Italy, progress to wanting to buy an Italian place of their own. However, you might be one of the few who enjoy the renting experience and decide to rent permanently. That way you can retain your capital and if you rent out your own property in your home country, you could find that after paying your rent in Italy, you are still making money. Of course, some foreigners who rent permanently in Italy do so because they are expatriate workers who have their accommodation arranged for them as part of their job package.

Prospective buyers of Italian property usually have to make their own arrangements to find somewhere they can stay for the length of time it takes to explore a region and view the properties for sale there and ultimately choose the one they will buy. In Italy it is possible to rent every kind of property from a studio apartment (*monolocale*) to a large villa.

There are other possibilities for finding somewhere to stay depending on how long you wish to remain in one locality. For instance, some prospective purchasers might prefer to move around a particular region staying in hotels, hostels, *agriturismos* (working farms that take paying guests), colleges and religious guest houses, etc.

LONG-TERM RENTALS

A long-term rental is a rental for three months or longer. For this duration, it will be much cheaper to rent than to pay the weekly rates for vacation rentals. Typical prices might be €1,000 (£660) per month for a furnished flat in Florence. Accommodation in a rural area of Tuscany might be €700 per month. Outside Tuscany and Umbria you should pay even less.

Rentals for longer than a year are usually unfurnished (*nonammobiliato*) and long-term furnished (*ammobiliato*) properties are difficult to find.

Italians sometimes prefer to rent to non-Italians because the strict rental laws in Italy mainly protect tenants rather than landlords. It is very difficult to evict Italian tenants, even if they have defaulted on rental payments. Non-Italians can be easier to deal with. However, this is not always the case as one person found out when she first tried to rent an apartment for her Italian husband, herself and two small children to stay in while they went house-hunting in Le Marche:

> ### BELINDA SCABURRI DISCOVERED THAT:
> *Despite there being an enormous demand for rental properties, the laws are still such that landlords are not protected and are therefore nervous and reluctant to enter into rental agreements which, in many instances, end in the law courts. We imagined that we would appear the ideal tenants – a mummy, a daddy and two adorable children. In actual fact, we presented the very worst type of tenant risk. We were not employed, we 'claimed' to be looking for a house to buy and, being foreigners (my husband, being a northern Italian, constituted as much of a foreigner as myself), we could say we had nowhere to go should we decide to stay at the end of the tenancy. A combination of luck, timing and a telephone number spotted on an internet site meant that we did find ourselves a house to rent, but it is by no means the hassle-free, legally sound procedure to which we have all become accustomed in the UK.*

SHORT-TERM RENTALS

If you are looking for short-term rentals there is a great deal of choice. There are apartments, cottages, villas, chalets and even castles. However, as mentioned the best prices are out of season and if you want to rent for a couple of months this is the best option, especially if you are good at negotiating and come to an agreement with the owner/agent about the rent. Also, if you are renting in the off season, you should check out the property first to make sure that if you stay there during winter, the heating is adequate (i.e. there is central heating or a wood-burning stove with a local supply of wood).

AGENTS

Vacation rental agents offer long-term rentals based on a monthly rate that is cheaper in the off season (i.e. November to March). It is worth contacting agencies to ask about this as a renting possibilty. You can find a list of vacation property agents and the properties they offer for rental on the internet.

Useful sites include:

www.brianfrench.com (Umbria and Le Marche)
www.casa.it
www.housearounditaly.com (Abruzzo)
www.initaly.com (all regions)
www.knowital.com (mainly Lucca, Tuscany)
www.laportaverde.com (Umbria)
www.smithgcb.demon.co.uk (Piedmont)
www.tuscanhome.com

Dealing With Agents

If you decide to rent a farmhouse or a villa in a rural setting similar to the kind of property you hope to buy, and you arrange it through an agent, you will have to pay the agent a month's rent as a fee for his services, and if it is a long-term rental then you will be asked for 10% or 20% of the first year's rent. It is a good idea when the contract is drawn up to include a clause that will let you terminate the contract if anything unforeseen crops up.

Many tenants are asked to produce proof of income such as a bank statement, or pay-slips to show that they are solvent. You will be asked to pay a deposit, which is refundable upon departure if the house is in good condition. You will also have to pay the utilities and other expenses, these include, gas, water, telephone, electricity and maintenance. It is also likely that you will have to pay a rubbish tax as well.

HOME EXCHANGES

Although not involving renting, home exchanges can serve the same purpose in that you have a place to stay while you look for somewhere to buy. However, it is well known that Italians are spoilt for choice when it comes to foreigners wanting to stay in their houses and apartments, and that they are very choosy about the locality of the home they exchange with. If you are American, the areas most popular with Italians are New York or California.

Most countries have their own home exchange agencies. Homelink International has branches worldwide.

Exchange Agencies

Home Base Holidays: 7 Park Avenue, London N13 5PG; ☎020-8886-8752.

Homelink International: Box 650, Key West, Florida, 33041, USA; ☎305-294-7766 or 800-638-3841.

Homelink International: Linfield House, Gorse Hill Road, Virginia Water, Surrey GU25 4AS.

Homelink International: Casa Vacanze, Via San Francesco 170, 35121 Padua, Italy.

Intervac International Home Exchange: Via Oreglia 18, 40047 Riola, Bologna, Italy.

ADVERTS

Long-term Rentals

Apart from following up *affittasi* (to let) signs posted outside apartments, the obvious place to look for advertisements in in the classified sections headed *appartamenti da affittare* (flats to let), of main local papers. It is possible to contact the private Italian owners of properties to let direct. They advertise in 'local' papers like the daily Roman paper *Il Messaggero* and Milan's paper *Seconda Mano* which is published on Mondays and Thursdays, and supplements that come with

property magazines. For other newspapers see the *Media* section of *Living in Italy.*
Adverts in the city papers above are likely to be mainly for city rentals.

You can also consult the local expatriate communities' websites for long-term
rental listings. For example The Grapevine (www.netemedia-net/grapevine) is the
local network for northern Umbria.

Short-term rentals

Adverts for short-term rentals can be found in the same places as for long-term
rentals. However there are additional sources including adverts in the British
newspapers including *The Sunday Times, The Sunday Telegraph* and *The Observer*,
magazines and on internet sites. The internet has numerous sites covering every
Italian region including www.italianbreaks.com, www.italianencounters.com and
uliviera@hotmail.com (e-mail for Tuscan rustic apartments). The Italian Tourist
Office (www.enit.it) and local tourist offices are other sources well supplied with
contacts for short-term renting. Also check out the Italian publication *Casa per
Casa* (www.casapercasa.it), a weekly free property magazine published in regional
editions. The *English Yellow Pages* (www.englishyellowpages.it) is another useful
source of adverts of properties to rent.

Below is a glossary of rental terms. Notice that there are three words that mean
tenant, two words for rental and for lease and two ways of saying sublet.

GLOSSARY OF RENTAL TERMS	
Affittasi	to let
Affitto	rental/lease
Canone mensile di locazione	monthly rent
Conduttore	tenant
Contratto	contract
Contratto di locazione	rental contract
Dare la disdetta	to give notice of termination of the contract.
Deposito cauzionale	deposit (against damage)
Inquilino	tenant
Locale	room
Locatario	tenant
Locatore	landlord
Locazione	rental
Mora	in arrears
Pattuizioni	stipulated agreements
Pianterreno	ground floor
Primo/ seconda/terzo/ quarto piano	1st/2nd/3rd/4th floor
Rata	instalment
Risarcimento danni	payment for damage
Riscaldamento	central heating
Servizi	kitchen and bathroom
Sublocare	sub-let
Unità immobiliare	a unit of property
Utenze	utilities, services

TENANCY LAWS

Obtaining a tenancy agreement is usually easier if you are a non-resident, since anyone with *residenza* status is protected by state laws from being evicted (*sfrattato*). The length of rental contracts varies. When the landlord or landlady (*padrone/padrona*) wishes to have the property back, the tenant (*inquilino*) will be sent notice to quit.

If you sign a rental contract, make sure that you understand all the conditions which will include the following:

- The landlord must be allowed access to the property.
- When the tenant hands the property back to the landlord it must be in the same state in which he or she found it.
- Tenants have to pay for any damage.
- Tenants may not make any alterations without the landlord's permission.
- If the tenant's proposed improvements are approved by the landlord, the landlord is not obliged to pay for them.

Failure of the tenant to keep to the terms of the contract means that the contract can be terminated.

Tenants' Responsibilities

Tenants also have responsabilities, such as obtaining an annual certificate to confirm that the central heating boiler and gas heaters conform to European Union requirements. The tenant is liable for the cost of the certificate. Check with other expatriates as well as the landlord to find out exactly what is expected of you and what the landlord is responsible for as local conditions and rental contracts vary, as does the quality of the landlord.

Holiday Lettings and Furnished Lettings

The rental laws and protection for tenants do not apply to holiday or furnished rental properties. For holiday rentals, the client and the owner's agent agree terms regarding the deposit etc. and although this is normally a written agreement rental contract laws do not apply to it.

If the owner has not made an inventory of the contents, it is a good idea to do this and to check that all the appliances work, with the owner, before signing any agreement. Rent is usually paid monthly or by direct debit (*bonifico bancario*), cheque or cash. Most contracts require 6 months' notice in writing regarding termination. If the tenancy is less than a year, then three months' notice is adequate.

If you are renting a flat in a condominium (apartment building where all communal charges are paid by the members), you should have an agreement with the owner about who is going to pay the communal charges set out in the building's convenant.

OTHER ACCOMMODATION

If you do not want to arrange a rental in one spot so that you are free to move around the region on your house hunt, the following accommodation options may be useful.

Hotels (Alberghi) and Guest Houses (Pensioni)

Hotels are classified according to quality standards based on cleanliness, service etc., which are given a star rating from one to five. The more stars, the higher the price. If you stay during the low season or stay for longer than two weeks, you may be able to secure a lower rent. Cheap hotels with one or two stars in large cities are often used for long-term accommodation. An up-to-date list of hotels can be obtained from the *Aziende di Promozione Turistica, Ente Per Il Turismo Uffici I.A.T.* (tourist information offices) in the main cities.

Agriturismo

Agriturismo is a type of rural lodging based at a working farm and is increasingly popular in Italy. It stems from a government initiative to shift rural entrepreneurial activities from agriculture to tourism. Prices are based on location, season and the type of accommodation offered. Full board is customarily provided which limits your exploration of the region, but the meals are all made from local produce. Rates are in the region of €25-€30 per day. Information about *Agriturismo* can be obtained from the local tourist office and the website www.tuttoagriturismo@tatt ilo.it. There is also a magazine *Tutto Agriturismo* published every two months.

Religious Guest Houses

Orders of monks and nuns may sometimes offer hospitality in their communities. This is usually just bed and breakfast but some communities may also offer an evening meal. The rates are usually very reasonable. A typical example is the Benedictines of the Tuscan monastery *Abbadia di Monte Oliveto Maggiore* who offer bed and breakfast for €20. A global guide to religious community guest houses *Itinerantibus in Toto Orbe Terrarum* (To Wander About the World) by Don Giovanni Munari is available from bookshops.

Youth Hostels

Youth hostels are amongst the cheapest lodgings in Italy and there are over 50 to choose from. Italian hostels have good standards and are often situated in stunning locations; others may be in old palaces or castles which have been restored and adapted for young people. Membership can be obtained from the International Youth Hostel Federation in your own country. In the low season long stays are permitted.

FEES, CONTRACTS AND CONVEYANCING

CHAPTER SUMMARY

○ **Professional Assistance.** The official appointed to handle property sales in Italy is a *notaio*. This is a dignified profession and you should always try to be punctual for appointments at his or her offices and bring all necessary documents with you.
  ○ Most notaios like to be paid in cash.
  ○ You will also need the services of a *geometra* (surveyor). Geometras are familiar with both the legal and technical aspects of land and buildings.
○ **Third Parties' Right to Buy.** In Italy, certain third parties have pre-emptive rights to buy (*prelazione*). To avert the possibility of a *prelazione*, you have to obtain a disclaimer (*renuncia)* from any interested party.
  ○ Without a disclaimer the price could be bumped up if an interested third party used their prelazione to make you buy thcm off.
○ **Imminent Planning Threats.** It is possible to pay the local council (*comune*) to have some types of road plan diverted from proximity to your property.
○ **Beware the Vendor.** You should always check the vendor's identity and that he or she owns the property and is financially solvent.
  ○ If the vendor goes bankrupt within two years of selling you a property, it will revert to his estate and you will be merely a creditor.
○ Any contract or official translation in Italy requires official ID and an italian tax code number (*codice fiscale*).
  ○ Plastic codice fiscale cards can be obtained from the comune or local tax office.
○ **The Deposit.** The main deposit on a contract to buy, is a *caparra*, which is governed by law and is 20% to 30% of the agreed price.
  ○ If the vendor fails to complete, he must pay double the deposit

to the buyer.

○ The deposit should be paid by banker's draft or non-transferable cheque.

○ **Under-declaration of the Price.** Under-declaring is common practice in Italian conveyancing deeds as a means to reduce tax on capital gains.

  ○ Capital gains tax was abolished in Italy in 2002 and there may be disadvantages to under-declaration. Consult your notary.

○ *Rogito.* The *rogito* is the final contract and the date for signing this at the notary's office is booked well in advance as all parties have to be present.

  ○ The title does not officially change hands until the contract is filed in the land registry by the notaio.

UK-BASED PROFESSIONAL ASSISTANCE

LAWYERS

The official usually appointed to handle a property sale is a public notary (*notaio*) who in Italy acts for both the vendor and the purchaser, as they do in other European countries, such as France. There are also some lawyers (*avvocati*) who are qualified to handle property transactions. Foreigners, who are generally not versed in Italian property buying procedures, may wish to appoint both a *notaio* and an *avvocato*. This way, an expatriate can have a competent professional who works for them directly explain the process to them fully and completely, and not someone who is supposed to be an impartial administrator. Italian lawyers based in the UK can represent expatriates in Italy (see names and contact source below) when you are buying Italian property, alternatively your embassy or regional consular office

should be able to supply a list of local lawyers who speak your language.

Specialist lawyers based in the UK:

Bennett & Co Solicitors: 144 Knutsford Road, Wilmslow, Cheshire SK9 6JP; ☎01625-586937; fax 01625-585362; e-mail: internationallawyers@bennett-and-co.com; www.bennett-and-co.com.

Claudio del Giudice: Rivington House, 82 Great Eastern Street, London EC2A 3JF; ☎020-7613 2788; fax 020-7613 2799; e-mail delgiudice@clara.co.uk; www.delgiudice@clara.co.uk.

Giovanni Lombardo: 020-7256-7467; g.lombardo@lombardolawfirm.co.uk.

The Italian Law Centre: Unit 2, Acorn Business Centre, Livingstone Road, Hessle, Kingston-on-Hull, HU13 OEG; ☎01482-350850; fax 01482-542799;

John Howell & Co: 17 Maiden Lane, Covent Garden, London WC2E 7NA; ☎020-7420 0400; fax 020-7836 3626; www.europelaw.com.

Roberta Crivellaro: ☎020-7597 6491; r.crivellaro@studio-lea.com.

LOCAL PROFESSIONALS

The key local professionals indispensable to the purchase of a property in Italy are the surveyor (*geometra*) and the notary (*notaio*). The *geometra* performs the functions, which we associate with an architect, – making drawings and specifications, supervising work etc. Architects (*architetti*) also exist in Italy, and it is worth explaining the difference between an *architetto* and a *geometra*.

Comparison of Geometri and Architetti

A *geometra* does all the work we expect of an architect, up to a certain level. An *architetto* has a more prestigious title and operates on a higher plane both financially and artistically. A *geometra* qualifies by passing the requisite high school exam, and then, following another exam after two years of apprenticeship, he is fully fledged at twenty-two. But an *architetto* has to do a five-year university course and is usually 28 before qualifying. The result is that *architetti* know a lot about the artistic and theoretical but little about the practical side of building; they charge much more, seldom visit sites – and the *geometri* get most of the work. There is a state of mutual hostility between these two branches of the same profession. *Architetti* often exploit *geometri* and *geometri* are resentful of this.

The *geometra* is now a threatened species; the system is about to change in Italy to conform with the rest of Europe: they will all become *architetti*. As it stands in 2003 you would only consult an *architetto* if you were involved in a large project or on a listed building, or if you were looking for an artistic modern treatment for the interior of an ancient building. *Architetti* are employed by the Fine Arts Commission (*la sovrintendenza delle Belle Arti*) of the Province, which is a sort of local style-police appointed by the Culture Ministry of Rome (*il Ministero dei Beni Culturali*).

THE GEOMETRA

An alert and vigilant *geometra* should pick up on any faults in a building, which might be used if possible to negotiate a lower price. But certain considerations which are important in the British Isles, such as rising damp, woodworm or rotten timbers, are taken for granted in unrestored properties in Italy, where the price is dictated by the broader picture – the rarity value or the location or the beauty of the environment.

The *geometra* is familiar with both the legal and technical aspects of land and buildings, and it is vital to have him check all the points listed below before you arrange for the legal side of your purchase, for which you will require the services of a notary or *notaio*, and more checks.

Checklist for the Geometra

So, at the normal domestic level of house buying you would employ a *geometra* for the purpose of inspections or surveys. A site visit is called a *sopralluogo*. A technical survey is called a *perizia*. A checklist for an apartment or town house should include the following points:

- architectural drawings? (*La planimetria*)
- floor space in square metres? (*i metri quadri*)

- type and number of rooms? (*tipologia e numero vani*)
- year of construction? (*anno di costruzione*)
- which floor? (*piano*)
- type of condominium (*tipo condominio*)
- lift? elevator? (*ascensore*)
- porter/janitor? (*portineria*)
- utilities and services ok? (*impianti a norma*)
- garage? how big? (*box*)
- parking space? (*postauto*)
- cellar? how big? (*cantina*)
- store room? how big? (*ripostiglio*)
- balconies? how big? (*balconi*)
- terrace? how big? (*terrazzo*)
- doors and windows? in what state? (*infissi*)
- floors? in what state? (*pavimenti*)
- plumbing and bathrooms? in what state? (*sanitari*)
- leaks? (*infiltrazioni*)

A checklist for a country property should add the following points:

Access roads? (*strade di accesso*) (What are they like in winter? How much to repair and maintain? Whose responsibility? Normally they are *strade vicinali* neighbourhood roads, but don't count on the neighbours making a contribution to any repairs.)

- electricity (see *ENEL* in *Services* chapter).
- water (*acquedotto*) (see *Services* chapter)
- gas (*gas metano*) (see *Services* chapter)
- cracks? (*crepe*)
- subsidence? (*assestamento*)
- roof? (*tetto*)
- rotten beams? (*travi marce*)
- rights of way? (*diritti di passo*)
- earthquake risks? (*rischio seismico*) (what architectural reinforcements are required by local building codes?)
- Radon gas risks? (*rischio gas radon*) (this applies to the Dolomites and other granitic areas, Tufa areas might be at risk. Remedial architecture is available.)
- flooding risk? (*rischio allagamento*)
- landslide risk? (*rischio frana*)
- If you are putting in a bore-hole for water (*pozzo artesiano*) or an in-ground swimming pool your *geometra* must obtain a *svincolo idrogeologico* or a hydrogeological clearance from the provincial authority.
- sewage (*fognatura*) Is it mains (*comunale*) or a private septic tank? (*fossa biologica*) Does it need repairs or replacement? Periodic emptying?

CHECKLIST FOR THE BUYER

Verbal agreements. No verbal agreement has any value in Italian law. Handshakes in the market place belong to a past age.

Inspection of Property. Don't accept the definition of property 'as seen' (*visto e piaciuto*), and do not accept it 'in the state of fact and law in which it is at present found' (*nello stato di fatto e diritto in cui attualmente si trova*) without visiting and carefully checking everything.

Appurtenances. In particular check that all appurtenances (*pertinenze*) are specified, such as cellars, attics, garages and sheds. Attach a *geometra's* drawing of the property to the contract, signed by both parties and specify such appurtenances in writing.

Utilities and Services. Examine the utilities and services with the help of an expert. Water, gas, electricity, oil, boilers, pumps – (*impianti*). Yearly service contracts and guarantees should be obtained from the vendor.

Furniture and Fittings.   Make an inventory (*elenco*) of all the items you and the vendor are agreed on for you to keep. Check that all rubbish and all the items you do not want are removed before the sale. Some unscrupulous owners remove all fittings, door handles, switches, radiators, boilers, etc. To avoid this, include them in the inventory. As an extra precaution, arrange with the owner for a final check-up on the day or the day before the final contract. The same argument applies to plants, shrubs, tubs and planters etc., which you might or might not want to keep.

Mortgages. Mortgages (*ipoteche*). Be aware of the fact that even if you buy a property on which the previous mortgage has been completely paid off, this does not mean it has been officially cancelled. You need to know how much the necessary formalities would cost to cancel the mortgage in the land registry (*La conservatoria dei registri immobiliari*).

Alternatively you can take over the vendor's existing mortgage. (see *Mortgages*).

PRELAZIONE – THIRD PARTIES RIGHT TO BUY

Il diritto di prelazione – pre-emptive rights, designed to protect the small working farmer of yesteryear, are still available to people who are officially registered as *coltivatori diretti*, literally direct cultivators, who are *confinanti*, contiguous neighbours, giving them the right of first refusal on any non-urban land adjacent to their own. They are entitled to buy this at the declared price. Sitting tenants and individuals, who are conducting a business in the property also have a right to buy.

The state – or the *comune* or other state bodies also have the right to buy, or requisition in certain cases, for example, in the case of an archaeological find, and in the case of listed buildings in the *beni culturali* category.

To avert this threat you have to obtain a disclaimer (*rinuncia*) from any interested party. For this you need the co-operation of the vendor, or of your own professional, *geometra* or *avvocato*.

Inherited or Donated Property. Beware of property acquired by donation or inheritance. A group of siblings often inherit a property, which they decide to sell, but at the last minute one of them refuses to sign. This is often used as a ruse to jack the price up, and is a frequent cause of disappointment for buyers. The only solution to this problem is for the *notaio* to assemble all the owners of the property at the early *compromesso* stage and obtain their signatures on the *compromesso*.

A *certificato di provenienza* – a certificate of provenance such as a will or a donation attests to the legal owners of such property.

Vacant Possession. Check that there are no tenants or squatters in a property supposed to be vacant, including the owner himself. It takes six to ten years to evict a tenant or squatter, going through the Italian legal process. Make sure that all goods and chattels not required by you are removed from the premises.

Tenanted Property. If the property is tenanted it can be as much as 30% cheaper than an untenanted property and could be regarded as an investment.

It is advisable to talk to the tenant and find out his intentions. You have to give him six months written notice to get him to leave. If he decides to stay, the Italian legal system will take an average of six to ten years to evict him.

You must get from the vendor: the tenancy lease, the tenant's deposit money and any advance rent already paid (*il contratto di locazione, il deposito cauzionale, and i canoni anticipati*).

Restrictions and Limitations on the Property. Itemise all restrictions (*vincoli*) and limitations (*servitù*), rights of way (*diritti di passo*) and other burdens (*oneri*) on the property. Make the vendor responsible for any expenses required for eliminating any declared or undeclared restrictions.

Planning Regulations. The validity of a property sale contract in Italy requires documents proving that any illegal improvements have been sanctioned. The local council (*comune*) can issue a document specifying all the permissions they have granted to the property, although not many councils are aware of this. The sanctioning of illegal work is called a *condono edilizio*. Building permission is: *concessione edilizia*.

Imminent Planning Threats. If possible go with your *geometra* or an interpreter to the *Ufficio Tecnico* (planning office) of your local Council (*Comune*), which is normally open to the public two mornings a week.

Ask to see the P.R.G, the master zoning plan, (*piano regolatore generale*) to check the scenarios: housing estates (*zone edificabili*), industrial developments: (*zone industriali*), quarries, clay pits (*cave*), roads (*strade*), roundabouts (*rotatorie*), overpasses (*sopraelevate*), railways (*ferrovie*), dumps (*discariche*), composting plants (*impianti di compostaggio*) and golf courses (*campi da golf*). There are many long term projects, such as the *Grosseto-Fano* road link, which has been long in abeyance, but is apt at any moment to bring large scale road works to the most hidden valleys of Tuscany, Umbria and the Marches.

The *ufficio tecnico* can provide you with copies of its plans, and the status of your target property, whether it is listed (*schedata*) and what the neighbours might be up to. The word *zoning* has entered the Italian language.

These researches are not automatically carried out in Italy, certainly not by lawyers or notaries. The key professional to commission for the task is the local *geometra* who will be familiar with the *comune* involved.

WHAT MONEY CAN DO

Some house-owners in Italy, when they find their property is threatened by certain municipal planning use their resources and resourcefulness to get things changed. Methods include:

Road Diversions. Roadside houses can be given the priceless advantage of privacy by diverting the road to by-pass the property at a distance. You can only do this if you own, or can buy, the land on which to locate the new road; and then only if the old road is a *strada bianca* – a dirt road, literally a 'white road'. You have to negotiate with the local council if the road is a *strada comunale* (a road which is the responsibility of the *comune*), or with the provincial planning office it is a *strada provinciale* (provincial road).

An unthinkable amount of political clout would be required to change the course of a *strada statale* (a road which is the responsibility of the state). On the other hand a *strada vicinale* – a neighbourhood road – would only require the assent of the neighbours who used that road, plus the planning consent of the local council.

The 2002 cost of a *strada provinciale* diversion (*strada bianca*) was about €110,000 per kilometre.

Burying Electricity or Telephone Wires. There are three types of electricity cable *alta, media* and *bassa tensione* (high, medium and low). *Alta tensione* pylons are impossible to move but *media* and *bassa* are no problem, and indeed encouraged for aesthetic reasons. You simply apply to the Electricity board, the ENEL, who will do the work for you. The conduit alone costs €3,000 per 100 metres. To bury *media tensione* cable costs €140,000 per 250 metres. For telephone lines apply to the telephone company, SIP.

Improvements Without Planning Consent. Many house owners carry out improvements regardless of planning permission. They simply pay the fine when challenged, and get the work *condonato* (amnestied) at a later date. Be aware that Councils have been known to issue legal injunctions to stop or demolish *abusivo* work, in particular when they have received complaints from the public, and especially in the case of swimming pools. To achieve your objectives in all these cases you need the services of a *geometra* who is familiar with the planning offices involved. You will also need plenty of money (*un sacco di soldi*).

In the Event of any Dispute. It is wise to put into the contract an agreement to settle any eventual disputes by means of a preferably quick and cheap arbitration. A notary (*notaio*) can be appointed for this task; it is his job to be impartial. Alternatively the local *Tribunale* or law court can be named. This arrangement is called *una clausola arbitrale*.

Beware of the Vendors. Establish first that the vendor(s) have the right identity, and that they own the property. Is the vendor of sound mind? Is he under age? Is there a spouse lurking in the background with a claim to the property? Is he bankrupt?

If he goes bankrupt within two years of selling the property, the property reverts to his estate, on which you will figure as one of the creditors.

If you buy from a company it is even more imperative to check – in the local chamber of commerce – whether the company is still registered or struck off, or encumbered with debt or insolvent (*fallito*). Bankruptcies (*fallimenti*) are common. You and your professional advisers have to be extremely vigilant.

Fraud (*Truffa*). Beware of con men (*imbroglioni*). A single property was once sold to three different buyers on the same day at different notaries. The first notary to register the property in the *catasto* yielded the only legal owner.

In Bologna two flats were rented out to 26 different tenants at the same time, at a deposit of €43.8 per head, which the fake estate agents pocketed and then disappeared into thin air. The gang was recognised by one of the victims when its leader appeared on a TV quiz show.

That particular gang consisted of Italians and Colombians – but the con man could equally be British or German or American, preying on his own compatriots.

THE NOTARY

The *notaio* is a representative of the state whose duty it is to register all contracts, deeds, and titles in the appropriate registry office, and collect all appropriate taxes and duties on behalf of the state; responsible, if in default, for making good any deficit out of his or her own pocket. Women are increasingly evident in the profession. A *notaio's* office is an august and serious place and much dignity and prestige is attached to the profession. Beware of being late or casual with your appointments, and always be sure to bring all your documents and identifications. Despite this dignified appearance fees are negotiable and notaries compete for business. Many prefer to be paid in cash (*contanti*).

The buyer has the right to choose the notary. Normally the agent (*mediatore*) will supply one, your friends in the district will recommend one, or you can find one in the yellow pages. Not many notaries speak English – despite the high academic qualifications that are required for the job, so bring an interpreter if you don't speak Italian.

By law, the notary must be sure that you understand Italian, i.e. that you understand what you are signing in the contract. If he thinks you do not understand, a notarised translation of the contract must be supplied. The notary himself will arrange this for you at a cost.

Power of Attorney, Proxy (procura, delega)

If the vendor has a power of attorney, it needs careful checking by the *notaio*. Is it original? Is it a properly notarised copy? What powers does it confer? Is it of recent date?

If you require a power of attorney yourself, i.e. someone to sign for you, the two main requirements are that he should be (a) trustworthy and (b) understand what he is signing, i.e. an Italian speaker you know and trust.

The drawing up of a proxy document can be done at the *notaio's* office or in an Italian consulate anywhere. You need a valid passport or ID and if possible an Italian *codice fiscale* number. The following information is also required:

- personal details about the procurator (name, surname, place and date of birth, address and occupation, nationality);
- list of functions the procurator is to perform (e.g. buying or selling property), this can either be specific or general. A specific proxy deals with a specific transaction – in the case of property the land registry details should be given.

Powers of attorney in English can be translated and authenticated by the Consulate.

Documents required from the Vendor by the Notary

Deed of provenance (*atto di provenienza*). This is normally the previous contract of sale (*rogito precedente*), but could be a will or a donation.

Land registry details (*scheda catastale*): ground plans, plot numbers etc. These should be checked thoroughly in the inspection of the property to ensure that they correspond with the reality.

Land registry tax certificate (*certificato catastale*). This gives details which include the rateable value (*la rendita catastale*).

Condominium rules (*regolamento condominiale*) – if applicable.

A photocopy of the passport or ID and *codice fiscale* – Italian tax code number of the vendor(s).

Any planning sanctions and permissions (*condono fiscale*), if applicable.

Marital status document (*estratto per sunto degli atti di matrimonio*) issued by the vendor's Comune. This document is necessary if the owners are in a nuptial joint ownership regime, whereby the sale is invalidated if one of them refuses to sign.

Any rental contracts (*contratti di locazione*) or recent cancellations of same.

The latest income tax return of the vendor, (*dichiarazione dei redditi*) proving that the property has been declared to the tax authorities.

Further documents: certificate of habitability (*certificato di abitabilità*), heating and electrical certificates (*certificati impianti*).

Documents you need for the Notary

○ Passport or other valid ID.

○ Italian civil code number (*codice fiscale*).

○ If you have obtained an Italian residence you will also need a residence certificate (*certificato di residenza*) in order to avail yourself of certain tax reductions.

THE CODICE FISCALE

Any contract or official transaction in Italy requires, along with your identification details, an Italian tax code number (*codice fiscale*) which is made up according to a formula of letters and numbers taken from your name, date of birth, birthplace and sex. Plastic *codice fiscale* cards are issued by your local comune or tax office (Ufficio delle Imposte Dirette). They can also be obtained through Italian consulates. Numbers can be worked out for you on the internet (www.codicefiscale.com).

Deposits (acconto-anticipo-caparra)

The first deposit (*acconto*) you will be asked to pay is by the estate agent for his so-called 'irrevocable proposal to buy' *proposta irrevocabile d'acquisto* or *prenotazione*. This has the merit of showing that you are not a time waster (*perditempo*), it engages you to the agent and prevents you from any collusion in a private deal with the vendor, but it is no guarantee that you have secured a property. Its purpose is to give the agent a fixed amount of time, normally a month, to obtain an agreement from the owner to sell you the property. If this agreement is not forthcoming your deposit is refunded.

Agents have been known to collect several deposits from different candidates for the same property and then proceed to an auction, awarding the property to the highest bidder. To avoid falling into traps like this and to limit the risks, four precautions are recommended:

Get the 'irrevocable proposal to buy' drawn up by the notary who you have engaged to handle the conveyancing. In fact this proposal must contain all the details of the definitive contract.

Limit the period in which the proposal is irrevocable to 24 or 48 hours maximum, This is quite enough time for the agent to contact the owner of the property.

Make this deposit minimal: a hundred odd euros. The real deposit will be paid later, at the *compromesso* (preliminary contract). No deposit should be made out to the agent, but to the vendor direct.

Get the agent to specify his commission and/or expenses on a separate sheet; they are nothing to do with the deposit. The true deposit in the contract is called a *caparra*, which is governed by the civil code. It is normally 10% – 30% of the final price.

If the buyer is in default he loses his deposit. If the vendor fails to complete he has to refund the buyer double his deposit. Both parties can take the other to court to enforce the contract.

There are two kinds of *caparra*: *caparra confirmatoria* and *caparra penitenziale*. The *caparra penitenziale* allows for either party to withdraw from the deal on their own terms, jointly agreed, and the contract is not enforceable.

It is advisable to pay any deposits by banker's draft or non-transferable cheque (*assegno non trasferibile*) and to keep a photocopy of the cheque(s).

Full Declaration versus Under-declaration

Under-declaration of the price is common practice in Italian conveyancing deeds. The lowest you can get away with (*il minimo consigliabile*) is quantified at 100 times the figure given for the *rendita catastale* in the *certificato catastale* (the rateable value in the land registry document). Declare any less than this and you will attract the attention of the tax assessors, who have three years in which to re-assess your declared valuation.

The advantage of this practice is that you pay less tax on the sale. Before the abolition of Capital Gains Tax (INVIM) in 2002, the tax evaded was much greater. But the practice is still embedded, as part of the Italian way. Indeed you can consult with your notary as to the correct figure to declare.

The disadvantages of underdeclaring the value – apart from the inconvenience of carrying banknotes around in brown envelopes are: the minor risk of tax reassessment at a future date, and the risk of falling prey to any party who might have a right to buy (*diritto di prelazione*) at the declared price. This could be a tenant of the property, a neighbouring 'farmer' (*coltivatore diretto*) or the state itself. (see *Checklist for Buyer 6, Prelazione*). In a recent case in Southern Tuscany, a Sardinian shepherd's wife – whose husband had signed a disclaimer (*rinuncia*) – made such a claim – and had to be paid off for a large sum.

As for declaring the full value, the law (30/97) enabled compromessos to be registered by a notary at the land registry (*conservatoria dei registri immobiliari*). Lawyers and estate agents encourage this 'correct' way, which safeguards the buyers from other purchasers, prevents any price increase and gives you peace of mind if there is going to be a long gap between the *compromesso* and the final contract (*rogito*) as the registration is valid for up to three years.

The framers of the new land registry system (the N.C.E.U or *Nuovo Catasto Edilizio Urbano*) which came into force on 1 January 2000 instructed their tax assessors to base the rateable valuation of real estate on current market prices, which, when it happens, will remove this anomaly.

The Dangers of Under-declaring the Purchase Price

There are inherent dangers in under-declaring the amount you are paying for your property, which is sometimes advised by notaries as it enables you to pay less money in notarial fees and taxes associated with purchasing. However, if you sell the property within five years, and you have under-declared on the purchase price you will end up paying higher taxes on the *plusvalenza* (value added to the property by the time you sell) (see *Tax on* Plusvalenza).

There is also the shock of under-declaring at the *compromesso* stage and then finding yourself paying nearly double the amount you expected at the *rogito* (final act of purchase) stage. This is what happened to Mr. B. He was advised by a notary to declare a price of sixty thousand euros on the property he was buying. However, he wrote cheques to the value of one hundred and forty thousand euros. At completion (the *rogito*), the notary acting pointed out the difference between the declared price and the actual price as denoted by the cheques and Mr B. found himself paying the equivalent of €17,400 instead of the €8,000 purchase costs, that he had been expecting to pay. The moral of this story is that if you do under-declare then your cheques must correspond to the amount you have declared. Note that cheques can be traced by the tax police (*guardia di finanza)* should they wish to take a special interest in your financial affairs.

Completion Date

Stipulate a completion date (*data del rogito*) as soon as possible after the *compromesso*. Two or three months is the normal time. Anything could happen in between. If the time has to be longer it is all the more imperative that you have a properly notarised and registered *compromesso*. Even then the vendor might be tempted by a higher bidder *and* afford to give you back double your deposit.

The Rogito Notarile

The *Rogito* – or final contract – is the Big Day for which the *compromesso* has been a rehearsal. The time and date will have been booked well in advance. All you will need are your identity documents and the money.

It is advisable to book the *rogito* appointment for the morning or early afternoon while the banks are open, just in case there is a hitch with the payment formalities, which a trip to the bank might immediately rectify. All parties have to be present, naturally, to sign the contract. The estate agent or *mediatore* will also probably be there (with his hand out) and it is advisable to have an interpreter to help you check all the details of the contract, which the *notaio* will read out, (unless you have previously arranged for an official English translation).

Ask the *notaio* to reassure you that he will file the contract in the Land Registry without delay – it is only then that the title officially changes hands. The Land Registry will then take about two months to furnish a certificate of your title.

SUMMARY OF ITALIAN CONVEYANCING

The sale of real estate in Italy (*La compravendita di un immobile*) is governed by the Civil Code articles 1754-1765 and also by laws (*leggi*) 39 of 3 feb 1989 and 452 of 21 dec 1990.It consists of two stages:

The *Compromesso*, the preliminary contract or *preliminare di vendita*, whereby the buyer pays a deposit called a *caparra*, or earnest money, on an agreed price on a specified property, the contract to be completed by a specified date. It can be a privately signed deed between the buyer and vendor, but it is recommended that it should be done with a notary, publicly registered, and regarded as seriously as a final contract. If the buyer fails to complete he forfeits his deposit. If the vendor pulls out of the contract he must pay back the buyer double his deposit.
Il rogito – the final contract and transfer of title, registered in the Land Registry office (*Ufficio del Registro* or *Catasto*) by the *notaio*.

Before you sign anything remember that an estate agent, however honest, is not guaranteed to be impartial. You are advised at this stage to get the help of a lawyer or a notary.

- **O** an *avvocato civilista* – of the status of the international practitioners mentioned above.
- **O** a *notaio*. Employ a *notaio* from the very beginning, and you will get the documentation and the wording right, and avoid possible complications. A *notaio* is professionally qualified to make all the necessary checks that are required for the filing of a contract.
- **O** The *Compromesso* is the important and binding part of this contract.

ENGLISH TRANSLATION OF THE COMPROMESSO (SALE CONTRACT)

To explain this document in detail a translation of an Italian *compromesso* form follows. What is being translated is the official contract for property sales in Italy. The full Italian text can be found on the website www.casa24.ilsole24ore.com (click *vendita, modulista* then *preliminare di compravendita*)..

Preliminary Sale Contract (Compromesso)

Article1: Mr.............born at............in the province of ....date of birth..........., fiscal code number........... marital status............pre nuptial agreement..........(shared/separate) in the quality of................ hereinafter named the 'vendor'.

AND

Mr.................born at..................in province...................date of birth............ ......citizen of ....Italian fiscal code number..................pre nuptial.................. hereinafter named 'the buyer'.

AGREE UPON AND STIPULATE THE FOLLOWING:

Article 2: The vendor promises to sell to the buyer, who promises to buy, for himself, or for a person, body or company, to be nominated at the final contract, the portions of real estate hereinafter called 'the property' situated in the Comune of............, identified as follows: Street...... number........, comune of.........., situated on the floor...... and consisting of........ rooms plus services (bathroom and kitchen) and with additional space:........... The whole premises are specified in the N.C.E.U. (the new urban building register – nuovo catasto edilizio urbano) as follows: sheet:.... map:....... subsection:.... scale:....... plan:....... homogeneous territorial zone:....... census zone:........ category:...... class:....... rooms/land registry square metres......... land registry value.......... The vendor to give the buyer a copy of the deed of provenance, a copy of the land registry specification and a copy of the condominium rules affecting the property.

Article 3: The vendor declares that he has full ownership and power to dispose of the property in full accordance with law no. 151/1975, and that the property will be free of persons and things from... date, except for the present tenant (if rented).

Article 3B: Millesimal tables (if a condominium share of expenses)

property:-....

heating....

water.....

other...

ADMINISTRATIVE AND TECHNICAL DOCUMENTATION REGARDING THE SAFETY OF THE INSTALLATIONS. (*IMPIANTI*)

....
....

PUBLIC SAFETY CERTIFICATE AND GAS/ELECTRICITY CERTIFICATION.........
....

Article 4: The vendor declares that the property is unencumbered by any mortgages, current lawsuits, liens, fiscal privileges, unpaid condominium expenses and other burdens and encumberances of any kind, except for the items specified in the deed of provenance or the condominium rules with the exception of ....

Article 5: The vendor declares that the condominium committee has not/has authorised works to be done, extra expenses to be paid, of which he attaches a copy of the relevant minutes. These expenses are to be paid by the vendor/buyer.

The vendor declares that the condominium administration holds/does not hold a reserve fund for extraordinary expenses...... .

The vendor guarantees that, in the event of his legal separation, no entitlement to the enjoyment of the property has been awarded to his spouse.

Article 6: The property will be transferred in the state of fact and law in which it is found, seen and accepted by the buyer, in the same way as it reached the vendor (Mr....).... of whom the vendors are the heirs by virtue of the above mentioned deed or provenance.

Article 7: The property includes a share in the ownership of the communal parts of the building, as specified in the abovementioned condominium rules and millesimal tables, which the buyer is bound and obligated to accept.

Article 8: The final contract (*il rogito*) will be completed before the ......date, at the request of the buyer, with a notary which the buyer has the right to choose (or at the notary's office of Dr .... + address......).

Article 9: The expenses of the notary's deed, the registration tax, the mortgage, land registry and/or IVA (value added tax) charges are to be paid by the buyer.

The task and expense of finding any documentation concerning the property is the responsibility of the vendor (plus any INVIM – value added tax or future equivalent).

Article 10: The ownership and enjoyment of the property will pass to the buyer at the moment of the notarised deed of the final contract (*il rogito notarile*). From that point the buyer shall be responsible for all rights and burdens, especially the condominium dues with the eventual exception of the items specified in article 4, including any tenancy agreements, the details of which have been notified to the buyer.

The vendor will supply proof of payment of condominium expenses for the full period involved, i.e. up to the date of the final contract.

From that date the buyer must pay any interest on any mortgage he has taken over; whilst any current instalments of the mortgage, up to the date of the final contract, must be shared between the two parties.

Article 11: The sale will be 'as a whole' and not 'by measure', at the price agreed upon by all parties of .....euros, which the buyer commits himself to pay by the following means and at the following dates:- ....euros (in figures and letters)................ are paid by the buyer at the signing of the present deed by means of a bank draft (or cheque – *assegno circolare*) number... ...- particulars........... and date...... which the vendor accepts as an earnest money deposit (*caparra confirmatoria*) and first instalment.

In the case of default by the vendor he must pay back double this deposit to the buyer.

In case of default by the buyer, he loses his deposit,

€...........euros is also now paid as an instalment of the sale price.

Article 11B:...........................

Article 11C: The balance of ....euros will be paid by bank draft at the moment of the final contract (*rogito*).

Article 12: The vendor declares and guarantees not to have carried out on the property any unauthorised works, i.e. not in compliance with the laws and with current planning regulations, with the exception of the following.............

Article 13: The vendor shall pay any eventual fines, cash settlements or concessions regarding the property or resulting from his actions or omissions up to the date of the final contract. Equally he must be responsible for any burden incurred for regulations or restrictions not declared in the present private contract. In any case, all rights guaranteed to both parties by Article 1385 of the Civil Code, shall be recognised.

Article 14: The vendor declares himself aware of his obligation to supply the notary with a statement at the signing of the final contract, to the effect that he has declared the land registry rent of the property in his income tax returns.

Article 15: (*if the property has been sold through an agency*).

Article 16: (*if the property is rented*).

Article 17: (*if tax reductions for primary residence are required*).

Article 18: (*if the construction of the property was started after 1 September 1967.*

Date

Signatures

Buyer   Vendor

....
....

In accordance with articles 1341 and 1342 of the Civil Code, we specifically recognise articles 4, 6, 8, 9, 10, 10B, 10C, 12 and .... of this private contract.

Buyer   Vendor

....

Translation of the Official Italian Notes on the Compromesso

Article 2:

- Note that this is a *promise* to sell/buy in the *future*. The phrase sells/buys would denote a final contract in *the present*, which would be of no validity until registered. Beware of inexpert wording.

- The formula '*for himself or for a person to be nominated in the final contract*' creates the possibility for the 'buyer' to transfer the property to a third party. This could be advantageous in a family group in which the nominee could have special mortgage or tax advantages for the purchase of a primary residence. Equally the formula could be exploited by a 'buyer' who wanted to speculate on the property and sell it on at a higher price. The vendor might prefer to cancel this formula, to prevent such speculation.

- If the property is not registered in the Land Registry or if the class of building and the rateable value is not specified – you have to get this corrected by an expert (*geometra*).

○ If the plans on the registry document are inaccurate or the internal subdivisions have changed, or if the appurtenances have been left out (cellar, attic etc.), the vendor should submit an updated plan to the registry office signed by a *geometra* which definitively identifies the extent and layout of the property and its appurtenances. An authenticated copy of this plan should be given to the buyer.

Article 3:

○ Avoid the common formula 'will be transferred at the registry of the title free and available'. The buyer needs to know the *immediate* availability, whether it is lived in or rented. This information should be clearly specified in this article, plus the eventual evacuation date.

Article 3B:

○ The *millesimi* table -of shares in the condominium expenses – has to be accepted in total by the buyer (except for rare exceptions) – and is an important source of information on the running costs of the property (and should be compared with the most recent condominium accounts). According to Law DPR 447/91, article 9, paragraph 2, the vendor must give the buyer, at the signing of the final contract, all documentation regarding the safety of the gas and electricity installations (*impianti*). It is reasonable for the buyer to have this information earlier, at the signing of the *compromesso*, bearing in mind the expense of bringing, the *impianti* into conformity with the legal standards. It is also in the interest of the vendor, who could see himself sued in court by the buyer for a reduction in price if the *impianti* are not in order and certified as such.

Article 4:

○ *Mortgages* give the mortgager the right to sell the property to recover the loan. A *privilege* is the right of a creditor to be paid off first by the debtor. Note that the State has the first option (fiscal privilege). It is easy to calculate the privileges that private individuals have on the property but very complicated to work out the possible tax demands of the State regarding unpaid tax, etc. A servitude (*servitù*) is a real right of enjoyment of a property owned by others, such as a right of way to reach your own house. Transcription (*trascrizione*) is the official registration of deeds to make them publicly valid – for example a son might be the owner of a house but his mother might have the right to live there. Between two real rights precedence is given to the one that has been transcribed first. Restriction (*vincolo*) is a limitation imposed on a property by a public body (e.g. archaeological environmental restrictions). Burdens or encumbrances (*oneri o pesi*) are generic terms for limitations on the property imposed by one person in favour of another.

○ If there is a mortgage on the property, at the bottom of article 4, after 'with the exception of....' add the phrase 'a mortgage, of which the residual capital is.......'. Then choose between the following two clauses to be added to article 5b, to make your own case: 'The vendor declares that he will cancel the mortgage before the final contract' or 'The buyer declares that he has included the mortgage in the price'.

○ If you opt for taking on the mortgage add the following clause to Article 4B: 'For x euros, depending on further checks at the final contract, the buyer agrees to pay the residual debt of the vendor to ....financial institution or bank, concerning which the vendor shall produce the advice note of the last half yearly payment. The interests owned on this mortgage shall be paid by the vendor up to the date of the transfer of title' (*rogito*).

○ There is the possibility that one of the previous half-yearly instalments has not been paid by the vendor, in which case the buyer risks having to pay out of his own pocket. For this reason you should check on the last payment advice the vendor can produce.

○ If there are liens or sequestration orders on this property, you should check with a lawyer (*pignoramenti a sequestri*).

Article 5:

○ It is good for the buyer to know whether the condominium committee has agreed to any particularly onerous expenses for extraordinary maintenance or renovation of the buildings and installations which he will have to pay from his own pocket. He could be happy to benefit from this; but if he didn't know he could be in for an unpleasant surprise, especially if he had no money.

○ The reserve fund for extra expenses set up by the administrator of the condominium: the vendors share in this should be transferred to the buyer, and the following phrase should be inserted after 'extra expenses':- 'in which the buyer will take on all the effects'. Alternatively, the following phrase could be added: 'whose share will be reimbursed to the buyer on the signing of the contract'.

○ The buyer risks finding the house occupied by the separated spouse to whom it has been assigned. Even though the Court of Cassation has the right to evict this spouse, but it is not a pleasant thing for either party.

Article 6:

○ The 'state of fact' is how the property presents itself at the present moment, with all its installations, doors, window and sanitary ware. Unscrupulous vendors sometimes dismantle boilers, sinks and even door handles, doors and taps. The only way for the buyer to safeguard himself against this improbable occurrence is to draw up an inventory signed by both parties. The 'state of law' provides that there should be no changes in the property, the ownership, and in its compliance with planning laws.

Article 7:

○ An examination of the Condominium rules before signing the *compromesso* could be very useful: for example for someone who wanted to set up a medical surgery which was expressly forbidden by the rules.

Article 8:

○ The buyer has good reason to distrust too long a gap between the preliminary and final contract. Anything could happen between the signing of the *compromesso* and the transfer of title.

Article 9:

○ In general the registry tax is paid by the buyer, but it can be ascribed to the vendor by special agreement to that effect.

- Clarify also who is to be responsible for finding the various certificates and for paying the expenses, in order to avoid useless arguments. There are no doubts about who is responsible if the final contract is delayed for want of documentation: it is nearly always the vendor.
- If the construction of the property was started after 1 September 1967, fill in article 18. If the construction was started before that date it is better to attach an affidavit (*una dichiarazione sostitutiva di atto notorio*) to the effect that work was started before that date.

Article 10:

- The vendor owns the property up to the date of the transfer of title. If he allows the buyer to start renovation work after the *compromesso* he is taking a big legal risk (for example injuries to third parties during work) or even a criminal risk (for example if the work required planning permission). On the other hand, if the vendor stays in the property after the transfer of title he could in theory demand to become a tenant and pay the legal rent (*l'equo canone*). If the worst comes to the worst, it is possible to share the ownership (which passes to the buyer at the transfer of title) and the possession and enjoyment (which stays with the vendor up to a certain date following the actual transfer of title): you must anyway consult a notary for the clauses you must add for this.
- It is better for the buyer before signing the *compromesso*, to telephone the administrator of the *condominium* and ask if the owner has fully paid the condominium dues. The condominium administrator could demand a reimbursement of the expenses, not only of the current year but also of the previous one. (Civil Code, article 63).

Article 11:

- The sale 'as a whole' is one that recognises the property as a single unit. It is not a good idea to sell 'by measure' (by the square metres) because of possible disputes regarding the calculations of the area of the property.
- The deposit/instalment (*caparra*) can be *confirmatoria* or *penitenziale*:
- If it is *confirmatoria* and the buyer fails to fulfil the contract the vendor has the right to pocket it. If the vendor defaults the buyer has the right to be paid back double the deposit.

In both cases a repayment of any damages can be claimed. Alternatively a judge can be asked to enforce the contract itself, over and above the damages.

- A *caparra penitenziale* gives both parties the right to withdraw from the contract on payment of an agreed sum, without the obligation of fulfilling the contract. The same criterion applies: the buyer pays single, the vendor pays double.
- The *caparra* is usually 10% of the value of the sale price. The lower its value the less the risk for the buyer if the vendor is up to no good. The vendor often refuses to pay back the *caparra* when in default. Sometimes the vendor demands an instalment on the sale price which is greater than the *caparra* itself, in which case it is wise to split the two sums and specify how much is to be *caparra* and how much is to be an instalment.

- It is advisable to give the *caparra* to the vendor and not to the estate agent (who might later claim it as his fee).
- It is absolutely essential to clarify the conditions of payment. The buyer should safeguard himself by ironclad contracts, checked by an expert, against banks and/or financial institutions which promise to pay out mortgages on a certain date and then postpone, claiming documentation problems. This can delay the date of the transfer of title till after the deadline and cause trouble between the parties.

Article 12:

- The details of any request for amnesty (*condono*) must be specified at the foot of the article.

Article 13:

- The purpose of this clause is to protect the buyer as much as possible (contractually, normally the weaker party) from vendors who have made false declarations in articles 3, 4, and 12.

Article 14:

- If the rent of the property has not been declared in the last income tax return the notary will make you attach a declaration to the final contract, which will be sent to the tax office. In the absence of such a declaration the Deed is null and void.

Article 15:

- If the property is being bought through an agency, add this clause to article 15: 'The parties give notice that Mr...... of the .... agency, registered no. .... in the Brokers' Registry of the ....Chamber of Commerce, is entitled to a commission at the moment of .... from both parties of the agreed total of ....euros equal to ....per cent of the sale price plus IVA (value added tax) for which he will issue a separate receipt"

Ask the agent to countersign the margin of this clause.

If you want the agent to keep hold of the deposit money (*caparra*) (which is not to be recommended), add the following clause to article 11, after the words 'in the hands': 'of Mr ..... of the agency.....,as an interest-bearing deposit, until the drawing up of the Deed of Sale. The agency must issue a receipt and recognise that it cannot withhold any of this money in payment of its eventual fees or expenses'. A signature is also required by the agent in the margin of this clause.

Article 16:

If the house is rented:

- Add the following clause to Article 16:
- 'The vendor declares that the premises have been rented to Mr............ until date .... for the rent of ....euros (per month, year, quarter.) and the caution money deposit of .... euros, and undertakes to give the buyer this caution money plus interest and any eventual rents or instalments for expenses received in respect of periods following the date of the transfer of title'.

Article 17:

- If you want to benefit from tax reductions on a primary residence (*prima casa*):

These reductions benefit the buyer (who pays a registration tax of 3%).

Article 18

○ If the construction of the building starts after 1 September 1967, it is advisable to add a clause to Article 18 to the following effect: 'The vendor specifies that the property was built according to building/planning permission......in...... by the borough council (*comune*) of ....and/or passed by the retrospective legislation of law 47/85 and further improvements were also passed as shown by the attached documentation.

The detail of the building permit must perforce be included in the final contract, otherwise the contract is null and void. It is best, however, to declare them in the *compromesso*. If the final contract is annulled it will be on the basis of the *compromesso* that the buyer can claim his rights of compensation.

Signing twice: Make a separate list – with the help of the notary – itemising all the clauses in the compromesso to do with the payment of money, and get all the parties involved to sign it. Signing twice is a double guarantee and reminder for everyone.

MONEY TO COMPLETE THE PURCHASE ETC.

Make sure to give yourself plenty of time, months not weeks, to transfer the necessary funds to a local bank in Italy. See the section *Importing Currency* in the *Finance* chapter for the different ways of doing this. It is wise to have a chequebook and to get the notary to write out the cheques you have to sign on completion day, with his prior agreement. In many cases wads of banknotes are required – even for the notary – combined with banker's drafts (*assegni circolari*). It is always preferable to pay by personal cheque rather than carry large sums in brown envelopes. In Italy you can make out a cheque to yourself and countersign it on the back, which is as good as cash and does not name the recipient. You should not exceed €10,000 for each cheque. When larger sums are deposited they are subject to the strictures of the anti-money laundering measures (*anti-riciclaggio*) put in place to combat organised crime.

TAXES AND FEES

Taxes and duties vary on a property sale

If the house is to be a principal residence and the vendor is a private individual (*prima casa*).

○ Registry Tax – (*imposta del registro*) 3%
○ Fixed mortgage tax – (*imposta ipotecaria fissa*) 129.11 euros
○ Fixed Land Registry Tax – (*imposta catastale fissa*) 129.11 euros

If the property is a second house (*seconda casa*) the total tax is 10%

○ Registry tax – 7%
○ Mortgage tax – 2%
○ Land Registry tax – 1%

If it is a primary residence being bought by a developer the taxes are:
- IVA (Value added tax) – 4%
- Fixed mortgage tax – €129.11
- Fixed Land Registry tax – €129.11

The above taxes are levied on the value declared in the deed of sale. This value cannot be less than the rateable value (*valore catastale*), which is obtained by multiplying the *rendita catastale* by 100.

Typical notary's fee (*onorario*); depending on property:

Value of property	Fee
€50,000	€1,400
€250,000	€2,000
€300,000	€2,200
€500,000	€3,000

increasing by €100 for each additional €25,000 of value. This is the fee on the *rogito*. The fee on the *compromesso* is 50% of the above. In addition the notary will charge for the following:

- accessory rights (*diritti accessori*)
- indemnities (*indennità*)
- searches (*visure*)
- authentications (*autenticazioni*)
- expenses (*rimborso spese*)

It is essential to ask the *notaio* for an estimate of his charges at the very start. His fees may be fixed, but with all those extras he has plenty of room to negotiate. In a typical transaction the total notarial expenses will be minimum of €8,000 for a *Rogito notarile*.

POST-COMPLETION FORMALITIES

It is the duty of the notary to file and register the transfer of title and pay all taxes due, with all possible speed. Within 48 hours the local police – the *carabinieri* in a *comune* – or the *questura* in a provincial capital – must be informed of the change of ownership. The notary can do this himself or supply you with the relevant form. You will also want to transfer the utilities into your name, (electricity, water, telephone, gas, etc.) and arrange for new contracts (*volturazione delle utenze*), for which a photocopy of your contract will be useful.

LAND REGISTRY (ACCATASTAMENTO)

The *catasto* is an official register, created for taxation purposes, which files details of ownership, boundaries, mortgages and rateable values.

This register is divided into two parts:

O   *Nuovo Catasto Terreni* (N.C.T.), New Land Registry.

O   *Nuovo Catasto Edilizio Urbano* (new urban building registry).

The new system came into force on 1 January 2000 by presidential decree. Each census zone of the national territory is divided into 'microzones', and each property is classified in categories. Valuations are based on current market values, and revaluations are possible after any permanent 'socio-economical, environmental or urbanistic' change. The system, recently digitalised, is still in the throes of computerisation.

In theory anyone can apply for a search in any registry office on payment of a search fee (*visura*) of about 6 euros. Generally this search is done by the *geometra*, the *notaio* or their minions. But if you are doing the search yourself remember to start early and be prepared to shuttle from one office to another as is the case in all bureaucratic endeavours in Italy. Searches via the internet are becoming the norm for accredited professionals and their associations. (www.visurmet.com).

REAL ESTATE GLOSSARY

Abitabilità	literally 'habitability' certificate issued by the Comune ensuring that ceiling heights, window, safety regulations etc. are complied with.
Agente immobiliare	Estate Agent.
Acconto	Refundable deposit.
Bucalossi	A tax on renovation work named after the minister who introduced it in 1977 which is not refundable.
Buona fede	Good faith (ignorance of encroaching on another's right).
Caparra	non-refundable deposit – essential guarantee of a sale contract.
Catasto	Office of the Ministry of Finance which acts as a Land registry for updating land maps and plans of real estate.
Catasto certificate	Certificate giving land registry details, ownership, rateable value.
Catasto categories	Buildings are classified by letter:- A. Dwellings B. Collective institutions such as barracks or schools C. Commercial buildings such as shops D. Industrial buildings E. Special buildings Under categories:- A1. de luxe, A2 civil, A3 economy, A4 popular, A5 ultrapopular, A6 rural, A7 small house, A8 villa, A9 historical building.

Centro storico	The ancient centre of a town or city. Often used as a reference point.
Clausola penale	Penalty clause specifying amount payable for defaulting party.
Compromesso	Preliminary sale contract.
Comuncazione di cessione d fabricato	Document which must be presented within 48 hours of purchase or rental of a property, to the Comune or Carabinieri.
Comunione dei beni	Joint ownership in the case of a married couple.
Concessione edilizia	Planning permission from the comune essential for any building work.
Condómino	Owner of property in a condominium.
Condono edilizio	Amnesty, by payment, for legalising past illegal building work, essential for the validity of the sale contract.
Conduttore	Tenant of a rented property .(legal word)
Delega	Power of attorney.
Dichiarazione ici (see ici)	Declaration to the Comune for tax purposes to be made by June 30 of any acquisition of a property.
Diritto di abitazione	Right to live in a house – limited to a person or family. No sub-letting or sale allowed.
Diritto di uso	Right to use a property – mainly in an agricultural context, limited to the needs of a particular farmer or family.
Diritto di usufrutto	Right of usufruct – which does not exceed the life time of the beneficiary – but can be tranferred.
Fallimento	Insolvency, bankruptcy.
ICI	Imposta Comunale Sugli Immobili. Council (Comune) tax on property, levied according to the Catasto value of the property.
Imposte	Registration
Ipoteca	Mortgage on a property.
Ipotecarie di registro e catastali	taxes payable by the buyer at the moment of sale, according to the catasto value of the property.
Inquilino	Tenant of a rented property (normal word).
IRPEF	Imposta sui redditi delle persone fisiche; Income tax payable on the catasto value of the property – or on the rent, if rented, even if the rent is not collected.
Libero al rogito	'Free on completion' – meaning the property will be freed of its occupants on completion of the sale.
Locatario	Tenant of a rented property.
Locatore	Landlord contract for a property.
Locazione	Rental contract for a property
Mutuo	Long-term loan or mortgage.
Multiproprietà	Time sharing.

Ónere	Burden, limitation.
Percentuale	Percentage – commission.
Perizia	Technical survey.
Permuta	Exchange – or house-swapping – governed by articles 1552-1555 of the civil code.
Pertinenze	Appurtenances – such as garage, attic, cellar or outhouse – belonging to an apartment or house.
Piano regolatore	Development plan drawn up by the Comune for zoning the district into building, industrial, green etc. areas.
Procura	Power of attorney.
Preliminare di vendita	The same as compromesso or preliminary contract of sale.
Provvigione	Commission.
Rendita	Annual rateable value for a property established by the Ufficio tecnico erariale or Tax office.
Ristrutturazione	Renovation, rebuilding.
Rogito notarile	Notarial deed signifying the final contract.
Separazione dei beni	Separate ownership (of married couples).
Sopralluogo	Site visit.
Supercondominio	Complex of more than one building with shared facilities such as access road, car parking, garden etc.
Tabella millesimale	'Table of thousandths', showing the exact share of the expenses of a condominium for each member.
Trascrizione	The public registration of any real estate contract, governed by article 2643 of the civil code and lodged in the local land registry (Ufficio dei Registri Immobiliari).
Trattative	Negotiations.
Ute	Ufficio Tecnico Erariale – the tax office which gives a rateable value to real estate.
Valore catastale	Catasto value – obtained by multiplying by 100 for dwellings, by 50 for offices and by 34 for shops, the basis for the calculation of the sale and ICI taxes.

Part IV

WHAT HAPPENS NEXT

SERVICES

MAKING THE MOVE

BUILDING OR RENOVATING

MAKING MONEY FROM YOUR PROPERTY

SERVICES

CHAPTER SUMMARY

- ○ Arranging for an isolated property to be connected to mains services can be very expensive.
- ○ **Electricity.** ENEL is the main supplier of electricity in Italy and bills are sent out every two months.
  - ○ Electricity bills are estimated, and adjusted twice yearly after a meter reading.
- ○ **Plugs and Light Fittings.** Most Italian plugs have either two or three round pins. All electric bulbs are screw fitting.
- ○ **Mains Gas.** Mains gas is supplied in most large towns and cities by SIG or Italgas.
  - ○ Mains gas is not available in rural areas.
- ○ **Gas Tanks.** Many foreign residents in remoter areas have a refillable gas tank for central heating and there are strict regulations regarding installation.
- ○ **Bottled Gas.** Bottled gas is commonly used in rural areas but also in towns and cities, especially for cooking.
  - ○ One bottle of gas, used just for cooking should last an average family six weeks.
- ○ **Water.** Italian water tends to have a high calcium content, which builds up deposits in pipes and equipment.
- ○ **Drought.** Water is plentiful in northern Italy but in central and southern parts drought is common.
  - ○ In cases of drought, water may be rationed to a fixed number of litres per house regardless of the number of occupants.
  - ○ In rural drought areas water used in the house is recycled for watering the garden.
  - ○ On a grander scale you can install a purifier and a special tank to recycle all water from the house to use on the garden, orchard, lawns etc.
- ○ **Wells and Bore Holes.** If you have a property with a well or underground water supply you may need to employ a water-diviner to pinpoint the best place to sink a bore hole.
  - ○ Well water should be scientifically analysed to confirm it is

> safe to drink.
> O **Telephone.** The Italian public utility is known as SIP.
>   O It can be very expensive to connect isolated property to the telephone system.
> O **Security.** Italian cities have a very bad reputation for petty crime but even in rural areas you should lock up your property.
>   O Owners of holiday homes are often glad to have reliable people stay for free in the winter to keep the property occupied in return for maintenance, gardening etc.

It is important for anyone contemplating a move to Italy to ascertain whether or not their property is connected to the main services – water, electricity, gas, sewage and telephone. The further away the property is from the nearest telephone line or mains, the greater the cost of connection. Such costs can add considerably to the price of an Italian property and you should therefore expect to pay a lower price for property without services/utilities than would be asked for a property with them. Most houses and flats in cities are connected to mains services. Another important consideration when purchasing a rural property is the provision of a well-made access road. Many roads to rural properties are at best a rocky path the majority of which are not suitable for any vehicles other than four wheel drive, tractors and diggers. A good road is essential and if shared with other properties (*strada vicinale*) it is a good idea to draw up an agreement about the upkeep and the division of costs with the help of your *geometra* (surveyor) or direct consultation with the neighbours involved.

ELECTRICITY

The national electricity company *Ente Nazionale per l'Energia* commonly known as ENEL/Enel (www.enel.it) had the monopoly for supplying electricity before privatisation in 1998; even so there is still little competition. Enel monitors your consumption of electricity every two months and sends estimated bills (*bollette*): your bill is adjusted twice a year when meters have been read. Bills show your account number (*numero intente*), amount payable (*importo lire*) and due date (*scadenza*). You can pay your bill at the bank, post office or the electricity board's own offices but the easiest way to pay bills is by direct debit from your bank. You can read your own meter and dial your meter reading (*gli scatti*) or report breakdowns on telephone number 800 900 800.

You can also find more information on services provided on the website www.prontoenel.it. The cost of electricity in Italy is relatively high. There is a standing charge (*quota fissa*) of €3,70 for every two months and the consumption charge is based on the power rating of the property, the maximum being 6KW. The charge per Kilowatt hour (*scatto*) is €0.13 on a 6KW power rating. Changing your power rating from 3KW to 6KW can be costly. Out of 22 million electrical service contracts in Italy 18 million are for 3KW, including most apartments.

Arranging a Contract with ENEL. After purchasing your property and if the estate agent hasn't arranged for the electricity to be transferred to your name, you will have to sign a new contract (*volturazione delle utenze*) at the local ENEL office. You need to bring identification with you either your passport or residence permit (see the *Residence and Work Permits* chapter) the registration number of the meter and the previous owner's paid electricity bill.

RESIDENT AND NON-RESIDENT TARIFF

Note: If you are supplied with electricity on a resident basis and the property is your main residence (*prima casa*) you get a reduction, non-residents pay a premium rate.

Power Supply

The electricity supply is limited in Italy to between 1.5-6 kW (the maximum) per house. This means that appliances with a high wattage (e.g. washing machine/dishwasher) cannot be running at the same time. The system will overload and there will be a power cut. If you rely on electricity for operating a computer, fax and other such equipment you need to seriously think about the installation of a back-up generator or solar power system as frequent power cuts can damage appliances.

Before you can be plugged into electricity an ENEL inspector will have to verify that the wiring you have had installed meets ENEL specification. Make sure that all electrical work is carried out on your property by a fully qualified electrician (*elettricista*). The electrician should be registered at the local Chamber of Commerce (*La Camera di Commercio*). As part of safety regulations new electrical systems in your property are checked every year and a certificate of inspection is issued.

Remote Properties. The cost of providing electricity to a rural property can be prohibitive especially if the property is over 500 metres or more from an electricity pylon. It is possible to install a generator or solar power but this means weak current and not enough power to work washing machines, dishwashers, televisions etc. The diesel to run the generator can be costly. In the long-run and for your own comfort and convenience, mains electricity is a priority.

Meters. Most meters are now installed outside the property for easy access for the meter reader. In some old properties and apartment blocks there is a common meter and the bill is equally shared among the apartment owners. This is not good for the owner who is absent, especially in winter.

Plugs. Most Italian plugs have two or three round pins so if you are bringing electrical appliances from another country you need to purchase plug adaptors. The two-pin plug has no earth wire so large appliances using a high wattage must be plugged into earthed sockets.

Fuses. When there is an overload in the electrical system, a circuit breaker is tripped. The fuse box is usually situated by an entrance. For this reason, it can be a good idea to keep a torch on or near the box. Before inspection and reconnecting one must make sure that all high power appliances are switched off.

Bulbs. All electric light bulbs in Italy are screw fitting. You can buy adaptors to change appliances such as lamps from bayonet to screw fittings.

GAS

Most cities and large towns in Italy are supplied by the (*Società Italiana per il GAS*) (SIG) or ITALGAS (www.italgas). If you purchase a property with mains gas you should contact SIG in order to have your meter read and get connected. Mains gas is costly. You receive a bill every two months and you can pay at the post office, bank or SIG offices or by direct debit (*domiciliazione*) from your bank account. Gas appliances have to be approved and installed by a registered GAS company. It is advisable to have gas water heaters checked annually, as gas leaks can be fatal.

Unfortunately the SIG network does not penetrate rural areas where many foreign residents buy homes. For inhabitants of these areas who wish to have central heating, the solution is a gas tank known in Italian as a *bombolone*. Gas tanks can be loaned from the larger gas companies for example Agip gas, Shell gas, and Liquigas, and installation is governed by strict regulations. For obvious reasons, the tank should not be immediately adjacent to the house or road, it must be at least 25m away. The tank can be sited underground and pipes laid to connect it to the house. The contract with the gas company supplying liquid gas will stipulate a minimum annual purchase usually in the region of €1,200. The size of your tank depends on your needs.

Bottled gas

The gas bottle (*bombola*) is commonly used in rural areas but can be used in towns and cities. Bottled gas is mostly used for cooking though it can also be used for portable gas fires. You pay a deposit on your first purchase of bottled gas and then you exchange your empty bottle for a full one. The bottles weigh 10 kg and 15 kg and a 10kg bottle costs €17, plus a delivery charge if necessary. A bottle used just for cooking will last an average family six weeks. The bottled gas is sometimes kept outside with a connecting pipe to the cooker. If you choose this method you must buy propane gas and not butane as propane can withstand changes in temperature – butane is for internal use only. For those who do not wish to go to the bother or expense of arranging connection with mains gas, particularly if you are only using your Italian home for holidays, the *bombola* is a useful alternative to mains gas.

WATER

The water supply is under the control of the local commune, eg CIGAF and there are conditions governing the various uses of this precious commodity. There is usually plenty of water in the North of Italy but in central and southern parts there may be only a meagre supply. For this reason it is essential if you live in a rural area especially in the south to have a storage tank (*cassone*) which can be topped up when the water supply is on or filled by tanker, though this is expensive. For flat-dwellers in the main cities a 500 litre tank may be sufficient. In remote rural areas it may be necessary to store several months of water in huge underground tanks. Water shortages can be made worse whatever the region by the poor infrastructure; much water is lost because of old leaking mains water pipes. If water in your area is metered it may be rationed to a fixed number of litres per house, regardless of the number of occupants.

Recycling Water. Due to the shortage of water in some areas, there are restrictions on watering the garden and a ban on swimming pools. However, if you are clued-up and possess a little ingenuity there are solutions. It is possible to recycle water used for washing and bathing for the garden by draining it into a separate tank (*serbatoio*).

Another method of recycling your domestic water, both white and grey is to install a water purifier (*depuratore*). This is a large tank, which is made up of sections. It is placed underground and in a position where the treated contents of the septic tank spill into it. This water passes through an aerated section. The aeration is done by means of an electric pump, programmed to work at least 16 hours a day. This pump passes oxygen into the water to feed the 'good' bacteria which in turn eat the 'bad' bacteria. The filtered water collects in the last section and overflows into another tank; this water can be used for watering or irrigation and is especially beneficial for an orchard, or large lawns that you want to keep green. The total cost of a *depuratore* is €9,500 (about £6,270). This includes the tanks, pipes, pump and labour.

When is a Swimming Pool not a Swimming Pool? Answer, when it's a *vasca*. The way round the swimming pool ban is to build an artificial water basin (*vasca*) common in rural areas and ostensibly for domestic use when the mains water is cut off. The idea is that it fills up during the winter when rain is plentiful; it may also be fed by a spring or well. With a proper lining and some kind of filtering system to keep the water clean, a vasca could be used as a swimming pool, the less obviously the better.

Wells and Water Diviners. It is a good idea when you buy your house that if it states there is a well (*pozzo*), that you have it confirmed by an expert, that there is plenty of water and that it is not likely to dry up. Also make sure who owns the well and your rights to use it, e.g. that it cannot be stopped or indeed diverted or drained away by your neighbours. If you are lucky enough to have a well on your land, this can make your life easier. You may even wish to call in the services of a water-diviner (*rabdomante*) to detect where the water is and put markers down for future bore-holes. A *rabdomante* can usually determine the depth of the water, with a high degree of accuracy. If you buy a property with a well – you can take a sample to be tested by the local water authority to make sure it's safe to drink. In general water is hard in Italy and has a high calcium content. The water stains sinks and deposits settle in taps, kettles etc, which require cleaning with *anticalcare*. It is possible to install a water softener – this has many benefits and prevents furring of appliances and pipes.

Turning Off the Water. If you are moving into a new house or apartment it is a good idea to check where the stopcock is situated, so that in an emergency the supply can be turned off. If you are absent from the property during the winter it is a good *security* measure to turn off the water as burst pipes can cause untold damage, and if the water hasn't been turned off you are in default of your insurance conditions.

TELEPHONE

Installing/Getting Connected. The Italian telephone service (*Telecom Italia*) was privatised in 1997. In 1998 deregulation meant competition was introduced. The public utility is called *Società Italiana per l'Esercizio delle Telecomunicazioni* known as (S.I.P). To get a new telephone line (*nuovo impianto*) installed in your home you must first apply at the local Telecom Italia office; there, you can fill in the application form. You need to bring your passport (and a photocopy) for identification purposes. Note that if you live in a remote rural area the cost of a telephone line, especially if your nearest connection point is miles away is likely to be prohibitive. If you manage to get connected the cost of installation will appear on your first bill.

Bills. Billing payments can be paid by direct debit from your bank. Bills can be wildly inaccurate, a problem for which there is little remedy. You could try installing a metering device (*indicatore di conteggio*), but should you ever convince the company of your right to a rebate, it is doubtful whether you would ever manage to obtain it.

Directories and Yellow Pages. If you have a private phone – you are given a copy of the local telephone directory (*elenco*) www.paginebianche.it and a copy of the

Yellow Pages (*pagine gialle*) www.paginegialle.it annually. There is also an *English Yellow Pages* (EYP) which can be bought.

The EYP contains names, addresses, postcodes, telephone and fax numbers plus e-mail and website addresses. You can contact EYP, www.englishyellowpages.it. There is also the Into Italy information website (www.eypdaily.it).

Mobiles. The Italians have taken to mobiles (*telefonini*) and the number of providers is growing as is the quality and coverage of the services. For more information see *Communications* in *Living in Italy*.

SECURITY

Italy has a bad reputation for petty crime but this is mostly confined to the cities. However, even in rural areas securing your home is important and it is always advisable to lock your house even if you are only going to the local shops as a competent burglar can empty a house in a few hours and have driven away with all your possessions, which the police (*carabinieri*) are unlikely to recover.

Clever lighting can be a good deterrent, lights that come on intermittently and radios and televisions fitted to a time clock make the would-be intruder think the house is occupied. If you are a permanent resident, a dog can be useful to scare away unwanted visitors. Even a warning sign with a picture of a fierce dog may be sufficient.

Home Insurance. Another important consideration is the insurance requirements – no insurance company will settle a claim if the property is not secure. Most insurance firms insist on:

- An external door, which should be strong either made of steel (*porta blindata*) or have a steel-rod mechanism. Some policies insist on two locks on external doors.
- Windows to have internal lockable shutters with iron cross-bars fitted. Bars on all windows and doors less than ten metres from ground. Grilles can be fitted externally which allow for open windows in the heat of the summer and prevent intruders.

You can have an alarm fitted and this too will reduce your insurance premium. There are several different systems and there is even one that can monitor your property from another country although this is costly.

House-sitters

For temporary absences for a month or more, it is a good idea to employ house-sitters who, unlike a caretaker, would be expected to stay on the premises at night. For your own peace of mind you could invite friends to stay or employ trustworthy locals perhaps recommended by the local priest or doctor.

Lucy, an expatriate widow with a large villa near Florence, who was vacating her property for a month's holiday in Australia was delighted when her local priest found two university students who were only too glad to house-sit as they needed peace and solitude to study. The payment they received was a welcome bonus. Their only duties were to care for two dogs and three cats thus ensuring their employer could go on holiday assured her home was protected.

Owners of holiday homes are often glad to have reliable people stay for free in their houses during the winter in return for some kind of useful work: chopping and stacking wood, garden clearing, looking after animals, painting and decorating etc. The owners then relax knowing their house is thereby secure and heated.

STAFF/CLEANERS

Immigrants

There is no need for Italians to do menial jobs e.g. gardener, cleaner, handyman etc. as for the last decade or more there has been an invasion of immigrants (*extracomunitari*) from Sri Lanka, the Philippines, the Balkan States, Africa, India and South America and also 65,000 from other EU countries. The number of official immigrants is 1.5 million, while the unofficial (*clandestini*) number is estimated at an additional 250,000 and growing. An amnesty (*una sanatoria*) in 2002 allowed immigrants to register and so come into the system.

Employing Immigrants. The drawback of most immigrants is that they cannot speak the language and as a result don't integrate into society. However, if they are employed as domestics, handymen etc., they are recognised by the authorities. You can also sponsor someone from Sri Lanka etc., and employ them as a carer (*badante*). There are special laws in their favour and application forms for sponsorship are at the post office.

Finding a Gardener. It is possible to find a gardener/handyman by talking to locals and employing someone on a recommendation. The ideal arrangement is to find a retired person who is looking for an allotment in which case you can give him part of your land. He in turn looks after your garden and supplies you with vegetables. You can also find gardeners in the Yellow Pages under (*Giardinaggio Servizio*) Gardening Services. These gardeners are usually attached to garden centres and can be employed on a regular basis. The advantage of using such a firm is that they are usually qualified gardeners and have all the latest specialist equipment. A gardener would expect to be paid €17-€20 (£11-£13) an hour. There are many expatriates of all nationalities working as gardeners, some of these are qualified garden architects or have certificates for differing degrees from horticultural colleges. The only way to find them is on the grapevine i.e. word of mouth.

Caretaker. In Italy it used to be possible to employ a married couple to caretake for you. The woman would clean and cook and do the laundry. The man would look after the property, tending the olives and vines and often arranging for any repairs to be done. Most couples now come from the immigrant population and are expensive to employ. They expect you to house them, pay them a decent wage including insurance and social security payments. Most people as a result make do with a cleaner who comes in for a few hours each week and a caretaker who does the same. Both would be paid in the region of €10-€12 per hour.

MS.

MAKING THE MOVE

CHAPTER SUMMARY

- Your removal firm will need a list of your goods and copies of documents pertaining to the ownership of Italian property, both stamped by the Italian consulate.
- You need to have a *Permesso di Soggiorno* (permission to stay document) before you can import belongings to furnish your new Italian home).
  - If you have not been in Italy long enough to get a permesso di soggiorno you can apply to the *comune* for an attestation to the effect that you have bought or leased property in Italy.
- **Cars.** Non-residents from the EU can drive back and forth to their Italian holiday home with their own national documents.
  - You can drive a foreign registered car in Italy for six months before it has to be registered in Italy.
  - To register a foreign vehicle in Italy, it must pass a *collaudo* (MOT).
  - There are agencies (*agenzie pratiche auto*) which can carry out all the bureaucratic run around involved in importing a car.
- **Customs.** Items must be imported within 6 months of entering Italy.
  - Make sure new items show some wear and are not still wrapped in their factory packaging.
- **Pets.** To import a pet you need a Certificate of Health issued by a vet registered with your country of origin's ministry of agriculture.
  - If entering with a pet by air, it can normally travel as excess baggage (i.e. on the same flight as the owner).
  - Anyone wishing to take their pet back and forth between Italy and the UK can do so with a 'pet's passport' arranged with a DEFRA registered vet.

REMOVALS

Moving the Contents of Your Home to Italy.

The amount of possessions that an expatriate will take with them to Italy is likely to vary considerably. Generally speaking, anyone moving to a new home in Italy will want to export a large enough quantity of bulky possessions to require the service of a professional removal company with international expertise. This being Italy, there are a number of bureaucratic formalities to be dealt with before the shipping company can deliver your possessions. If you live outside the EU the first step before you leave for Italy is to submit a list of the items you wish to import into Italy to the nearest Italian Consulate, who will officially stamp it. All nationalities must also apply for their *permesso di soggiorno* (permit to stay – see *Residence and Entry* chapter for addresses) from the *questura* (police station) in Italy once you have arrived. Once the permit is issued you can then import your belongings.

The removal firm will require both the list stamped by the consulate, the *permesso* and copies of documents relating to your ownership of property in Italy or proof of address. If you have not been resident in Italy long enough to have obtained the *permesso* you can obtain an attestation from the *comune* to the effect that you have purchased or leased accommodation in the area. This should allow the shipping company to import your belongings successfully.

Shipping personal belongings internationally is always best done by a professional and reputable company that has, most importantly, experience in dealing with the system of the country you are going to. When leaving Italy it is also important to make sure you use a company that is experienced in that process too, as there are procedures such as cancelling your residence permit to be undertaken so that you can export your possessions again.

Removal Firms

There are a number of large firms that specialise in international removals and it makes sense to consult one of these. UK residents can obtain a list of such companies from The British Association of Removers (3 Churchill Court, 58 Stations Road, North Harrow, Middlesex HA2 7SA) in return for a stamped addressed envelope. Be sure to ask for a list of international movers as these are a subgroup of the association's members. The BAR also publishes a free leaflet of handy hints for those contemplating removals overseas, available from the same address.

Residents of other countries should consult the membership directories of the international associations listed below. Most of these organisations also maintain their directories online.

Household Goods Forwarders Association of America: www.hhgfaa.org
International Federation of International Movers (FIDI): www.fidi.com
Overseas Moving Network International: www.omnimoving.com

Useful addresses

Baxter's International Removers: Brunel Road, off Rabans Lane, Aylesbury HP19
	3SS; ☎01296-393335. Specializes in removals to Italy and Germany.

Interdean: Worldwide removals (UK 020 8961 4141; USA Headquarters , 55 Hunter Lane, Elmsford, New York 10523-1317; tel: 914-347 6600; fax: 914-347 0129; Chicago 630-752 8990, fax 630-752 9087; Dallas 817-354 6683, fax 817-354 5570; Houston 281-469 7733, fax: 281-469 9426; Los Angeles 562-921 0939, fax 562-926 0918; Raleigh/Durham 919-969 1661, fax 919-969 1663; San Francisco 510-266 5660, fax 510-266 5665; www.interdean.com). Interdean have offices in a number of European countries (including Italy) and the Far East, which can be found via the website. They also offer relocation services.

Importing a Car

Whereas non-residents may freely drive back and forth between the UK and their Italian holiday home with British car registration documents and an EU or International Driving Licence, residents are obliged to either officially import their British registered vehicle or buy one in Italy. For drivers moving to Italy who are already resident in Europe (except UK and Irish residents who will have right hand drive cars), taking their own car with them is often a good idea. This is because you have to be a resident before you can buy an Italian car and therefore have to manage without private transport for a number of months, unless you can afford a rental car for that length of time. UK and Irish residents, who know far enough in advance that they are moving to Italy, may want to buy a left hand drive car in preparation for their relocation. Second hand left-hand drive cars for sale in the UK can found online on the Exchange and Mart website (www.exchangeandmart.co.uk).

Insurance for a UK Registered Car. When taking a UK registered car to Italy it will be necessary to ensure that the insurance cover purchased in the UK will be applicable for a long stay abroad. In the past, failing to notify the insurance company that the car will be used predominantly outside the UK for an extended period has been grounds to refuse an insurance claim. 12 month Europe-wide car insurance can be secured through *Stuart Collins & Co*, 114 Walter Road, Swansea SA1 5QQ; ☎01792-655562; fax 01792-651126.

Registering a Foreign Vehicle in Italy

To register a foreign vehicle in Italy it must first pass a *collaudo*, the Italian equivalent of an MOT. From then on the process becomes the usual Italian paper chase. No wonder most people are happy enough to call on the services of one of the specialist agencies (*agenzie pratiche auto*) that wade through the necessary procedures on your behalf. Once the *collaudo* has been obtained it must be taken with all the car documents and a residence certificate, to a *notaio* who will apply for the car registration at the local (*Uffizio della Motorizzazione Civile e dei Trasporti in Concessione*) and register the vehicle with the local *Pubblico Registro*

Automobilistico. The car will then be issued with a registration certificate (*carta di circolazione*). Licence plates (*foglio di circolazione*) are issued by the *Pubblico Registro Automobilistico*. Registration costs vary according to car size but in any case will not be less than £100.

CAR TAX

Following registration you become liable for car tax. Note that it is not necessary to display a car tax disk (*bollo*) on the windscreen. You will also need an insurance badge (*contrassegno*). There are additional taxes for diesel driven cars and radios (but not cassette players).

For further information about driving in Italy, the rules of the road and insurance the following addresses may be useful.

Useful addresses

Automobile Association (AA): Import Section, Fanum House, Basingstoke Hants RG21 2EA; ☎01256-20123; www.automobileassociation.co.uk. Information is supplied only to members of the AA. Ask for information on the permanent importation of a vehicle into Italy. For membership details contact your nearest AA office.

Automobile Club d'Italia (ACI): Via Marsala 8, 00185 Rome; ☎06-49981; www.aci.it.

IMPORTING PETS

Many pet owners find the thought of leaving their pets behind when they move overseas heartbreaking. Children, especially, can find leaving the family pet behind a traumatic experience. It is a reasonably straightforward process to transport your dog or cat (and other species not on the endangered species list) with you to your new home in Italy, providing you take care to follow the regulations.

To the Italians, who reserve all doting pride for their children and grandchildren, a dog tends to me more of a fashion accessory than a faithful companion.

To import domestic pets it is necessary to have a certificate of health issued by a veterinarian registered with the ministry of agriculture in the country of origin. A list of vets who have this designation is usually available from the ministry of agriculture. However, in some countries it is necessary to visit the local offices of the ministry of agriculture to obtain the necessary Health Certificate, or have one issued by a veterinarian stamped and approved by the Ministry of Agriculture. In addition to the Health Certificate, which must be translated into Italian, the animal must have received a rabies inoculation not less than twenty days and not more than eleven months prior to crossing the Italian border – a rabies certificate attesting to this is also required. Finally, the vaccination record (sometimes known as an animal passport) of the animal is required to show that the animal has received the standard vaccinations required for the particular animal – as prescribed by a veterinarian. These vaccinations are usually required to have been administered not less than thirty days prior to entering the country. Always check with Italian embassy to ensure the current requirements as regulations can change suddenly, as was the case following the foot and mouth epidemic in the UK in 2001; dogs and cats can be carriers of foot and mouth even though they do not display symptoms.

Transporting Pets by Air. If the animal is to enter the country by air, it can often accompany passengers as excess baggage, though it is necessary to book cargo space in advance as airlines often limit the number of animals to two per flight. Airlines can also advise on the current bureaucratic requirements for importing an animal, as they are responsible for checking the paperwork before accepting the animal on board their aircraft. Taking a dog or cat as excess baggage is often easier than sending the animal as air cargo independently from the owner as customs officials are less worried that the animal is being imported for commercial reasons.

Regulations and Practices in Italy. Regulations now in force in most areas of Italy compel owners to have their dogs tattooed on the body as a means of checking their registration. An alternative to the tattoo is for the dog to have a tiny microchip inserted under the skin of the neck. Any loose dog without either a tattoo or microchip is liable to be destroyed. The tattoo/microchip insertion can be done by a vet, or in some areas by the *Unità Sanitaria Locale*. Dog insurance against claims for damages is advisable for those with unpredictable animals and those, whose canines have no traffic sense.

Rabies vaccinations have to be given yearly and a log-book will be provided by the vet for the purpose of recording these. Apart from rabies, which is reputedly prevalent in the far north of Italy, hazards further south are more likely to include encounters with porcupines and snakes. For animals (and human beings) it is advisable to keep a supply of venom antidote in the fridge, but make sure that it is regularly renewed before the expiry date has been reached.

UK Pet Passport Programme. UK resident pet owners who wish to take their pet back and forth between Italy and the UK and avoid subjecting their animal to quarantine should be aware that the Passport for Pets scheme only applies to cats and dogs. There are also a limited number of entry points where an animal can be returned to the UK as part of the programme. Consult your veterinarian well in advance of departure from the UK as it can take up to six months to fulfil the requirements necessary for your pet to qualify for the scheme. Residents of Italy can take their cat or dog to the UK for a holiday without having to place them in quarantine if they have fulfilled the necessary requirements as outlined below.

In addition to having an up to date pet passport, the animal should also have a microchip inserted under the skin of their shoulder and be vaccinated against rabies. A blood test one month after the vaccination to prove immunity is also required. It is also necessary for the animal to be given anti-parasite medication the day before entering the UK – i.e. when entering by ferry from France. Though the animal does not have to undergo quarantine it can take a number of hours after arrival in the UK for the animal to be cleared through customs.

Current details about the scheme and a number of factsheets can be found on the website of the *Department For Environment, Food and Rural Affairs:* www.defra.gov.uk/animalh/quarantine/index.htm. DEFRA also has a PETS helpline: 0870-241 1710 (or +44 20 7904 8057 from outside the UK) – open 8.30am to 5pm, Monday to Friday. Further information about the quarantine rules can be obtained from 020-7904 6221.

Useful Addresses:

Independent Pet and Animal Transportation Association International Inc.: www.ipata.com. A directory of members, as well a advice on transporting pets, is contained on this website.

D.J. Williams: Animal Transport, Littleacre Quarantine Centre, 50 Dunscombes Road, Turves, Nr Whittlesey Cambs PE7 2DS; ☎01733-840291; fax 01733-840348. International pet collection and delivery service, will deliver overland or arrange air transport. Will collect from your home and arrange all the necessary documentation. For those people whose pet is not covered by the PETS scheme, they also provide quarantine services.

CUSTOMS

The good news for those importing household goods into Italy is that there are no regulations about how long they must have been in your possession. However, a large selection of expensive, pristine equipment would undoubtedly arouse the suspicions of the customs officers. It is advisable that any new items show a few obvious signs of wear and tear in order not to attract import duty and VAT – another way to lessen the interest of customs officials is to make sure that the items are not perfectly wrapped in their factory packaging.

The most important regulation regarding the import of personal possessions is that the items must be imported within six months of taking up residence in Italy. The Excess Baggage Co lists current import regulations on their website: www.excessbaggage.co.uk.

If you decide to take a loaded van of furniture and other items for your home from one European Union country to Italy, you should have no problems, especially if the country is inside the Schengen area. If you are driving from an EU country through Switzerland to get to Italy (which is not strictly necessary) and you are stopped by Swiss customs, you should inform the Swiss customs that you are in transit to another EU country. An employment contract, rental agreement or ownership document would undoubtedly help convince the Swiss officials of your legitimacy.

If you are going to drive your possessions from a non-EU country into Italy you should have your consul stamp and *permesso di soggiorno* in your possession at the point of entry. However, you should also ensure that you have the necessary paperwork required to transit through any country *en route*.

Italian Customs and Your Foreign Registered Car. On arrival at customs, the owner must present the registration documents, proof of insurance and a certificate of residence. After checking the vehicle against the documents the customs will issue a customs receipt (*bolletta doganale*). The owner may then drive the car with foreign plates for up to six months before the car has to be registered in Italy. There is no duty or VAT levied on cars imported in this manner, but it is a once in a lifetime concession. The problem with this procedure is that now the Schengen agreement has been implemented there are, as often as not, no customs officers present at the point of entry into Italy. In this case it will be necessary to find a customs office and apply for your customs certificate soon after your arrival in Italy.

BUILDING OR RENOVATING

CHAPTER SUMMARY

- ○ You will need to employ a *geometra* (surveyor) to obtain any planning permission and to oversee the building work.
  - ○ It is essential to have a building plan produced in conjunction with the geometra before you begin.
- ○ Recommendations for a *geometra* and all other artisans can be obtained from the local builder's merchants.
- ○ The building trade in Italy is predominantly manned by immigrant labour.
- ○ Each building firm has its own style – you should inspect some finished work to make sure you know what you are getting.
- ○ Having the employer on the spot encourages the workmen.
- ○ **Water.** In Italy, water arrives in your house from the mains via a pump in the basement. This is a disadvantage if your pump breaks down.
  - ○ Only the kitchen is supplied with water direct from the mains.
- ○ **Heating.** The standard heater system is gas-heated water pumped through radiators.
  - ○ Underfloor heating is popular and very economical needing only a small boiler.
- ○ **Doors and Windows.** In Italy doors and windows are tailor-made to the openings and not vice versa.
  - ○ Italian windows have integral shutters (*scuri*).
  - ○ Local hardwoods are best for the windows and shutters.
  - ○ The woodwork expert may also be able to make shelves and tables to order.
- ○ **Marble.** Marble and dressed stone are widely used in Italian building.
  - ○ Marble-working is an uncomfortable and risky occupation yet Italy produces beautiful marble work at reasonable prices for bathrooms, kitchens etc.
- ○ **Compulsory Building Notice.** You are obliged to put up a notice supplied by the *comune* when any building work is being done. This is a measure against illegal building work.

> **○ Swimming Pools.** Swimming pools are governed by strict regulations relating to aesthetic and environmental aspects.
> **○** If a trespasser falls into your pool, you are liable under Italian law so you should get insurance to cover this.

HIRING THE PROFESSIONALS

Once you have bought your property the key person for the initiation of any major building or renovation work is the *geometra* (surveyor). You need him/her to pilot your planning application (*il progetto*) through the planning office (*l'ufficio tecnico*) of your local borough council (*comune*). You probably already have a *geometra* involved in the purchase of the property who will oblige. You now have to give him a signed authority to act on your behalf without which, thanks to new privacy protection laws, he will be unable to access the registry details of your property. With the *geometra* you now make an agreement with regard to their duties and fee. The duties will normally be to submit drawings and obtain planning permission (*la concessione edilizia*) from the *comune*, draw up a specification (*un capitolato*) of the work to be done and supervise its correct execution by site visits (*sopralluoghi*), coinciding with stage payments (*stadi di avanzamento*) every two or three months. For this the fee will be at least 6% of the value of the work done.

Geometra. Should you not have a *geometra* and your friends and contacts have failed to come up with one, your search should begin by visiting the builders' merchants (*fornitori edili*) nearest to your property, who you will find by consulting the yellow pages of your province (*pagine gialle casa*) under the heading of *edilizia – Materiali e attrezzature* (Building – Materials and equipment). Find the boss of the establishment and ask him to recommend not only a *geometra* but also a building firm (*un'impresa edile* headed by an *impresario*) – or, depending on the size of the project, a builder (*un muratore*), who must be good (*bravo*). The builder's merchant, by the nature of his job will know all the builders and tradesmen who come to him for supplies, and how good they are. In you he will see a future customer, and it will be in both of your interests to forge a relationship. Ask him to set up an appointment with the *impresario* or the *muratore*, possibly in his own office to discuss the project, and the name of a good local *geometra* will soon emerge.

Other Tradesmen. The same builders' merchant will be able to recommend all the other tradesmen you need: the sandblaster (*il sabbiatore*), essential for restoration work, the bulldozer man (*il ruspista*) or the digger man (*U.S. backhoe*) (*lo scavatorista*) for the ground work, the plumber (*l'idraulico*), the electrician (*l'elettricista*), the carpenter or joiner (*il falegname*), the painter (*l'imbianchino*) and so on. If you wish to co-ordinate these tradesmen yourself, this is an excellent way to find them. If on the other hand you do not have the time or inclination – or the language or other skills to do this job – you are better off relying on the services of an *impresario* who will co-ordinate his own team of tradesmen. It is likely that you will also need a go-between – usually a resident expatriate who speaks your language – who is experienced in this kind of work and who will charge you for his/her time and expenses.

Builders and Craftsmen

This whole process looks simple, but it is not. It is normally a nightmare. If anything can go wrong it will. Builders the world over are in the habit of taking on more work than they can manage; they park their materials on your land and treat the site jealously as if it were their own property – then they disappear to another job. The building trade in Italy is now predominately manned by immigrant labour, mostly Albanian, North African, even Polish, who soon pick up the language and do the drudgery and donkey work in a brisk and workmanlike fashion, but are not over zealous in the detail. Sometimes with the connivance of their *impresario*, they will skimp. Given the licence to be rustic they will be slapdash. To get the job done as you want it, constant vigilance and forethought are needed.

First, before you take on any building firm or tradesmen, ask to see their work. Each firm develops an individual style. The ideal style is a strict respect for the local vernacular. The more local craftsmen you employ the more likely you will be to achieve this. Make sure that there is at least one master veteran mason working on your project. Having satisfied yourself that you like their way of working, tell them so and convey your enthusiasm. One of the main motivations for buying a place in Italy, is after all, aesthetic. To be in a position, now, to commission craftsmen to work for you is the realisation of a dream. By being on the spot yourself you fulfil three desirable objectives:

- You savour in person the realisation of your dream.
- Your enthusiasm encourages the workmen.
- Your vigilance averts mistakes and corrects omissions.

Making a Plan

Secondly – before you lift a brick: think out a master plan of your project in such a way that you *get it right first time*. To chop and change during the course of the work is demoralising and expensive. The best ideas occur as you go along? No they don't. Don't make any knee-jerk changes. Only do things you have though through and slept on.

To make this master plan the *geometra* is crucial. He will keep you within the guidelines of local requirements and building codes:

- ⊙ the anti-seismic reinforced ring around the eaves (*il cordolo*)
- ⊙ the aerated cavity beneath the basement floor (*l'intercapedine*)
- ⊙ the minimum area of windows required for bedrooms (one eighth of the floor space)
- ⊙ the ante-chamber required for bathrooms (*il disimpegno*) and so on.

But it is you who must provide the life-style choices, which you will have thrashed out with your spouse, partner, children, friends and architects – amateur and professional:

- ⊙ A multi-cook gourmet kitchen large enough to live in? Or a galley – kitchen tucked away in a corner?
- ⊙ A kitchen leading onto a terrace?
- ⊙ A bathroom en suite with every bedroom?
- ⊙ Walk-in closets/dressing rooms?
- ⊙ A study/computer room/library?
- ⊙ A larder?
- ⊙ A wine cellar?
- ⊙ An integral garage? Many *comunes* allow these to be underground.
- ⊙ A south facing living room for winter sunlight?
- ⊙ A dead-end sitting room with a fireplace?
- ⊙ A separate TV room?
- ⊙ A children's room?
- ⊙ A fitness room?
- ⊙ An imposing entrance? Space for hospitality?
- ⊙ An artist's studio?
- ⊙ A separate guest wing? .... and so on.

Local Tradesmen

Then come the decisions regarding the plumbing (*l'impianto elettrico*), heating (*il riscaldamento*), wiring (*l'impianto elettrico*) and the doors and windows (*infissi*).

With all your ideas clear in your head you should make an appointment with the *geometra* and the *impresario* or *muratore* for a *sopralluogo* – a tour of the site. Armed with a canister of aerosol spray paint or coloured chalk, you mark the required position of every single socket (*presa*), switch (*interruttore*), conduit (*forassite*), wall light (*applique*), sink (*lavello*), basin (*lavabo*), bidet (*bidè*), WC bowl (*vaso*) and radiator (*radiatore*). There is a standard height and position for each fixture, which a qualified tradesmen will adhere to; insist on uniformity. Thus the centre of a WC bowl must be at least 35cm distant from the side wall, a light switch 110cm from floor level and so on. If the plumber or the electrician does not know these standards you should not be employing him. Ask the *geometra* to make a detailed diagram of these fixtures and fittings as a blueprint for the workers.

If you are directly employing these tradesmen it is advisable to ensure that they know each other, so that they can co-ordinate their work between themselves. Thus the electrician – unless he is doing external wiring with the wire or conduit pinned to the wall – will expect to find all the conduit (*forassite*) and switchboxes (*scatole*) already cemented into the wall by the builder before he does the wiring. The electrician simply feeds the wires into the conduit and fixes them into the switchboxes and sockets. Similarly the plumber will expect the builder to have fixed all the waste pipes (*gli scarichi*) into the wall or floor – and all the tiling done – before he can fit the sanitary ware (*i sanitari*).

The Plumbing

The plumber's main job – connecting the water supply to the bathrooms and kitchen and fitting the central heating – is different to what you might be used to in other countries as pumps take the place of gravity. The water arrives from the mains or your own well into a water tank in the basement or garage from whence it is pumped on demand by a pump under constant pressure (*l'autoclave*). The kitchen alone must have a direct supply of drinking water from the mains, (in order to qualify for the certificate of habitability (*il certificato di abitabilità*). The pressure of the water for washing purposes therefore is powerful and constant throughout the house. The showers are power showers: no need for booster pumps. But the disadvantage of this system is that it is entirely dependent on the electricity supply – no electricity, no water. The *autoclave* also breaks down or gets airlocked or clogged up once every three years on average, which requires professional attention. A simpler, more foolproof, water supply system must exist, but this is the way they do it in Italy.

You have more of a choice with the toilet flushes (*sciacquoni*) on offer. In favour at the moment is the Swiss Geberit method. The cistern is hidden in the wall fronted by a small divided push panel. You press the small section for a small flush (to save water) and the big section for a big flush. Other flushes are available operated by push buttons in the wall or under an eye level cistern. The pull chain flush is still available, with a plastic cistern, but has not been restored to the Victorian glamour it enjoys in England. To finish the selection there are close-coupled bowls and cisterns (*a zaino*) and a WC/bidet unit in one bowl. You take your pick. The favourite combination at the moment is a cantilevered bowl (*il vaso sospeso*) combined with a Geberit flush.

Heating

The standard heating system is gas (rarely oil-fueled) hot water pumped through radiators, placed under windows, or walls, in niches (*nicchie*). Aluminium radiators deliver instant heat, but cast iron ones are still manufactured and sometimes preferred for their heat retention and classic look. For buildings which are going to be used all winter underfloor heating is now found to be spectacularly economical, kept on permanently from October to April at a temperature of 32°C (90F), requiring only a small wall-mounted domestic boiler. Underfloor heating raises the dust slightly; it can be placed in the walls instead – it consists of a serpentine zigzag of copper or plastic pipes encased in a slab of poured concrete – which can be tiled or carpeted. Under the floor it is important to have at least 5cm of expanded polyurethane insulation. (This is the minimum of insulation that you must insist on in the roofs and external walls too).

Doors and other Woodwork

Nowhere is the traditional Italian system of building more different from the English than in the fitting of doors and windows. In Italy the doors and windows (*infissi*) are tailor-made to fit the openings and not vice versa. The carpenter will need to know the measurements of the empty spaces (*il vuoto*) he has to fill. It is better that he should measure these himself.

The longest and most craftsmanlike of all the jobs required for the renovation of an Italian house is the woodwork (*la falegnameria*), which is still done mostly in local family-run workshops, well mechanised, certainly, but with a limited rate of production, You will almost certainly prefer solid wood (*legno massello*) to plywood (*compensato*) doors, and will be given a choice of wood, in which you should favour local hard woods such as chestnut (*castagno*), larch (*larice*) or cypress (*cipresso)* for the windows (*le finestre*) and shutters. Internal shutters are called *scuri*, which are an integral part of the window. External shutters are *persiane*. Traditional windows open inwards. Woodwork should be treated and varnished or painted, or both, before delivery by the *falegname*. *Impregnante* is the name given to the wood treatment, varnish is *copale*, and paint is *vernice*, stain is *mordente*. The traditional colour for doors and windows is grey, for external shutters brown, green, grey or ochre. Some local councils enforce a favoured colour or choice of colours.

Not all buildings have to be restored using traditional styles and materials, although it is desirable and sometimes compulsory to use them in old houses. Upkeep-free plasticised aluminium shutters – and windows – are increasingly replacing wooden ones. Throughout Italy there will be local factories fulfilling this demand. And it goes without saying that double-glazing (*vetri termici*) is now standard. Similarly you will not have to go far to find a factory making insect-screens (*zanzariere*), which can either be rolling (*avvolgibili*), sliding (*scorrevoli*) or swinging (*ad anta*). Some joinery works incorporate the (*zanzariera*) into the window frame itself. It is always worth getting the factory to measure *and* fit the insect screens, resisting the temptation of doing it yourself.

So the *falegname* is a very important artisan for the aesthetically inclined renovator and you should count yourself lucky if you find a good one: He might also be able to make shelves, tables and furniture to order, effortlessly conforming to the local style which is so right for your house.

Rates of Pay

The *falegname* will deliver the *infissi* but he will prefer to leave it to the *muratore* (builder) to fit them. The *muratore's* other skills will include tiling, paving, plastering and particularly bricklaying and masonry work. To help him he will have a labourer (*un manovale*). Specialists in all these skills are often called in; thus a tiler is a *piastrellista*, a floorer is a *pavimentista*, a plasterer is an *intonachino*; very often they are on a piecework basis (*a cottimo*) and are called *cottimisti*. As a rough indication as to the going rate for these workers, in central Italy in 2003 (cheaper in the South), a *muratore* gets €23 per hour and a *manovale* €21. Plastering (*intonaco civile*) – i.e. rendering and skimming with a lime-based plaster, excluding materials, is €14 per square metre, floor tiling is €18 per square metre, and wall tiling is €20.

The plumber and the electrician – normally quick, skilful and efficient – are not paid by the hour but will charge for the job. The standard minimum call out rate is €50. These specialists spend much of the time on the road and the advent of the mobile phone has been a godsend for them.

IN PRAISE OF ITALIAN BUILDING WORKERS

Italian building workers have a glorious history behind them stretching back to the legionaries of ancient Rome. The proportion of Albanians and North Africans in the mix is probably the same now as it was then. The physical type – especially the men from Campania and Lucania – i.e. small and nimble is the ideal *physique du role*, for building work, to which is added a mercurial mind, a spirit of improvisation and a strong aesthetic sense. The phrase '*l'occhio vuole la sua parte*' – the eye has to have its share – is often used to describe a felicitous juxtaposition of materials, and an eyesore is called '*un pugno nell'occhio*' literally a punch in the eye. Another talent in evidence is a skill in instantly justifying a mistake by conjuring up reasons why it is actually better that way. Italian building workers in general are also probably the most punctual and orderly in Europe; they do not belong to the drinking culture of some of their Northern European counterparts. They will arrive in good time to start at 8 o'clock in the morning, work without a break till 12. No question of any tea or coffee break, perhaps just a drink of water. They will have brought a carefully prepared lunch which they will light a fire to heat, possibly taking a short nap after lunch, and then an afternoon of working without a break until as late as 7 o'clock.

Il Marmista

Another specialist in Italy who deserves special praise is the marble man (*il marmista*). Marble – travertine, dressed stone – is used extensively in Italian buildings for thresholds, worktops, sills, cladding, columns, paving, for shelves, tables and even sinks. Most large towns will have at least one *marmista*. Marble working is an extremely unhealthy and uncomfortable job, with a high risk of silicosis, hernias and work accidents, and yet Italy cheerfully produces and exports the most beautiful marble work, some of which can be used to beautify your own house in its county of origin at a very reasonable price; for example the cladding of bathrooms and shower enclosures with slabs of polished marble in preference to tiles.

BUILDING WORKERS' OCCUPATIONS

Costruttore	builder
Decoratore	interior decorator
Elettricista	electrician
Fabbro	locksmith or blacksmith
Falegname	carpenter
Ferramenta	hardwear shop owner
Idraulico	plumber
Imbianchino	painter (whitewasher)
Ingegnere	engineer
Intonachino	plasterer
Muratore	builder or mason
Pavimentista	floor tiler
Piastrellista	tiler

Permits and Supervision

Finally, before any work is done, and after you have obtained the work permit (*la concessione edilizia*) you are obliged by law to put up a notice – supplied by the *comune* – specifying the type of work and the professionals involved. If you are employing direct labour and working yourself it is called *in economia*, in economy. The type of work is described as renovation (*ristrutturazione*) or ordinary or extraordinary maintenance (*mantenuzione ordinaria* or *straordinaria*). The *geometra* or the *muratore* will put you right on this legal obligation. If you are seen working without such a sign the carabinieri – or a neighbour – can report you to the borough council. Illegal building work is rife, especially in the south where no one takes a blind bit of notice, but as a foreigner it is unwise to take such liberties.

Supervision of the work is important. The eye of the master fattens the pig (*l'occhio del padrone ingrassa il maiale*). If you cannot be on the site yourself make sure your visits are regular and strategic. It is amazing how galvanised and focused the workforce become when they know that the *padrone* is coming. The visits should coincide with the stage payments (*stadi di avanzamento*) and if possible, the *geometra* should be involved. The work done should always be checked for its conformity with the requirements of the local building regulations. The object being to obtain a *certificato di abitabilità*, 'a certificate of habitability'.

Indeed, a recent law makes this certificate the responsibility of the *geometra* in charge. He must certify the *impianti*, the electricity, the plumbing and the sewage, to prove that the house is habitable. Without this certificate you will not get an official licence for bed and breakfast or rental operations (see the chapter *Making Money from Your Property*).

DIY AND BUILDING TOOLS

If you are keen on DIY it is not a good idea to meddle or interfere with the work of the builders while they are there. However well meaning, your attempts to help will usually hold back the work. But DIY activity can save money. A properly paid mason and his labourer cost over £200 a day: a huge saving if you can do the same work yourself. Tools and materials are cheap at your friendly builders' merchant. You will find there all you need: tile cutters, angle grinders, drills, trowels and floats. It is no longer necessary to order sand and cement and have a cement mixer – dry mortar mixes are supplied by the bag – €7.20 for 40kg – which can be mixed in a bucket effortlessly if you invest in a purpose built electric mixer (*un mescolatore*). Weber & Brountin is the best of the several firms supplying the building trade with mortar mixes, etc. Their mortar (*malta* or *intonaco*) is tinted with ochre to reproduce the colour of traditional lime mortar. They also make an excellent macroporous synthetic mortar SANAMUR, which solves for ever the problem of rising damp and damp walls by breathing out the moisture faster than it rises. So effective are these products that they should be specified by name in the geometra's *capitolato*. (www.weber-broutin.it). The amateur DIY person requires rudimentary plastering skills to apply these materials – cellars, outhouses, garages can be improved beyond all recognition, given that traditional Italian building came late to the principle of a damp proof course. Throughout Italy the ancient drama of rising damp and peeling stucco giving way to pristine *intonaco* in muted limewash colours specially designed to tone in aesthetically with historic centres. This technology is extremely recent.

Building Tools

The DIY woodworker will find local suppliers of timber cut to measure under *Legno, compensatie profilati* in the yellow pages (*Pagine Gialle* – casa). You will also find DIY outlets under *Bricolage* – *fai da te* (do it yourself), in places like *Mister Brico City*. In the shopping malls mushrooming throughout Italy *Brico Centers* are a popular novelty. But your local hardware shop (*ferramenta*) and carpenter (*falegnameria*) should not be neglected. Through them you can find a product for ageing new wood: emulsionable oil (*olio emulsionabile*), normally used for metal lathe work, which digests the surface resins of the wood and is a godsend for house restorers. Small shopkeepers in Italy are very knowledgeable and helpful about such products, and they support local industries.

This is a distinctive and reassuring feature about Italy, how local everything is.

Italian building tools and materials

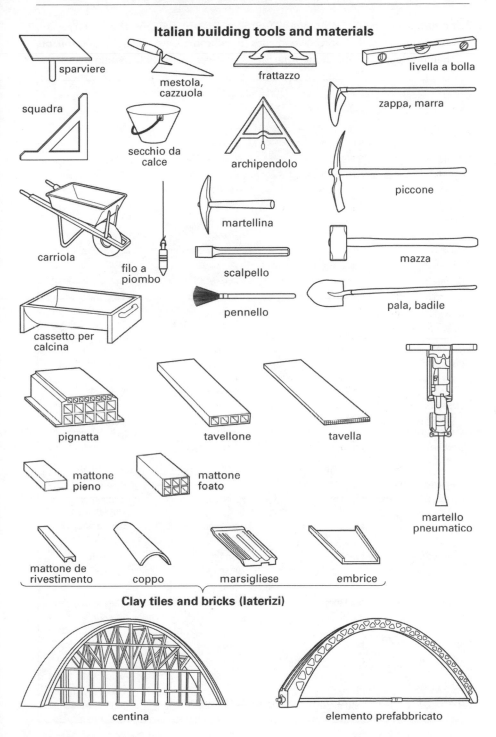

sparviere

mestola, cazzuola

frattazzo

livella a bolla

squadra

secchio da calce

archipendolo

zappa, marra

piccone

carriola

filo a piombo

martellina

scalpello

mazza

cassetto per calcina

pennello

pala, badile

pignatta

tavellone

tavella

mattone pieno

mattone foato

martello pneumatico

mattone de rivestimento

coppo

marsigliese

embrice

Clay tiles and bricks (laterizi)

centina

elemento prefabbricato

For example in a recent bathroom in Southern Tuscany the taps, the sanitary ware, the travertine slabs, the cypress woodwork, the chrome ware, the lights and mirrors were all produced in workshops or factories within a radius of forty kilometres.

BUILDING GLOSSARY

Addolcitore	water softener	Paralume	lampshade
Boiacca	slurry, grout	Parapetto	wall
Brillante	gloss	Pavimento	floor
Cannella	tap, faucet	Pennello	paintbrush
Carta da parati	wallpaper	Piccone	pick
Cavo	cable	Pittura	paint
Cisterna	water tank	Plafoniera	ceiling light
Coibentazione	insulation	Pozzo	well
Colla	glue	Pozzo artesiano	bore hole
Colore	paint, colour	Pratino	lawn
Colmo	ridge	Presa	socket (electric)
Coppo	round, Roman roof tile	Radiatore	radiator
Corrente	current (electric), also rafter	Riscaldamento	central heating
Depuratore	water purifier	Rubinetto	tap
Forassite	electric tube/ conduit	Ruspa	bulldozer
Forcone	pitchfork	Sabbia	sand
Fossa biologica	septic tank	Sabbia fine	fine sand
Frattazza	plastering trowel/ float	Sabbione	coarse sand
Gettata	poured concrete, reinforced concrete for floors	Satinato	satin finish
Giardino	garden	Scalpello	chisel
Gomma	hose pipe	Scavatore	excavator (machine) digger
Gronda	eaves	Scavatorino	mini-digger
Grondaia	gutter, downpipe	Smalto	oil paint
Imbianchino	painter	Soffitta	attic/loft
Imbiancare	to whitewash	Soffito	ceiling
Imbiancatura	painting	Solaio	attic
Imbrice	flat Roman roof tile	Spina	plug (electric)
Intercapedine	cavity wall, dry wall lining	Spugna	sponge
Interruttore	switch	Stuccare	to point or grout
Intonacare	to plaster to render	Stucco	plaster
Intonaco	render, plaster	Tassello	plug (wall plug)
Intonachino	plasterer	Tavola	board, plank
Isolamento	insulation	Tavolone	big plank

Isolato	insulated	*Tegola*	roof tile
Lampada	lamp, bulb	*Tegola di colmo*	ridge tile
Lampadario	chandelier	*Tempera*	wet paint
Lavabile	washable (of emulsion paint)	*Termosifone*	central heating radiator
Mazza	sledge hammer	*Tetto*	roof
Mazzetta	club hammer	*Tinta*	die, shade
Mazzuolo	mallet	*Tinta unita*	single colour
Mestola	trowel	*Traspirante*	breathing, microporous
Muretto	low wall	*Trave*	beam
Muro	wall	*Travicelli*	rafters (small beams).
Orcio	large oil jar	*Tubo*	
Orto	vegetable garden	*Valvola*	valve
Pacciamatura	mulch	*Vanga*	digging spade
Pala	shovel	*Velo*	final skim coat of plaster
Pannelli isolanti	insulation panels	*Zappa*	mattock, hoe
Pannelli solari	solar heating panels		

POOLS

Swimming pools are expensive to build and run, and they require constant attention, however if you wish to rent out a country property in Italy in June, July and August, they are indispensable. But planning permission is required, and might be refused. Before buying the property you should therefore check with you surveyor (*geometra*) or directly with the planning office (*ufficio tecnico*) of your local council (*comune*), to ascertain their rulings on the subject. Some councils have strict aesthetic and environmentally conscious restrictions such as:

- the pool must be rectangular in the proportions, 3 to 1.
- the pool must be finished in natural materials such as stone or marble or in natural earth colours.

or safety restrictions such as : a pool with a depth of over 1.40m (4ft.8ins) in a property which is used by the public must have a *Lifeguard* on duty when it is in use.

Many owners welcome these restrictions; a shallow pool is cheaper to build, and natural colours are less of an eyesore than the traditional bright blue.

> If a trespasser falls into your pool, you the owner are responsible according to Italian law. To combat this it is wise to include the pool in your insurance cover; and fence it in, especially if it is out of sight and a hazard for children.

As for the building of the pool, there are numerous specialists in this field in Italy, consult the swimming pool magazines such as *La Piscina* (published by di Baio editore) or *Piscine Oggi* for ideas and addresses, or the yellow pages (*Pagine Gialle – casa*) under the heading *piscine ed accessori*. Remember the importance of after sales service; give preference to the specialists who are nearest to your property. Italian building firms are also capable of building reinforced concrete swimming pools to order, but a reputable firm such as Culligan (www.culligan.it) must be employed to put in the filtration system, pool cover etc.

A 50ft x 16ft (15m x 5m) pool with landscaping costs about €30,000 in 2003.

Siting and Building a Swimming Pool

A decent sized pool 50ft x 16ft (15m x 5m) requires a flat area of at least 70ft x 36ft (20m x 10m), The ideal orientation is for a sun terrace or *plage* overlooking the water in the direction of the afternoon sun (south west); the pool, if rectangular, being aligned on a NE.SE axis. The *plage* should be at least 10ft wide (3m) to allow for sun beds and gangway. The arc from the NE to the NW should be screened off from the north winds (*maestrale and tramontana*) by windbreaks or hedges (see gardening). Deciduous trees near pools should be avoided; debris in the pool can be a nuisance. A raised pool surrounded by a low 18in (45cm) wall for sitting on can prevent this, and be advantageous for safety and comfort. A motorised roller cover is also recommended. A waterfall effect, a natural pond with a swimming area, fountain, a paddling pool, a poolhouse – all these should be considered, as well as the options of solar heating and ozone filtration. Some permanent residents, especially arthritis sufferers, hanker after a heated indoor pool which can be used throughout the winter, perhaps with a counter current (*controcorrente*) swimming system. If you have a superfluous barn or building on your site consider this option.

> Should your local council refuse you permission for a pool you can install an out-of-ground 'temporary pool' which requires no permission. These can cost as little as €3,000.

As for the siting of the pool, there are two schools of thought. Pools generate a large amount of noise when children are at play. Some older people therefore prefer to locate them as far away from the house as possible – perhaps with a poolhouse, equipped with kitchen, bathroom, fitness room etc. Others, especially younger parents, want the pool as near to the house as possible so that they can keep an eye on their children at play, and be spared the long trek back to the house if they have forgotten something.

Water

You will choose according to your terrain, your pocket and your instincts but you must not forget to check on the obvious requirement: water. If you are in a drought-prone area with a hosepipe ban and no spring, well, or rainwater tank of your own, and there are no local suppliers of water by the tankful, what do you do? Call in a waterdiviner (*un rabdomante*) and a geologist (*un geologo*) and a well-digger (*un pozzaiolo*), sink a borehole, find water and put in the largest underground water tanks you can afford, one for the borehole water, the other for the rain water, which you will capture from all your roofs. After a long dry summer you can still run out of water. Pools need refilling every few years and need topping up throughout the season: Be very careful before you make the investment. The *geometra* is required by law to furnish a 'hydro-geological clearance' (*svincolo idrogeologico*) with the local provincial authority before permission for a pool is granted. This safeguards against environmental damage.

Useful Websites
www.culligan.it – for water purifying installations.
www.gruppoazzurro.it – 24 pool and service companies throughout Italy.
www.assopiscine.it – 150 associated pool industry companies.

GARDENS

A garden – or at least a terrace or courtyard – is a priority for most house hunters, especially in Italy, where life outdoors is so favoured by the climate: a place to grow your own herbs and to enjoy the sun in winter and the shade in summer. If you have pets or children or give parties, or want to practise the healthy and creative hobby of gardening, a garden is indispensable.

There are varying hardiness zones and soil qualities in Italy which the potential buyer should be aware of. The climate ranges from the frost-free Southern coastal and island regions where the lemon tree grows, to the permafrost of the Alps. In between are the continental climate of the Po valley with extremes of heat and cold and the milder climate of the central regions where the olive tree grows.

The soil; most of the country is mountainous or hilly, and calcareous; heavy clay soil predominates, sometimes granite. There are fertile volcanic plains in Campania, Lazio, Sicily. Puglia has a deep productive soil, and the Po valley yields a rich alluvial tilth, especially in the Lugo area where the peach orchards grow. Acid microhabitats by the lakes in the north promote the growth of massive camellias, azaleas and rhododendrons, while much of the southern uplands is sheer and barren rock, and scrub *macchia*, as is Sardinia.

The problem of water is another decisive factor. If there is a shortage of water – and the equivalent of a hosepipe ban on public water is universal throughout Italy you should radically reconsider your project. Why buy a house in a desert? It is no fun living through the heat of the summer without an abundance of water. Gardens in hot climates depend on rills, pools and fountains and lush shady greenery for their charm. Tropical jasmines, mandevilleas, bougainvillea, Chinese hibiscus, lemons, gardenias and plumbagos, only luxuriate with abundant irrigation. They depend on constant attention and labour.

But if you find yourself stuck with a shortage of water and labour – which is the normal situation for the house buyer in Italy – do not despair. The recent science of *xeriscaping*, pioneered in the droughts of Arizona, makes a virtue of indigenous – and exotic – plants which thrive in arid conditions and only need watering to establish themselves in the first year. These plants are: rosemary, oleander, cypress, santolina, lemon verbena, rue, curry plant, artemisia (listed below for their insect repellent qualities) and:

- lavender planted in rows, or clumps of three.
- teucrium fruticans, planting as lavender.
- saltbush (atriplex halimus) – *(porcellana del mare)*.
- crepe myrtle or pride of India (*lagerstroemia indica*). Go for the white and red varieties.
- Pomegranate (*melograno*). Go for the dwarf variety (*nana*).
- Jerusalem sage (*phlomis fruticosa*).
- Cistus (*cisto*).
- kitchen sage (*salvia officinalis*). Go for the common thin-leafed variety for the best flavour.

For climbers:

- the potato vine (*solanum jasminoides*) flowers profusely until the winter and comes back even when cut down by the frost, like a scentless jasmine, blue tinged.
- the Banksian rose – (*rosa Banksiae*) the only rose that requires no attention, used for pergolas, thornless, flowers in spring, shady insect free foliage.
- the strawberry grape – (*uva fragola*) known as the Concord grape – the only grapevine that requires no insecticide, large leaves.

For trees:

- the carob (*carruba*) in the south.
- the Fremontodendron, a fragrant evergreen, from California and Mexico, with showy yellow flowers in Spring.
- the olive (*ulivo*)

Olives. We finish with the olive. If you have land and are at a loss what to plant, plant an olive grove. For this you need holes a cubic metre in volume, dug with an excavator, refilled and heavily manured, at five metre intervals in a regular quincunx formation. Plant three-year-old potted plants from a nursery in the spring, with the final earth level at least a hand's breadth above the rootstock. Choose the *Taggiasco* in Liguria, the *Correggiola* in central Italy or the favourite type of your region (and a pollinator). The olive tree is attractive even when neglected and superbly rewarding when tended to: it will yield oil for centuries. For more information there is an excellent English-speaking website at www.olivematters.com.

Ilex. You may also consider either a *lecceto* or ilex grove – mophead ilexes planted regularly as above, with a three-metre spacing; will form a dense shaded area screening against sight and sound – or a walnut grove, an investment yielding valuable timber in twenty five years time.

Grass. For grass sow a mixture of rye grasses, (*loietto* and/or *lolium perenne Manhattan*) and Bermuda crab grass (*gramigna* and/or *cynodon dactylon Uganda*), thickly in autumn. The crabgrass is green in summer and brown in winter. The rye grass is green in winter but dies back in the drought of summer. For large areas such as olive groves, invest in a ride on mower.

Planning Your Garden

It is wise to make your garden a priority and not an afterthought. The factors listed above should stimulate you to decide what possibilities are viable. Seek out the local nurseries and garden centres as soon as possible; ask them to make a plan and an estimate for supplying and planting what you want. At least aim to get the windbreaks, screening, shade and orchard plants into the ground in the first year. It is surprising how soon they will work their magic and give you no cause to regret years later that you didn't plant things when you first came.

For terraces – *tufo blocks* are best (soft porous sandstone), set on a screed of sand or grit; sweep a mixture of dry sand and cement into the cracks and water in with a hosepipe.

The aesthetic side of gardening depends on taste and fashion; one man's yew is another man's Leylandii. But certain design rules are immutable, and the enemies of the garden are the same for everyone. These should be borne in mind from the very start when sizing up a potential property.

The design rules are governed by the dimensions and quantity of the humans, animals and machines using the garden, and by the orientation of the sun and the direction of the winds.

- Paths must be wide enough for a wheelbarrow or a wheelchair – 3ft/90cm.
- Ramps for wheelchairs should not exceed an 8% gradient.
- Lintels or arches should be at least 6ft 6in/2m.
- The headroom for pergolas at least 8ft 6in/2.5m.
- A terrace for twelve people dining, with barbecue and side tables, needs an

area of at least 20ft x 12ft/6m x 4m.

O The terrace should have a fall of 1inch in 6ft/3cm per 3m to carry off the rain.

O Risers and treads of all steps must be even and regular conforming to pre-ordained proportions (Wren's 15 inch tread to a 5 inch riser is the ideal).

O A wall to sit on should be 16in-24in/40cm – 60cm high.

O A safety railing or wall should be 3ft/90cm high.

O A tennis court needs an area of 120ft x 60ft/36m x 18m.

O A car park for six cars needs an area of 50ft x 33ft/15m x 10m, and shade.

O A 40ft/12m swimming pool and its surround needs at least 66ft x 33ft/20m x 10m. (See the section above on swimming pools).

O Hedges and windbreaks should be on the north side to protect against the *tramontana* wind.

O Shade trees should be on the south of the house.

O Large trees (*piante di alto fusto*) must be planted no less than 10ft/3m and hedges (*siepi*) no less than 20inches/50cm inside the boundary (by law).

O Boundary hedges and fences must not exceed 6ft 6in/2m in height (by law).

O The natural flow of human pathways should be respected and retained.

O Dead-end and shaded areas, which are not in a corridor, should be provided, for privacy.

O Water and electricity should be laid on for irrigation, garden machinery and lighting.

O Terrace, pathway and step lighting are desirable.

O An easy access tool shed big enough for a lawnmower.

O A covered wood store.

O A compost emplacement.

All these should be visualised in the first survey of a potential garden.

Enemies of the Garden

Enemies of the garden in Italy are: neglect, drought, frost, wind, fire, water, insects, animals, prying eyes, thieves and vandals, slippery and dangerous surfaces and noise.

Neglect. To combat neglect you should foresee yourself or someone else tending to the garden, closing it down for the winter, mowing, weeding, cleaning, sweeping, for at least one hour a week, especially during the season of most rampant growth between March and July.

Drought. Then comes the time of almost certain drought when the plants have to be watered, between June and September. An automatic irrigation system supplied by your own rainwater, springwater, or purified sewage water will prove cheaper in the long run than paying a person to do the watering. Such an installation is familiar to most Italian plumbers, who benefit from the spin-off technology of the Italian horticultural industry.

Frost. The next most dangerous time for plants is the winter when temperatures can dip below -10c and frost can be a killer. A *limonaia* or an orangery is the traditional solution to this problem: a large glazed room facing south – or a small greenhouse – into which lemon trees and other tender plants in pots are wheeled for the winter. Otherwise individual plants must be wrapped in fleece, bubblewrap or hessian where they stand.

Winds. The arsenal of the Italian climate also contains withering winds which need guarding against: the *tramontana* from Siberia – from the north-east – at its worst known as the *Bora* in Trieste. Steep hills and buildings in that quarter are worth noting as valuable protection. A shelter belt or a windbreak will also help: a wire or netting fence 5ft/1.5m or 6ft 6in/2m high, with a screen of shading fabric firmly attached, is the quickest and cheapest solution, preferably incorporating in its lee – to take over in the future – a row of hedging plants. The most robust of these would be the live oak or ilex *quercus ilex/leccio*, although bay *alloro*, *arbutus(corbezzolo)*, *eleagnus ebbingei*, or a combination of these could be considered, and the cypress (*cupressus sempervireus pyramidalis*) planted close would be expensive but superb; excellent also around a tennis court, (make sure you get the grafted *d'innesto* pencil thin cypress and not the seedlings which branch horizontally).

For an instant windbreak, a hedge of bamboo is recommended (get only *phyllostachys aurea*) known as *canne d'India;* an old favourite in Italian villa gardens. You need to dig a trench 20ins/50 cm in depth and width preferably by means of a minidigger *scavatorino*, mix in a lot of humus and fertiliser *concime* and line both sides with an impenetrable vertical barrier 20ins/50 cm. Fibreglass *vetroresina* cut to size from the roll by your local hardware shop, *ferramenta* is the best material for this. When confined in this way the bamboo becomes a neat, dense, constantly sprouting hedge, instead of a dreaded colonising monster thicket. It is self-mulching, the right height and of a cheerful green colour, swaying and singing in the breeze. It will not grow in heavy clay, needs watering the first year and responds to frequent fertilising. When grown on both sides of a broad path *phyllostachys aurea* creates a green shady tunnel.

Fire. The next hazard, fire, decimates hectares of Italian woodland every summer. Commonsense precautions are to keep your garden clear of combustible dry undergrowth, refrain from lighting bonfires in the summer and be careful with barbecues and cigarettes.

Water. Heavy rainfall and flash floods are very common in Italy. Lanes become riverbeds, floods have been known to wipe out freshly planted groves. Storm drains must be provided. Heavy duty cast-iron grilles set into concreted gulleys must be placed at regular intervals on gravel access roads, and in front of houses and garages.

Insects. Insects in Italy are at least as virulent as they are in north America; stagnant water should be filled in – or stocked with Koi carp to eat up the mosquitoes. Italian country folk are puzzled by the English habit of growing creepers on their house walls. They attract insects and *animali*. This is particularly true of the wisteria (*glicine*) which hornets love and which is bad for asthmatics – and should with all its ilk be banished to the farthest reaches of the garden. You should surround the house with plants that repel insects such as:

◎ The oleander (*oleandro*) is actually poisonous to animals as well as to insects.
◎ The cypress, (*cipresso*) – the classic *cupressus sempervirens pyremidalis* mentioned above), has a pleasant smell for humans and birds but not for insects. Its wood was prized as a moth repellent for wardrobes. Originating from Afghanistan, it loves the arid conditions at the base of a house wall exposed to the sun and it grows into a neat aromatic evergreen column which only needs occasional clipping.
◎ Cotton lavender *santolina* – needs clipping.
◎ Lemon verbena *Lippia citriodora* (*cedrina*) seems to die in the winter, but grows back in the summer with intensely aromatic leaves to over 8ft/2.40m.
◎ Rue (*ruta*).
◎ Curry plant *helichrysum italicum*.
◎ Artemisia.
◎ Rosemary (*rosmarino)* a plant whose life is lengthened to thirty years or more by annual clipping, is excellent as topiary, growing to the height of a man, and is ideal on either side of a kitchen door, being an essential ingredient of sauces and roasts, also good ground cover for escarpments (*scarpate*).

Another plant to avoid in the garden is the umbrella pine (*pinus pinea*) which as well as attracting the toxic processional caterpillar plays havoc with terraces with its roots. Further precautions against insects – fill and point all cracks in brickwork, stonework, remove all loose piles of rubble, where scorpions might lurk – and spray all surfaces with insecticide.

Animali. Animals to guard against are porcupines (*istrici*), wild boar (*cinghiali*), roebuck (*caprioli*), pine martens (*faina*). Porcupines will dig out and eat any bulbs or rhizomes – lilies, iris, tulips, narcissus etc. Wild boar will rootle and wallow destructively. Roebuck love feeding on roses, flowers and any tasty young shoots. All can be kept out by a stout fence of rabbit wire, or chain link. 5ft or 6ft 6in/1.5m or 2m high. But the pine marten (*faina*) is a mysterious loner, which climbs on to roofs and dislodges tiles in search of eggs, often at dead of night. Feral cats on the other hand are to be welcomed for their elimination of mice, rats, and other vermin. Bats are beneficial for their consumption of insects, but their bite can be lethal and they frighten people, so should be discouraged by screening off their entrance holes to attics, sheds and cellars. Snakes are also frightening; mostly they are harmless long green grass snakes (*serpi*), but adders (*vipere*) which are short and dark are occasionally found. They love sunning themselves and hiding in piles of stones. Country householders are recommended to keep viper serum in the fridge as an antidote to bites. *Il siero anti-vipera* can be acquired at the pharmacy (*farmacia*). But the best protection against snakes is to point or grout all cracks and hiding places, get rid of all piles of stones and bricks, beware of all gaps or spaces beneath decking, and lay ashes and grit to deter slugs and snails.

Prying Eyes and Thieving Hands. Prying eyes are a psychological discomfort which can be screened off by a double layer of bamboo slatting (*cannicci*) or preferably by evergreen plants or trees. The variety and ingenuity of the screening used on the Ligurian Riviera shows what can be done for the preservation of privacy at close quarters – much of it being *pittosporum tobira*, which thrives there. As for thieves and vandals, even in apparently law abiding areas, there is always the first time. In the countryside, near Siena, for example an Italian couple, who had proudly planted a new olive grove found that their olive saplings were disappearing at the rate of four or five a night, and there was nothing they could do about it. Similarly terracotta pots of lavender or jasmine in village streets are a temptation to passing kleptomaniacs and have to be chained firmly in place. Tools have to be locked up in cars and sheds. 'Not like in the old days when you could leave your …..' is a sentiment as common in Italy as anywhere else. Stout wire netting fencing around your whole property is your best defence.

Noise. Noise, finally can be muffled by evergreen thickets – Italian neighbours are characteristically noisy, they are part of the music of the country – but the sound of roads, motorways, or factories is a form of pollution which could become unbearable. The only really effective barrier against noise is a mound of earth three metres in height (to test this go to the old Roman amphitheatre at Roselle near Grosseto.) This remedy should be considered before any landscaping operations take place (such as digging out the pool). With careful forethought hundreds of cubic metres could be redeployed for this purpose which would otherwise go to waste.

RECOMMENDED NURSERIES

Name and Location	Website and Speciality
Montivivai (Lucca)	www.montivivai.com
	Specialises in indigenous and old-fashioned fruittrees. Full landscaping service and plants garden centre.
Rose Barni (Pistoia)	www.rosebarni.com
	Online shopping for bare root roses. Rugosa, chinensis etc. Worth visiting for container -grown roses in winter.
N. Sgaravatti e C. Sementi Valdarno (Arezzo)	www.Sgaravatti.net/uk
	Excellent seeds, grass seed mixes, bulbs etc. branches at Ancona, Mestre and Rome garden centres.
Sgaravatti Mediterranea sardinia.com	www.sgaravattimediterranea.it
	four nurseries in Sardinia. Commercial landscaping. Specialises in Mediterranean plants for xeriscaping.

Otherwise consult the yellow pages – *pagine gialle* (yellow pages) for *vivaio* (nursery) or 'garden center'.

GARDENING GLOSSARY

Abete	fir tree	*Melo*	apple tree
Albicocco	apricot	*Mirto*	myrtle
Alloro	bay (laurel)	*Mortella*	myrtle
Arancio	orange tree	*Nespolo*	medlar, loquat
Argilla	clay	*Noce*	walnut
Arnesi	tools	*Nocciolo*	hazel
Badile	shovel	*Oleandro*	oleander
Boschetto	grove	*Oliveto*	olive grove
Bosso	box	*Pacciamatura*	mulch
Calce	lime	*Paiolo*	pail
Carciofo	artichoke	*Pala*	shovel
Carriola	wheelbarrow	*Pero*	pear tree
Cedrina	lemon verbena	*Pesco*	peach tree
Cedro	cedar	*Potare*	to prune
Cesoie	shears	*Pratino*	lawn
Cipresso	cypress	*Pino*	Pine tree

Corbezzolo	arbutus (strawberry tree)	*Pineto*	pine grove
Cotogna	quince fruit	*Querce*	oak
Cotogno	quince tree	*Rastrellare*	to rake
Falce	scythe	*Rastrello*	rake
Falcetto	sickle	*Rovere*	oak
Fico	fig	*Sabbia*	sand
Forbici	scissors/secateurs	*Sabbione*	coarse sand
Forca	pitchfork	*Secchio*	bucket
Fragole	strawberry	*Spuntare*	to trim
Frutteto	orchard	*Topinambur*	Jerusalem artichoke
Grappolo	bunch of grapes	*Tufo*	soft sandstone
Lampone	raspberry	*Uva*	grapes
Leccio	ilex, live oak, holm oak	*Vanga*	spade for digging
Lentisco	lentisk	*Vite*	vine
Limonaia	orangery	*Viti*	vines
Limone	lemon	*Vigna*	vineyard
Mandarlo	almond	*Vigneto*	vineyard
Mazza	sledgehammer	*Zappa*	hoe, mattock
Melagrano	pomegranate		

MAKING MONEY FROM YOUR PROPERTY

CHAPTER SUMMARY

- Bed and breakfast is very popular in Italy but it is almost unheard of for foreign residents to offer it.
- If your property is a working farm, orchard, riding centre etc. you may be eligible to take in paying visitors under the Italian government *Agriturismo* scheme which helps farmers supplement their income.
- There are a great many openings for skilled professionals who are computer literate to run a business from home in Italy.
- Chambers of commerce can help with the initial stages of starting a business.
- If you are a sole proprietor running your business from home, you have to register within 30 days with the business registry of the town where you are operating.
- **Renting Out.** For security reasons it is advisable not to let your property remain unoccupied for long periods.
  - The income you can expect varies according to the degree of luxury offered and whether it is high or low season.
- **Tax on Rental Income.** You are liable to pay tax on your rental income in Italy.
- Long-term rentals over a month have to be registered with the authorities.
- You can advertise the property and handle the clients yourself, or you can appoint an agent.
- **Selling On.** You may need to change the interior or exterior of the property to maximise its selling potential.
- If you sell your property after restoration as a business venture, the best time to sell is usually spring.
- If you have spent a small fortune restoring your property you may not recoup the money, let alone make a profit, unless you paid a bargain price for it.
- You can either handle the sale yourself and save the commission

> or appoint an estate agent.
> O **Sole Agency.** Sole Agency gives the agent exclusive right to sell the property in return for a small percentage.
>> O If you give the agent sole agency and then decide to sell the property yourself, you will still have to pay the agent's commission.

B & B

Bed and breakfast is alive and well in Italy and is known as *casa per ferie/casa per vacanza* and also *affittacamere*. Bed and breakfast is often provided by the landed gentry, widows, groups of locals and single people. Surprisingly perhaps it is almost unheard of for foreign residents to offer this type of accommodation. Perhaps it is a jealously guarded source of extra cash. If you wish to try to break into this market, note that bed and breakfasts require a certificate of habitability (*certificato di abitabilità*) and a licence from the local commune in order to operate. Bed and breakfasts are very popular and you often see the B & B sign as you drive along. Prices are very competitive and start from as little as €15 a head. The breakfast is usually a feast of local produce including jams, cheese, a selection of hams and fruit.

Agriturismo

The government started giving subsidies for *agriturismo* in 1965 to farmers to help subsidise their dwindling income. In fact most *agriturismos* are run by women, many of them farmers' wives. The subsidies granted led to abuse of the system and lots of people advertised themselves as *agriturismo*, when in fact they did not meet the criterion for claiming a government grant. The grants are for working farms only and *agriturismo* is now somewhat better regulated against fraud than it was a couple of decades ago. There are approximately 11,000 *agriturismos* throughout Italy, and their annual turnover is €700 million. They cater for families, couples (young and retired) groups of friends and singles. The aims of *agriturismo* are as follows:

O To preserve the environment.
O To have direct contact with guests making sure they have a peaceful stay in the tranquil surroundings of the countryside.
O Speak foreign languages.
O Make friends with the guests and allow them to use cooking facilities.
O Make the guests feel at home.

Owners of *agriturismos* are passionate about the countryside. They enjoy cooking and cleaning and get great satisfaction knowing they have created a haven of peace and quiet away from the rat race of the towns and cities.

The Diversity of Agriturismo

La Selva. A very successful *agriturismo* called 'La Selva' in Montebenichi, Bucine, Arezzo is run by a single woman, Riccarda Caipini, in what was previously her family home where she and her family spent many happy days. Riccarda suffered a serious illness and was struggling to make ends meet. When she returned from hospital she decided to make her old family home into an *agriturismo*. There was a great deal of work involved but finally Riccarda Caipini brought her old home back to life. Her *agriturismo* has a swimming pool, horse-riding facilities and wonderful walks and Riccarda is a supreme hostess who loves to cook. She makes new friends through her business and has attracted a lot of Belgians and Dutch people to her *agriturismo* www.laselva.net.

Santa Scolastica. Near Rome at a place called Subiaco a group of Benedictine monks have turned part of their monastery (Santa Scolastica) into an *agriturismo*. Their guests enjoy a 'truly sacred welcome'. The monks offer pastoral activities as well as spiritual and prayer meetings, and they state that the visitor will benefit from their experience. The monastery has a neo-classical church and a library that contains the first printed books in Italy.

Subiaco is near Tivoli and the Villa d'Este which has a glorious Renaissance villa with breathtakingly beautiful frescoes. Multiple intricate working fountains with magnificent sculptures fill the formal gardens. The hot springs are also nearby at Fiuggi. Full board €44 per person, a night stay is €34, excellent value for money. Telephone tel. 077 485 569; www.benedettini-subiaco.it.

Agriturismo for Foreign Residents

Generally, foreign residents in Italy do not utilise *agriturismo* as a way of making money from their property and this is mostly due to the fact that few foreign residents own property that has the necessary qualification of being a working farm. However, in theory there is no reason that they cannot join the scheme depending on their circumstances. A productive olive grove or a riding establishment would both qualify as a working farm and these are both types of agribusinesses that foreign residents might be involved in.

The other use of *agriturismo* is as a way of seeing the country and checking out your possible location for buying a property and becoming familiar with the Italian way of doing things, the climate and the people, not to mention learning the language. Some *agriturismo* offer Italian lessons. You couldn't do better than visit these excellent establishments see www.paginegialle.it/biricoccole.

RUNNING A BUSINESS FROM YOUR PROPERTY

All EU citizens have the right to work in Italy provided they apply for a *libretto di lavoro* (see the *Residence and Entry* chapter) and are free to nail up their nameplates if they wish to launch out on their own.

Before setting up your own business in Italy it will undoubtedly have helped to gain experience in running a business in your own country or running someone else's abroad first. Many entrepreneurs have already had a successful business or professional career working for someone else when they set up on their own and this experience is even more useful when setting up in a foreign country.

If you are a skilled professional, computer literate and contemplating starting up a business from your property in Italy there are a great many openings because competition is not as great in Italy as in the US and Britain. A website giving good advice and information on starting up your own business from home is www.entrepreneur.com. *102 Lavori* is an excellent publication for those who wish to work from home using their computer; produced by the Minister of Employment, it contains ideas for work connected to the Internet. It deals with all aspects of business.and produces a newsletter for a worldwide market.

Many highly-qualified and skilled people have started up their own businesses and have been extremely successful (e.g. artist, writer, website designer). For instance Georgina, a single Englishwoman in her early twenties, rents an apartment in Montisi, a hilltop village in Southern Tuscany; she makes her living solely by selling her paintings and accepting commissions. Georgina has been successful because she produces work that appeals to tourists and her prices are reasonable. She also arranges exhibitions of her work locally and in centres such as Cortona. She is now well known in the area and her talent and good business sense means that she can afford to stay in Italy, which she says is paradise for a landscape artist.

ADVANTAGES IN WORKING FROM YOUR OWN PROPERTY

- You do not have to find business premises. (Italian banks are not forthcoming with financial assistance unless you are a well-established business).
- As an EU citizen you are free to advertise your business on your property. However you should check to see if you need any special registration for your particular profession. You can ask at the Italian Consulate in your own country, or in Italy at the Chamber of Commerce (*camera di commercio*).
- A home-based business means you do not have to be fluent in Italian although a knowledge of the language is beneficial.

Doing Business with Italians

If your business is likely to involve dealing with Italian commercial companies it would be unthinkable to attempt this without learning the language, mainly because being a commercial success in Italy probably depends more on socialising than in most other countries. The ability to communicate in Italian is therefore imperative for anyone contemplating co-operation with Italian ventures. In addition to speaking Italian, as when starting a business in any country, it is also important to:

- Have a sound business plan
- Carry out an in-depth feasibility study of the practicalities of running your proposed business in the area your are considering.
- Have a thorough knowledge and experience of the type of business you are intending to run.
- Have the personal stamina and determination to succeed.

Many people decide to launch a business using their property as a base. However, if the property already has a business running from it which you are taking over, you can avoid most of the bureaucracy involved in setting up from scratch; but an existing business usually comes with staff and Italy's protective labour laws may make a shake- up or dismissal of staff extremely difficult. On balance there is probably more to be said in favour of starting up an entirely new business.

Ideas for New Businesses

The website www.allbusiness.com gives a list of the most successful home-based businesses who have registered with them:

- Computer – repair technician
- Massage therapist, physiotherapist, yoga instructor, chiropractor, osteopath.
- Computer tutor/ language tutor
- Writer
- Artist/sculptor
- Website designer
- Home-made specialities e.g. (chocolate, honey, soap, candles)
- Plantsman/nursery specialists.
- Estate agents. There is a short supply of estate agents who speak English and as there is a large demand for English-speaking agents from American and British buyers. Now that currency restrictions have been abolished in Italy, Italians are also beginning to buy up property in France, Spain, Portugal etc. and it would certainly be worth the while of estate agents with international contacts looking into this area of business.

Peter, a 24-year-old qualified technical engineer and his friend Francis, an ex-Microsoft employee, bought a property in Umbria two years ago and set up as website designers, advertising mainly on the internet. They have all the technical expertise needed to succeed. Due to computer technology the whole world is their market place and they have a turnover which gives them a very comfortable lifestyle.

Many expatriate professionals find they do better if they look for customers amongst their own nationality. Those who are medical and dental practitioners (but not for some reason physiotherapists and osteopaths) mostly operate in the Milan area where there are an estimated 30,000 expatriates. Expats working as estate agents usually find themselves based in the north, Rome, Tuscany, Umbria or the Marches.

Sources of Information

In the initial stages of setting up a business in Italy you will probably be dealing with the British Chamber of Commerce in Milan (www.britchamitaly.com) or the American Chamber of Commerce (www.amcham.it). These can provide you with contacts and make introductions. The British Chamber of Commerce also has an online newsletter *Britaly* available to subscribers and publishes:

- *Focus on Italy* – the guide to business and pleasure in Italy with facts, figures, articles, contacts and information on doing business in Italy.
- *Speak to the World* – an annual brochure of the Chamber's English Language Consultancy Service. It has a print run of about 5,000 copies. To advertise in these publications you should access www.britchamitaly.com.

The branches of the British Chamber of Commerce will be able to provide local advice and information for prospective entrepreneurs.

If you are running a business and are the sole proprietor then you have to register within 30 days with the business registry of the town you are operating your business from. If you are registered as self-employed in your own EU country and take up work on a self-employed basis in Italy, you may be exempt from paying the Italian Social Security contributions for up to 12 months providing you continue to pay your own national contributions and hold an exemption certificate. (See the *Finance* chapter).

Owing to the complexity of the Italian tax system it is essential to have expert fiscal advice from an accountant *(commercialista)*. A *commercialista* is a qualified professional registered with the local *Albo dei Dottori*.

Foreign Professionals Practising in Italy

Foreign professionals who have located in Italy, and who have set up successful businesses include lawyers qualified in international law, accountants, veterinarians, landscape gardeners and interior designers.

Sophie: A woman in her late 30s, who graduated as a mature student and is an artist/potter – began a cottage style industry from her small house in a village near Siena. She made a selection of bowls, plates etc. which were painted in earth colours and the finished product had a lustre within the colour. She displayed these bowls in her house and at any local *festas.* Some Japanese tourists were so pleased with Sophie's dishes that they placed an exceedingly large order – it was an unrealistic proposition for Sophie as she did not have the room or manpower to produce on a large scale, so the Japanese bought the patent and made Sophie a director. Sophie says that her success is beyond her wildest dreams and has now moved to a larger house. The saying *'pensare in grande, cominciare in piccolo'* (think big – start small) really does apply to Sophie and proves there is plenty of opportunity for home-based businesses in Italy.

RENTING OUT YOUR PROPERTY

Once your Italian property is finished if you are not making it your permanent residence but merely using it as a holiday home you may think about renting it out. This is usually done from spring to autumn keeping perhaps a slot for yourself in either June or July. August is very hot and the majority of businesses close down as Italians go on their holidays.

Renting is a useful way of recouping some of the cost of restoration and it is also wise not to let your property remain unoccupied for long periods especially for security reasons and insurance cover. The income you can expect will vary according to the degree of luxury offered, and whether the let is in the high season (July and August) mid-season (June and September) or low season (April, May and October). Rentals range from £300 for a one-bedroom apartment, to upwards of £6,000 for a luxury villa for one week in the high season.

To rent a villa in Southern Tuscany during July and August would cost £4,500 a week. For this you get:

- A villa and converted barn (*capanna*) which sleeps 16 people.
- Swimming pool – pool house with gym.
- Bedrooms en suite.
- Large gourmet kitchen.
- Panoramic view.
- A daily cleaner who also cooks, as an extra.

In the high season it is usual for people to book for two weeks. The lets are mostly to foreigners e.g. Americans and British.

Of course not everyone relishes the idea of a constant stream of strangers marching through their house inflicting additional wear and tear, but most tenants behave responsibly and you can always stipulate no animals or children. It is probably a good idea not to fill your home with irreplaceable antiques. If you decide to rent out your property, be it a villa, farmhouse or apartment, there is no shortage of holiday rental companies that can be approached – the Italian State Tourist Office can provide a list or check out websites such as www.estate.net.

Considerations Before Renting Out

Before you place an advert for your property in a newspaper or magazine you must make sure that you meet all the requirements that make your house/apartment a suitable rental.

- A swimming pool is fairly essential.
- If your property is near a major city or place of interest you can charge more rent.
- Well-equipped kitchen.
- Provide bed linen and towels.
- Have a cot and highchair for young children.
- Central heating or another form of adequate heating.
- Washing machine/dryer (laundry room).
- Place to hang washing.
- TV, video, radio, CD player.
- Bicycles – badminton – table tennis etc.
- Garden space with private corners for guests to sit.
- Barbecue area – eating area suitable for up to 12 diners, equipped with crockery, cutlery – fridge for cold drinks,.

With holiday letting you are free to make your own rules e.g. period of rent, deposit and number of occupants.

> You will be liable to pay tax on your rental income in Italy; and long-term rentals over a month should be registered with the authorities. Some *comunes* require all guests whatever their length of stay to register. This is a requirement of Italian bureaucracy which some *comunes* will not waive.

Advertising Your Property

If you decide to act as your own agent there are many ways you can advertise your property. The newspapers in the UK which contain holiday rental classifieds from homeowners in Italy are, *The Sunday Times, The Sunday Telegraph, The Observer,* and *Dalton's Weekly* and niche magazines such as *The Gay Times.* Another possibility is to create your own website but this is costly. A well produced brochure with internal/external photographs and a few paragraphs about the local information, the attractions, the facilities and shops etc. A map on how to get there is also a good idea and of course your contact details, and clear instructions about the cost, paying the deposit and balance. When you have had a satisfied client – then word of mouth will be your best advert.

Agents

If you don't have much time to do the renting yourself you can decide to use an agent or (agents). The agent takes care of everything, They deal with the clients and they sort out any problems affecting the visitors during their stay. The agent charges commission of 20-40% of the gross rental income. The agent often has a catalogue/ brochure or internet site on which they advertise properties. If you are considering going down the renting road contact the rental company the summer before you want your renting to begin. Letting agents turn down as many as nine out of ten properties that are sent to them. Needless to say it is of the utmost importance to employ an agent who is conscientious, efficient and honest and comes recommended.

> You do not have to have a special licence to set up as a holiday rental agent in Italy and some have gone bust owing their customers thousands of euros.

A company that has been trading for a number of years and can show you other villas and apartments on their books is the best bet. It is usual to sign a contract with the agent and this is renewed annually. The services of the agent should include:

- Meeting the guests – handing over the keys.
- Tour of the property and how main appliances work.
- Arrange for cleaners and linen changes between rentals.
- Arrange for a gardener and for the pool to be cleaned.
- Give guests contact phone number for emergencies.
- Check property occasionally when not rented during contract period.
- Arrange for payment, deposit etc.

Because of the immense competition in renting your villa, farmhouse or apartment in Italy it is possible that all your vacancies will not be filled. At best you can expect 20 weeks especially if your property is of a high rental standard and with good staff. However, geopolitical problems and changing fashions can have a devastating effect on a rental season. At the moment Italy is extremely popular because of its abundance of history and art treasures combined with good food and *simpatico* people.

SELLING ON

When you buy a property in Italy – it could be that you are considering living there for the rest of your life. On the other hand you may be buying the property as a business venture and intend to restore it and then sell it on. It may be that life in Italy did not live up to your expectations and you want to sell and leave, whatever the reason you must ask yourself some questions:

- What is the state of the property market?
- It is a good time of year to sell?
- Should I get more than one valuation?
- How do I find a reliable estate agent? Where will I find one that speaks

English. Should I consider sole agency?

- Do I need to change the interior or exterior of the property to improve its chances of selling?
- Shall I sell the property myself?
- Where shall I advertise my property?
- Who can give me advice about the legalities of selling a house in Italy?
- What reasons do I give prospective buyers for selling my house?

There are advantages to selling the property yourself:

- You do not have to pay commission.
- You have already been through the buying process and can advise any interested parties what to do.
- You can explain the layout of the property and clearly explain about the water, gas, electricity and telephone, which will facilitate the purchase.
- It may be that your staff i.e. cleaners, gardener, handyman/caretaker etc. would be glad to remain in employment at your property. This provision would be very welcome to most buyers.

Note that if you have thoroughly restored your property, even if you have spent a fortune (or more especially if you have) and it looks immaculate, unless you paid a bargain price for it, you will probably not recover all the money you have spent. To maximise your chances of getting the best price it is a general rule that a good time to sell your property is in spring. However, a lot of purchasers like to see the property in the winter. This is a good idea because by seeing it at its bleakest, they know what to expect.

It is a good idea to get at least two or three valuations. You can also look at similar properties for sale and set a realistic price. If you ask too much you will price yourself out of the market. The valuation should take into account that buyers might ask you to drop the price; you don't want to deter them because your price is not negotiable (*trattabile*).

Tax on Plusvalenza

Although capital gains tax (INVIM), was abolished in Italy in 2002, there is a tax which operates in a similar way on *plusvalenza* (literally 'plus value') and is levied at 30% less deductions for some costs (see below). It is applied to property sales that occur within five years of purchase.

Plusvalenza (literally 'plus value') is the difference between the declared purchase price of a property, and the declared sale price, minus deductions for renovation and notarial fees. This means that if you expect to sell the property within five years you should plan ahead so that you minimise the tax on the *plusvalenza*. You should ensure that the declared price on the conveyancing documents when you buy is as high as possible.

Estate Agents (Agenzie Immobiliari)

It might be beneficial to use the estate agent who sold you the property as he will be familiar with it. If this is not possible or desirable, there are lists of Italian estate agents on the internet including www.grimaldi.net, www.arpnet.it, www.casa.it and www.findaproperty.com. All estate agents must be registered and have a document attesting to their legality. An estate agent must have a signed authority from the owner and come to an agreement whereby either the estate agent has sole control over the sale; or, seller has the right to deal with other agents and private individuals.

> ### SOLE AGENCY
> N.B. The benefit of a sole agency agreement is that the percentage is usually lower. If however you sign an estate agent's authority without stipulating that you have the right to find your own buyer then you still have to pay the agent's commission even if you sell the house yourself.

Selling Through an Estate Agent

Always scrutinise any contract and make sure you understand what you are signing. Contracts will specify the estate agent's commission and this is not paid until completion although sometimes the commission is paid at the *compromesso* stage. Agents' fees vary; the rate of commission can be anything from 3-8% depending on the area and the market. The cost is usually shared between the vendor and the buyer. If you are selling a property include the estate agent's fee in the price; if the estate agent used another person to procure a buyer then it is up to the estate agent to share the commission.

Before putting your house on the market it is important to make sure that the exterior and interior are up to a high standard. The interior should be bright and clean. The kitchen and bathroom should be modern and of the best quality. It is not necessary to spend a fortune on designer products as it is unlikely you will recover the amount spent. The price of buildings in Italy is based on the link between the cost per square metre, times the area m2 e.g. 300m2 @ 1,000 euros per m2 = €300,000.

Your estate agent will advise you about any improvements that would attract buyers. He will be up to date with buyer's preferences. If you are forced to sell your home and it is not fully restored, this should be reflected in the price. The house should also come with any planning permission needed for renovation and an estimate for the cost.

Selling your own property

If your home is in a good location and is very desirable and you have set a realistic price, then it is possible that you will have no problems selling it yourself. Good advertising is the best guarantee that you will sell. Access to a computer means you can place your advertisement with various agents who specialise in overseas property e.g. www.knightfrank.com – international agency with associates in Tuscany and North America and www.piedmontproperties.com – specialist in marketing villas in the Monferrato and Langhe regions of Piedmont.

A useful publication is *Ville e Casali* (www.villecasali.com) a national property and decoration magazine in Italian. The classified property advertisements are listed in both Italian and English.

A 'For Sale' (*vendesi*) sign at the entrance to your property can be useful, if only as a signpost indicating the location of the property. An advertisement put into newspapers or magazines is also a must. Italy is now attracting buyers from America, Canada, Australia and their Europeans neighbours, the Italians too are also buying property mainly restored as holiday homes in fact they are buying back what was once theirs.

It is a good idea to compile all the documents, guarantees etc. that pertain to your property. Certificates such as *il certificato di abitabilita*. This is to certify that your house meets the standards required. Any architectural drawings (*planimetria*) are useful and a list of local plumbers, builders and electricians. The guarantees for the boiler and information on the gas *bombola* and where to locate the pump for the water are important.

When selling your home yourself you will need the services of a notary (*notaio*) to give you sound legal advice, prepare the contracts and conduct the completion. It is your choice whether you engage the services of an estate agent or sell the house yourself. If you give an estate agent exclusive rights – you get a guarantee of quality and service. The agent's commission takes care of the costs of advertising the property and he or she will have personnel to pay who deal with telephone calls, letters and the preparation of documents for the *notaio*. An estate agent will also use forms supplied by the organisation of Italian Estate Agents (*Federazione Italiana Mediatori Agenti d'Affari*) F.I.A.M.A.A. If you give an estate agent sole rights he will be more committed to advertising and do his utmost to get you a buyer.

CASE HISTORIES

FRANK LEE

Frank Lee is a retired doctor aged 69 from Edinburgh who lives in Tuscany with his wife, Moira.

What made you choose Italy for your retirement ?
The Mediterranean climate had always appealed to me, and my wife and I had spent many holidays visiting neighbouring countries. When the time came for my retirement, we considered living in either France or Italy. To begin with France looked to be winning. Housing was cheaper in France, its cuisine was renowned, there were many pretty towns and some beautiful scenery. In addition we both spoke the language, whereas neither of us knew Italian, a considerable drawback.

Nonetheless Italy appealed to us, especially Tuscany with its wooded hills and valleys, the architectural traditions of its charming towns and cities. In addition, Italians have a spontaneous friendliness towards foreigners; their cuisine is simple but excellent, healthier because it is based on olive oil, and their restaurants are reasonably priced. The most compelling factor, however, was that we had some very good friends living in southern Tuscany, friends of long standing who were in the business of renovating and selling houses. We knew they would be of great help to us, and we were not disappointed.

Three years on, we still enjoy living here. Life is slow and easy-going: at our age this usually suits us. We live in a renovated farmhouse with five bedrooms and three bathrooms. Like most retired people we wanted to scale down, so we also acquired twenty-two hectares of non-arable land, including three olive groves with a hundred trees. Well, it is a change from city life, and our elevated position compensates with some idyllic views across valleys, woods and ravines.

How do you find the health services?
There is a large modern hospital in Siena. The health services are good, and also free for those with *residenza*.

How do you cope with Italian bureaucracy?
Any foreigner can buy a house or two in Italy, but he cannot buy a car without first obtaining both permission to stay *permesso di soggiorno* and residence *residenza*. there are other bureaucratic quirks to tease the embryonic expatriate, but you soon learn it needn't upset your life style.

You speak the language reasonably now. How did you learn it?
During our first winter we attended weekly classes in Italian from October to March, augmented by the study of grammar books at home. Italian grammar is like its bureaucracy: too much unnecessary paper work. At home we continued to speak English to each other. Outside we conversed largely with expatriates. It took time to break out of our cocoon of timidity and laziness by socialising with local Italians, and availing of the friendliness shown by tradesmen and shop assistants. Instead of stifling ourselves with grammar, we needed to communicate. That was the quickest way to learn, as well as being more enjoyable.

What do you miss?
There are some things that we miss from our home country. Quite a few of our friends holiday in Tuscany and come to see us, but few visit on a regular basis and others do not stay long. We too enjoy returning to our native city.

What do think of Italian TV?
Much of Italian television is disappointing: a mixture of chat shows, old films dubbed in Italian, quiz programmes, bimbos hoping to be discovered and frequent advertising. Of course there are some programmes of quality, and one is kept informed of world events and local news.

Do you find it inconvenient not living in a city?
City people frequently complain about traffic congestion. Here there are no such problems, but we spend far more time travelling by car. The principal supermarket is 23km away, my bank is 20km, to the North, the butcher and the dry cleaners are in another town to the west. To visit our dentist we travel 70km; medical specialists are usually in Siena, 30km from here. Shops generally open at 8.30am and close at 1pm. They re-open from around 5pm until 7.30pm. Banks and professional people work different hours, and it is all too easy to drive to town and arrive at closing time, or find it is a local holiday.

But these are minor and often temporary inconveniences. We can still enjoy the healthy ambience of freshness and tranquillity, the warmth of the sun and the gentle beauty of the countryside.

What about theatres, concerts and other amusements?
You cannot expect the wide variety of entertainment, shopping and the arts that a big city can offer, but the towns and villages hold a large number of *festas* throughout most of the year. The Palio horse race takes place twice in Siena during July and August. The larger towns offer a fair selection of attractive shops. Top class professional musicians are imported to play classical concerts. There are art and sculpture exhibitions; the many artisans of the region offer ceramics, metalwork and other crafts. Tuscany is steeped in the history of the arts, and

proud of the harmony and splendour of its architecture.

Would you consider relocating to another country?
What for?

CHARLES BUTTERNO

Charles Butterno is a freelance writer and wine consultant aged 52 from Capetown, South Africa, who now lives in Valdarno.

Why did you buy a house in Italy?
I don't know really. I never intended to: the idea of owning a property here, with all the consequent niggling and purposeless bureaucracy, fiscal obligations, dealings with intransigent council authorities, opportunistic maintenance trades people, horrified me.

Besides, I was living in a place lifestyle magazines habitually write about – a restored 400-year-old barn on a remote olive farm 450 metres above a Tuscan valley with the pre-Apennines as a spectacular, sometimes snowy, backdrop. I'd been there for fifteen years as a tenant and felt perfectly at home, having (albeit laboriously) established an acceptance within the tiny local community, a harmony with the environment and a highly productive vegetable garden.

And despite being seemingly cemented to the place I had the delicious option of being able to pack up and leave any time I chose, having few cumbersome possessions and even fewer obligations.

And so why did I buy a house in Italy? Maybe because I believe those of us who truly love country environments don't live in them. But it doesn't really matter why, I'm just glad that I did!

So what happened ?
With barely time to plan or consider the consequences I found myself owning a small second floor apartment smack bang in the main thoroughfare of the town of Valdarno in the valley below. From the natural serenity of the Tuscan woodlands I was faced with neighbours, traffic, urban noise… in other words, all those things many dream of leaving behind.

What changed your mind about buying your own place in Italy?
It happened in an unexpected flash. A non Italian-speaking foreign friend had asked for some help in finding a property 'somewhere in Italy', firstly for his family to live in for a year, secondly, to rent out when they weren't here. He had ideas of life deep in rural Arcadia, the *real* Italy, communing with Nature and the locals, interrupted only by idyllic picnic lunches in the fields. But knowing his manual clumsiness and his chronic and dominating urban habits, I had other ideas.

What he and his family needed was convenience – to be close to a major rail link, close to an *autostrada*, close to restaurants, shops, banks, communication facilities, yet feel an integrated part of Italian life without having to learn local rural dialect, the phases of the moon, and which mushrooms are the deadly ones.

And so the search quickly concentrated on medium-sized characteristic Tuscan towns and, ultimately, on a 70 square metre apartment in the phase of being restored, above a grocer's shop and opposite a bar in the main street of an historically famous town built on the banks of the Arno River 700 years previously.

But instead of him buying it, I did: he hadn't even contemplated its suitability before I had signed the *compromesso*.

Is that gazumping or is it called something else?

Who cares – I wasn't interested in propriety, having been overtaken by an uncharacteristic and urgent impulse. Firstly the price seemed ridiculously cheap. But probably more than that the sheer convenience of urban living struck me with lightning clarity after having lived 15 years a hard 30km round trip drive from the nearest commercial centre. Buying a loaf of bread could become a two-minute exercise on foot rather than two hours involving a car.

The town had three cinemas, a few restaurants, bookshops, music stores, specialist food shops, wine merchants, a weekly market, fancy clothes shops and plain ones. It was 30 minutes by train to Florence, almost the same to Arezzo and only three hours from Rome.

Who needed a car! Who needed the country!

As well, I was able to guide the restoration to my own tastes, moulding it to suit my particular, and hitherto merely imagined, needs. And the size was perfect for my individual needs – efficient, intimate living with no wasted space, superfluous rooms or indulgent playthings.

Within six months I was ensconced, blessing the impulse and suffering the cries of foul from the other would-be owner.

How did you deal with the buying process?

The purchase was simple, particularly because I had no need of a mortgage: cash on the contract. Luckily the agent from whom I bought it was a trusted, capable and credible friend and the architect overseeing the restoration soon became one. Had I not had such assistance, nor spoken the language, undoubtedly it would have been an exercise riddled with misgivings, mistrust and fear of falling into a ruinous bureaucratic, legalistic trap.

My friends handled it all, presenting me with strangely-worded and formatted papers to sign and suggesting procedural short cuts which would made it easier for all of us: trusting them implicitly I calmly registered my moniker on all the dotted lines.

Having previously restored a Tuscan farmhouse on commission I was well aware of the unspeakable frustrations and difficulties or trying to co-ordinate the many trades necessary to bring a place back to scratch and grapple with medieval regulations.

I was also aware of the incredible and seemingly never-ending costs of maintaining a rural retreat, access roads particularly, but also land and dwellings and the inevitable environmentally objectionable swimming pool. The four windows are the only things in my little apartment, which might need attention, the rest is shared within the condominium.

Is your property intended to be an investment to sell on or rent out?
It's been three years since I moved in and in that time the property has appreciated by nearly 25%: I could sell it tomorrow, or even more easily, rent it. But I have no intention of doing either.

What about security?
An extra advantage is that it has a single entrance, is on the second floor, and has neighbours on all sides, as well as above and below and is on the main street of the town. With a security door the likelihood of burglaries is absolutely minimal and so, when I have to leave the country on work for months on end, I close and lock the door with tranquillity. No house-sitters needed.

BELINDA SCABURRI
Belinda is English, married to an Italian and at the time of interview was looking for a house to buy in Le Marche.

You are house hunting in Italy; why now?
We figured the time was right; the children were six and three years old, my Italian husband was keen to return to *la patria* and I did not much fancy living out the next ten or fifteen years doing school runs or taxiing teenagers up and down our Wiltshire valley. 'Change is the evidence of life' someone quoted at me and I was happy to embrace this concept even if it did occur to me later that maybe it had been made with reference to the amoeba!

What made you choose Le Marche?
Between us we knew both Tuscany and Umbria well, but we also knew that we could not afford the prices now commanded by those two regions. For some time the name on the block had been Le Marche, which, despite bordering both Umbria and Tuscany, neither of us knew at all. It seemed that no sooner had we organised and booked our first exploratory trip, an article appeared on the front cover of one of the weekend travel supplements with a photograph of Urbino underneath which read the caption 'Is this the new Chiantishire?' We hoped not, or we hoped not until we had got a foot in the door.

Why do you think Le Marche has gained popularity with buyers?

We knew that one of the reasons why Le Marche was opening up and becoming more interesting to British buyers was because of the attractively-priced flights offered by Ryanair from London Stansted to Ancona. Stansted may be convenient for those living in or north of London, but from Wiltshire and with the daily, nail-biting crawl that is the M25 at around 9am, we arrived at check-in with semi-shot nerves for what was a more than reasonable flight time. Depending on which part of Le Marche one favours, a BA flight from Gatwick to Bologna may be a better option as the journey from Bologna to Urbino is a straightforward two-hour drive.

You are based in Italy for your house hunt. How did you organise that?

It seemed logical to rent a house in Le Marche while we looked for a property, and having established that our house in Wiltshire would be easy to rent out, we assumed that the rental market in Italy would be equally efficient and offer as many possibilities. We were wrong.

Was it easy to arrange renting a property in Italy?

Despite there being an enormous demand for rental properties, the laws are still such that landlords are not protected and are therefore nervous and reluctant to enter into rental agreements which, in many instances, end in the law courts. We imagined that we would appear the ideal tenants – a mummy, a daddy and two adorable children. In actual fact, we presented the very worst type of tenant risk. We were not employed, we 'claimed' to be looking for a house to buy and, being foreigners (my husband, being a northern Italian, constituted as much of a foreigner as myself), we could say we had nowhere to go should we decide to stay on at the end of the tenancy. A combination of luck, timing and a telephone number spotted on an internet site meant that we did find ourselves a house to rent, but this is by no means the hassle-free, legally sound procedure to which we have all become accustomed in the UK.

There is a lot of paperwork involved in getting residence in Italy. How did it go?

Once all the family was in situ at the beginning of September, it seemed that we spent a good six weeks settling in. Paolo and I spent most days during that time attempting to obtain all the various permits and documents required to educate, transport and ensure our family's health. Not being new to the bureaucratic merry-go-round that is Italy, we were however amazed to find that the simplest matters are still hampered and made hugely complicated for no apparent reason. Countless times I have sat in dreary municipal buildings waiting to see someone about a bus pass for my daughter or an authorisation for my son to avail himself of the school *mensa* (canteen), only to be told that I should in fact be at a different office. In my hot-headed youth, I would regularly be driven mad by these episodes, but there is no point in getting agitated as nothing happens any faster or more efficiently even if you are blue in the face and steaming from your ears.

What about school, health care arrangements etc?
We were pleasantly surprised at the open-minded attitude of the School System. There truly is the credo here that everyone has the right to be educated. Not so the Health System which one might have been forgiven for thinking might embrace the same attitude but which is, alas, a minefield of red-tape and absurd regulations. Contemporary Italy is in the process of having to get used to the presence of many foreigners: North Africans, Albanians and a smattering of oddities like us and other Northern Europeans (the latter still chasing the Mediterranean dream). Culturally it is a struggle for the natives and, as a nation of emigrants, they are surprisingly baffled at the number of foreigners fetching up on their shores.

What about bringing your car from the UK?
Anyone thinking of coming from the UK to Italy with their car for more than the standard green card allowance time should make other plans. No Italian insurance company will insure an English-plated, right-hand drive car. Once English insurance cover runs out, one is obliged, by law, to have the number plates changed to Italian ones and to have all the car's documentation translated into Italian via the nearest consulate office to where you are based. Who said that being part of the EU made things easier?

How is the house hunting progressing?
Six months on we have yet to find a house that we like sufficiently to buy and this, in part, is because properties are more expensive than we had anticipated. We have all but made a joint career out of looking at houses and often this has been highly enjoyable and has enabled us to get to know this beautiful region. The faith is there, we have only to make the leap. In the meantime our children jabber away in Italian – a source of enormous delight and satisfaction – and we have met some incredibly friendly and kind people.

Any regrets so far?
All the annoying things about Italy are still annoying – the slowness, the bureaucracy, everything being closed on Mondays. However, all the good things are as good as ever – the food, the wine, the countryside, the light and the ease and charm with which the Italians live their lives.

BIBLIOGRAPHY

Alighieri, Dante – *The Divine Comedy, The Inferno.*

Arnaldi, Girolamo – *L'Italia e I Suoi Invasori* (Publisher Laterza).

Braudel, Fernand – *The Mediterranean and the Mediterranean World* (Harper Collins 1966).

Boccaccio, Giovanni – *The Decameron.*

Cary, John – *The History of Rome.*

Castiglione, Baldassare – *The Courtier* (1518).

Columbia University Press – *The Columbia Encyclopedia*

Croce, Benedetto – *History as the Story of Liberty* (and other works)

Diaconus, Paulus – *The History of the Lombards.*

De Agostini – *Calendario Atlante de Agostino 2003.*

Dundes, Alan & Falassi Alessandro – *La Terra in Piazza* (1975 University of California Press).

Follett (Chicago) – *Follett's Vest Pocket Dictionary of Italian.*

Guicciardini, Francesco – *Storia d'Italia.*

Gibbon, Edmund – *The Decline and Fall of the Roman Empire.*

Heurgon, Jacques – *Daily Life of the Etruscans.*

Highet, Gilbert – *Poets in a a Landscape.*

Il Vespro Editore – *Regioni in Bocca* series (20 books) 1976-1981.

Machiavelli, Niccolò – *The Prince (Il Principe 1532), The Discourses.*

Montanelli, Cervi – *L'Italia del Millennio (Sommario)* published by Rizzoli.

Montanelli, Indro – *Storia d'Italia* (Fratelli Fabbri publishers).

Newspapers – *La Repubblica; La Stampa; La Nazione* (weekly regional guides 2002-2003); *Il Sole 24 Ore* (Publications Casa 24 Website: www.ilsole24ore.com).

Piccolomini, Aeneas Sylvius – *Secret Memoirs of a Renaissance Pope.*

Russell, Bertrand – *The History of Western Philosophy.*

Stille, Alexander – *Excellent Cadavers* (Barnes & Noble 1996).

Smith, Denis Mark – *Modern Italy, A Political History* (Yale Press 1997).

Touring Club Italiano – *Guida Blu, Le 300 Spiagge Più Belle d'Italia.*

Laterza 2001 – *Ritratto dell'Italia.*

Wayland Kenneth & Elizabeth Young – *Northern Lazio, an Unknown Italy.*

Zanichelli Dictionaries – *Italiano/Inglese Italiano.*

FURTHER READING

Christ Stopped at Eboli – Carlo Levi. Devastating.

The Diaries – John Evelyn (circa 1680). A 17th century trip described by a gifted English diarist.

Diary of Montaigne's Journey to Italy in 1580 and 1581 – Michel de Montaigne. 16th century impressions by the great essayist.

Italian Backgrounds – Edith Wharton (1905). Delightful travel book by American novelist.

Italian Food – Elizabeth David (1954). The founder of the food revolution homes in on Italy to educate the British about real food.

Italian Journey – Johann Wolfgang von Goethe (1816). The original German romantic explains the lure of The South.

The Italians – Luigi Barzini. A glorification of Italian flair and panache.

The Leopard – Giuseppe de Lampedusa (1958). Famous historical novel. Everything has to change to stay the same in Sicily.

Mussolini: my part in his downfall – Spike Milligan.

Old Calabria – Norman Douglas. An Edwardian's fascination with the South, newly revered in a recent Italian translation.

Pictures from Italy – Charles Dickens (1846). The great novelist's take on Italy.

Portal to Paradise – Cecil Roberts (1955). Matchless raconteur renovates in the Riviera.

A Roman Journal – Stendhal, Marie Henri Beyle (1829). The Italophiles' Italophile as a tourist.

A Tramp Abroad – Mark Twain (1879). Irreverent debunking.

A Traveller in Rome, In Southern Italy – H.V. Morton (1964). The master travel writer.

Travels Through France and Italy – Tobias Smollett (1776). A Scottish novelist and curmudgeon on the road in the 18th century.

A Tuscan Childhood – Kinta Beevor (1993). Evocation of English symbiosis with Tuscan country people.

Tuscan Retreat – Vernon Bartlett (1961). Renovating a farmhouse in Tuscany. One of the first and best of the genre.

Twilight in Italy, Etruscan Places, Sun Sea and Sardinia – D.H. Lawrence. Deeply articulate empathising with Lawrence's favourite kind of people.

INDEX